Different Drummers

MUSIC OF THE AFRICAN DIASPORA

Guthrie P. Ramsey, Jr., Editor

Samuel A. Floyd, Jr., Editor Emeritus

1. *California Soul: Music of African Americans in the West,* edited by Jacqueline Cogdell DjeDje and Eddie S. Meadows

2. *William Grant Still: A Study in Contradictions,* by Catherine Parsons Smith

3. *Jazz on the Road: Don Albert's Musical Life,* by Christopher Wilkinson

4. *Harlem in Montmartre: A Paris Jazz Story between the Great Wars,* by William A. Shack

5. *Dead Man Blues: Jelly Roll Morton Way Out West,* by Phil Pastras

6. *What Is This Thing Called Jazz?: African American Musicians as Artists, Critics, and Activists,* by Eric Porter

7. *Race Music: Black Cultures from Bebop to Hip-Hop,* by Guthrie P. Ramsey, Jr.

8. *Lining Out the Word: Dr. Watts Hymn Singing in the Music of Black Americans,* by William T. Dargan

9. *Music and Revolution: Cultural Change in Socialist Cuba,* by Robin D. Moore

10. *From Afro-Cuban Rhythms to Latin Jazz,* by Raul A. Fernandez

11. *"Mek Some Noise": Gospel Music and the Ethics of Style in Trinidad,* by Timothy Rommen

12. *The Memoirs of Alton Augustus Adams, Sr.: First Black Bandmaster of the United States Navy,* edited with an introduction by Mark Clague, with a foreword by Samuel Floyd, Jr.

13. *Digging: The Afro-American Soul of American Classical Music,* by Amiri Baraka

14. *Different Drummers: Rhythm and Race in the Americas,* by Martin Munro

Different Drummers

Rhythm and Race in the Americas

———

Martin Munro

UNIVERSITY OF CALIFORNIA PRESS

Berkeley   Los Angeles   London

University of California Press, one of the most distinguished university presses in the United States, enriches lives around the world by
advancing scholarship in the humanities, social sciences, and natural
sciences. Its activities are supported by the UC Press Foundation and by
philanthropic contributions from individuals and institutions. For more
information, visit www.ucpress.edu.

University of California Press
Berkeley and Los Angeles, California

University of California Press, Ltd.
London, England

Library of Congress Cataloging-in-Publication Data

Munro, Martin.
    Different drummers : rhythm and race in the Americas / Martin
Munro.
        p.   cm. — (Music of the African diaspora ; 14)
    Includes bibliographical references and index.
    ISBN 978-0-520-26282-9 (cloth : alk. paper)
    ISBN 978-0-520-26283-6 (pbk : alk. paper)
    1. Blacks—Caribbean Area—Music—History and criticism.
2. African Americans—Music—History and criticism.   3. Brown,
James, 1933–2006—Criticism and interpretation.   I. Title.
    ML3550.M86   2010
    780.89'960729—dc22   2010005646

Manufactured in the United States of America

19   18   17   16   15   14   13   12   11   10
10   9   8   7   6   5   4   3   2   1

This book is printed on Cascades Enviro 100, a 100% postconsumer
waste, recycled, de-inked fiber. FSC recycled certified and processed
chlorine free. It is acid free, Ecologo certified, and manufactured by
BioGas energy.

For Cheralyn

CONTENTS

Acknowledgments   *ix*

Introduction: Slaves to the Rhythm   *1*

1. Beating Back Darkness: Rhythm and Revolution in Haiti   *24*

2. Rhythm, Creolization, and Conflict in Trinidad   *78*

3. Rhythm, Music, and Literature in the French Caribbean   *132*

4. James Brown, Rhythm, and Black Power   *182*

Conclusion: Listening to New World History   *214*

Notes   *227*
References   *251*
Index   *269*

ACKNOWLEDGMENTS

I wish to thank Ramsey Guthrie for his interest in this project and for sharing his expertise. I am very grateful to Mary Francis for her encouragement and guidance, and to Eric Schmidt and Suzanne Knott for help in the production stages. Sincere thanks to John Cowley for information on Trinidadian music, to Charles Forsdick for many useful reading suggestions, to Laurent Dubois for very helpful comments on the manuscript, to Celia Britton and J. Michael Dash for continued support, and to Martin Chisholm and Pat Crowley for enduring friendship. Many thanks to Bill Bollendorf for help and advice on Haitian art. Love to Jean, Gary, and Alan Munro. My deepest gratitude as ever is to Cheralyn, Conor, and Owen for companionship, love, and sharing thoughts on music new and old.

Introduction

Slaves to the Rhythm

The Burt Lancaster film *The Swimmer* contains a scene in which the white suburbanite protagonist, Ned Merrill, emerges from the woods at the entrance to the home of one of his wealthy friends. At the same time, the friend's Rolls-Royce car arrives at the gate, and Merrill runs forward to catch a ride up the lengthy driveway. As the car draws up, Merrill calls out the chauffeur's name ("Steve"), and the car stops. It is only when Merrill moves close to the car that he realizes he had mistaken the chauffeur for his predecessor. "You're not Steve," he says. "No," the driver replies, without giving his own name. The unnamed driver agrees to take Merrill the short ride through the verdant property up to the house. By this point, we viewers see plainly that the driver is a brown-skinned man, and we might also hear that his accent has a slight Caribbean intonation. The implication is that the white protagonist cannot distinguish between one person of color and the next, that "they all look the same." The driver's wry facial expression suggests that he is aware of Merrill's complacent racism but accepts it, as if it is not the first time his identity has been confused with that of someone else of similar skin color.

Driving up to the house, Merrill makes small talk with the driver and finds out that he has been working for the family for two years. Merrill asks what happened to Steve, and the driver discreetly says nothing. "Man, what a character," Merrill says of Steve, "did he mangle the English language. We told him he should have been on television." Steve, moreover, had a "big bass voice." "You should have heard that guy sing," Merrill says to the driver, who has appeared unmoved to this point in the conversation but cannot resist asking: "And a natural sense of rhythm?" Unaware that the driver is mocking him, Merrill nods enthusiastically, saying "Yeah, that's right."

1

The Swimmer was released in 1968, the year that Martin Luther King, Jr. was assassinated, race riots broke out in major cities across the United States, and James Brown recorded "Say It Loud (I'm Black and I'm Proud)." The brief exchange between Merrill and the unnamed brown-skinned chauffeur gives some sense of the contemporary tensions between, on the one hand, longstanding, often complacently held white assumptions about race and the essential qualities of black people, and, on the other, a growing African American tendency to challenge centuries of racial caricaturing and assert black identity on its own terms. The scene also suggests that rhythm, and specifically the idea of innate black rhythmicity, was one of the key elements at stake in this uneven, discordant discussion between the races in 1960s America. The driver's evocation of rhythm seems to suggest his weariness with the stereotype and, by implication, his need to reject or otherwise rework the tired idea that all black people sing, dance, and have natural rhythm.

In the Carnival tradition of Trinidad there is a masquerade known as *sailor mas,* during which players dress up in nautical-related costumes and act out various roles associated with the mas. Although its roots lie in the earliest post-Emancipation period, its contemporary forms were strongly influenced by the presence of mainly white American servicemen in Trinidad during World War II. This period saw the emergence of the "Fancy Sailor" bands, which used expensive materials and elaborate decoration to create a flamboyant spectacle, the underlying aim of which was in part to emulate and appropriate elements of the Americans' dress style and general demeanor. Just as important, and true to Trinidad Carnival tradition and its tendency to mock any show of class or race power, the sailor bands also parodied the Americans. The mockery of the white Americans is made plain in the way masqueraders shower each other with talcum powder, whitening their faces to emphasize the play on racial difference. This playful caricature of the American sailors is, however, most prevalent in the idiosyncratic dances of the sailor mas. Just as they designed new costumes during World War II to comment on the American presence, so sailor masqueraders invented new dances, different kinds of "fancy footwork" that in their own ways were playful commentaries on the Americans, their mannerisms and behavior. Out of these new steps emerged the Fireman and King Sailor dances, which have remained synonymous with the mas until today (Gibbons 2007, 156).

These dances and others associated with sailor mas differ from other carnival dances in that they are composed of a complex set of rhythmic and arrhythmic movements: in one sequence (called the Marrico), the sailor dancer gyrates his hips in a circular movement and then pushes out his buttocks to the back in an exaggerated, ungainly way. In another, known as the Camel Walk, the player stands erect with a walking stick in his hand, facing the ground, walks heel and toe with one of his knees slightly bent, rotating his shoulders and moving backwards and forwards to the calypso music. In both cases, the dancer tries to get with the beat but fails, either because he is trying too hard or because he is physically unable to move in time with the music. The spectacle of a mass of talcum-powdered Trinidadians moving uncertainly to the beat amounts to a mockery of the white Americans' inability to dance in time. It also implicitly asserts that the ability to move rhythmically is one of the primary attributes of the black Trinidadian, a quality that differentiates black from white. In short, it suggests that rhythm is a fundamental component of black identity.

These two examples seem to tell conflicting stories. In the first case, the black chauffeur subtly mocks and implicitly rejects (as a racist stereotype) the idea that all black people have natural rhythm. In the second case, rhythm is also evoked as a key element in differentiating blacks from whites, but this time black people themselves assert their rhythmicity and claim rhythm as a marker of their racial and cultural distinctiveness. Which of these characters is right: the casually racist wealthy white, the exasperated black driver, or the sailor masquerader? Are they all correct in some way, or indeed are they all wrong? What is the relationship between blackness and rhythm in the Americas? This book focuses on these questions and traces the history of the discourses on rhythm and race in four key American places and times: Haiti from the revolution to the mid-twentieth century; Trinidad from the early nineteenth century to the 1940s; Martinique from the 1930s to 1980s; and the United States in the civil rights era.[1]

If rhythm—in music, dance, and work patterns, for example—was a fundamental aspect of slave experience, and if it is still one of the most persistent features of circum-Caribbean cultures, it remains also perhaps one of the most misunderstood and under-theorized elements of American historical and cultural experience. There is generally a reticence among critics of the circum-Caribbean to mention rhythm—especially, it seems, among nonblack, nonnative observers. The reason for this reticence no doubt lies in the long-standing negative, stereotypical image, evoked by Merrill in *The Swimmer*, of the naturally rhythmic black, and in critics' unwillingness to be construed as essentialist, reductivist, or, worse, racist. Another reason for the critical neglect of rhythm is that rhythm is most closely related to the outmoded cultural nationalist ideas of twentieth-century movements such as Negritude, Haitian Indigenism, and Black Power. Few authors would declare now, as the great Martinican poet Aimé Césaire did in 1961, that rhythm "is an essential element of the black man" (quoted in Ngal 1994, 152). Indeed, most critics would quite rightly question such an assertion, much as both René Ménil and Frantz Fanon did in *Tracées* (1981) and *Peau noire, masques blancs* (1952), respectively. Fanon, in particular, has had a profound influence in directing critical attention away from the more mystical, Africanist elements of Negritudist thought, including the idea that rhythm and blackness were in some way related. In the post-Fanon era, rhythm has almost become a taboo subject for critics wary of racial and cultural essentialism. But to ignore rhythm completely is to neglect a fundamentally important feature of circum-Caribbean aesthetics, history, and indeed contemporary lived experience. A more engaged, interdisciplinary criticism is required if we are to arrive at a sophisticated understanding of rhythm and its relationship to race and culture in the Americas. Moving through slavery, revolution, Emancipation, world wars, nationalist uprisings, the end of colonialism, dictatorships, and various black power movements, this book breaks the critical taboo of discussing race and rhythm together, and it shows how, in diverse locales and at different times in New World history, rhythm has been one of the most persistent and malleable markers of race, both in racist white thought and in liberatory black counter-discourse. As the chapters show, rhythm has also been a dynamic force for change and renewal at virtually every major turning point in black New World history. Rhythm has its own obscured yet real and important history in this region that has long been ignored by historians and social and literary critics alike but that demands now to be understood as part of our broader attempts to engage with the evolution of races, nations, cultures, and thought in the Americas.

HEARING RHYTHM, FEELING SOUND

Sounds are the most powerful stimuli that human beings experience, but they are also the most evanescent, dissipating quickly into nothing. We experience sounds as waves of air molecules that strike against our eardrums, creating vibrations inside the body. If the sounds are loud enough, the waves strong enough (the sounds of a large drum, for instance), the vibration may be felt beyond the ears and into the viscera of the gut (B. Smith 2004, 389). Sound is therefore something that is not only heard but also felt, with palpable physical effects. Rhythm, too, is an element of sound that can produce physical, indeed psychophysical effects, particularly when it accompanies religious rituals (or even secular dances), and it induces a heightened state of consciousness or a state of trance.

Typically characterized by repetition, rhythm is heard and felt simultaneously. Depending on the receptivity of the listener, various parts of the body—the hips, the feet, the head, the arms, even the fingers—may move in time to it. As one critic puts it, "It was always the whole body that emitted sound: instrument and fingers, bend. Your ass is what you sing. Dedicated to the movement of hips, dedicated by that movement, the harmolodically rhythmic body" (Moten 2003, 39–40). Indeed, rhythm appears to predate music, or at least to have extra-musical beginnings: Plato attributed rhythm to the "artful motion of bodies" (quoted in Filmer 2003, 96). Rhythm seems then to originate in the body, from psychophysiological urges, from the impulse to perform continuous, regular movements, which in turn create "the awareness of greater ease and gusto through constant evenness in motion" (Sachs 1965, 112).

The human body itself can be seen as a set of rhythms that are different but that act in harmony with each other, particularly when the body moves in time to music (Lefebvre 1992, 31). The bodily response to rhythmic music occurs in the sympathetic and para-sympathetic nervous systems, which govern human emotions and are involved in the restoration and maintenance of homeostasis— that is, the metabolic equilibrium operated via the autonomic nervous system to counteract disrupting changes (McNeill 1995, 6).[2] The rhythmic movement of the muscles, as they work through the nervous system, may also "provoke echoes of the fetal condition," when the major external stimulus to the developing brain was the mother's regular heartbeat. As such, "prolonged and insistent rhythmic stimuli may restore a simulacrum of fetal emotions to consciousness" or else bring back a state of consciousness left behind in infancy, when most psychologists agree little distinction is made between self and surroundings (McNeill 1995, 7). More obviously, participating in rhythmic singing or dancing brings about noticeable physiological changes: the pulse rate may quicken, respiration deepens, adrenalin flows, and a general feeling of satisfying physical exhaustion may occur (Robinson and Winold 1976, 4). Rhythm can to some extent be considered a sense in its own right; the common term a "sense of rhythm" suggests a general awareness that the sensory experience of rhythm is not quite hearing, not quite touching or feeling, but an amalgam of these (and possibly other) senses.

Rhythm also plays a fundamental role in bonding societies and groups and in structuring the collective experience of time. All societies seem, at every stage of their evolution, to have integrated the concerted, rhythmic social movements of song and dance with other significant social activities, principally work (Filmer 2003, 92–93). A society's notion of time becomes "second nature" to its people through collective, rhythmic interactions. People learn how to keep together in time through various forms of movement socialization, and these movements are mediated by rhythm.[3] Moreover, this rhythmic process is far older than language: prolonged and rhythmic movements throughout human history have created a "euphoric fellow feeling" that provides the basis for social cohesion "among any and every group that stays together in time" (McNeill 1995, 4). Moving and singing together in time enables collective tasks to be carried out far more efficiently. Fundamentally, keeping together in time was important for human evolution in that it allowed early human groups to "increase their size, enhance their cohesion, and assure survival by improving their success in guarding territory, securing food, and nurturing the young" (McNeill 1995, 93). Rhythm in this sense, and in the way it facilitated the creation of stable human communities, was essential to the emergence of human beings as the dominant species (McNeill 1995, 156–57).

If rhythm is therefore considered to be primarily an element of sound—in *rhythm as malleable* (margin annotation)

speech, music, and poetry—it is a malleable concept that may be applied to other patterns of repetition and regularity, be they natural (the rhythms of the body, time, and the seasons) or manufactured (rhythms of work, machinery, industrial time, everyday life).[4] In this book I consider each of these kinds of rhythm as they have manifested themselves at different points in New World, circum-Caribbean history, and the possible connections between them—between, for example, the enforced, policed rhythms of plantation labor and the apparently freer, more liberatory rhythms of slave dances. Like the critic Henri Meschonnic, I seek not to limit too restrictively the possible definitions and applications of the trope of rhythm; as he says, "rhythm criticism involves going beyond the definition of rhythm" (Meschonnic 1982, 172). The principal interest lies, however, in music, dance, and literature, and in tracing the history and evolution of rhythm and the discourse surrounding it in each of the four New World places and times. Just as the geographical scope of the book is broad, so the analysis stretches over time, from the late eighteenth to late twentieth centuries. This temporal and geographical span leads to a diachronic understanding of how the trope of rhythm has changed (or not) as historical, political, and cultural situations have evolved. It was in these circum-Caribbean places and at these times that two great primary rhythmic systems—broadly, European/"modern" and African/"traditional"—met, clashed, and creolized, creating new, hybridized peoples, cultures, and societies. What were these Old World rhythms, what did they have in common, how did they differ, and how did they reflect specific notions of culture, civilization, and existence?[5]

RHYTHM AND TIME IN EUROPEAN MUSIC

First exchange (margin annotation)

The exchange of African and European cultural forms predates the Atlantic slave trade. In 1451, a witness to a royal wedding in Lisbon recorded that "'negroes and Moors' performed . . . their tribal dances and songs" during the processions (Russell 1973, 228). The music and dance cultures of African peoples were brought first to Portugal in the fifteenth century, and then to Spain, and soon became a part of local high and popular culture. As the music spread, European authorities moved quickly to control it, seeing it as a subversive and moral threat. As early as 1461, slaves were forbidden to hold parties in the Portuguese town of Santarém (Reiss 2005, 3). In Spain, African or Creole dances such as the *guineo*, the *calenda*, and the *chica* arrived in the late sixteenth century and were commented on by Golden Age writers such as Miguel de Cervantes, Lope de Vega, and Francisco de Quevedo. Such was their popularity and their perceived threat to morality that they were censured several times by the Spanish Inquisition (Benítez-Rojo 1999, 202). Around the same time, the Afro-Latin dance musics *zarabanda* and *chacona* emerged. These music and dance cultures were fundamentally rhythmic in nature and were liable to induce in listeners and dancers states of abandon that

censorship (margin annotation)

were considered immoral and potentially dangerous to fixed social hierarchies of class, gender, and race (Reiss 2005, 5).

class, gender, race

When Europeans began to settle in the New World, they brought a wide array of musical styles, ranging from traditional folk songs of white indentured laborers (characterized by the rhythmic, repetitive song structures typical of oral cultures) to religious and military music and the more stylized, less overtly rhythmic "art music" developed for and by the emerging bourgeois classes. In the early days of the French Caribbean colonies, the planters, who lived essentially like French country gentlemen, would listen after dinner to courtly airs sung by the women or to music played by women and children on the harpsichord or the pianoforte (Rosemain 1986, 16). The ability to play these instruments was a sign of social prestige and of the players' artistic education, which was a privilege reserved for the wealthiest. There was also constant awareness of the latest developments in French music, because Parisian music teachers, poorly paid in France, came to the islands to teach the children of the colonial elite contemporary dances, airs, and the rules of musical art (Rosemain 1986, 17). Wealthy colonists lived, in effect, "in tune" with Paris and followed scrupulously the latest trends in European music, which quickly became a "social requirement and a distinctive sign of the bourgeois family" (Rosemain 1986, 45). Moreover, music became an indicator of power, a means of demonstrating the bourgeois white Europeans' social, cultural, and racial superiority and of gaining respect for European ideas of order and civilization (Rosemain 1986, 34).

music as power

In the eighteenth century, European art music was transported to the New World to be heard and appreciated in respectable salons across the circum-Caribbean, and it was held up as a musical embodiment of all that was putatively civilized about European culture. In contrast to the more primitively rhythmic European folk forms, this European art music was characterized by distinctly teleological structuring processes. The music typically builds tension and anticipation, leading to a climax and a conclusion that are experienced as the "natural" ending of a piece of music. In classical European music theory and music psychology, the music is structured hierarchically: it must be divisible into more or less closed parts, and it must progress from one part to the next in teleological fashion. Although there have been other, less linear musical styles in the history of European music, the teleological model holds a privileged place in this tradition among musicologists and the bourgeois listening public, which from the eighteenth century to the present has come to expect unity, development, and linearity in its ideal of musical form (Danielsen 2006, 150).[6] In Leonard B. Meyer's classic theory, for instance, tension in the musical piece is necessarily followed by climax, release, and resolution. In his *Style and Music* (1989, 37), he explains this structure in terms of the demand for "closure," which is regarded as a common attribute of all musical styles. For Meyer, tempo, texture, figuration, and instru-

folk vs art

mentation are largely "secondary parameters," as they cannot specify "definite points of termination" or bring about closure in musical structure (1989, 15).[7] In fact, he draws a distinction between sophisticated art music and "primitive" music (which includes for him European popular forms). The essential difference between the two forms, Meyer says, lies in "speed of tendency gratification" (1994, 32). The primitive person cannot tolerate uncertainty or suspension and seeks almost immediate gratification. This apparent failing is further attributed to a lack of maturity, both of the individual and of the culture (Meyer 1994, 33). The mature person, in contrast, exhibits control and suspends gratification, and these tendencies are signs "that the animal is becoming a man" (Meyer 1994, 33).

It is not too great a leap to see in this theory of music reflections of the temporal and philosophical contexts from which they first emerged. The penchant for tonality and functional harmony may be interpreted in the context of eighteenth-century Europe's "mechanistic worldview," whereas the later dramatic developments in nineteenth-century music can be read in relation to the "conflicting forces within the newly invented psychological subject" (Danielsen 2006, 152). More generally, too, the promotion of linearity, teleology, and synthesis in music seems to reflect the modern model of time and progress. In her analyses of nineteenth-century European music, Susan McClary makes a similar point, and she argues that music prepared society for the constraints and discipline inherent to eighteenth- and nineteenth-century notions of progress and civilization. In particular, she argues that, though in any tonal composition the expected arrival of closure is initially postponed by various strategies, the closure does finally reward patience and come inevitably, thereby confirming the belief that rational, systematic effort will always result in the attaining of objectives. "The self-motivated delay of gratification," McClary argues, "which was necessary for the social world to come into being in the eighteenth century, worked on the basis of such habits of thought, and tonality teaches listeners how to live within such a world: how to project forward in time, how to wait patiently but confidently for the pay-off" (2000, 67). In its New World contexts, this music carried with it self-legitimizing structures of civilization and progress, and in a sense it provided one soundtrack to the plantation, at least as it was heard in respectable society. Listening was a habit to be acquired and cultivated; gratification was not instant but deferred (yet inevitable); all that was required was an investment of effort and patience. This emphasis on projecting rationally forward in time, allied to the unshakeable belief that the ends always justify the means, echoed in many ways the practices of work on the plantation, the harnessing of many millions of dispensable Africans to a process that was always driven by the profits and power that were, for the planters, the payoff for good planning and patient deferral of gratification.[8]

This modern European art music, however, provided only part of the soundtrack to the plantation. Outside of the salons, the music was decidedly more rhythmic and more rooted in repetitive folk structures. The African input to this external, communal, rhythmic music was the most significant, but European settlers did also bring their own ancient rhythms that were close in form and function to the ostinato rhythms of the Africans. Indeed, the first new rhythms to penetrate the plantations of the circum-Caribbean were European in origin, primarily the folk rhythms of Spanish and French settlers. These early European rhythms resembled the later African rhythms in their repetitive structures and in their history of repression by official religions. With the arrival of African slaves, the colonies became a place of encounter between the ancient "cosmogonic rhythms" of Europe and Africa—that is, between the pagan rhythms that were appropriated by European Christianity and the animist rhythms of the Africans (Rosemain 1990, 34).

Europe had, in fact, been relatively late in incorporating the drum into its musical forms. The first use of the word "drum" in English was recorded only in 1540 (Sublette 2007, 73). European pagan rhythms had long been repressed, from Ancient Greece to the early Christian era. The "savage, delirious" dances and sounds of pre-Christian rituals in Europe were systematically suppressed as the Church sought to establish order and orthodoxy (Rosemain 1990, 35). The Church was scrupulous in its control of dancing and dance music in Europe; it acted as a "rhythmic retardant," suppressing not only percussion but all instruments. Musical instruments were played in Europe but only by the "rabble" and in folk music forms (Sublette 2007, 74).

The "crusade against rhythm" continued unabated in the colonies (Rosemain 1990, 37). On the plantations, all rhythms—whether of European or of African origin—were subject to this anti-rhythmic impulse: because they were seen as savage and dangerous, and because they accompanied the dances of cults not recognized by the official religion, they were prohibited. These prohibitions applied equally to European folk and pagan rhythms as to the rhythms of African rituals. Only with the growth of the slave trade and the influx en masse of slaves did the putative dangers of rhythm and dance become attributed to uniquely African sources (Rosemain 1990, 34). It is not a coincidence that, during this same period, racial thinking began to solidify, white indentured labor in the colonies became unacceptable to white elites, and forced manual work was increasingly seen as a fate to which Africans alone were to be condemned (Stein 1979, 9–10).[9] And yet, despite these religious prohibitions and the ever more rigid race and color divisions, the popular rhythms of Africa and Europe persisted in the colonies, blending and fusing with each other, because they were "basically the same" and were sung and danced at the same occasions: during the festivals of the Catholic Church and in the rituals of the Afro-Creole religions celebrating the gods of life, death, and fertility (Rosemain 1990, 37).

In truth, repetitive rhythm is not an exclusively African phenomenon. Cyclical views of time and history, normally attributed to non-European peoples, were also widespread in pre-industrial Europe. These now-suppressed rhythms of time and history in European cultures were in many ways similar to the religious and cultural beliefs found across the circum-Caribbean in African diasporic communities, in that they observe the "periodic regeneration of biological and agricultural systems" (Snead 1984, 65). Thus, early European settlers and African slaves both observed cyclical ceremonies, and their rhythmic chants had much in common in terms of form and function. If these rhythms are now less immediately prevalent in European societies, it is because they have been "domesticated and systematized," supplanted by what Antonio Benítez-Rojo calls "scientific rhythm" (1992, 170). This rhythm was, Benítez-Rojo says, emptied of its "cosmological and social signification during the European process of political Christianization" (1992, 170).

As the colonial period advanced and notions of civilization and culture solidified around rigid racial demarcations, pre-modern, nonscientific rhythms became almost exclusively associated with Africans and with concepts of "black culture."[10] Rhythm became one of the primary markers of this culture, and it featured prominently in contemporary dualistic, racialized debates and conflicts over what was civilized and uncivilized culture in the New World. From the earliest days of slavery, Europeans in the New World (forgetting their own traditions of rhythmic folk music) came to associate drumming with Africa and black culture and thus disorder, otherness, and danger.

The European idea of black culture has historically been a means of self-definition through perceived contrasts with the black other, and as such it is a decidedly unreliable concept. The modern idea of a distinct black culture may be traced back to some of the great works of eighteenth- and nineteenth-century European philosophy. In the eighteenth century, Voltaire (however inadvertently) laid the groundwork for some of the more overtly racist thought of the nineteenth century. Although he was against slavery in principle, Voltaire was more directly concerned with serfdom in France than with the enslavement of Africans in France's colonies (Miller 2008, 76). Crucially, too, Voltaire's polygenic beliefs led him to suggest that different groups, different species of humans, had their own essential characteristics, and this justified in his mind the enslavement of Africans. "Nature has by this principle subordinated different degrees of genius and character among the nations, which are rarely seen to change," Voltaire said, adding that this is "why the Negroes are the slaves of other men" (1876–83, 12: 381). In this sense, Voltaire embodies some of the contradictions of Enlightenment discourse and lays bare the contemporary tension between a profound belief in equality and the "social limits on its articulation" (Malik 1996, 40). As many critics have observed, the modern discourse of race (and racism) has its roots in the tensions and paradoxes of the Enlightenment era.[11]

Perhaps the most significant figure in promoting the idea that black and white cultures were irrevocably different was Hegel, who, in *The Philosophy of History*, drew a distinction between European and African conceptions of time, history, and being. Hegel, notoriously, declared that the "Negro . . . exhibits the natural man in his completely wild and untamed state" (1956, 93). The African, to Hegel's mind, had little or no conception of justice or morality and was a fundamentally "sensual" being (1956, 95). In Hegel's view, slavery in the Americas was for the African an improvement over his existence in Africa, where it was impossible to attain a "consciousness of . . . freedom," and he was inevitably "an object of no value" (1956, 96). The African's way of relating to the world was irrevocably strange and other to Hegel. Moreover, as one critic has suggested, because the African in Hegel's scheme was "unfixed in orientation towards transcendent goals and terrifyingly close to the cycles and rhythms of nature," the black other "overturns all European categories of logic" (Snead 1984, 63). Most notably, perhaps, the African disrupts the European idea of time; the African, to Hegel, had "no idea of history or progress" but instead allowed "accidents and surprises" to take hold of his fate (Snead 1984, 63). For Hegel, then, European culture was teleological and seemed to progress through time to reach its "transcendent goals" (Snead 1984, 63). African culture, by contrast, had no concept of progress but experienced time and history in cycles.[12]

Hegel's notion of a distinct black (and white) culture was echoed to some extent in Artur de Gobineau's contemporary theories of the "natural" differences between human races. Although Gobineau was far from the first European philosopher to argue that natural hierarchies existed among different categories of humans, he went to new extremes in assigning essential characteristics to each group. He argued, again notoriously, in his *Essai sur l'inégalité des races humaines* (1853–55), that there were three distinct human races: the black, the yellow, and the white (1983, 339). The black was placed at the bottom of the scale by virtually every measure, including moral sensitivity and intellectual capacity (339–40). All civilization, Gobineau wrote, "flows from the white race" (345). Yet he also attributed to the black race an aptitude for the arts and poetry. Gobineau believed that ancient civilizations such as Assyria and Egypt were characterized by contact between whites and blacks and that the latter brought to the arts of these places their "striking taste for that which comes from the imagination, that vehement passion for all that could invoke the aspects of intelligence that are easiest to inflame, that devotion to all that falls beneath the senses" (467). Taking this idea further, Gobineau argued that the source from which the arts have emerged was "foreign to civilizing instincts" and that this source was "hidden in the blood of the blacks" (472). It follows, he said, that in any society the extent of the power of the arts over the masses will be determined by the "quantity of black blood" that flows through their veins (473). Of all the arts, music is, Gobineau said, the one preferred by the black man because it "caresses his ear with a succession of sounds, [and] demands nothing from the thinking part of his brain" (474). Similarly, dance is "the object of the most irresistible passion" for the black man, for in dance, sensuality "counts for everything" (476). In these ways, Gobineau concluded, the black man possessed to the highest degree the "sensual faculty without which there is no art possible" (476).[13]

Such racialized understandings of culture and race form the ontological basis for the history of the drum, percussion, and rhythm in the circum-Caribbean. The fear that underlies Hegel's idea of black culture—"terrifyingly close" to natural rhythms—repeats itself endlessly in this history. Gobineau's idea that the black man was naturally inclined toward art, music, and dance persists even today and has been echoed by critics and commentators, both black and white.[14] In colonial times, Christian missionaries in particular opposed the drum, slaves' rhythmic dancing, and their association with non-Christian rituals.[15] In Europe, the fiddle was decried as the "devil's instrument," whereas in the New World, the drum was the symbol of pagan excess (Cowley 1996, 6). This white or European fear is, however, a complex phenomenon. It is not only a fear of black revolt— the drum was always associated with slave insurgency—but also a dread of (or unconscious desire for) "contamination" by blackness. The European fear also certainly masked an attraction to the drum, the dance, and the abandon that civilized European sensibilities were supposed to abhor but that had long been an important if suppressed aspect of European cultures.

AFRICAN RHYTHMS

Even if creolized circum-Caribbean cultures are polyrhythmic, in the sense that diverse peoples each brought their own music and rhythms (not only the Europeans but also, for example, the East Indian people and the *tassa* drum), and notwithstanding the difficult question of where rhythm comes from—Jacques Derrida talks of the "incalculable origin of a rhythm" (1996, 81)—the great traditions of music here, from kaiso to ska, soca to dancehall, belair to zouk, jazz to hip-hop, have emerged from predominantly African origins.[16] The black cultures of this region have evolved from the "common trunk" of Africa and, in terms of rhythm, have conserved "definite filiations with the continent of origin" (Barthélemy 2000, 171). One can also say that rhythm still plays a significant role both culturally and existentially in many sub-Saharan African societies.[17] This is not to say, however, that a single conception of "African rhythm" exists, even in sub-Saharan Africa. Drums, for example, do not figure prominently in the traditional music of southern Africa, and even within West Africa—arguably the hub of rhythmic African music—there is a complexity of styles in which rhythm figures to varying degrees.

contrast

That said, rhythm is undoubtedly a prominent feature in many West African musical forms and, indeed, in everyday life there, in contrast to European (art) music's general neglect of rhythm as a specific field of inquiry.[18] John Miller Chernoff's seminal study, *African Rhythm and African Sensibility* (1979), addresses the functional importance of rhythm at all levels and all ages in West African existence: "African children play games and sing songs displaying a rhythmic character . . . [and] learn to speak languages in which proper rhythmic accentuation and phrasing is essential to meaning. . . . Facility with rhythms is something people learn as they grow up in an African culture, one of the many cultural acquisitions that make someone seem familiar to people who have also learned the same things. Rhythms are built into the way people relate to each other" (94). Chernoff examines the sociocultural significance of African rhythm and music and its deep "integration into the various patterns of social, economic, and political life" (35).

If, as the musicologist Francis Bebey argues, many West African musicians use sound not just for a pleasing aesthetic effect but to "express life in all its aspects through the medium of sound" and to "translate everyday experiences into living sound" (1975, 5), these sounds are characterized by distinctive rhythmic elements. In the West African tradition, music has strong functional elements, is integrated into the structures and movements of daily life, and is traditionally used to mark out the rhythms of work, mourning, celebrations, and religious ceremonies as well as to express ideas that could not otherwise be voiced (White and White 2005, 40). In *The Music of Africa* (1974), Ghanaian musicologist J. H. Kwabena Nketia discusses some of the basic features of "African rhythm," by which he means the rhythms of the Akan people of West Africa. Most essentially, he says, different rhythmic patterns are interrelated in strict time and are controlled by a fixed time span, which can be divided into an equal number of segments or pulses of varying densities (126).[19] In other words, West African rhythmic patterns, though they may have several interrelated layers, typically have a fixed length in time, and the patterns are repeated (Danielsen 2006, 43). The ethnomusicologist Simha Arom calls this organization of West African music into invariant, repetitive units *isoperiodicity* and asserts that "the basic temporal principle of rhythm is bringing back a form" (1991, 212).

The interrelated layers of rhythm in West African music are organized as "rhythmic dialogues" between two, usually complementary, figures (Danielsen 2006, 52). This rhythmic structure is in turn closely related to traditional West African antiphonal (or call-and-response) forms. Chernoff argues that, in a West African context, it is inconceivable that a band would play a single rhythm; there are always at least two rhythms playing, and playing off against each other (1979,

51). Musicians keep time according to the rhythmic relationship with other musicians rather than by following a stressed beat. The music emerges through the combined rhythms, and the only way, Chernoff says, to hear the music properly, to find the beat, is to listen to the two rhythms simultaneously (51). In contrast to much European music, where rhythm is something to "respond to," in West African music rhythm is something to "get with" or become more fully part of (55). The participatory, dialogic aspects of West African music are complemented by the dancing, handclapping, and stomping feet of listeners—to the extent, Chernoff argues, that the drums accompany the dancers rather than vice versa (50).[20]

If rhythmic repetition is the dominant mode of West African (and African diasporic) music, the repetitions are never quite identical: even as the music repeats itself, it introduces and highlights difference and variation. In the participatory mode of musical performance, repetition is less a static phenomenon than a dynamic, ongoing process of production. In this mode, "the complete rhythmic pattern is neither played nor experienced at once; it is instead experienced over time. Every gesture has to be effected, and in one sense, repetition is like a kind of continual re-*petition*, a re-appeal or request that requires a follow-up" (Danielsen 2006, 164).

Rhythm in West African music has a strong verbal basis. As Bebey argues, the "prime motive of the instruments is to reconstitute spoken language" (1975, 115). A further element of spoken culture, oral poetry, is the rhythmic foundation of the drum patterns used by master drummers in many cultures of West Africa. The rhythms and pitches of the drums combine with the contrasting timbres of the instruments to create what Olly Wilson calls a "heterogeneous sound ideal" made up of "mosaics of tone color and pitch" (1992, 331). These rhythmic processes are controlled in much West African and western Congolese music by the time line, the pulse created by handclapping or in the rhythms of an idiophone such as a bell. The time line is an essential part of many musical forms of the region, against which the other instruments play the multilinear rhythms that make up the "exciting, interlocking, cross-rhythmic, and polyrhythmic configurations of African music" (Floyd 1995, 28). Given that more than three thousand African ethnic groups exist, and notwithstanding the important regional variations, there is a surprising homogeneity in song style. And the fundamental elements common to these styles are rhythm and repetition (Lomax 1975, 46).

The complex timbral and rhythmic range of West African drumming can be partly attributed to the ways in which the drum is traditionally used as a means of communication. By reproducing phonetically the sounds of the words themselves, West African drummers developed a sophisticated rhythmic sense and became particularly sensitive to timbral subtleties. The drum is more than a mere musical instrument; it is used for praise, to console, to celebrate, and as a means of discovering the innermost self (Martins 1983, 28).[21]

While rhythm permeates in these ways the daily, secular life of many West African societies, it is also an integral part of religious ritual. Indeed, perhaps the retention of rhythmic aspects of ritual such as antiphony, bodily movement, and drumming in much West African (and African diasporic) religious practice is the single most important factor in perpetuating the rhythmic qualities of these societies. Because rhythm is not excluded from religious ritual (as it largely is in European religious practices), it is validated as an important element of existence and is integrated into the individual's whole experience. In traditional West African societies, dance, drum, and song have long been central elements in religious ritual. In some of these societies, it was believed that "ritualistic dancing can increase and generate *ache* or life force in the individual" (Gonzáles-Wippler 1985, 12). The dance generates a power that is intensified in the trance states of possession, when the gods take possession of the consciousness of the believer. This trance state is largely brought about by the songs and drumming of the group, and each of the gods has its own songs and rhythms (Raboteau 1978, 15).

Although the foregoing discussion has focused on "European" and "African" rhythms, it is important to note that these are not in themselves stable, fixed categories and that their encounter in the New World rendered them ever more unstable and unreliable. Circum-Caribbean cultures are inevitably hybrid creations, and the Caribbean itself bears close comparison to modern, "Western" societies in terms of its work and trade patterns, industrialization, political formations, even its sports. Moreover, the Caribbean does not simply mimic these Western processes but has historically made a major contribution to their creation. Famously, profits flowing from the plantations of the Caribbean have been seen as the fuel for European industrial expansion and social change.[22] Thus, the Caribbean does not stand in contradistinction to the West but is part of it; conversely, too, the West as we understand it could not exist without the Caribbean.

SLAVES TO THE RHYTHM

With the mass influx of largely West African slaves to the circum-Caribbean, rhythm became a marker of racial difference and cultural inferiority, on the one hand, and a sign of resistance and impenetrable black subjectivity, on the other. As slave ships left the coast of West Africa, many distressed slaves would throw themselves overboard, beat their heads against the walls, or try to suffocate or starve themselves to death. Once Africa was out of sight, however, as one slave trader reported, the slaves could be cheered up through the playing of music (Savary 1675, 140).[23] In this sense, music was also a source of comfort and a means of making the experience of slavery to some extent bearable. For newly arrived slaves, music and rhythm soon became some of the strongest markers of identity. Even if the sounds of their songs initially seemed "absurdly out of place" in the

New World, gradually the "reassuring texture of their own words" and the "resonance of the music's pulse"—in other words, its rhythm—"transported them to a place where something other than their appalling conditions mattered" (White and White 2005, xi). In terms of musical modes, the diverse African peoples brought to the New World the apart-playing, polyrhythms, cross-rhythms, timeline, elisions, hockets, ululations, tremolos, vocables, grunts, hums, shouts, and melismatic phrasings of their homelands (Floyd 1995, 38). Just as drums communicated messages or "talked" by imitating the rhythms and tonality of speech, so too some of the wordless calls, howls, and hollers of slaves functioned as an "alternative communication system," conveying information through sounds in ways that whites "could neither confidently understand nor easily jam" (White and White 2005, 20). Although African music and dance were often viewed with suspicion and suppressed by whites, slave masters soon learned that their slaves worked more effectively when they sang, and they appointed a lead singer for each group of working slaves. Indeed, when slaves were auctioned, singers with the strongest voices attracted the highest prices (Kebede 1982, 130). In work songs, pronounced, regular rhythms at once echoed the repetitive nature of much of the work and helped slaves endure its monotony. Thus, one contemporary observer of plantation life in pre-revolution Saint-Domingue wrote of the "abundance" and "peace" of the place and of "the dutiful Africans working in cadence" (Popkin 2007, 70). Game and social songs were also marked by regular meters and consisted of simple additive rhythms and repetitive pentatonic melodic constructions, with accents on the offbeat (Floyd 1995, 51).[24]

Slavery had many discordant sounds: the cracking of overseers' whips; the cries and screams of slaves; the pealing of bells and the sounding of conch shells to mark out different periods of the slaves' working day; the grating, mechanical noise of the sugar refineries; the call-and-response singing of working slaves; the genteel sounds of the masters' dances; and the drumming, singing, and clapping that accompanied slave dances on weekends and holidays. Many of these sounds, both musical and industrial, were rhythmic and repetitive, sonic accompaniments to lives that were themselves governed by repeated routines and rhythmic patterns of work.

If it is true that circum-Caribbean music has evolved from largely African sources, the African understanding of rhythm cannot, however, be directly transposed onto the Caribbean or other New World locales where slave culture developed. The transported slaves undoubtedly took with them to the New World their intimate relationship with and deeply felt sensitivity to rhythm. Indeed, on the plantations, slaves accompanied virtually every kind of work with songs, chants, and movements that were primarily characterized by rhythm. However, in the New World, African rhythm inevitably clashed, meshed, and creolized with other musical styles and other rhythms that shaped, structured, and stunted slaves' lives in ways that they could never have foreseen in Africa.[25] From the regular beating of the Atlantic waves on the hull of the slave ship to the constant push and pull of the ship's oars in calm waters, rhythm became more than a benign social and cultural element—a sign of common identity. It also came to mark submission, alienation, and loss of identity.[26]

On the plantation, too, repression had its own rhythms, not least the steady crack of the master's whip—a fixed number of thrashings meted out in time according to a system of control whose broadest functions were stipulated by rhythms, repetitions, and routines. Most fundamentally, plantation life engaged slaves in a cyclical, year-long system of work that was dictated by the rhythm of the crop itself. The slaves' experience of time in the New World was figured around the cycle of planting and harvesting, a "natural," agrarian rhythm that was nonetheless altered and manipulated by the planter to enhance productivity and to keep slaves occupied at all times. The natural rhythm of the crop created changing periods, alternating rhythms of work and rest, but in order to maintain regular work habits the planter implemented a constant, unrelenting rhythm of work, a deadening routine of repetitive tasks. During the fifteen- to eighteen-month cycle between planting and harvesting sugar cane, field rotation was scrupulously structured so that the planting of one crop would be quickly followed by the harvesting of another. The slaves' work routine was polyrhythmic, a multilayered loop of repetitive functions (Tomich 2000, 422). Moreover, this work indicates something of the relation between social convention and repetition as well as the way that the former depends on the latter (in work, habits, ways of thinking) as a means of perpetuating itself.[27] Yet this kind of enforced, unending repetition was also a sign of deep insecurity, a tacit recognition of the "unnatural," ultimately untenable practices of plantation slavery.

In the Caribbean, the slaves' monotonous, rhythmic experience of time was compounded by the largely constant year-round duration of the day in the tropics. The slight variations in daylight from one month to the next created a temporal continuity that reinforced the unending repetitions that structured work. In the American South from the 1830s onward, slaveholders adopted a mechanical "clock-dependent time consciousness" that was communicated to slaves through the regular, rhythmic soundings of bells and horns. Because the slaves or their forebears had come from societies in which clocks were virtually absent, where the sense of time was "task-oriented" and "natural," they had to adjust themselves to the strictures and demands of the clock-regulated world, to the plantation's "mechanical regulation of life and thought" (M. Smith 1996, 143, 152, 157, 158).[28] It is significant in this regard that a contemporary observer in colonial Saint-Domingue remarked how two slave foremen wore pocket watches "to distinguish themselves" from the field workers. It was as if the mastery and domination of people went hand in hand with the control of time (Popkin 2007, 41).

In Saint-Domingue, slave drivers would wake up the slaves half an hour before sunrise with the crack of a whip, the ringing of a bell, or the blowing of a conch shell, repeated sounds that structured the passing of days and that were auditory reminders of their subjugation to the alienating rhythms of the plantation (Dubois 2004, 38).[29] Starting work between five and six o'clock in the morning, the slaves would work for nine or ten hours, until sunset. Daytime was the unit of measurement for slaves' work, but the divisions between different parts of the day were less fixed and were subject to the judgment of the overseer, who was himself under constant pressure to maximize production. In the French Caribbean, divisions between successive periods of the day—rest times, lunch time—were marked by the blowing of a whistle or conch shell, the ringing of a bell, or, most often, the cracking of the overseer's whip. The use of the whip—the source of rhythmic flagellation—to mark time emphasized the motifs of control and punishment that structured slaves' experience of time. Moreover, it strongly suggested that time and existence itself were lived as punishments.

In terms of religion, too, there was temporal conflict on the plantation. African and European systems of belief structured the calendar around regular observances of holy days and seasons. Yet these calendars followed quite different rhythms: the African gods are related to calendrical events and are identified with natural cycles, such as the spring new year festivals, whereas the Christian calendar is shaped less by natural factors than by the cycle of holy days. In effect, the African system often had to adapt to the Christian cycle, and slaves came to perform their African ceremonies on major Catholic feast days: rituals of purification were held during the Christmas season, and departed ancestors were honored on the Feast of All Souls (Desmangles 1992, 10). Time and culture in the plantation world were structurally interrelated and interdependent and were always "mediated by rhythm" (Filmer 2003, 91).

During the harvest season, the regular routine of the workday was superseded by another irresistible rhythm: the mechanical workings of the mill and the regular flow of the boiling house, whose machines took the place of the overseer in that they dictated the rhythms of life during this hectic period, when the processing of ripe cane had to be carried out within strict time limits. On larger estates, shift systems divided the day into seven and a half hour periods, thereby creating a continuous flow of time, a never-ending workday shaped by the rhythmic cutting of cane and the grinding, pounding, swirling machines of the mill. In a very real sense, slaves were machines, too, driven by endlessly alienating rhythms.[30] In his classic work on the colonial French Caribbean, *Nouveau voyage aux isles de l'Amérique* (1722), Jean-Baptiste Labat writes in great detail of plantation machinery and presents humans as both driving and being driven by the machinery (Garraway 2005, 139). For Labat, sugar production was the most demanding of all contemporary industries, requiring fully eighteen hours of work, and therefore leaving the workers, the slaves, a mere six hours in which to eat and sleep (Labat 1722, 2: 194). In this Caribbean factory, slaves had to keep up with the rhythm of the machinery or else "be consumed by it" (Garraway 2005, 140). The slaves' consciousness of their machine-like status is suggested in an episode that took place in April 1784 in colonial Saint-Domingue when, emulating the French scientific pioneers who one year previously had sent the world's first balloon into the sky, a group of Saint-Domingue whites, including a man called Odeluc, the administrator of three plantations, launched a balloon 1,800 feet into the sky above the sugarcane fields south of the city of Le Cap. In contrast to the "deep admiration" of the white onlookers, the black spectators are reported to have "called out tirelessly" at the "insatiable passion of men to submit nature to his power" (Moreau 1958, 1: 289–90). As Laurent Dubois surmises, the slaves were likely thinking about and commenting on their own position (2004, 91), their own status as natural beings submitted to the power of men and dehumanized science.

The planters' view of slaves as dehumanized, consumable entities and as parts of the rhythmic machinery of the plantation is confirmed in a statement made by the administrator Odeluc. In a letter he wrote in 1785, he wondered how the plantation could produce a lot of sugar "when we work only sixteen hours [per day]." The only way he could think of doing this was "by consuming men and animals" (quoted in Dubois 2004, 93).[31] More than a century earlier, Jean-Baptiste Du Tertre had written frankly of the effects of the plantation machine on slaves: "We feed them however we want," he wrote, "we push them to work like beasts, and with their consent or by force, we draw from them all the service of which they are capable until their death" (Du Tertre 1973, 2: 462).

The principal effect of this machine-like, monotonously rhythmic existence was that the more natural cycles and rhythms of slave lives were violently interrupted. Even on the Gallifet plantation, reputed to be the most advanced in Saint-Domingue in terms of slave living conditions, very few slaves lived over the age of sixty, and few even reached forty years of age. Out of a group of fifty-seven African slaves who arrived on the Gallifet plantation in February 1789, twelve were dead within a year. Similarly, rhythms of reproduction were significantly distorted: the birthrate among slaves was unnaturally low, and out of those children who were born, a third died in infancy (Dubois 2004, 93).[32] Suicide, abortion, and infanticide were widespread among the slaves, even though these acts were severely punished. For example, the bodies of suicides were mutilated (by whites, apparently conscious of this aspect of Vodou belief) so that they would be disfigured in the afterlife, on their posthumous journey back to Africa (Bell 2007, 15). It is significant, then, that as the slave revolt in Saint-Domingue spread across the colony in August 1791 the insurgents not only set light to the cane fields and the masters' homes but also, in many cases, "smashed to pieces" all of the machinery related to sugar manufacturing. Throughout the northern region where the insurgency first took hold, rebel slaves destroyed the "manufacturing installations, sugar mills, tools and other farm equipment, storage bins, and slave quarters; in short, every material manifestation of their existence under slavery and its means of exploitation" (quoted in Dubois 2004, 96).[33]

The end of the cane harvest brought a temporary break in the rhythm of the plantation. Slaves were rewarded according to their endeavors in the harvest with, among other things, money, meat, syrup, and sugar. Two days of dancing released the slaves from the tyranny of industrial time and returned them fleetingly to their more benign, organic rhythms.[34] In the mechanized world of the plantation, such dances were rare moments of escape and seminal episodes in the creation of Caribbean social relations and aesthetics. It was through dance and rhythm—chiefly the language of the drum—that slaves began to (re)form an idea of themselves, an identity other than, if not entirely different to, that of the deadening machine of the plantation. As Gérard Barthélemy states, "music through dancing and especially rhythmic motions were to constitute . . . the only means of socialization since rhythm allows the emergence of collective expression while foregoing any pre-established structure" (quoted in Lahens 1998, 159). Implicit in Barthélemy's argument is the idea that the rhythm of the dances was completely divorced from the everyday working existence of the slaves. However, given the ways in which repetitive rhythms structured daily routine, the insistent rhythms of the dance are perhaps better considered not as untainted African cultural echoes but as doubled, distorted, creolized reverberations of the slaves' entire historical experience, from Africa through the Middle Passage to the plantation. It is possible to think of these early Caribbean rhythms not as an escape from the rhythms of the plantation but as cultural figurations of those very same rhythms, the pain of which is in part purged through the rhythmic intensity of the dance and the drum. If this kind of catharsis through dance and music were to be effective, it required the presence and consciousness of the source of suffering, not its forgetting. Or, at least, dances both erased and replenished memory. As one contemporary observer noted in colonial Saint-Domingue, dances such as the *chica* were the slaves' "only way of forgetting and of remembering" (Popkin 2007, 334). In a sense, therefore, the slave dances helped perpetuate the plantation system, as they were a means of releasing some of the tensions that forced labor inevitably created. Indeed, despite their reservations about the potential rebelliousness to which music and dance might lead, many slave owners permitted their slaves to hold their dances and to sing while working, "mov[ing] their bodies rhythmically to the beat of their songs" (White and White 2005, 55). Both on the plantation and at the dance, rhythm leveled individual identity and demanded the submission of the individual to a wider entity, be it the machine or the social collective that Barthélemy suggests.[35] In short, this early Caribbean rhythmicity seems to have been more than a straightforward cultural memory of Africa, in that it mirrored, echoed, and partially purged the alienating reality of slave existence.[36]

This idea—that slave dances were not simply means of escaping and forgetting the deadening rhythms of everyday life—is perhaps confirmed by the fact that, as one ethnographer recorded in the 1950s, the dances and rituals of Haitian Vodou *Petro* ceremonies were dominated by the constant sound of "the crack of the slave-whip," which was a "never-to-be-forgotten ghost" that called to memory the "raging revolt of the slaves against the Napoleonic forces" and the "delirium of triumph of the Haitian Revolution" (Deren 1953, 62).[37] In other words, the memory of slavery, at least in Maya Deren's interpretation, is not excluded from the ritualistic dance but is instead integral to its continuing purgative functions. It is reasonable to infer from this post-revolution dance that, in colonial Saint-Domingue and across the circum-Caribbean, slaves' dances were never simply diversions from everyday reality. Rather, they were intense magnifications and (partial) purgations of that reality. Also, more generally, the entranced, "possessed" state induced by rhythmic music and dance did not and does not constitute a loss of identity but is perhaps "the surest way back to the self, to an identity lost, submerged, and denigrated" by New World history (Dayan 1995, 74).

In this book, I seek out the connections between rhythms, music, dance, and the obscured, "denigrated" identities of circum-Caribbean black peoples and cultures. As chapter 1 shows, the repression and denigration of rhythm, music, and dance in the New World has not always been figured around dualistic black-white conceptions of race and culture. Probing into the post-revolution history and culture of Haiti, this chapter examines the paradox that the celebrated first black republic of the New World has, much like European colonial regimes, often repressed and devalorized as uncivilized and savage the rhythms of its popular culture. Arguing that social class and color divisions were constructed around cultural prejudices inherited from colonial times, I track the evolution of Haitian elite culture (chiefly in literature and art music) and popular culture (principally the sacred dances and music of Vodou) from the early post-revolution period to the 1940s, from rampant Francophilia to indigenist recuperation of the neglected "African" elements of popular culture. This evolution, as the chapter shows, may be figured around changing notions and representations of rhythm in literature, music, and ethnographic discourse.

Chapter 2 traces the more conventionally colonial history of rhythm and its suppression in nineteenth- and early-twentieth-century Trinidad. In the early part of this period, the drum and rhythmic popular music in general were systematically suppressed by the British authorities, who were fearful of slave insurrection, particularly because many of their slaves had arrived in Trinidad from the French Caribbean. I show how the British were often in conflict with the French Creole planter elite over questions of culture, especially Carnival. The history of Carnival is re-read in this chapter as a record of the attempted suppression of rhythmic, black popular music and the resistance of the masses to a succession of ordinances that banned the playing of African drums. At every point in the cultural history of Trinidad during this period, rhythm was momentarily silenced, only to return via new, improvised instruments such as bottles and spoons, biscuit tins, pieces of bamboo, and finally the steelpan. Repression of rhythmic music only strengthened the bond between rhythm and the popular black culture of the island.

Chapter 3 focuses more squarely on literature and on the persistence of rhythm in the literary and intellectual discourse of the French Caribbean islands of Martinique and Guadeloupe. Beginning with the Negritude movement's evocation of rhythm as an essential element of black culture and black being, I show how this rhythm-blackness equation was subsequently called into question by intellectuals such as René Ménil and Frantz Fanon, both of whom sought to demystify and de-racialize issues of culture and identity. Fanon's call for a more socially grounded engagement with French Caribbean existence was taken up by Joseph Zobel, notably in his classic novel *La Rue Cases-Nègres*. This more realist representation of Martinican life incorporated a reworked conception of rhythm as a living, evolving element in the lives of the island's poor. Subsequent readings of novels by Édouard Glissant and Daniel Maximin further show how rhythm has remained an important literary, theoretical, and sociocultural trope in the French Caribbean. In Maximin's case, rhythmic music is the single most significant phenomenon that links the cultures and peoples of the French Caribbean to those of the broader circum-Caribbean world and, in particular, to the great black musical traditions of the United States.

The final chapter develops the understanding of these links and the role played by rhythm in perpetuating them by shifting the focus from the Caribbean to the United States. Reflecting primarily on James Brown's development in the 1960s and 1970s of a distinctively rhythmic musical style, I demonstrate how Brown's rhythms were interpreted by black radicals such as Amiri Baraka as manifestations of living African aesthetics. The chapter also shows how this interpretation has been rejected by more recent critics such as Fred Moten, who places less emphasis on where the music has putatively come from than on what its performances and practices say about the lived present.

As the exasperated driver in *The Swimmer* seemed to realize, the question of whether there is a natural, biological link between black peoples and rhythm is a largely redundant one that has hindered discussion and clouded understanding of the diverse roles rhythm has played in diasporic New World cultures. In the chapters that follow, I consider how rhythm has been incorporated into conceptions of black culture and identity, and I ask new questions of rhythm: How has it been manipulated by various social, political, and cultural groups, and to what ends? How has rhythm shaped and defined history, societies, and cultures across the circum-Caribbean world? In each of the diverse though related and interconnected cases examined, rhythm is a contested concept that is sometimes vilified and repressed, sometimes glorified and valorized. As becomes clear, however, rhythm has been an ever-present aspect of New World cultural and social history, and it is a vital element in our understanding of where cultures in this hemisphere have come from and where they may go in the future.

Beating Back Darkness

Rhythm and Revolution in Haiti

In many crucial ways, the history of the modern Caribbean begins in Haiti in 1804, with Jean-Jacques Dessalines's declaration of independence. It was here that the fallible nature of colonial military power and, more importantly, of colonial ideology in the Caribbean was first exposed. The Haitian Revolution that began in 1791 dealt blows to the notion of innate European, "white" superiority, sending cracks through the colonial edifice that could never be repaired and that, over time, brought the whole enterprise crashing down. The events in Haiti effectively realized the lofty egalitarian ideals of the European Enlightenment: played out on the battlegrounds of colonial Saint-Domingue, the struggle between enslaving, domineering supremacism and liberating universalism demonstrated how notions of liberty, equality, and fraternity could not be applied exclusively but had to include every race, nation, and individual. For this reason alone, Haiti is the single most important point of origin for the Caribbean and perhaps also for broader New World black communities.

If Haiti is an exemplar for the postcolonial New World, it is also unremittingly, radically atypical. Haiti is at once the center of Caribbean history and an unknown entity, remaining on the outside, ignored, and misunderstood. To learn about Haiti is to come to know paradox, to understand how its truth often lies in contradictions and disrupted logic. This chapter explores one of these Haitian paradoxes: the way the fabled first black republic in the New World has long neglected and repressed, or else selectively appropriated, the "blackest" parts of its culture, chiefly its religion and its associated rhythmic music and dance. In postcolonial Haiti, rhythm, so long feared by the French colonists as an instigator of slave revolt, was subjected to renewed state control as the nation struggled to reconcile its modern, Europeanized idea of itself with its dynamic, African-rooted yet ever creolizing cultural traditions. Beginning in 1800 with François Dominique Toussaint Louverture's attempts to control Vodou dances, I consider some of the roles music played in the revolution and pay particular attention to the evolution of the Vodou religion in the nineteenth century and the roles of drumming and dance in religious rituals. Drawing on Haitian ethnography, literature, and musicology, I analyze the evolving relationship between the intellectual elite and Haiti's popular culture, from the nineteenth-century Francophile renunciation of it to the early- to mid-twentieth-century embrace of it as an authentic repository of the "Haitian soul." At every stage, rhythm has been an omnipresent albeit contested and shifting element of Haitian culture. In addition, I pay attention to how the rhythms and ideas of Saint-Dominguan refugees migrated to other Caribbean and New World sites and became integral parts of the emerging cultures there. Just as the ideas of the French Revolution could not be confined to France, so too those of the Haitian Revolution spread over the New World and blew across land and sea in pamphlets, tales, song, dance, and rhythm.

FREEDOM AND CONSTRAINT

In January 1800, Toussaint Louverture, one of the great leaders of the slave insurgency in Saint-Domingue, issued a decree that outlawed "nocturnal assemblies and dances." Peaceful cultivators, he said, had been led away from their work in the fields by men with "bad intentions" to gatherings and dances, principally "those of Vaudoux." Such practices were contrary to the principles of true "friends to their country" and were subversive activities that would henceforth be punished physically or by imprisonment (quoted in Dubois 2004, 244).[1] A year later, Toussaint's constitution brought further restrictions on popular black culture and declared that Catholicism was to be the only "publicly professed" religion in the land. Taking care to limit the extent of individual priests' "spiritual administration," Toussaint promoted Christian family values, "civil and religious marriage" and general "purity of habits" among the populace.

At the same time, Toussaint's administration, eager to reestablish the lucrative plantations that had made Saint-Domingue France's most profitable colony, was encouraging emancipated slaves back onto the land, often with a degree of coercion. Most of the newly freed slaves had been born in Africa, and once liberated their natural tendency was to return to the subsistence agriculture practices of African village life, not to the plantation. Toussaint was deeply concerned about this tendency and about the numbers of the newly freed who had adopted an itinerant, wandering way of life (Bell 2007, 203). "Work is necessary, it is a virtue," Toussaint had said in March 1795, and "all lazy and errant men will be punished by the law." A few months later, he wrote to the French general Étienne Laveaux, saying that he was "busy gathering the cultivators, the drivers, and the managers, exhorting them to love work, which is inseparable from liberty" (quoted in Dubois 2004, 188). In 1800, the plantation, long the site of slaves' violent subjugation, was being reimagined by Toussaint in benevolent, familial terms as a "factory that requires the union of cultivators and workers; . . . the tranquil refuge of an active and loyal family, whose father is necessarily the owner of the soil or his representative" (quoted in Dubois 2004, 244). The common cultivators, as members of the plantation family, were not permitted to leave the "home" of the "father," the owner of the soil, who in many ways assumed the power and status of the planters that the slave armies had taken such pains to remove. In a final, cruelly ironic twist, Toussaint stated his intention of taking the "appropriate measures" to bring new cultivators from Africa to bolster his own workforce, which had been seriously depleted during the course of the revolutionary wars. In effect, Toussaint was contemplating cooperating with merchants to transport men and women from Africa to work as cultivators on Saint-Domingue's plantations (Dubois 2004, 244–45).

Toussaint's constitution was articulating a classical political claim, which drew on the previous policies of both Republican France and Republican Saint-Domingue and which asserted the responsibility of citizens in supporting and sustaining their nation. As Laurent Dubois says, however, such claims, in the power they gave to a "potentially abusive state" to define citizens' responsibilities, inevitably created contradictions between liberty and obligation. In the case of Saint-Domingue, these contradictions were particularly striking, as Dubois argues:

> On the one hand, the project that all of the people of Saint-Domingue were called upon to support was a project of emancipation, of freedom from racial hierarchy, of liberty for all in a land once dominated by slavery. At the same time, ex-slaves were given very particular responsibilities that were defined by their old status: those who had once worked as slaves were now free, but they were required to work as cultivators. To defend freedom, they had to surrender their freedom to the new state. (2004, 245)

RHYTHM, MUSIC, AND MILITARISM
IN THE REVOLUTIONARY ERA

A similar paradox existed in terms of culture and rhythm. Toussaint's 1800 decree prohibiting Vodou dances meant that, in order to be free politically, the ex-slaves had to surrender their cultural freedom to Toussaint's state, which amounted to a perpetuation of the racist policies of popular cultural suppression that had characterized French colonial rule. Indeed, the control of Vodou ceremonies was nothing new in the colony. They had already been prohibited by the Code Noir of 1685, and the Catholic Church had worked assiduously toward eradicating African "superstitious" practices. Its missionaries were responsible for a series of police rulings that restricted the movements of slaves and controlled the use of objects associated with Vodou rituals (Gisler 1965, 78–79). In particular, the Police Rulings of 1758 and 1777 prohibited the slaves "under penalty of death" from meeting during the day or night under the pretext of celebrating weddings or marking the deaths of fellow slaves. Drum playing and singing other than when engaged in field labor were also prohibited. The 1758 ruling stipulated, moreover, that slaves were not to gather either "near the house of their master or anywhere else, and even less in and around remote places" (Desmangles 1992, 36). In 1765, the dancing of the *calenda* was expressly forbidden, and a special division of the rural police was set up to ensure such dances did not occur (Garraway 2005, 355, n. 30). Following Toussaint, Jean-Jacques Dessalines and Alexandre Pétion were to prohibit dances, fearing, like their predecessor, that the dances might disrupt the good order of the new Haitian state (Barthélemy 2000, 159).

The uprising begun in 1791 had spectacularly swept away the institution of slavery, but many of the racist ideas and cultural prejudices that had underpinned slavery remained strong, both among slave leaders such as Toussaint and among those in French politics who promoted the interests of the plantation owners. For example, in early 1795, less than a year after slavery was abolished in the French colonies, Marie-Benoît-Louis Gouly, a planter and representative from the Indian Ocean colony of Ile-de-France, made a speech at the French National Convention in Paris that portrayed the former slaves of Saint-Domingue in crudely racist terms. His portrayal made a direct link between blacks' intellectual inferiority, their sensory limitations, and their cultural practices. To grant freedom and citizenship to people whose souls were accessible "only through the organ of hearing," who were animated only by the "loud sounds of a drum or a voice expressed with force," whose eyes had no "vivacity," and who generally presented the "image of stupidity" was, Gouly argued, patently absurd (quoted in Dubois 2004, 194). Although there was nothing new in Gouly's pro-slavery racism, it is interesting in terms of music and dance that he connects the heightened (or perhaps, in his view, overactive) auditory sense of the ex-slaves with the purported deficiencies of their other senses and faculties. Dance, drumming, and rhythm, he implied, functioned contrarily to the other senses and dulled the intellect. Toussaint's 1800 decree seemed informed to some extent by this kind of long-standing racist view of black musical practice. Moreover, it seemed to negate or deny (or, at best, fail to recognize) the crucial role that popular culture—dances, songs, drumming, religion—played in fomenting the spirit of revolt and common black identity that had helped the slave armies hold strong against the many and diverse adversaries they had faced since 1791.

It is significant in this regard that the founding moment (or perhaps founding myth) of the Haitian Revolution was a ceremony of music, dance, drumming, and religion. Even if the truth of the Bois-Caïman ceremony has been clouded by a lack of reliable contemporary sources, most historians agree that, in mid-August 1791, Dutty Boukman, a Vodou priest and former driver and coachman, led conspiring slaves in a secret gathering on a plantation in northern Saint-Domingue, somewhere between the Gallifet plantation and the town of Le Cap.[2] Dubois suggests that there may have been two ceremonies in August 1791, and he argues for Bois-Caïman's importance as a symbol less of a specific, historically knowable event than of the achievement of Saint-Domingue's slave insurgents and the "creative spiritual and political epic that both prompted and emerged from the 1791 insurrection" (2004, 102).

Music and religion were closely intertwined in this "spiritual and political epic." Religious practices and ceremonial dances facilitated the organization of the rebellion and fostered a sense of community and identity among the diverse ethnic African groups and between them and the Creole slaves (that is, those born in the New World). In contrast to the whites, whose dances were held strictly on secular, social occasions, the blacks incorporated dance and music into their religious rituals (and vice versa), their funerals, and their wakes, and therefore music was less of a social entertainment than a link with a metaphysics and an identity that had their roots in Africa but were inevitably mutating and being translated into their new context. Even as African cultures and religions were transported across the Atlantic, they were changing: religions fused with the rituals and symbols of Catholicism, and the Christian saints' identities were often doubled with African deities in the new syncretic religion. Thus, one white observer noted in 1777 that at the community of La Fossette, just outside Le Cap, there was a burial mound called Croix bossale where unbaptized Africans, or *bossales,* were buried. Near this site, he noted, the blacks held their dances on Sunday nights or holidays, so that it became "a theater of fury and pleasure" (Moreau de Saint-Méry 1958, 2: 543–44).[3] These dances can therefore be read as acts of memory, as a means of remaining close, spatially and culturally, to the dead. It is significant that the observer juxtaposes the apparently contradictory states of fury and pleasure: the dance and the music, it seems, were means of expressing and partially exorcizing anger and thereby of attaining pleasure. In the alienating, mechanized world of the plantation, religious ceremonies, music, and dance offered slaves more familiar rhythms and rituals as well as a group identity that the plantation owners and colonial administrators sought largely, though not consistently, to negate and nullify. The Code Noir had specifically prohibited slaves of different masters to gather "under the pretext of weddings or otherwise," especially in rural areas, but the regulation was never enforced completely or consistently by masters, some of whom apparently considered slave gatherings as harmless diversions or perhaps as events that purged to some extent the slaves of their frustrations and in this way helped ensure a less agitated and more compliant workforce (Sala-Moulins 1987, 122–24). Religion, rituals, dances, and music became for slaves a "space of freedom" (Dubois 2004, 43) in an otherwise restrictive society, and they helped create the social networks and consciousness of difference that proved vital to the future success of the revolution.

Partly because of its close association with African ritual, music was a source of fear for white Europeans. The auditory aspects of the slave armies' style of warfare were intended to unnerve their adversaries and included the beating of drums, howling, whistling, and trumpeting on large conch shells (Arthur and Dash 1999, 39). The slave armies' auditory elements were particularly striking to one French soldier, who reported how the slaves advanced to the accompaniment of rhythmic African music or else in a silence that was broken only by the "incantations of their sorcerers" (quoted in Dubois 2004, 101). Similarly, French naturalist Michel Étienne Descourtilz, who visited Saint-Domingue in the late 1790s, wrote of African fighters marching into battle "with a supernatural intrepidity, singing Guinean songs, as if possessed by the hope that they would soon see their old acquaintances" (quoted in Dubois 2004, 295–96).[4] The close connection between religion, music, and slave insurrection was further confirmed in the account of another contemporary, who described how, before battle, religious leaders prepared *ouanga,* or fetishes, and thereby "exalted the imagination of the women and children, who sang and danced like demons" (quoted in Dubois 2004, 101). In addition to songs and drums, and when more conventional instruments were not available, slave armies would fill pots with stones to increase the noise that accompanied their attacks and thereby, it seems, spread fear and confusion among the enemy ranks (Dubois 2004, 140). The whites' fear of slave music and the music's capacity to unnerve whites were heightened in one particular case in October 1791 when, in the initial stages of the insurrection, a group of whites were taken prisoner by slave insurgents and led to a camp in which the highest ranking slave leader was the notorious Jeannot Bullet (commonly known simply as Jeannot). One of the white prisoners, a local official called Gros, wrote later of how the prisoners were kept chained and given only basic rations. Moreover, he wrote, the "terror" of the prisoners worsened at nights because of the black insurgents' "sad songs, accompanied by instruments, [which] seemed to be a prelude to new tortures" (Dubois and Garrigus 2006, 104). Later, too, when Jeannot had some prisoners taken to be executed, "chopped to pieces or strung up and bled to death," the death march was accompanied by the sound of a drum (quoted in Dubois 2004, 123). And when the slave leader Boukman was decapitated and his body burned in view of the rebel camps by the French in mid-November 1791, the insurgents immediately began a three-day *calenda* dance (Dubois and Garrigus 2006, 107). The insurgent slaves' music in these cases seems to have been used deliberately to heighten the mental torture of the white prisoners, who had long feared the hidden messages and meanings of slave music and its capacity to retain and incite a sense of black subjectivity and resistance that could not be completely nullified by the processes of slavery. The music contained, in a sense, a prophecy of defiance and overcoming that was being realized graphically in the grotesque reversals of torture and suffering at Jeannot's prison camp.

In addition to the African drumming and songs that often accompanied slave armies, distinctly European musical forms were used in the revolutionary battles. From the earliest days of colonial Saint-Domingue to the present, social and cultural life have been marked by a pervasive strain of militarism. This is the result of a complex set of factors, including the military backgrounds that many first-generation slaves took with them to Saint-Domingue, the organization on some plantations of slaves into militaristic "national" structures, the slaves' long experience of serving in the French (and British and Spanish) colonial military, the protracted fight for independence itself, and the Haitian army's postcolonial domination of social, economic, and political life (Averill and Yih 2000, 268, 271).[5] From the early colonial era to the twenty-first century, this persistent militarism has influenced Haitian culture, especially its music. European military practices in the eighteenth century used music—chiefly drums—to communicate commands during battle. In central Africa, drums and trumpets were used to regulate the movements of armies in battle (Forbath 1977, 97). And, many of the slave groups in Saint-Domingue had their own militaristic dances and songs. The Ibo nation, for instance, which was renowned for resistance to slavery, is honored in Vodou ceremonies with a dance that evokes its military prowess. Another Vodou dance, the *nago,* is performed for Ogou, the deity of war, and is considered a war dance (Averill and Yih 2000, 276).

It is likely that European and African systems of military music (and dance) syncretized in Saint-Domingue and constituted a kind of common language among soldiers of all colors. In Saint-Domingue, a musical corps was assigned to each military division, the light infantrymen or chasseurs, the grenadiers, the artillery, the sharpshooters, and the palace guard. Port-au-Prince alone had sixteen such musical corps, and many more were in the provincial towns (Averill and Yih 2000, 272). In addition to these units, the Haitian army also had fife, drum, and bugle corps that had more formal functions, such as playing in public ceremonies (for example, the consecration of Dessalines as emperor in 1804), calling reveille, and serenading leaders and other distinguished persons (Averill and Yih 2000, 274). A further Haitian musical style, still used today to serenade the powerful in Haitian society, is called *ochan* (from the French military call "aux champs") and has retained European military signal style in its drum rhythms. In contrast to the polyrhythmic style of Vodou drumming, *ochan* drumming is played to a single underlying rhythm, in "heterophonic rhythmic unison" (Averill and Yih 2000, 279). The practice of war in Saint-Domingue was therefore an important force in syncretizing culture, and rhythmic appropriation and mixing was one of the principal means of translating diverse (though in many ways similar) European and African military music into the Caribbean context. Allied with other rhythmic military activities, such as drilling, music established group cohesion among the armed forces. After all, keeping together in time was often a condition for surviving military engagements (Filmer 2003, 95).[6]

MUSIC, DANCE, AND RITUAL
IN COLONIAL SAINT-DOMINGUE

Evidence of the importance of religion, dance, and music to slave life in Saint-Domingue is provided in Médéric-Louis-Élie Moreau de Saint-Méry's remarkable study of the pre-insurrection colony, *Description topographique, physique, civile, politique et historique de la partie française de l'isle de Saint-Domingue* (1796). In his description of the slaves of French Saint-Domingue, Moreau divided them into two groups: those born in Africa (who made up two-thirds of the slave population), and those born in the colony, the Creole slaves. In general, Moreau believed the Creole slaves to have superior moral and physical attributes than those born in Africa (Moreau de Saint-Méry 1958, 1: 59). When it came to dance, however, Moreau observed that both groups of slaves shared a common passion and would travel great distances, often at night, to satisfy this passion (1: 63). The principal dance Moreau discussed was the *calenda*, a dance that he said came with the slaves from Africa and that even Creole slaves learned from a very young age. Two drums made from hollowed-out wood were required for the dance: one that was left open, and one over which stretched the skin of a sheep or a goat. The shorter drum was called *bamboula* because it was often formed from bamboo. A male slave sat astride the drums, playing them with fingers and thumbs, one to a quick rhythm, the other more slowly, and this "muted and monotonous" sound was joined by the rhythmic shaking of calabashes filled with little stones or seeds. For a fuller sound, the percussion instruments were sometimes accompanied by the *banza*, a crude, four-stringed type of violin that was plucked.[7] The rhythms of the male players were regulated by the women, who gathered in a circle, clapping their hands in time and responding in unison to the one or two female singers who repeated or improvised the songs. Black people, Moreau believed, "have the talent of improvisation," which showed itself in their skill for verbal duels (1: 63).

Dancers moved in pairs to the center of the circle and danced the *calenda*, which involved highly stylized, animated movements and had, Moreau said, "a precise rhythm" that lent it a real sense of grace (1: 64). The rhythmic aspects of slave dances were further affirmed in Moreau's description of the *chica,* another dance of African origin, which had its own song and strong, marked rhythm. This dance, which again was passionately performed by both African and Creole slaves, involved a female dancer moving her hips and buttocks while keeping her upper body immobile; a male dancer approached her in a rhythmic, seductive movement that became, for Moreau, first a "voluptuous" then a "lascivious" spectacle (1: 64).[8]

Although the *calenda* and the *chica* appeared to have no religious function, the third dance that Moreau described, the *vaudoux,* was closely connected to religious rituals and had a particular status in what Moreau called "institutions where superstition and bizarre practices have an important role" (1: 64). It was this dance that Toussaint specifically targeted in his 1800 decree and that was associated with the Rada people in the colony, the African-born group that maintained, as Moreau said, the "principles and rules" of *vaudoux* in Saint-Domingue (1: 64), even if the religion had already become a syncretic form and had integrated certain Creole and European beliefs and practices (1: 65). The *vaudoux* ceremonies, especially those that had most retained their "primitive purity," took place in secret, away from "all profane eyes" (1: 65). Moreover, they were far more elaborate and regimented than the other, secular dances. Only after rituals of exhortation and invocation and oaths of secrecy did the *vaudoux* dance begin. It would start with the admission of the *récipiendiaire,* the person to be initiated into the society, into a circle, around which the rest of the group gathered, singing a repetitive African song. As the initiate began to tremble and dance, he was "mounted" by the gods and lost himself in convulsive movements that were stopped only by the king (the *Roi Vaudoux*), who then led the person out of the circle to swear his allegiance to the sect (1: 67). Further dancing followed, characterized by "violent shaking" and what Moreau judged to be a general delirium; he called it a "disgusting prostitution" between various members of the group (1: 67–68).

One remarkable aspect of Moreau's description of the *vaudoux* dance is his reporting that the "magnetism" of the slaves' dancing had sometimes been felt by whites spying on the ceremony. Those whites who had been touched by one of the members of the group would begin to dance uncontrollably, a "punishment" from which they could release themselves by paying the *Reine Vaudoux,* or Vaudoux Queen (1: 68).[9] Remarkably, too, Moreau suggested that to appease the "alarm" that the "mysterious cult of *Vaudoux*" caused in the colony—he talked of the police "war" on the religion—slaves would affect to dance the *vaudoux* in public with drums and clapping and even to serve a meal afterward. As Moreau saw it, this was merely a ruse to escape the vigilance of the magistrates and to ensure the success of the "shadowy meetings" that were not sites of pleasure or entertainment but a "school where the weak-spirited go to give themselves over to a domination" (1: 68). The domination Moreau spoke of is not only that of the gods but that of the Vaudoux leaders, who exercised a great deal of power over the other members of the group. In Moreau's opinion, nothing was more dangerous in Saint-Domingue than the Vaudoux cult, which was founded on the "extravagant" idea that the Vaudoux leaders know and are capable of everything, which was an idea that could be used as a "terrible weapon" (1: 68–69). For Moreau, as for Toussaint later, it was the question of power and authority that was troubling in Vaudoux, the realization that, through rhythmic dance, chanting, and drumming, slave religious leaders could build hidden networks of influence that had the capacity to weaken the structures of colonial and state control.

Moreau also described other, less threatening black dances among the house slaves, who, he said, liked to imitate mockingly the whites in dancing the minuet and the contredanse. Whereas the rhythmic *vaudoux* dances evoked fear in Moreau, the slaves' play on and modification of the European dance forms seemed to amuse him; they were enough, he said, to brighten up the most serious face, even if the changes to the dances appeared at times "grotesque" (1: 69). Moreau observed, moreover, that the slaves had a "keen ear" for music, which enabled them to be first-class musicians. In particular, the blacks excelled in playing the violin, even if they had no formal training in the instrument and must have learned it solely through practicing and listening to other players (1: 69). Such modes of learning created, however, mere "fiddlers," players who in their "noisy sounds," their heavy drinking, and their talent for falling asleep while still playing could not rival the violinists of Paris (1: 69).[10] Slaves' musical improvisation was also evident in their playing of another unnamed instrument, which Moreau described as being made of a small wooden board, steel or brass wire, and very thin reeds or pieces of bamboo. The instrument was played by plucking on the reeds, and its "shrill, monotonous" sounds, accompanied by those of the Jew's harp and of the triangular cymbal and the little scales, completed what he called the instrumental music of the blacks (1: 70).

Music, and sounds in general, seem to have been for slaves means of expressing thoughts that were taboo or outlawed in straightforward linguistic discourse. Moreau described, for example, how the blacks of Le Cap interpreted the melody of the church's funeral bells as saying "One good white is dead. The bad ones are still here" (3: 1253). As Dubois argues, this was perhaps a subtle way of saying that the only good white man was a dead one (2004, 11). It also demonstrates how sounds and music became repositories of a muted though profoundly felt black resistance. At the same time, a propensity for dance linked the blacks to the free coloreds of Saint-Domingue, especially the mulattoes (those who had, according to Moreau's elaborate system of color classification, more or less equal European and African ancestry). The mulattoes, he said, were ruled by their pleasures:

dance, horseriding, and "voluptuousness" (1: 103). Indeed, in Moreau's opinion, there was a common penchant across all colors and classes in Saint-Domingue for pleasure. White Creole women enjoyed singing and, in spite of the climate and the "weakness of their constitution," had a keen enthusiasm for dance, which "revives their existence" and made them forget the indolence that Moreau said they seemed to cherish (1: 41). The white Creole women dictated the rhythm of the dance, which they followed precisely but "without constraint." That is, the women were thrown into a kind of "delirium" by the dance, so that a foreign spectator might believe that dance was the pleasure that "holds the greatest sway over their souls" (1: 41). It seems that, in the Saint-Domingue that Moreau described and across the society's highly stratified groups, races, and colors, there was a shared passion for rhythm, dance, and abandon. For different reasons and in different ways, dancing, singing, and music were used as means of temporary escape and release. Although the abandon of the white Creole women was confined to the controlled spaces of the plantation or town house and was tolerated and even cherished as a distinctive feature of the "most endearing portion of the human species" (1: 39), the *vaudoux* dance, music, and rhythmic escape of the slaves were viewed unequivocally (and with some justification) as profound threats to the colonial society and, later, to Toussaint's nascent state.

Moreau's descriptions of slave dances also indicate a further, fundamental role of rhythm in colonial Saint-Domingue. Moreau was aware of the subtle play within the dance between individuals and the collective group. In spite of the tumult and confusion of the dance that arose from individuals' displays of joy, Moreau said that the dance itself established "a kind of togetherness and simultaneity that ends up controlling them" (1: 64). In this sense, Moreau suggested the ways in which the disparate identities of individual slaves of the more than fifty African ethnicities present in Saint-Domingue were collectivized through the insistently single rhythm of the dance. The fractured identities of the African peoples were brought together through dance, through the "immediate universality of rhythm," creating the "bonding dimension" (Barthélemy 2000, 157) in which individual identity was subsumed into a new, rhythm-driven consciousness of place and time. In the absence and impossibility of more extensive group structures, dance and rhythm had important socializing roles that were crucial factors in adapting to and surviving the plantation world (Barthélemy 2000, 159).

RHYTHMS OF VODOU

Many of Moreau's observations on music, dance, and rhythm in colonial Saint-Domingue are echoed, developed, and given ethnographic validity in Alfred Métraux's modern study of Haitian religion and ritual, *Le Vaudou haïtien* (1958). The scientific perspective of the French ethnographer allows for a fuller, more perceptive description of Haitian music and dance than is found in the colonial author's study. Métraux is particularly sensitive to the relationship between drums, rhythm, and religion. The drum on which the dance rhythms are played, he says, symbolizes Vodou. Moreover, the term "to beat the drum" signifies in the popular language "to celebrate the cult of the *lwas* [deities]." The political importance of the drum is shown in the way that it has been regularly prohibited by the state in its campaigns against "paganism." Even if he is not a *serviteur* (one who serves the gods) himself, the drummer is the "mainspring" of every Vodou ceremony; his "science of rhythm" and vigorous beats determine the ardor of the dancers and the intensity of the "nervous tension" that allows the dancers to attain the desired trance-like state. An unskilled drummer, one who does not completely master his "rhythmic formulas," will create disorder in the dance and prevent the epiphanies of the spirits (159). Vodou drummers have, Métraux says, a fine sense of rhythm and a "vast musical memory" that, allied with their uncommon "nervous resistance," allows them to play their instruments throughout an entire night with an often frenetic passion. Drummers rarely, however, enter into the trance state or are possessed by the spirits. Implicitly, if they are possessed by anything, it is the rhythm itself (159).

Rhythm, Métraux observes, is also one of the principal means of differentiating between the main Vodou rituals. The drums associated with the *Rada* rituals are reproductions of the Dahomean drum. These drums are always played in groups of three, and, though they are identical in shape, they are of three different sizes. The *adjountò* or *manman* is more than a meter high; the *hountò* or *ségond* is smaller but larger than the *boula*, which is between forty and fifty centimeters high. Each of the drums is played differently and is beaten by hand or with various percussive implements (160–61). The largest drum, the *manman*, is given preeminence in the orchestra; it has in its rhythm an "intensity and a freedom" that attracts the spirits (161). The drums used in the *Petro* rituals, in contrast, are played in pairs and are smaller than the *Rada* drums. The *Congo* orchestra comprises three differently sized drums, and in their cylindrical form they resemble European drums. The *djouba* or *Martinique* drums are used only when the peasant divinity Zouka calls out via a *serviteur* for the *djouba* dance to be executed. The rhythm of the dances is emphasized by the *tchatcha*, an instrument made out of a calabash filled with seeds (162).

The drum in Haitian Vodou is more than a mere musical instrument. It is also, as Métraux says, "a sacred object and even the tangible form of a divinity" (163). Believed to contain a "mysterious power," the drum is the first of the sacred objects that the *serviteurs* salute before the ceremony starts, and the priests themselves, the *houngan* and the *mambo*, will in the course of the ceremony kiss the earth before the drums and pour libations on them. Like all divinities, the drums need to be revitalized through sacrifices and offerings. Métraux describes a specific ceremony called *bay manger tambour* in which the instruments are placed on banana leaves close to the *vèvè*, the ritual drawings that represent the drums symbolically, offerings of food and drink are made, and chickens are immolated (163). The ethnologist Milo Rigaud further observes that the ceremony is accompanied by "funereal chants" and that the participants affect a great sadness, because the funeral music announces the departure of the drums to Africa to renew their powers (1953, 387).[11] This is interesting in terms of rhythm because it suggests that the Vodou adherents (quite predictably) consider Africa to be the source of the drum's rhythms, and hence its power, and that the fact of being in the New World somehow diminishes that power and weakens the rhythms.

The most sacred of all the drums is the *assoto*, which stands at more than two meters tall and is played only on solemn occasions. Its importance is suggested in Métraux's observation that most of the *assoto* disappeared—they were destroyed—during the state- and Church-led anti-superstition campaign of the 1940s (1958, 164).[12] Such is its sacred significance that Métraux believes it could be called an "idol" or a "fetish" (165). Jacques Roumain similarly described it as more than an instrument, as a "powerful Afro-Haitian God" (2003g, 1078). The fabrication of the *assoto* takes place in strictly controlled conditions: only prescribed trees can be used, the trees must be cut at full moon, and the skin that covers the drum must be placed on it at exactly midday. Once made, it then undergoes a "baptism" attended by seven or three-times seven "godfathers" and "godmothers," who chant the baptismal song:

> Assoto micho
> We call Jean
> Jean Assoto, I call you
> So that we may baptize the Assoto drum
> God the Father, God the Son, God the Holy Ghost,
> After the Good Lord I baptize you
> You have left Africa
> To come to see the Creoles
> We are happy to see you, Assoto micho,
> I baptize you Assoto.
>   (Roumain 2003g, 1079–80)

This ceremony is similar to the one described above by Rigaud, in that the drum is venerated as an African object that, much like the people, is in exile from the mother continent. Even if the drum has been made in Haiti, it is still considered to have come "to see the Creoles," like a long lost part of themselves. In its adaptation of the Christian baptismal sacrament, this ceremony clearly shows the syncretic nature of Haitian Vodou, and this aspect is further demonstrated in the subsequent acts of honoring the various *lwa*—Legba, Aïzan, Loco, Ogou—and in tracing a cross on the *assoto* with the blood of a sacrificed goat or bull. The ceremony continues with dances, singing, and many possessions by the *lwa rada,* and the *assoto* is beaten in turn by seven *hounsi* (Vodou initiates) with a special drumstick fitted with a nail until the drum skin is punctured (Métraux 1958, 166; Roumain 2003g, 1126).

The syncretic nature of the ceremonies is also apparent in the chants that accompany the dances and ritual acts, and whose melodies are often of European origin (Métraux 1958, 166). The songs themselves belong to African tradition and are part of an "ancient repertoire" even if new songs are created in special circumstances. As in many other African diasporic musical forms (and as Moreau recognized), improvisation is an important element in Haitian ritual music; songs improvised in certain situations pass into the repertoire and are diffused according to the prestige of the *houmfo,* the Vodou temple (Métraux 1958, 167).

The rhythms of the dances and the drums are the primary elements that draw in the spirits; this is why the rhythms are given a "dominant place" in almost all Vodou ceremonies (Métraux 1958, 168). Moreover, if music and dance please the spirits to the point of restricting their resolve, it is because the spirits are themselves dancers who let themselves be carried away by "the supernatural power of rhythm" (Métraux 1958, 168–69). Each *lwa* has its own drum rhythms and dances, which are classified according to ethnic group—Dahomey, Congo, Ibo—but which also include other dances of different origins. Improvisation plays a role in dance, too, in particular when the *manman* drum is beaten with redoubled energy and introduces in the orchestra "breaks" to an off-beat rhythm, which interrupts the movement of the dance and creates a paroxysmal state similar to that attained when being mounted by a *lwa*.[13] Rhythm is, ultimately, the means by which the state of trance is attained. It is linked to the ancestral past as well as being a way of connecting with and living fully in the present and of sensing one's physical, bodily being. In Henri Lefebvre's interpretation of rhythm (1992), the body is an entity neglected in philosophy but one that is made up of rhythms: respiration, the beating of one's heart, the circulation of blood, the flow of one's speech. It is only in music, Lefebvre says, that a perfect accord between all the body's rhythms is achieved and that one "thinks with one's body, not in the abstract, but in lived temporality" (31–32). In Haitian Vodou, rhythm connects believers at once to their community and to their individuality, to the past and to the present.

Haitianist ethnographers like Métraux and Roumain (and others like Melville J. Herskovits and Harold Courlander) observe largely similar music, dance, and religious practices to those recorded by earlier writers like Moreau. The essential differences between the earlier and the later writers lie in perspective and context. Moreau's view of popular culture was clouded by the prejudices of his time and by the fearful recognition that rhythmic music and dance had played significant roles in the Saint-Dominguan slave uprising. The ethnographers were influenced by their own intellectual context, which encouraged openness, curiosity, and scientific observation, and also perhaps by the realization that Vodou dances in the twentieth century had largely lost the capacity to transform society in the way they had before.

TRAVELING IDEAS, TRAVELING RHYTHMS

In the late eighteenth to early nineteenth centuries, however, in Saint-Domingue and across the plantation world, African-derived music and dance were potent tools for insurrection, both in reality and in the white, European imagination. By this time, too, what had started off in Saint-Domingue as a local challenge to French imperial authority by colonial whites, then mutated into a conflict over racial inequality, then became a war over the institution of slavery (Dubois 2004, 3), had become an event of major international importance. Some of the principal means of spreading news among New World slaves about the uprising, and of disseminating the "idea of Haiti," were music, song, and dance.[14] Indeed, one month after the August 1791 uprising, slaves on the neighboring island of Jamaica were singing songs about it. By 1800, when Toussaint had established himself as the effective ruler of Saint-Domingue, slaves sang on the streets of Kingston, Jamaica, "Black, white, brown, all the same" (quoted in Geggus 2001b, x). Informal networks, oral communication, and traveling songs soon spread news of the revolt across the Caribbean, to Virginia and Louisiana in the north and to Brazil in the south. In Trinidad, too, the year after Haitian independence, slaves parodied the Catholic mass and sent ripples of fear through the ranks of nervous planters in the song "Pain nous ka mange/C'est viande beké/Du vin ka boué/C'est sang beké/Hé St Domingo/Songé St Domingo" (The bread we eat/Is the white man's flesh/The wine we drink/Is the white man's blood/Hé St Domingo/remember St Domingo) (quoted in Cowley 1996, 14).

The various stages of the revolutionary war in Saint-Domingue sent successive waves of planters and their slaves from the colony into other New World territories, and these migratory movements helped to disseminate further the news of and the ideas behind the revolution. Across the Americas, the 1790s recorded the highest frequency of slave revolts, and all of the major uprisings took place during the forty years after 1791. Although many different factors were at play in these revolts, historians have consistently found connections to the Saint-Dominguan uprising. From the 1790s, "French" slaves and free coloreds were implicated in revolts in English-, Dutch-, and Spanish-speaking territories (Geggus 2001b, xii). In early-nineteenth-century Trinidad, the British colonial authorities were particularly wary of the newly arrived French Caribbean free coloreds, even if relatively few of them had migrated from Saint-Domingue. White planters across the Caribbean considered the free coloreds to be the true agents of Saint-

Domingue's demise, and in Trinidad the first British governor of the colony, Sir Thomas Picton, urged caution with regard to the island's French Caribbean free coloreds, who, he said, had borne arms and taken part in "Jacobinical outrages and violation" (quoted in Brereton 2006, 128). The Shand Estate Revolt of 1805 was purported to be planned not by free coloreds but by slaves who had come to Trinidad from the French territories and who had plotted a Saint-Dominguan-style uprising on Christmas Day. In the Guadeloupean dependency of Marie-Galante, a few weeks before the Lamentin revolt in Guadeloupe of 1797, a crowd marched to the main town crying out that "they should cut the throats of all the whites and do what was done in Saint-Domingue, where all the leaders were black or *de couleur*" (Dubois 2001, 116).

Similar patterns were repeated across New World plantation societies. In Curaçao in 1795, Francophone slaves led a rebellion in alliance with a local slave who had adopted the name of the Saint-Dominguan revolutionary André Rigaud. In Venezuela that same year, the leader of the Coro rebellion was a sharecropper who had visited Saint-Domingue and who called for the "law of the French." In Barbados in 1816, rebel slaves conspired to spread fire "the way they did in St. Domingo." And in 1822 in Virginia, Denmark Vesey, the rebel freedman who had worked briefly in Saint-Domingue, vowed to his followers that they would have the support of Haitian soldiers once they had taken the city of Charleston (Geggus 2001b, xii).

Quite naturally, the blacks, whites, and free coloreds driven out of Saint-Domingue had cultural impacts on the new territories they settled in. These impacts varied, however, in terms of extent and duration. In Jamaica and the eastern seaboard of the United States, for example, the Saint-Dominguan refugees bolstered existing Catholic communities and impressed their hosts with their culture and worldliness, but this influence was transitory and was absorbed into the broader fabric of the new societies, leaving only faint traces behind (Geggus 2001b, xiv). In Charleston, South Carolina, at least five hundred Saint-Dominguan refugees arrived between 1791 and 1793, and by early 1794 there were French schools, a French theater, and a whole district in which French or Creole were the main languages. By 1816, there were an estimated three thousand French or French Creoles living in the city (Geggus 2001a, 232). The influx of Saint-Dominguan refugees with distinctly Caribbean mores concerning miscegenation and endowment of illegitimate children gave new impetus to the expansion of Charleston's "brown" middle class (Geggus 2001a, 235). In the more northerly city of Philadelphia, as many as five thousand Saint-Dominguan refugees had arrived by the end of the eighteenth century. Paradoxically, in contrast to their counterparts in the southern city, the Saint-Dominguan free coloreds and slaves seem to have had more difficulty in assimilating into Philadelphia, a city in which the law for the gradual abolition of slavery had been enforced since 1780 (Branson and Patrick 2001, 194). Largely ignored by Philadelphia's Protestant black elite, the black émigrés formed a discrete group: "Language, religion, and culture appear to have created a distinct and unassimilated group of black people who identified with one [an]other as black Catholics from Saint-Domingue" (Branson and Patrick 2001, 204).

In Trinidad, by contrast, Saint-Dominguan refugees (along with the more numerous migrants from other Francophone islands) were quickly integrated into the emerging plantation society and established a distinctive French Creole culture that prevailed there throughout much of the nineteenth century. Most notably, perhaps, and most enduringly, the Catholic French émigrés revitalized the pre-Lenten celebrations in Trinidad, and French Creole folklore still features in many modern evocations of Carnival characters. In Cuba, where thousands of Saint-Dominguan refugees helped to develop the nascent sugar and coffee industries, more tangible traces remain of French Creole culture, especially on the eastern side of the island, where dance, folklore, festivals, and religion retain important traces of Haitian influence. In effect, migration and the corollary movements of rhythmic music created in this circum-Caribbean world a kind of "musical Fertile Crescent" that stretched from Saint-Domingue to Cuba and west to New Orleans (Sublette 2007, 107).

SWINGING NEW ORLEANS

The Haitian Revolution had a profound influence on Louisiana. In 1791, at the beginning of the Saint-Dominguan revolt, the total free and enslaved population of Spanish Louisiana stood at approximately forty thousand. Events in Saint-Domingue influenced Napoleon Bonaparte's decisions first to obtain Louisiana's retrocession from Spain in 1800 and then to sell it three years later to the United States. Indeed, Saint-Dominguan refugees played an important role in defending New Orleans in 1814 against the British attack at the end of the War of 1812 (Lachance 2001, 221). The decline in sugar exports from Saint-Domingue in the 1790s was an important factor in many Louisiana planters' conversion from tobacco and indigo production to sugar cane (Lachance 2001, 209). Much as in Cuba, but on a considerably smaller scale, sugar production established itself in Louisiana during the Haitian Revolution. By 1804, sixty to seventy sugar plantations had been established on the banks of the Mississippi River above and below New Orleans, and by 1840 Louisiana was producing 8 percent of the world's sugar (Lachance 2001, 211).

The abolition of slavery in Saint-Domingue in 1793, which had been confirmed by the French Convention and extended to all French colonies the following year, also inspired several slave rebellions in Louisiana in the 1790s. Consequently, slaveholders in Louisiana began to take seriously the prospect of major slave revolts and moved to suppress them quickly when they occurred. In October 1791, just a few months after the beginning of the Saint-Dominguan revolt, Pierre Bailly, a free mulatto from New Orleans, was tried on hearsay evidence that he had declared that he and his fellow conspirators were awaiting word from Saint-Domingue to stage a coup d'état similar to the one mounted in Le Cap. In 1795 and 1796, a series of slave conspiracies were discovered, and this led to a ban on slave importations that was not lifted until 1800, and even then it was still prohibited to import Saint-Dominguan slaves (Lachance 2001, 211–12). Later, at the end of Saint-Domingue's war of independence, more than ten thousand sought refuge in New Orleans, profoundly influencing the city's commerce, society, and culture (Lachance 2001, 210).[15]

New Orleans was not the preferred destination for refugees from the Haitian Revolution. Fleeing colonists from 1791 to 1803 naturally sailed to the closest open seaports—to Jamaica, Cuba, and the eastern seaboard ports of the United States—or else sought refuge in Santo Domingo, the Spanish part of the island. Some Saint-Dominguan refugees did go directly to New Orleans in the 1790s and around the time of Haitian independence, but, for most of the approximately fifteen thousand migrants, New Orleans was a secondary destination. The doubly displaced Saint-Dominguan refugees arrived in New Orleans from the eastern United States and the Caribbean, especially Jamaica, from which a thousand Haitian migrants came in 1803–4. The largest wave of migrants came from Cuba in 1809–10, and these ten thousand refugees doubled at once the population of the Crescent City.

Composed of three numerically equal groups of whites, slaves, and free people of color, the waves of immigrants left a significant impression on the social fabric and culture of Louisiana (Dessens 2008, 28). Each group imported specific cultural traits to Louisiana society, which in the early nineteenth century was distinctly undeveloped, especially in comparison to Saint-Domingue. The Saint-Dominguan whites were influential in developing education (for all three classes of the population), journalism, architecture, and the theater, and they also brought their strong tradition of Freemasonry. They opened book stores and music stores, and they established and controlled all of the newspapers of early American Louisiana (Hunt 1988, 53–54). Yet the white Saint-Dominguan refugees retained a "visceral attachment to slavery" and, as New Orleans grew in the first half of the nineteenth century, they were the most active of all property-holding groups in the city in perpetuating and investing in slavery. They also reinforced the institution of slavery by keeping alive the memory of the Haitian Revolution as an event characterized by black brutality and injustice (Lachance 2001, 223–24).

Saint-Dominguan free people of color seem to have had a more nuanced understanding of the historical meaning of the revolution (Lachance 2001, 224) and brought their own dynamism to the cultural and economic expansion of nineteenth-century New Orleans. The many skilled artisans in this group became prominent in New Orleans in confectionery, house building, and furniture making (Hunt 1988, 50–51). Culturally, too, the free coloreds left a deep impression: some of the best known early Louisiana poets and writers (Louis Victor Séjour, Michel Séligny, Camille Thierry, Armand Lanusse, and Rodolphe Desdunes) and musicians (Edmond Dédé, Constant Debergue, Eugene Arcade, and Samuel Snaër) were Saint-Dominguan free colored refugees or were descended from them (Dessens 2008, 30).

The migrant Saint-Dominguan slaves, for their part, influenced many aspects of Louisiana vernacular culture, from cooking and clothing to medicine and oral literature, Vodou, and the Creole language. In effect, the Saint-Dominguan migrants "both re-Africanized and re-creolized the whole material, psychological, and spiritual matrix of New Orleans," adding to existing Louisiana society and culture "another beat in-between" (Cartwright 2006, 105, 114). Perhaps most significantly, the slaves brought with them their music and their rhythms, which infused and blended with Louisiana music and gave birth to a new, very specific musical style that would mutate and creolize with other traditions into early jazz (Dessens 2008, 30).

Jazz, it should be remembered, "started out as dance" (Daniels 2003, 113) and has deep roots in the traveling aesthetics of the Saint-Dominguan refugees, notably in Vodou ritual and rhythm. Indeed, connections between jazz and perceived Vodou primitivism have long been a feature of negative critiques of swing. In 1921, for example, the *Ladies' Home Journal* attacked swing as "the accompaniment of the voodoo dancer, stimulating the half-crazed barbarian to the vilest deeds" (quoted in Determeyer 2006, 17).[16] Before swing became a noun of the jazz age, denoting both a dance style and the music's steady, pulsing rhythm, it was a verb that referred to the rhythmic movement of bodies and objects in ritual ceremonies. In Haitian Vodou, the verbal equivalent is *balanse*, to balance or swing ritual objects and bodies back and forth, the purpose of which is not to achieve equilibrium but to heat things up in the ritual dance, to "activate or enliven" the ritual (Brown 1995, 222). The practice of *balanse* or swinging, heating things up in the ritual dance, is also evoked in nineteenth-century descriptions of New Orleans voodoo ceremonies. One observer of a voodoo rite in 1885 noted that a celebrant lifted a *serviteur* up and spun him around several times before sending him whirling. The observer was sensitive to the rhythmic, swinging aspects of the ritual and noted how the dance's "rhythmical shuffle, with more movement of the hips than of the feet, backward and forward, round and round, but accelerating . . . as the time of the song quickened and the excitement rose in the room . . . made it almost impossible for the spectator not to join in the swing of its influence" (quoted in Tallant 1965, 42, 40). Swing in this case is more or less synonymous with rhythm and has a primary function in "heating things up" for the voodoo *serviteurs,* providing for them much of what makes religious belief and *konesans* (knowledge) possible. The faithful serve the spirits by first learning to embody the rhythmic, ritual spirit of swing (Cartwright 2006, 112). For the Saint-Dominguan refugees, therefore, rhythm and swing were closely connected to religious belief and practice. However, their rhythms did not remain confined to the religious sphere and soon crossed over into secular dances. In general, too, the creolizing rhythms of the traveling émigré culture confirmed New Orleans as a unique New World cultural crossroads, and Congo Square was a privileged site in this new process of creolization.

Since the late 1750s, African slaves, Native Americans, and some free people of color had gathered for recreation and trading in New Orleans' Place des Nègres, an open area that had been a sacred site for the Houma Indian corn feasts. The site later became known as Congo Square and was noted in particular for the encounters it staged between the essentially rhythmic dance and music traditions of the various African and Native American groups. It became the most important public site for performances of African or Afro-Creole dances, such as the *bamboula, calenda, coujaille,* and *pile chactas* (Turner 2003, 133). To some extent, however, the Congo Square performances seemed to "de-Africanize" the dances and the music. The presence of a nonparticipating audience—in Vodou ceremonies all those present also participate at various points—placed the African music into a new, modern frame of representation. The Congo Square performances modified the music's relationship with religious ceremony: the music became more markedly a form in itself, one that could exist without religious functions. For the authorities, there were certain advantages in effecting this break and in secularizing the music and dance. Most obviously, the performance could not be so easily harnessed to the Vodou metaphysics that had long been feared as a potential incubator of black revolt. The further consequences of this new, significant (if not definitive or complete) break between African music and African metaphysics were twofold, as Michael Ventura points out: "On the one hand, something wonderful was lost. On the other, only by separating the music from the religion could either the music or the metaphysics within it leave their origins and deeply influence a wider sphere" (1985, 123–24).

Congo Square thus helped to free African music, rhythm, and dance from religious ritual, and perhaps this is partly why it is often invoked by musical historians "as the originating locus of American jazz" (Kodat 2003, 2). Musicians, too, speak of Congo Square as the matrix of jazz. Sidney Bechet, for instance, wrote a biography of his enslaved grandfather who, much like the Haitian drummers observed by Métraux, would "beat out rhythms on the drums at the square— Congo Square they called it. . . . No one had to explain notes or feeling or rhythm to him" (Bechet 1960, 6). Bechet's evocation of his grandfather's "natural" feel for music and rhythm echoes what Moreau had said about the slaves in Saint-Domingue and indeed what countless other white observers had noted in other New World locales. The fear of rhythm and its potential to provoke and energize slave revolt also traveled to New Orleans. In 1817, the New Orleans City Council officially sanctioned Congo Square as the site for slaves' Sunday dances, which had previously been held in various locations, thus "allowing for simultaneous release of enslaved black energies and for their policed observation" (Cartwright 2006, 111).

By the 1820s, Haitian Vodou had firmly embedded itself among New Orleans' Afro-Creole population, and the new tradition of Congo Square performances reflected both the strong influence of Saint-Dominguan refugees on the religious life of the city and New Orleans' status as the foremost site for Vodou worship in the United States (Turner 2003, 125–26). Before the arrival of the Saint-Dominguan migrants, Louisiana's Afro-Creole religious practices drew predominantly on the rituals and beliefs of Senegambian slaves, who had creolized their practices with Catholicism and indigenous Amerindian beliefs. New Orleans' first recorded Vodou queen was a free "quadroon" from Saint-Domingue, Sanité Dédé, who is believed to have established St. John's Eve (June 23) as the most important fete of the year and to have chosen Lake Pontchartrain's shores as the site for the annual ritual (Cartwright 2006, 108). The success of Saint-Dominguan migrants in establishing their culture in New Orleans is further suggested in an episode recalled by a fifteen-year-old white who was brought to Dédé's house one night in 1825 and who witnessed a scene of possession induced by the rhythmic beating of drums, shaking of gourds, banjo playing, and a "lithe, tall black woman, with a body waving and undulating . . . to sway on one and the other side" as the lead drummer chanted "Houm! Dance Calind!/Voudou! Magnian!/Aie! Aie!/Dance Calinda!" (Asbury 1936, 264). The *calenda,* the rhythmic Saint-Dominguan dance described by Moreau, had therefore been successfully transplanted to New Orleans (indeed, it may already have been introduced there before the arrival of the Saint-Dominguan refugees) and was closely harnessed to the growth of Haitian Vodou in Louisiana. In a further echo of Moreau's account of Saint-Dominguan culture, the New Orleans fifteen-year-old reported seeing among the black and colored *serviteurs* "half a dozen white men and two white women" (Asbury 1936, 261).

By the 1850s, the instruments used in Congo Square—including banjos, tom-toms, violins, jawbones, and triangles—were complemented by the regular rhythms coming from the bells and shells attached to dancers' arms and legs. By this time, too, further diverse influences, notably from Cuban and Mexican musicians and their waltzes, contredanses, *danzones,* and habaneras, had added to the musical complexity of New Orleans. For one contemporary white observer, the exact rhythmic sense of the dancers was the most striking aspect of the performance: "In all their movements, gyrations and attitudinizing exhibitions," he wrote, "the most perfect time is kept, making the beats with the feet, heads or hands, or all, as correctly as a well-regulated metronome!" (Creecy 1860, 20–21). Rhythm in these cases seems to have formed a durable, constant, and quite tangible bond between different groups of people who had been separated by history and who occupied different times and places. Today, rhythm acts as a kind of cultural and historical repository that contains, performs, and perpetuates the musical and ritual affinity that existed between Saint-Domingue and New Orleans but has been forgotten to a large extent with the passage of time.[17]

POSTREVOLUTION RHYTHMS IN HAITI

While Saint-Domingue's rhythms—and the revolutionary ideas connected to them—were traveling, agitating, and evolving across the New World, those same rhythms enjoyed an ambiguous status in newly independent Haiti. Toussaint's decree of 1800 prohibiting nocturnal assemblies and gatherings, particularly "Vaudoux" dances, cast this ambiguity into sharp relief: the political impulse to control and regulate could not, it seems, exist alongside the cultural and religious freedom that had played a significant role in fomenting and ensuring the success of the slave revolt. Unlike Congo Square in New Orleans, where rhythm and music became secularized, in Haiti music, rhythm, and dance remained closely associated with religious practice and hence with a metaphysical, political, and cultural alterity that was considered the antithesis of the modern, essentially capitalist state envisioned by Haiti's first leaders. The twelve-year war of independence was a far more complex affair than the dualistic, black-white conflict that the Haitian Revolution still symbolizes for some. The revolution's leaders (unlike, perhaps, the majority of newly freed slaves) were never interested in returning independent Haiti to a preindustrial condition but had strikingly modern aspirations. As Eugene Genovese says, the revolution under Toussaint did not "aspire to restore some lost African world or build an isolated African-American enclave that could have played no autonomous role in world affairs. . . . Toussaint, and after his death, Dessalines and Henri Christophe, tried to forge a modern black state" (1979, 88). He argues that the fundamental objective of the revolution was the "Europeanization" of Haiti and yet that the new state also sought to compel Europeans to acknowledge the distinctly modern aspirations to freedom and democracy of colonial peoples. As such, Toussaint's revolution envisioned full "participation in the mainstream of world history rather than away from it" (92). Vodou and its rhythmic dance and music were, it seems, too closely associated with Africa and antimodernism to be incorporated into the new Haitian nation, which resisted "atavistic longings for a racial past" and whose impulses were "toward the future and not dwelling in mythical origins" (Dash 1998, 44–45).

For Dessalines, Christophe, and the other ultimately failed rulers who succeeded them in the nineteenth century, popular dance, music, and religion were considered obstacles to Haiti's development, even if, like Toussaint before them, their personal relationships to Vodou were quite complex and contradictory.

Toussaint's devotion to the Catholic faith was always apparent in his public life, and he celebrated most of the key moments of his career with Catholic ceremonies, even if the Church had been banned by the Jacobin government in France in the middle phases of the revolution. When, for instance, Toussaint accepted the keys to Ciudad Santo Domingo in 1801, he sought to reassure the Spanish citizens of his pious and civilized nature by ordering a Te Deum to be sung. And with the help of the Abbé Grégoire in France, Toussaint established four bishoprics in Saint-Domingue (Bell 2007, 194). Toussaint also expressed at times his abhorrence of Vodou, usually in the presence of white Europeans, who generally regarded the religion with a mixture of fear and disdain (and perhaps a little disavowed fascination). Nevertheless, Toussaint's pronouncements on religion were often ambiguous, and if and when he claimed to his audience that he was invested with a spiritual force, his Vodouisant listeners would have understood that this spirit was not necessarily or exclusively of Christian origin. Indeed, his listeners would not have considered the two religions to be mutually exclusive: as a syncretic religion, Vodou had already incorporated Catholic saints into its pantheon of gods, and Catholicism in Saint-Domingue accommodated to some extent African beliefs, so that the vast majority of the population would have seen the two faiths as "aspects of a single structure of belief" (Bell 2007, 196).[18]

Toussaint's concerns about Vodou religion, dance, and music were most likely to do with the conspiratorial potential of Vodou ceremonies and the religion's resistance to centralized control. He was keenly aware of how the hidden network of Vodouisant communities could "function as a cellular structure for rebellion and revolution" (Bell 2007, 195). This was why he complained in his correspondence to the French general Étienne Laveaux of how his own rebel commander Macaya would "hold dances and assemblies every day with the Africans of his nation" and "beat the drum too often" (Bell 2007, 130–31, 195). This was also why he sought to undermine and eliminate many of the more powerful and traditional African-born rebel leaders such as Biassou, who doubled as *houngans,* or Vodou priests (Bell 2007, 137). It is also true that, at times, Toussaint became exasperated with Catholicism. Shortly before his capture in 1802, he is reported to have said to the curé of Gonaïves, while holding a crucifix in his hand, that he "no longer wished to serve the Christian God. Then crushing this crucifix under his feet, he began to set fire to the church with his sacrilegious hands" (Pluchon 1989, 103). As his most recent biographer argues, although Toussaint's Catholicism was outwardly strict and exclusive, and although he sought to control the practice of

Vodou, he "served more than a single spirit" and was "the first of many heads of state to forbid Vodou publicly while practicing it himself in private" (Bell 2007, 288, 195).

Indeed, when Dessalines assumed leadership of the new Haitian state in 1804, he also sought control of the religious sphere and proclaimed himself head of the Church, with the authority to set the limits of each priest's jurisdiction and to appoint priests to vacant parishes. His policy of slaughtering white colonists during and immediately after the revolutionary wars had led to a shortage in priests, which he alleviated by appointing some of his ex-slave allies from the war. In addition, Dessalines's 1805 constitution further regulated the power of the Church by liberalizing marriage as a "civil act authorized only by the government" (Leyburn 1972, 119). The Vatican objected to the provisions of Dessalines's constitution, refused to recognize Haiti as a republic or to send priests there, and thus opened up a schism between Haiti and Rome that lasted for fifty-six years (Desmangles 1992, 42–43).

After Dessalines's death in 1807, the country became split between north and south and between two rival political factions led by Henri Christophe and Alexandre Pétion, respectively—two tyrants who maintained political control by military force. Just like Dessalines and Toussaint before them, these two figures implemented a militarized agricultural system that was deeply unpopular among the mass of cultivators forced to work in conditions barely distinguishable from those of slave labor. In particular, the socioeconomic systems instituted by Dessalines and consolidated by Christophe inadvertently created the rigid social structures—the disenfranchised black rural peasantry and the relatively privileged mulatto urban elite—that came to characterize Haitian society. The former free coloreds, who had largely lost their lands through state annexations, were now employed by the state as agricultural inspectors and plantation overseers or as bureaucrats overseeing the running of the state's functions. The new mulatto-dominated bureaucracy "used economic pressure to precipitate what Dessalines and Christophe vehemently resisted in Haiti: the creation of social classes on the basis of skin color" (Desmangles 1992, 40).

If Christophe had resisted the return of color-based social divisions, he, like Dessalines, publicly promoted the virtues of Catholicism and thereby denounced Vodou as a sign of the nation's cultural and moral backwardness. Under Christophe's leadership (which lasted until 1820), Catholicism became the state religion, and he attempted to restore the church to the preeminence it had enjoyed during the colonial period. Crowning himself the first king of Haiti, he created a nobility and revived the Church in order to lend his northern kingdom an air of respectability and dignity. In 1811 and 1814, he set up an archbishopric and three bishoprics; he also sent a delegation of young aspiring Haitian priests to Rome to be ordained, in the hope that they would return to train and ordain curates to fill the country's parishes. In these efforts, Christophe, much like his successor Jean-Pierre Boyer (1818–43), was frustrated by Rome's refusal to recognize Haiti. In religious and cultural terms, the most significant effect of this schism was that two generations of Haitian grew up with little or no formal instruction in the rituals of the Catholic Church. Consequently, Vodou developed further and instituted its own rituals, thus embedding itself ever more deeply into the fabric of Haitian society (Desmangles 1992, 43).

Vodou developed despite the official endorsement of Catholicism and despite the vigorous attempts by Haitian leaders, especially the black presidents, to suppress it. Again much like Toussaint, both Dessalines and Christophe were convinced that hard, controlled labor was the surest way to bring security and stability to the nation, and they knew only too well the potential for revolt that existed in Vodou ceremonies. As such, they attempted to suppress the nocturnal dances and assemblies with force, and all offenders caught were shot by the police. In 1801, Dessalines, then general inspector of culture in the Western Department, upon hearing that a Vodou ceremony was taking place in the Cul de Sac plain, led a battalion to the site of the ceremony and had fifty of the participants put to the sword (Price-Mars 1973, 231; Madiou 1989, 2: 112). Yet Dessalines was known as a Vodou adherent, and he is said to have entered the old Notre-Dame cathedral in Port-au-Prince in early 1803 wearing a red robe to resemble Ogou, the *lwa* of war, whom he served and considered to be his protector (Beauvoir-Dominique 1991, 59). As Vodou believers themselves, Dessalines and Christophe feared not only the political potency of Vodou but also the possibility that they could suffer the effects of "magic done against them" (Desmangles 1992, 45). The mulatto president Boyer's attitude toward Vodou is less apparent, though there is evidence to suggest that he believed the religion to be a "primitive aberration with no significant content" and that he was wary of acknowledging the widespread practice of Vodou for fear of jeopardizing the nation's ongoing negotiations with the Vatican (Desmangles 1992, 45). Similarly, the Haitian historiographers attached to the "mulatto school" that emerged in the 1840s seem to have excluded Vodou from their histories of Haiti. Thomas Madiou's *Histoire d'Haïti,* for instance, contains only fleeting references to "sorcerers," "magicians," "fetishes," and "spells," and a conspicuous absence of mentions of Vodou itself. Like Boyer, Madiou was all too aware of the "underlying organizational structure" of Vodou, and to acknowledge the existence of this in the contemporary climate would have been "to concede too much" (Pettinger 2004, 417).

In contrast to its harsh repression by Dessalines and Christophe, the Vodou religion flourished during Faustin Soulouque's presidency (1847–59). Leaving Catholicism to wane further, Soulouque revived Vodou and permitted ceremonies in which animals were sacrificed in the streets. For the first time in Haitian history, state officials could openly state their adherence to Vodou (Verschueren

1948, 333–34). Much as François Duvalier would do a hundred years later, the self-styled emperor made political use of Vodou's network of rural leaders to bolster his own authority and power (Pettinger 2004, 417). Significantly, too, the newly validated Vodou dances could now be held without fear of police suppression, and foreign visitors were able to witness, often to their chagrin, how deeply embedded Vodou rituals had become in Haitian society and culture. It was at this time that foreign writers began to associate Vodou (or "Vaudoux") with putative cases of cannibalism. Most notoriously, Spencer St. John, who was the British minister to Haiti during this period, wrote a chapter on "Vaudoux Worship and Cannibalism" in his *Hayti, or the Black Republic* (1884), in which he draws on local newspapers and the testimony of doctors and fellow diplomats to validate cases of cannibalism, many of which related to "Vaudoux" rituals from the 1850s onward. The persistence of cannibalism in Haiti represented to St. John all that was wrong about the nation. His hugely influential account of Haiti created a fascination for Vodou among subsequent European travelers, who increasingly presented the country in terms of darkness and impenetrability. In the imaginations of European writers and readers, the rhythmic aspects of the music and dances also became more closely associated with the primitive heathenism that Haiti apparently hid behind its veneer of civilization. As Alasdair Pettinger states, "foreign visitors now attuned their readers to the sound of distant drums, booming from the interior after nightfall" (2004, 419).

By the time Soulouque's successor, Fabre Nicolas Geffrard, came to power, the Catholic Church in Haiti was in such a miserable condition that it became easier to convince Rome of the need for intervention and cooperation. Special emissaries were sent from the Vatican, and a resolution to the fifty-six-year conflict was achieved when the Concordat was signed in Rome on March 28, 1860. The main stipulations of the agreement were that Port-au-Prince be declared the seat of ecclesiastical power in Haiti; an archbishop was to be named by the president; church officials could, in collaboration with the Vatican, reorganize the sizes of the various dioceses, appoint bishops and pastors; and Roman Catholicism was declared the official religion of Haiti and was to be supported by state funds. A scheme to reconstruct and refurbish the neglected Church buildings was also undertaken, and, by the end of the nineteenth century, the project was almost completed. The Church had been reestablished, its scope and influence greatly increased. In a crucial sense, though, the reinstitution of the Church had come too late. Despite the official suppression of Vodou, the near sixty years of isolation from Rome had allowed it to grow and further embed itself in national life. In the early eighteenth century, Father Jean-Baptiste Labat had bemoaned how "Vodou meetings or ceremonies mix often the sacred things of our religion with profane objects of an idolatrous cult" (1722, 4: 330–31). By 1860, Vodou had further syncretized with Catholicism, the Christian saints were closely associated with the

Vodou pantheon of *lwas,* and in general worshipers held that the belief in Vodou did not imply the denial of Catholicism, and vice versa (Desmangles 1992, 46–47). Equally significant in terms of how rhythm shaped the lives of the vast majority of Haitians were the communal work patterns that were, by this point, firmly entrenched in rural communities and that emphasized collective, reciprocal effort and people working (as well as singing, dancing, and worshiping) as one.[19]

The conflicts relating to Vodou during this early postindependence period and the official fluctuations between violent suppression (Dessalines, Christophe), ashamed disregard (Boyer, Madiou), and open promotion (Soulouque) of the religion suggest some of the difficulties that the nation faced in reconciling the urges to assume its place in the modern, global culture and yet to declare itself other and different. Among the elite, Vodou was associated with Africa and thus with barbarism and primitivism; the only civilization worth considering in the postindependence period was that of Europe (Nicholls 1979, 42–43). But early Haitian intellectuals were wary of being subsumed into this broader, European civilization. Haiti's uniqueness was held by some to lie in its distinctly hybrid culture. In 1836, for example, the author Émile Nau wrote of how both Haiti and the United States were "transplanted" nations, "stripped of traditions," and of how the particular fusion of European and African cultures in Haiti made it "less French than the American is English" (quoted in Dash 1998, 46). And yet, even if Nau did see Haiti as the primary exemplar of the "heterogeneous modern American nation" (Dash 1998, 46), the postindependence history of Vodou indicates the trouble the nation had in assuming this creolized identity and culture. Haiti's early intellectuals and authors seemed to hesitate before accepting the modern, hybrid nature of their culture and religion, which is ironic as Vodou was and is surely the most conspicuous example of Haiti's creolized culture. Vodou is a distinctly modern phenomenon, a new entity created out of the meeting of diverse Amerindian, African, and European cultural and metaphysical systems. It appears that Vodou, far from being embraced by Haitian intellectuals as a marker of their unique, creolized, and modern culture, became associated with a kind of internal otherness and a sign of the unresolved conflicts and contradictions between the nation's urban, light-skinned elite and the black rural peasantry.

RHYTHM AND NINETEENTH-CENTURY HAITIAN POETRY

From the early postindependence era, writing in Haiti has been closely associated with national identity and has generally been seen as a "strategy for achieving recognition in a modern global culture" (Dash 1998, 46). Literature has therefore been a primary form of Haitian interaction with the outside world, a means of self-interrogation and of legitimizing the new nation in its global context. Prominent nineteenth-century authors such as Anténor Firmin and Louis-Joseph Janvier used their writing as a means of promoting and rehabilitating Haiti in a world that was generally suspicious of and hostile to the new nation. Haiti was, to Firmin in particular, the most significant example of what the "black race" could achieve. Despite this, he expressed a concern common to nineteenth-century Haitian intellectuals when he wondered if "Haiti constitute[s] a sufficiently edifying example in favor of the race she is proud to represent among the civilized nations? What evidence does she offer that she possesses the qualities that are denied in African Blacks?" (2002, lvi). Thus, for Firmin, Haiti had to free itself from the negative images associated in European (and to some extent Haitian) minds with Africa and Africans, and to affirm its difference while asserting its "blackness."

Haiti was a modern state in terms of both its early postcolonial status and its hybrid racial and cultural composition.[20] This modern status was not attained through a steady process of change but through violent, cataclysmic change and upheaval. In a sense, Haiti's modernity was thrust upon it and was hurriedly and incompletely, if also enthusiastically and willingly, assumed. This was a new relationship with and conception of modernity—an early example of the "lived" modernity that Édouard Glissant associates with the Americas in general and that was not "developed over extended historical space" but "abruptly imposed" (1989, 148). This lived modernity in early, postindependence Haitian literature at times generated an exhilarating sense of freedom—the thrill of exploring in full and pushing to its conceptual limits the new entity that Haiti was—but also a tendency to retreat from that same freedom and occasionally to neglect or deny fundamental, especially "African," aspects of Haitian culture. The poetry of this period, much like its political history, provides valuable evidence of Haiti's fluctuating, abruptly assumed modernity and in particular of the changing conceptions of Vodou, dance, drumming, and rhythm that characterized the historical movement from Dessalines to Geffrard.

Rhythm is, of course, an essential element in all poetry. Conventionally, rhythm in poetry is seen as having a harmonizing effect, bringing regularity and predictability to the poetic form, which traditionally is conceived of as a fixed, codified system, determined by more or less inflexible rules. In French poetry from the classical period to the Romantic era, the predominant verse line was the alexandrine, the twelve-syllable line that consisted of six regular iambics, with a caesura after the third iambic. The rhythm of the alexandrine is therefore fixed, regular, and predictable. In the post-Romantic period, fixed poetic forms were often deliberately destabilized, most notably in Stéphane Mallarmé's experiments in free verse.[21] Since Mallarmé, the conception and function of poetic rhythm have been further revised and perhaps also liberated from their previously fixed status.

Twentieth-century poets and theorists of poetry have tended to further destabilize and reconceptualize the notion of poetic rhythm. In his influential work on poetic rhythm, *Critique du rythme* (1982), Henri Meschonnic carries out just such a process and specifically calls into question what he terms "the myth of rhythm compared to the movement-of-the-sea" (149). This "myth," Meschonnic says (drawing on Émile Benveniste), is founded on a faulty understanding of the etymology of rhythm: "The initial objection is that the verb from which rhythm is derived means to flow, and the sea does not "flow" (149–50). Meschonnic's objection is therefore to the "mythical" conception of rhythm as a sea-like entity that is fluid but fixed, contained, and bounded within the structure of the poem. The etymology of the verb suggests, however, that regularity and predictability are not inherent aspects of rhythm; rhythm is something that flows and is therefore freer, looser, and more irregular than the traditional sea-like notion of it suggests.

An important consequence of this reconceptualization of rhythm is that, rather than being a subordinate part of a fixed system, a formal imitation of meaning, rhythm takes on a new significance in the organization of any discourse, including poetry. Meschonnic argues that, after Benveniste's reconsideration of it as something that flows, rhythm can no longer be considered a "sub-category of form." Rhythm in itself organizes and configures the whole of the discourse; it is, moreover, meaningful, in that it orders meaning and accordingly "it is no longer a distinct, juxtaposed element. . . . Rhythm in discourse can have more meaning than the meaning of the words, or another meaning" (1982, 70). It follows that rhythm and meaning in poetry are no longer separable; rhythm assumes a different function whereby it can in itself determine meaning, destabilize the meaning of words, or indeed offer an altogether divergent meaning. Meschonnic also suggests that these ideas on rhythm were largely prefigured in Paul Valéry's theories of poetics. Valéry, Meschonnic argues, challenged the classical hierarchy that set sound and rhythm in dualistic opposition with meaning in poetry. Working against this dualism, which always privileged meaning over sound and rhythm, Valéry was interested in the auditory aspects of the words, their sounds, and their mutual relationships, which at times constituted their own meanings within a poem. It is to Meschonnic (and to Valéry) a "remarkable prejudice" to believe that the "meaning" of poetry is contained uniquely in its words and is more important than, or indeed separate from, its sound and rhythm. To understand poetry, says Meschonnic, is to have overcome this prejudice (1982, 174–75). Poetic rhythm therefore inheres in the flow of sounds, though this flow need not be measured or regular; rhythm can equally bring irregularity and disharmony to a poem. Moreover, rhythm is not subordinate to, or a simple reflection of, meaning but can itself constitute meaning or indeed destabilize what the words of a poem are apparently saying.[22]

Early Haitian poetry was largely based on European, notably romanticist models. The period from 1804 to 1915 is generally regarded as a distinct era in Haitian literature, a "period of apprenticeship" (St.-Louis and Lubin 1950, ii) during which Haitian authors generally mimicked contemporary French literature. In spite of their political independence, Haitian authors lingered over a "fairly sterile contemplation of France and French culture" (Corzani 1978, 3: 150). According to some critics, Haitian literature of this period had "no function," and "'art for art's sake' was the only literary credo" (St.-Louis and Lubin 1950, ii). Perhaps more perceptive, however, is J. Michael Dash's argument that this early writing established "the beginnings of a national and historical consciousness" (1981, 4). In particular, the modes and themes of Romanticism were used to explore notions of Haitian identity, which became closely associated with Romantic ideals of the power of the individual imagination and emotions. According to Jean Price-Mars, significant similarities in terms of politics and philosophy existed between Romanticism and nineteenth-century Haitian culture. In particular, Romanticism's "emancipatory philosophy" and its doctrine in favor of "the blossoming of lyricism" helped Haitian authors to express their own poetic sensibility. For Price-Mars, it was in this sensibility that the "distinctive mark of the Haitian soul" resided, which he said is "rich in emotive power [and] impressive in its affective resonance" (1959, 31).

During this period, Haiti's landscape was figured in terms of a Romanticized "untamed nature," and authors became preoccupied with "mapping a new space, inventing a new speech and recovering their territory" (Dash 1998, 47). Haitian historical consciousness was also tinged with Romantic ideals of the individual's capacity for rebellion. As the author Justin Devot said, Haitian intellectuals drew on the "glorious memories of an independence gained by the liberatory effort of human personality" (quoted in Hérisson 1955, 179). In effect, early Haitian writing "pompously sang" the praises of the Romanticized heroes of 1804 while "the perfume of our land embalmed the atmosphere of our poems" (St.-Louis and Lubin 1950, iii).

This idea of an "embalmed" literature is an apposite metaphor for Haitian writing's prolonged process of coming to life. In the early postrevolution period, Haitian poetry was often harnessed to the project of building national consciousness. As such, it tended to laud and glorify the "great men" who had brought about the revolution. A typical early work in this patriotic mode is Antoine Dupré's "Hymne à la liberté" (1812), which evokes the revolutionary ideals of the equality of men and the Christian notion of the fallen nature of humankind while stating its pride in Haiti's history of resisting tyranny:

> The noble author of nature
> Created man to find happiness.
> Man soon became cruel and untrue,
> Breaking the work of his maker.
> But Haiti, free and warlike,
> Reconquered its liberty

> And shows to the tyrants of the earth,
> The free and unbroken man.
> Honor and glory to the homeland.
> Let us brave the iniquity of kings,
> And if we must lose our lives,
> Ah! Let us die for liberty!
>   (St.-Louis and Lubin 1950, 1)

Dupré's poem demonstrates Price-Mars's conviction that Haitian poetry had been a receptacle for memories of the revolution: "In the past," Price-Mars stated, "our poets sang, exalted, glorified the heroism of our ancestors who transformed the group of slaves from whom we are descended into a nation" (1959, 13). The poem also shows how Haitian literature has often been used to build and reflect Haitian national consciousness, how it has largely been, as Price-Mars said, "the expression of the state of the people's soul" (1959, 13). It is significant, in terms of the Haitian people's "soul," that Haiti's gallant, ongoing fight for liberty is framed in specifically Christian terms: the idea of fallen, sinful, and deceitful human nature is clearly drawn from Christian theology. Typical of this period, Haitian poetry more or less excluded Vodou in its expression of the Haitian "soul," even if all across the nation Vodou was establishing itself as the predominant religion. In terms of rhythm, too, the poetry was restrained and formal, following regular rhythm patterns that did not significantly disrupt or indeed enhance the overt meaning of the work.

Dupré's poem, in its challenge to the "iniquity of kings" and its general impulse to assert selfhood, both individually and nationally, perhaps also further suggests the influence of Romanticism, which was to linger in Haitian writing to the end of the century. The recognition of Haiti's independence in 1825 by Charles X had increased contact and exchanges between France and Haiti, and Haitian poets such as Coriolan Ardouin, Ignace Nau, and Pierre Faubert were among the first to embrace Romanticism (Vaval 1971, 23). Dupré's work, and that of most other Haitian poets of the period, shared with early European Romantic poetry its genesis in a "patriotic cry," which at first exalted the notion of liberty and then sought to conserve and consolidate that liberty (Garret 1963, 21). Much as in European Romanticism, Haitian writing from this period valorized nature as the site in which this organic, coherent, "natural" selfhood could be quite literally rooted. The land as *terre mère* or motherland became associated with the harmony and natural order that intellectuals envisaged for the state itself. The ground, as Dash says, legitimized power and speech in nineteenth-century Haitian writing (1998, 48). The attraction of Romantic notions of nature and society to Haitian writing was suggested much later in Jacques-Stephen Alexis's essay "Du réalisme merveilleux des Haïtiens" (1956), where he states that Romanticism was revolutionary in that it understood that nothing lasts forever, "that one can always transcend the grandiose acquisitions of the past by relocating man in his experience of nature" (261).

The most celebrated of nineteenth-century Haitian poets, Oswald Durand (1840–1906), was also probably the writer most closely linked to Romanticism. In particular, Durand's work owed much to the poetics of Victor Hugo and had a strong patriotic element. Durand often invested Haiti's hinterland with sensual, feminine qualities, and, conversely, he often situated his Creole maidens in rural settings, singing their beauty with "melodious words and harmonious rhythms" (Garret 1963, 31). His best-known poem, "Choucoune" (1880), presents one such peasant Creole beauty who is the exoticized and eroticized object of the poet's desire but who spurns his advances in favor of the attentions of a French-speaking "p'tit blanc" or white foreigner (St.-Louis and Lubin 1950, 55). The drama enacted in the poem may be read in broader terms as an indication of the failings of the nineteenth-century Haitian nationalist impulse to appropriate the hinterland and its (feminized) meanings. The educated, urban poet encounters the rural, Creole-speaking peasant woman, who remains mute but who nonetheless is far from passive or inert (Dash 1998, 50) and who, in her rejection of the poet, suggests some of the incoherence and discord that exists between her and the educated urban elite. Tellingly, and in contrast to the formal regularity and closed lines of much of Durand's poetry, many of the lines in "Choucoune" end with ellipses, which seem to indicate the poet's uncertainty or confusion and the way that his desires are unexpectedly confounded by the resistant peasant woman. That she chooses the French-speaking foreigner over the Haitian nationalist seems to indicate the limitations of the male nationalist discourse and its suppositions of a common national subjectivity framed by and embodied in the imagined submissive, feminized, and homogeneous hinterland.

Durand's impulse to exoticize, eroticize, and feminize the hinterland—and peasants themselves—is strikingly apparent in his 1896 poem "Le Vaudoux" (St.-Louis and Lubin 1950, 52–53). Again, a physical and cultural distance between the male protagonist and the peasant community exists in the "green countryside," toward which he makes his way in the course of the poem. This distance is signaled in the opening line, which situates the man in the hinterland, "not far away," but still apart from the presumably urban milieu that is the poet's more common domain. Accompanied by a dog, the man follows a meandering path, and in the first part of the poem his senses are charmed by the surrounding abundant nature: in Romantic, Wordsworthian mode he looks to the skies to follow a lonely cloud; he takes in with every breath the perfume of flowers in bloom; and the sounds of woodpeckers and nightingales blend with other sounds of the forest to create one harmonic sonic entity (52).

In the second half of the poem, these sounds of nature are supplanted by human-generated sounds, which are themselves in apparent harmony with their

environment. These sounds come from a distant Vodou ceremony, the first indication of which is the "soft sound of a distant drum" (53). Significantly, it seems,
the man listens to the drum "to find his way," and, once he hears it, he is reas-
sured, pacified, and takes up the road again "with a lighter and more assured
step" (53). The suggestion seems to be that Vodou, its rhythms, and its sounds
can help reorient the errant Haitian urbanite, and that Vodou forms part of a
cultural hinterland from which national, elite culture has strayed somewhat.
This potentially compelling and progressive critique of Vodou's place in national
culture is, however, compromised to some extent by Durand's tendency in the
poem to eroticize the ceremony itself and to use it as a means of evoking the
charms of various color-defined categories of women. The man's senses are once
again evoked as he anticipates "see[ing] the negress" and "hear[ing] her songs full
of joy" (53). Once he reaches the site of the ceremony, the carefully prepared "circular ground," he sees the "griffonne" (one-quarter white, three-quarters black)
called Zoune, who is doing up her headscarf charmingly, "to please us" (53).
The remainder of the poem describes Zoune's dance in the circle and how her
shoulders "move to the sound of the words / that accompany the long drum" (53):

> She has her own law—it's a beautiful day!
> Brilliant, in her expressive dance,
> She embraces her partner,
> Spreads her arms, mad and lascivious,
> Around his neck like a collar.
> Oh! What rapture! Snakes
> Are less supple in their maneuvers
> Than Zoune in her sweet movements!
> And everyone rushes
> To dance with the griffonne,
> The griffonne who moves so charmingly. (53)

This final description of Zoune's dance is introduced by the poet's instruction
(or indeed command) to the reader to watch Zoune, to "see the dancer with
the white teeth" and "how she makes her hips sway!" (53). The poet wishes,
therefore, that the reader take notice of and acknowledge Zoune. By implication,
he reinforces the poem's subtle suggestion that Vodou (and peasant culture in
general) be incorporated into national consciousness and that the elite, instead
of looking constantly to France for its inspiration, should look inward to Haiti's
own neglected Vodou culture, which has been forgotten but which continues to
exist and thrive despite (or indeed because of) the elite's ignorance of it. Durand
himself was culpable to a certain extent in this regard, in that he borrowed so
heavily from European form.[23] Perhaps, then, this poem dramatizes some of the
difficulties and contradictions of representing Vodou (and its rhythmic music

and dance) in nineteenth-century Haiti. Durand evokes the forgotten culture but hesitates before it, turning it into a voyeuristic, eroticized event that exists principally to arouse in the (male) spectator lusty urges and to suggest the prospect of sexual abandon with the lascivious peasant women. In this sense, Durand does not fully take the ceremony seriously and does not follow through with conviction his suggestion that Vodou is a worthy and indeed vital element in Haitian culture. In terms of style and rhythm, too, he remains in a formally European mode, and no attempt is made to invest his own prosody with the rhythms of the drums that invigorate the dance itself.

Rhythm, for Durand and for other nineteenth-century Haitian poets, was generally subordinated to the desire to express the poet's soul, *his* individuality and *his* emotions. In this sense, again, the Haitian poets followed the Romanticist model of poetics. As the French critic Ferdinand Brunetière put it in the nineteenth century, lyrical poetry is "the expression of the personal sentiments of the poet translated in rhythms analogous to the nature of his emotion, lively and quick like joy, languid like sadness, fiery like passion" (1895, 154). In other words, rhythm is a secondary aspect of romantic poetry, which places a primary value on expressing the affective state of the individual. In the work of Durand and his Haitian contemporaries, rhythm is denied the primary, dynamic role that it plays in Haitian culture. In "Le Vaudoux," Durand went some way to rethinking and repositioning Haitian popular culture but was ultimately impeded by his own cultural reservations and his tendency to romanticize a tradition that was thriving and evolving dynamically in the hinterland while the urban elite remained fixated by Europe as the origin of all that was culturally worthwhile and civilized.[24]

The Haitian intelligentsia's tendency to look outward for inspiration reached something of an apogee in the late nineteenth and early twentieth centuries. During this period the literary review *La Ronde* emerged, the magazine of a new generation of young intellectuals who had attended the Lycée Pétion in Port-au-Prince and who included Dantès Bellegarde, Damoclès Vieux, Amilcar Duval, and Seymour Pradel. Established authors such as Georges Sylvain and Masillon Coicou supported the new generation, and other intellectuals such as Charles Moravia, Etzer Vilaire, and Edmond Laforest would later align themselves with the *La Ronde* group. The aims of the group were clear from the first issues of the review: to renew and purify literary style, and to distance this new generation from the overt, at times obsessive patriotism that had characterized Haitian writing for virtually the entire nineteenth century. In short, the aim was to modernize Haitian literature (Price-Mars 1959, 33–34).

In the broader Americas, this was a time of regeneration, of new ideas and conceptions of hemispheric identity, epitomized in the writings of Cuba's José Martí, of the Latin American writers José Enrique Rodó and Rubèn Dario, and indeed of Haiti's Anténor Firmin (Dash 1998, 52). The trend was toward looking beyond the nation, toward a cosmopolitanism that has been denounced by most subsequent critics as escapist writing or depoliticized aestheticism. Naomi Garret, for instance, judges this period to be one in which the "originality of the verse suffered as its richness improved" and in which "eloquence is banished, but affectations in language are common" (1963, 39). Nonetheless, there was an understated political aspect to the *La Ronde* group in that its embrace of a broadly American cosmopolitanism was largely a reaction against the growing U.S. influence in the region, both politically and economically. As Haiti stagnated in financial and political crises, the United States was thriving and becoming ever more aggressive in its activities in the Caribbean. In Price-Mars's view, Haiti's continued crises led to a general pessimism and disenchantment among the *La Ronde* authors. This was, he said, not so much their natural disposition as their inevitable reaction to Haiti's condition, and it was their sensitivity to their immediate political and social context that led them to attach themselves to the universal, which served as a "pivot" for their work (1959, 38).

La Ronde poetry is generally introspective, and it often indulges in extended contemplations of the human soul. In some cases, these meditations overflow into pious and moralistic commentary on contemporary Haitian mores, as in Vilaire's "Les Martyrs" (1901), which seems to condemn popular dance, music, and rhythm as well as those who engage in them (St.-Louis and Lubin 1950, 154–57). The poem recalls in some ways Durand's "Le Vaudoux" in its evocations of peasant dance and in situating the work on a country road, but it is strikingly different in its presentation of the event:

> On the cursed road of infernal life
> Close to the suicides, to the distraught and dying,
> Under some trees shaking with bunches of the hanged,
> Over some poisons in flower, passes a bacchanal.
>
> They are mute, deathly pale, wild, thick-lipped people,
> A frantic group, gripped by fever,
> Who turn pleasure into a dark omen
> And lose themselves in the flesh, like never-satisfied stryges. (154)

The difference is stark between Durand's romantic presentation of the Vodou dance and Vilaire's evocation of a carnivalesque, bacchanalian country scene. Whereas Durand's dance appears to be invigorating and morally innocent, Vilaire presents a deathly tableau with a cast of zombie-like dancers, whose physical characteristics, notably their thick lips, seem to mark them out as racially other to the poet. Although there is a discernible social and cultural distance between Durand's onlooker and the Vodou dancers, this distance is marked by a benignly voyeuristic fascination and leads to a desire to incorporate the peasant dance into the broader Haitian cultural consciousness. By contrast, in Vilaire's case, the dance and the black peasant dancers are presented as absolutely other and abject in terms of morality and culture. This impression of utter abjection is compounded in the two following stanzas, which evoke the dancers' rhythmic movements:

> They pass two by two; their snake-like torsos,
> Intertwined and moving, shake in unison,
> And their bodies fall apart in spasmodic shivers,
> Under bitter Voluptuousness—the untiring serpent—
>
> They groan, twisted, overcome with paleness,
> Slaves of desire, sensing in the bare flesh
> Their nerves live and die with an unknown intoxication,
> So strong that it becomes like pain. (154)

The rhythmic movements of the dancers, shaking "in unison," are therefore an integral part of the whole abject spectacle and are related in the poet's mind to sexual abandon and moral depravation, which in Vilaire's judgment "enslave" the people. As his description intensifies, the dance becomes an infernal scene of lust and damnation:

> Their blood—bitter dew that feeds infections,
> Styx where bathe fragments of poisoned nerves—
> Their bodies bent over under their languor, their cursed bodies
> Burn in their mortal kisses and destroy themselves.
>
> Confused, delirious, they are now but one
> In a savage rut, horrible like a madness.
> Their mute dialogue is an immense sigh,
> The odor of sweating flesh is their perfume. (155)

It is difficult to imagine a more condemnatory evocation of Haitian dance. Indeed, the poem reads something like a moralist European reaction to Vodou dance but without the redemptive aspect of exoticism, of partially enjoying the spectacle because it can be categorized as unequivocally other. In Vilaire's case, the dancers do appear as other, but they are also part of the same, of Haiti, and this creates the intense urge to expel and condemn. In a fascinating turn, however, Vilaire excuses the infernal dancers for their excess and turns his ire toward what he calls "Realism":

> However, do not condemn this bestial group,
> Drunk with lust, delirious with cynicism!
> Its hideous creator is your Realism:
> They are the child martyrs of the ideal!
>
> You have said to dreamers, to poets:
> "What good is it to be raised apart from man's animality?"

> To feel pity is madness, and to think is evil.
> What we all are—arrogant gods—you are too! . . .
>
> Matter, in our time, defeats ancient chimera.
> What we need is pleasure; practical science
> Is erecting a golden throne to Reality.
> Live in your century, live in your time. (155)

Vilaire therefore sees the true cause of the dancers' abjection as the "spirit of the time," the Baudelairean promotion of the "ideal," and especially the realism that, he believed, promotes a kind of atheistic, scientific primitivism that valorizes (and to some extent creates) the debauched dance he describes. This realism seems to promote a less condemnatory perspective on Vodou and its rituals, a scientific (or perhaps ethnographic) understanding of Haitian popular culture. In Vilaire's strictly Protestant mind, however, this openness leads only to further abjection and decline. The retreat from Christian piety degrades the nation, and the black peasant Vodouisants are ultimately martyrs to the cause of science. Moreover, in terms of style, Vilaire's strictly controlled meter and rhythm seem to function as counterpoints to the frantic, repetitive rhythms of the dance that he evokes in the opening section of the poem. His sober, restrained style appears to act in unison with the thematic urge to reinstate order and Christian godliness in Haitian society. Therefore, although Vilaire is perhaps an extreme example of the *La Ronde* poets' tendency toward introspection and away from specific racial and national notions of identity, we can sense that this Haitian cosmopolitanism was founded to some extent on a deep mistrust and misunderstanding of the rhythmic, African, peasant, Vodou culture that was part of the national reality but that had never truly been incorporated into elite consciousness.

RHYTHMS OF OCCUPATION

The pessimism of the *La Ronde* group developed in the context of unending social and political upheavals in Haiti: from 1860 to the present, only five Haitian presidents have been able to complete their terms. In the late nineteenth and early twentieth centuries, the Haitian government encouraged foreign investment in the country, and significant numbers of Haitian enterprises, including the National Bank, were controlled by foreign interests. In particular, U.S. corporations expanded into Haiti during this period. This apparent return of external, "white" economic power prompted intermittent attacks on foreign-owned businesses. Ultimately, the lack of commercial stability and the cycle of political instability precipitated the U.S. occupation of Haiti from 1915 to 1934.

In some limited ways, and according to a certain paternalist American narrative, the occupation had a positive effect: new roads were built; water distribution and drainage systems were implemented in cities and towns; schools and government buildings were constructed; the Université d'Haïti was restructured and operated more efficiently; large-scale sugar cane fields were reestablished; and the bourgeoisie prospered in an economic boom that Haiti had not enjoyed since the days of Pétion in the early nineteenth century (Desmangles 1992, 49). Law and order were reestablished, and merchants were able to conduct their businesses in peace as well as profit from the expenditure of around a thousand U.S. Marine Corps salaries (Schmidt 1971, 174).

Despite these improvements, the occupation was unpopular with the majority of Haitians. Price-Mars, for example, described it as "a veritable catastrophe" (1959, 41). The Marines installed a puppet president, forcibly dissolved the legislature, limited freedom of speech, and forced a new constitution on the republic, one that would facilitate foreign investment (Renda 2001, 10). The occupation was especially unpopular among the many thousands of peasants who were forced to abandon their small plots of land to work on the large-scale public projects. The return to forced labor evoked memories of the *corvée* system implemented by Dessalines and Christophe, and the surrender of individual freedom to foreign masters carried clear echoes of the colonial past. Under the leadership of Charlemagne Péralte, nearly five thousand peasant guerillas, or *cacos,* rose up against the Americans, and it took several years and many lives and resources to suppress the revolt. Apart from Péralte's *caco* revolt, and although the relationship between the Haitians and their American occupiers was often fraught, there was little further sustained resistance until 1929, when a student strike at the School of Agriculture at Damiens led to a series of sympathy strikes in Port-au-Prince.[25] It was out of this younger generation of politicized, patriotic agitators that the Haitian nationalist movement would emerge. Figures like Georges J. Petit and Jacques Roumain led the call to Haitian youth to overthrow the "white man," who had "trampled like a master over the sacred soil that our phalanx of heroes watered with their blood" (Petit and Roumain 2003, 463). Equally, the new generation criticized the "capitulations" of the "servile and cynical" Haitian elite (Petit and Roumain 2003, 463). The nationalist movement forced the Americans to change their policy, and in 1930 the Forbes Commission recommended that elections be held and that American troops be withdrawn. Further strikes followed in 1934, which helped to precipitate the exit of the Americans. The end of the occupation can, to some extent, be attributed to the activities of the literary, cultural, and political movements that had slowly gestated in the 1920s. Georges Sylvain, for example, had formed the Union Patriotique, and in his newspaper *La Patrie* he expressed the growing anti-American sentiment of the literate classes (Dash 1981, 52–54). Other nationalist groups such as La Ligue de la Jeunesse Haïtienne and La Société d'Histoire et de Géographie d'Haïti were also founded, with the shared aim of engendering national pride through promoting and valorizing Haitian culture.

The efforts of the diverse cultural and political groups to resist the occupation have subsequently been classed together as indigenism, though at the time the terms Africanism and Haitianity *(haïtianisme)* were also used. In sharp contrast to the thrust of much nineteenth-century Haitian intellectualism, Price-Mars's seminal indigenist essay *Ainsi parla l'oncle* (1928) aimed to legitimize Haitian folklore and peasant culture and to prompt a renaissance in Haitian arts; as he put it himself, his work led to a "spiritual revolution" (1959, 44). Artists and intellectuals from various fields—poets, novelists, historians, painters, musicians, architects, and sculptors—turned toward indigenous sources, inspired by the historic or prehistoric past, while sociologists and linguists reconsidered Haitian monuments, mores, and language to explain and define what was particular and unique about the Haitian way of life. In addition, new research on Vodou legitimized the religion and brought it into the intellectual sphere as never before (Price-Mars 1959, 44–45). In *Ainsi parla l'oncle,* Price-Mars devoted a chapter to "popular beliefs" and took care to situate his arguments on Vodou in the context of contemporary sociological thinking on religion, notably Durkheim's *Les Formes élémentaires de la vie religieuse* (Price-Mars 1973, 79–82). Price-Mars's objective, scientific approach to Vodou beliefs led him to affirm its status as a bona fide religion on three counts: Vodou is a religion because its adherents believe in the existence of spiritual beings that exist somewhere in the universe in close contact with human beings, whose world they dominate; Vodou is a religion because the system of belief calls for a hierarchized sacerdotal body, a society of believers, temples, altars, ceremonies, and an oral tradition that transmits the essential elements of the religion; and Vodou is a religion because, beyond the mix of myths and the corruption of fables, it still has a discernible theology, a system of representation that was used by African ancestors to explain natural phenomena and that underpins the "hybrid Catholicism" of the Haitian masses (1973, 83).

Evoking Moreau's earlier descriptions of Vodou ceremonies, Price-Mars reflected on how fundamental characteristics of contemporary Vodou practice have not changed since the colonial era. The most apparent of these basic traits is the state of trance that the individual enters into, a state that is attained to the accompaniment of the second fundamentally unchanging aspect of Vodou ritual: rhythmic music and dance. The tone of the ceremony is set by dance, which is structured by the rhythms of the drums and accompanied by the chanting of the Vodouisants (Price-Mars 1973, 178). Always anxious to downplay the exceptionalism of Vodou, Price-Mars constantly related Vodou practice to that of other world religions. In terms of dance and music, he argued that even the "most elevated" religions incorporated these elements: in Greco-Roman antiquity, dance often had a "sacred aspect"; the Nazirite Jews used music to provoke spirit possession and to have God speak through believers; and the importance of dance and music to the Hebrews is attested in various passages of the Bible (1973, 180).

What is fascinating, not to say slightly disconcerting, in Price-Mars' discussion of music and dance is that he considered these to be essential aspects of the black man. If dance and music are closely associated among all "primitive peoples," they have, according to Price-Mars, a power over the entire body that has a distinctly "biological" character. Developing his argument, Price-Mars restated his idea that music and dance are innate qualities of black people: "I mean to say that even in the form of a very simple melodic line, or the rhythmic step that are their most common expression, music and dance become *an organic need* for the black man, they become substantial if imponderable parts of his being that feed his nervous system, which bends under the weight of the most extreme kind of emotionalism. . . . [D]ance and music are the two tutelary muses that have a scepter-like primacy in the development of the black man in his primitive mode" (1973, 180, emphasis added).

In this passage, Price-Mars renounced momentarily his scientific engagement with Haitian culture and retreated into a form of racial essentialism that privileges biology as the major determinant in fixing the black man's intimate relationship with rhythmic music and dance.[26] The irony of Price-Mars's argument that the black man is innately, biologically musical and rhythmic is that it constitutes an unwitting affirmation of Artur de Gobineau's nineteenth-century theories of the "natural" differences between human races.[27] For Gobineau, there were three distinct human races—black, yellow, and white—and the black was considered inferior by virtually every measure, including moral sensitivity and intellectual capacity (1983, 339–40). Gobineau most clearly prefigures Price-Mars when he wrote of music and dance, at which the black race, being the most "sensual," excelled (1983, 476). For both Gobineau and Price-Mars, therefore, black people had an innate inclination toward and aptitude for music and dance. Unlike Gobineau, Price-Mars did not relate this aptitude to blacks' intellectual shortcomings, but he did echo the French author in his idea that the black man was often subject to the "most extreme kind of emotionalism" (1973, 180). Significantly, too, Price-Mars's essentialist conception of black being was reflected in François Duvalier's racial thinking. Referring explicitly to Gobineau's writings, Duvalier agreed with the idea that fixed biological traits differentiated the various races and that these traits were manifested in cultural differences. Tellingly, Duvalier, again echoing Gobineau, proposed that the black races were distinguished by sensitivity, subjectivism, and rhythm (Nicholls 1985, 53).

Price-Mars's work bears the imprint of European ethnography; *Ainsi parla l'oncle* includes many references to Leo Frobenius and Lucien Lévy-Bruhl as well as to their influential contemporary Maurice Delafosse. Although this influence is balanced to some extent by Price-Mars's drawing on Haitian intellectuals such as Hannibal Price, J.-C. Dorsainvil, Antoine Innocent, and Léon Audain, he does seem to have incorporated the idea, filtered through diverse European sources, that there is a natural, biologically determined connection between black people, music, and dance. In this way, Price-Mars diverged from his compatriot Anténor Firmin's earlier critique of Gobineau's biological racism in *The Equality of the Human Races* (1885). In that text, Firmin assiduously avoided biological explanations for apparent differences between various groups, and he suggested that art, poetry, and civilization in general are the products not of innate qualities but of multigenerational processes of change and development that are contingent on nonhuman factors such as the physical environment and the climate (Firmin 2002, 444).

Notwithstanding the questionable determinism of Price-Mars's ideas on race, music, and dance, his work profoundly influenced, indeed revolutionized, Haitian intellectualism across every discipline. As René Depestre states, *Ainsi parla l'oncle* was a veritable "declaration of identity" for black Haitians, an attempt to refigure Haitian culture on its own terms, which invited occupied Haiti to "refresh itself in the fertile compost of its origins" (1998, 33, 43). The occupation also had profound effects on the role of writers and of writing in Haiti. Price-Mars had asked in *Ainsi parla l'oncle* if Haitian literature really existed, and he had criticized at length Haitian intellectuals for ignoring Haiti's indigenous culture in favor of French civilization (1973, 255–56). More generally, the American presence and the newly dominated status of Haiti had, for many intellectuals, exposed the vanities of the *La Ronde* group's aestheticism and called into question the worth of Haitian authors' longstanding Francophilia. A more politically and historically engaged literature and culture was called for, and the works of figures such as Dominique Hippolyte, Frédéric Burr-Reynaud, and Christian Werleigh sought to recenter Haitian intellectuals in Haitian experience. In effect, the American occupation revitalized the literature of resistance in Haiti. Burr-Reynaud's poem "Trahison" (1930), for example, denounces the betrayal of those in the Haitian elite who collaborated with the Americans:

> They gnaw down to the bone your bruised body
> they stain your face with their bloody fingers
> and stretching out your dry, callous and withered skin
> they drum away to amuse the Whites.
> (Quoted in Dash 1981, 58)

This poem uses the image of the drum, constructed from the very body of the disenfranchised black man, as a metaphor for the Haitian elite's betrayal of the people and of Haitian culture itself. The poem also implicitly acknowledges the importance of the drum and drumming as distinctly Haitian cultural entities that have been betrayed through the elite's collaboration with the Americans. In fact, the poem prefigures the prominence that would be given to the drum and the drummer in this new nationalist phase of Haitian culture. Thereafter, the rhythm of the drum took on a new significance in Haitian culture as the educated elite rethought its relationship with Haiti's neglected though dynamic indigenous culture and sought to move, quite literally, to a different beat.[28]

One of the most marked developments in indigenist-inspired Haitian poetry written during and just after the occupation is the new enthusiasm for and representation of "African" elements, notably the image of the drum. As Roumain wrote in the first edition of *La Trouée* (1927), the movement for cultural resistance "explode[d] like the call of a drum" (2003f, 433). Similarly, rhythm ceased to be a neutral, colorless element of poetry; instead, it came to play a central role in constructing the new poetics of black, indigenous identity. Haitian poets of all colors and classes embraced and promoted their rhythmic Africanity. The contemporary poem "L'Africain" by the little-known poet Robert W. Scott epitomizes how the new racial pride drew on a revalorized image of Africa and Africans:

> I am African
> African, I bless my skin
> As the water sprite blesses the water.
>
> I bow down, joyous, before the black giant
> I have guarded the thrill of it in the long kisses of the evening
> And I have made of its eyes a limpid mirror.
>
> My brow is the torso of a slave
> Who wants to cast off his shackles.
> (Lubin 1965, 12)

The unequivocal opening declaration of the poet's African identity marks a departure from Haitian writing's long-held ambivalence about the African past. Dark skin now becomes a source of pride, and Africa, the "black giant," becomes a faithful mirror in which the Haitian finds his own clear reflection. Similarly, the long-neglected trope of African rhythmicity is evoked as a marker of this new racial identity:

> My heart is a famous tam-tam
> That beats a gracious rhythm
> My soul, like a negress,
> Becomes intoxicated by a caress.
> (Lubin 1965, 12)

In stark contrast to the introverted pessimism of much of the *La Ronde* poetry, Scott's poem strikes an affirmative, newly assured tone that leads to a final prophetic declaration of imminent renewal and rebirth:

> One evening will appear without veil
> The future [that] prepares itself. We see the star shining.
> The new day will, I believe, be beautiful.

> A two-edged sword sits on the hillside
> Your soul is reborn in sobs,
> Race. Like the swirling of the waves.
> (Lubin 1965, 12)

Although this poem provides evidence of the indigenist-inspired interest in Africa, rhythm, and race, it also illuminates a distinctly mystical bent to indigenist poetry, particularly in the later phases of the movement. In contrast to Price-Mars's largely scientific approach to race, much indigenist poetry tended to evoke a mystical vision of Africa, which in Scott's case is figured around the indeterminate "black giant" of Africa, the idea of an essentially black, rhythmic soul, and the image of the double-edged, almost Arthurian sword, which was presumably waiting to be raised again and to be used to ensure the coming of the new, glorious day of racial and national deliverance.

Just as Scott relates his heart to "a famous tam-tam," so the indigenist-inspired Haitian critic Maurice A. Lubin judges the drum to be the "symbol of the black soul" (1965, 16). This idea of the drum as a receptacle of blackness transmitting over time and place the essence of the race is given full expression in the poem "Le Tambour Racial" (1939) by Maurice Casséus, a work that begins with a supplication to the instrument:

> Ah! Tell us of your great African rhythm, your nocturnal voice,
> oh cone-shaped racial drum,
> tell us of your servitude and your acrid breath,
> DRUM, drum who gave rhythm to the surge of the naked, frizzy-haired packs
> all across the fatal night,
> beyond the shadowy glade.
> (Lubin 1965, 16)

Again the drum is related to the night, to the shadows, and therefore to mystery, hidden forces, and covert resistance. The drum is, moreover, a means of racial remembrance, containing the bitter memory of past servitude and, more positively, the memory of revolt during the "fatal night" of the revolution, which followed the initial insurrection at the "shadowy glade," an apparent reference to the Bois Caïman ceremony. However, the drum contains more than the memory of slavery and insurrection; it also connects the deracinated Haitian to "darkest Africa," to the "savage chant" that the speaker adores "secretly," to the "mystery of the distant hinterland" and to the "Guinean rhythm" that has come to be the "cry of an entire race" (Lubin 1965, 16).

As this invigorated Haitian poetry broke free from the more fixed forms of the past, rhythms and repetitions became integral, conspicuous aspects of the new, freer, and more irregular poetics. Jacques Lenoir (aka Paul Laraque) experiments with repetitive rhythm in his poem "Maintenant 'Nous Nègres'" which begins with an anaphoric structure that seems to beat its words of resistance like a drum:

> We who have not colonized Africa
> we who have not discovered America
> we who are the color of Satan
> we who are not the sons of Adam
> we who have eaten only the bread of ignorance
> we who are the swamps of the world.
>   (Lubin 1965, 13)

In terms of style and content, this opening echoes sections of Aimé Césaire's *Cahier d'un retour au pays natal* (1939): both poets use the repetitive stylistic device and share the desire to represent blackness in terms that at once reject historical, racist visions of black peoples and integrate some of those perceptions—putative depravity and backwardness—into their defiant assertions of black identity. In Lenoir's case, the new conception of blackness also involves a rejection of "white" notions of time and a re-incorporation of repetitive, rhythmic temporality into black Haitian consciousness. In contrast to the whites' mechanized, vertically directed experience of time—he says "the white man has made time into an escalator"—Lenoir's blacks exist in a more organic, rhythmic temporal sphere:

> We rise up
> and our dance is the earth that turns
> our chant that shatters the plate of silence
> is the nameless rhythm of the seasons
> the crossroads of the four elements.
>   (Lubin 1965, 13)

The rhythm, dance, and song of the blacks therefore connect them more vitally to the movement of the earth and the natural cycles of the seasons. This new rhythmic conception of black metaphysics and aesthetics also valorizes as never before in Haitian writing Vodou, or at least a version of the religion that could be appropriated into indigenism, which remained the intellectual elite's reaction to U.S. influence. The presence of a co-opted version of Vodou is suggested in the mention of the crossroads—in Vodou belief, sites that are haunted by evil spirits and ideal for the practice of "magical arts" (Métraux 1958, 89)—and, later in the poem, the speaker states that it is at the crossroads that the "thunder of our drums" is heard and where Ogoun, the *lwa* of fire and war, should "aim [his] slingshot well" to strike at the sun so that the night may be the people's "shield" (Lubin 1965, 13). In this Vodouesque darkness and shadow the people's revolt takes shape and accumulates its prophetic energy: "We are," the speaker says, "the new blood in the veins of the earth / Our laughter has chased away the old fear / suffering hides itself curled up like a cat" (14). As the poem moves to its prophetic climax, the figure of the drum reappears, "reestablishes communication between languages," and contributes to the rising, rhythmic sense of reinvigorated black identity (14). A further auditory element, the conch shell, is introduced, and this too is an echo from the revolutionary past, which "pierces the dark globe of the centuries with the single cry of liberty," and announces the new "dawn / when all black torches will be red torches" (14). This final image, of black torches being allied with red, indicates another important element of Haitian indigenism: the belief that the black struggle could be harnessed to the broader cause of internationalist socialism. Lenoir's poem demonstrates the hybrid nature of Haitian indigenism and the way in which it combined the mystical with the supernatural, how it drew on popular, African elements—in this case rhythmic music and Vodou—to construct its discourse of racial otherness (while remaining an esoteric and elite movement), and how sometimes the project of racial liberation was linked with Marxism.

The best-known literary text of Haitian Marxist-indigenism is not, however, a poem but is Roumain's peasant novel *Gouverneurs de la rosée* (1944), a work that presents the returning exile Manuel as the savior of a divided rural community who preaches communal action and cooperation to the fatalistic peasants. Like many indigenist intellectuals, Roumain's interest in Africa and Haitian peasant culture had grown over time and gradually supplanted his early focus on nonracialized issues of poetics and politics. Indeed, virtually none of Roumain's contributions to the seminal journal *La Revue indigène*, be they poems, short stories, or translations, corresponded to the indigenist aims of the journal (Hoffmann 2003, xl). It was only after returning to Haiti in 1927, in the middle of the American occupation, that Roumain began to assume his "double heritage," which he expressed in 1929 quite appropriately in terms of music and rhythm: "I like Beethoven, Bach, Wagner, Stravinski, their music enchants me, moves me, consoles me, saddens me, exalts me; but when the Vodou drum rumbles, when I hear the powerful voice of the Gods of my fathers call me imperiously, as if they were striking the goatskin impatiently with their finger . . . then, white men's music, so perfect, so fine, my heart is closed to you like the lips of a wound on the voice of my race" (2003d, 558).

Echoing, to some extent, Price-Mars's idea of a natural connection between black people and primitive instincts, Roumain argued in the same article that whatever his degree of civilization or culture, the black man will "always return in one way or another to purely black primitive sentiments" (2003d, 558). In an earlier essay, Roumain had expressed a similar idea and placed even greater emphasis on the importance of rhythm in allowing him to access his black, ancestral self: "Drums, conchs, the powerful call of the race! . . . [W]hen I hear you rumbling in the hills, my blood beats to your muted rhythm. I am no longer the incoherent mulatto who drives a 40CV . . . I am my Peuhl, Oulof, Asanti or Masai ancestor . . . living in the African bush" (2003b, 470).

Roumain's interest in the drum as a potent reminder of his and Haiti's African elements is signaled throughout his prose fiction. In his first published volume, *La Proie et l'ombre* (1930), for instance, the opening scene presents a crowd of lower-class Haitians leaving the "crushed mass of their houses" to go to the nearby countryside, drawn into the night by the "sinister and joyful voice of a drum, the voice of a thousand African kings, smiling and obscene, which cuts into the silence with little frantic beats" (2003e, 111). The drum, the hinterland, and the night offer respite from the silent, diurnal misery of the town. It also acts as a counterpoint to the jaded cynicism of the worldly bourgeois characters, whose conversations play out to the distant accompaniment of the drum. Set during the American occupation, the story evokes the drum as the "voice of our race" and, again, as a receptacle of memory, which recalls "all the pain of the slave on the plantation under the whip" (111). The Roumain-like figure Michel Rey promotes the values of indigenism, the need to "plant . . . in our soul" both Haiti's flora and the "black man's drum" (129).

Roumain also used music to reflect on Haitian society and culture under the American occupation in his second volume, *Les Fantoches*, published in 1931. There, Roumain focused more exclusively on the cynical, emasculated Haitian bourgeoisie, struggling to come to terms with Haiti's loss of sovereignty and its complicity in the nation's decline. At one point, Roumain suggested that the fascination with the past and with the revolution could do little to assuage the humiliations of the occupied present, and indeed that the fixation with the past had contributed to Haiti's downfall. He did this by using music again as a metaphor: at one point an old general takes out a gramophone record of the military march written by the famous composer Occide Jeanty, "1804," which the general says "gets them going, stimulates them" (2003h, 169). During the occupation, Jeanty's military march often sparked riots when played for Haitian audiences and became "an anthem for anti-American resistance" (Largey 2006, 90). When the record plays in Roumain's *Les Fantoches*, however, it sounds "worn out, scratched," and the notes come out of the machine "as if out of a grater, strangling themselves, making themselves hoarse" (2003h, 169). Roumain thus suggested that Haitian history is to some extent like an old record that plays itself over and again, that the constant return to the revolution as a counter to present frustrations only wears out the memory of 1804 and reduces the potency of the past to effect change in the present.

In addition to its worn-out fixation with history (with 1804 and the faded glories of the revolution), Haiti also suffers, Roumain suggests, from the elite's historical inability to recognize or validate the nation's cultural plurality. He implies this by presenting a bourgeois party scene at which young elite Haitians dance to a discordantly hybridized musical form. The orchestra plays "Blue Danube Blues," a "transposition of the famous waltz onto a black rhythm," in which "the Danube flowed between Louisiana river banks; a saxophone screeched like the wind above the somber bayous, and in the cotton plantations there swirled melancholically, instead of Viennese petticoats, the loose blouses of the black women" (2003h, 142). The effect of this hybrid music is, the narrator says, both "moving and ridiculous" (142). These two different musical forms do not fuse completely or harmoniously. An element of dissonance remains, which is further suggested in the way the music ends on a note that sounds like it was "shouted at the same time by a Tyrolian yodeler and a lynched black man" (142). The artificial, rigid atmosphere of the bourgeois party does not permit the black and white musical forms to creolize naturally; indeed, the privileged dancers seem oblivious to the hybridized nature of the music. To fulfill his deeply felt need to locate and represent the more organically creolized and authentically Haitian culture, Roumain would have to leave the middle-class salons and connect more directly with the rural peasantry.

In *Gouverneurs de la rosée,* Roumain focuses almost exclusively on rural Haiti and on peasant culture. In that work, the hero Manuel's life is sacrificed in order for the community to reunite and return to its previous, idyllic state of pastoral harmony, an idealized anterior world characterized by proto-communist work systems and Africanized cultural practices, of which rhythms, in work and in music, are an integral part. The organic, rhythmic connections between the people, the land, work, and the drum are established early in the novel when Manuel's father Bienaimé recalls the days of the *coumbite,* the collective, African-derived work system, which stands in sharp contrast to the impoverished, fatalistic present. Bienaimé's memory of the *coumbite* includes a vivid recollection of the role of the *simidor,* the drummer who beats out the rhythms to which the workers sing their work songs and raise their hoes "in one single sweep" (1944, 18). As Bienaimé recalls, the "rapid pulsations" of the drum course through the workers "like a more ardent blood" (18). The rhythms of Roumain's prose mimic those of the drum and the workers, who are taken over, almost possessed by the rhythm: "A rhythmic circulation established itself between the beating heart of the drum and the movements of the men: the rhythm was like a powerful flow that penetrated them right to the depths of their arteries and nourished their muscles with a renewed vigor" (19–20). Significantly, Roumain celebrates the practical, utilitarian role of rhythm in bonding workers and promoting group labor; if the workers are "possessed" by rhythm it is for materially useful, tangible ends. In an important sense, too, it is the rhythmic, reciprocal sharing of work and the synchronization of efforts that *create* the community in the novel. To work together is effectively "to espouse a collective pulsation, to vibrate in unison, to be united in a shared chant" (Bona 2004, 2).

Roumain's novel is thus sensitive to the ways in which rhythm continued to structure peasant life long after the revolution and the pressing need in colonial times to use rhythm on the plantations as a means of bringing together the ethnically diverse, culturally fragmented slaves. In the postrevolution period, rhythm, in the form of work songs, drums, and the repetitive movements of people and their work tools, helped people get back to working the land, the site of their previous forced labor. Collective, rhythmic work came to be organized by "sociétés de travail," or work societies, the principal attribute of which were the orchestras of four or five members playing the drum or bamboo trumpets as the work was carried out. Each society was distinguished by the kind of instruments played and the drum rhythms they preferred (Métraux 1960, 33). In this way, rhythm, work, and social organization were inextricably linked in postindependence Haiti. For the new Haitian state, this rhythmic counter-structure posed a threat to the rigid social and work organization that it sought to impose in the former plantations. For Pétion in particular, whose plans to reinvigorate the plantation system relied on the supply of a compliant, docile workforce, the societies were troubling. In effect, the conflict between the state and the autonomous work societies turned around rhythm: who had the power to impose the rhythm of work, the state or the workers themselves? In postcolonial Haiti, as in other places, the "master of rhythm" was the master of work (Barthélemy 2000, 165–66). Rhythm had been a supplement to slave life and had become, as in Roumain's novel, the motor of a model of self-sufficient labor generated by the people that operated outside the control of the state.[29]

Although Roumain evoked and promoted the rhythm-centered work of the peasants, he was more ambivalent about rhythm's role in Vodou possession. Manuel does participate in the ethnographically detailed Vodou ceremony that is held to celebrate his return, but this kind of rhythmic possession is ultimately dismissed as a waste of energy. Manuel says that he danced willingly at the ceremony, took his pleasure and responded to the drums "as a real black man," but for him Vodou is finally "foolishness" and "useless" (1944, 96). For Roumain, therefore, rhythm was of interest as an aspect of Haiti's ethnographic reality and as a means of structuring work and society. It was also, as for many Haitian indigenist intellectuals, a source of memory and a recurring, insistent counterpoint to the educated elite's complacently adopted Francophilia. Despite Roumain's misgivings about the practical benefits of Vodou, he and indigenism in general had recognized—and to some extent co-opted—popular culture as valid, politically potent elements of Haitian culture. The drum and rhythm were perhaps the primary elements of this culture, echoes of a past that had been forgotten by the urban elite but had continued to evolve dynamically in harmony with the changing lives of the Haitian masses.[30]

HAITIAN MUSIC, RHYTHM, AND INDIGENISM

At the same time as Haitian literature was taking its Africanist turn, the nation's elite musicians were effecting a similar, if less well-known, evolution in Haitian music, incorporating long-neglected popular rhythms, melodies, songs, proverbs, and instruments into their compositions. Significantly, too, middle-class musicians drew on Vodou and its music, with similar aims to the indigenist poets. That is, they infused their work with Africanized elements that would distinguish it more starkly from white, European, or North American music and thereby act as a conduit for resistance to U.S. domination.

The history of Haitian elite or art music has much in common with the evolution of Haitian literature in that, in both cases, one can trace a general trajectory from the nineteenth-century Europhile mimicry that ignored and denigrated native forms to the new nationalist indigenism of the early twentieth century, which sought to reincorporate aspects of the neglected peasant culture into its revitalized, racially charged aesthetic. Colonial Saint-Domingue had been an important venue for European musical performances; there were an estimated three thousand musical and theatrical performances in the colony between 1764 and 1791 (Largey 2006, 3). Just as European literature retained its privileged status among the Haitian elites after independence, so the same group continued to favor European music in the nineteenth century. In 1860, the Haitian government founded the École Nationale de Musique, an institution that followed the curriculum of the Conservatoire Impérial de Musique de Paris (Dumervé 1968, 40–41). Even before that, the Haitian elite, which generally regarded peasant music with a "mixture of wonder and fear," had sought at certain points to replace indigenous music with more European forms (Largey 2006, 36). General Guy-Joseph Bonnet, for example, recorded in his memoirs how he had tried to introduce the *calenda* dance accompanied by a violin; this was to be performed alongside the peasants' "African" dances, which were always accompanied by the drum. In 1820, Bonnet and a group of elite Haitians and French residents founded a society for "decent entertainment" in Port-au-Prince, the purpose of which was to "organize dances in the European style" (Nicholls 1979, 71).

At the beginning of the American occupation, as certain scenes from Roumain's short fiction demonstrate, Haiti's urban elite held sophisticated private balls and public dances for which the musical accompaniment often included a piano or a small French-style string orchestra with cello, bass, violin, clarinet, and trombone. The repertoire for these orchestras, called *okès bastreng,* included European couples and figure dances such as mazurkas, polkas, waltzes, lancers, contredanses, quadrilles, and the creolized dance *mereng* (Averill 1997, 35). Thus, in terms of music and entertainment, the urban elite's Europeanized tastes largely mirrored the intellectuals' reliance on European aesthetic and literary models.

Price-Mars, by contrast, recognized the importance of music as a primary example of indigenous culture. He was particularly sensitive to the threatened status of popular song, which he felt disappeared all the more easily because it was an oral tradition (1973, 27). Ironically, though Price-Mars was a great advocate of popular culture, he thought that popular song was too raw for elite consumption in its natural state, and he argued that the Haitian intelligentsia had to distill peasant culture into a national literature and music (Largey 2006, 52). The ultimate aims of this process of appropriation and interpretation of peasant culture were to assert the cultural and intellectual worth of the Haitian people and, by extension, the black race. In the final pages of *Ainsi parla l'oncle*, Price-Mars implicitly recognized the importance of indigenous-derived national music in the promotion of Haiti and the race: "[All those] who are obsessed with the problem of creating an original Haitian music, sensual and melancholic, all are guarantors who in the matrix of Time are preparing the work which will mark the capacity of the race for an individual art generating ideas and emotions" (1973, 183).

It is virtually impossible, however, to prescribe musical taste, and Haitian audiences during the occupation became enthused not by indigenous music but by foreign forms, swept in with the Americans and returning migrants. The occupying Americans did not influence Haitian literature directly (in that they did not bring new aesthetic examples), but they did have a significant impact on elite musical tastes. American troops, and elite Haitians returning from Paris, brought jazz, the Charleston, and the fox-trot to a receptive Haitian middle class in the 1920s. Jazz records were imported from the United States and France to be played in Haitian dance clubs, and the middle class took to the American music enthusiastically, "to the detriment," as one Marine noted, "of their native music" (Craige 1933, 168). Although jazz had arrived as a cultural aftereffect of the U.S. occupation, it was of course the music of black Americans, and, even if few Haitian jazz enthusiasts seemed to realize it, jazz had evolved from strong Saint-Dominguan-influenced roots in the dances at Congo Square. Thus, the arrival was also a return, a homecoming of a much-traveled, much-changed distant relative. Jazz was welcomed by politically conscious Haitians as an expression of the emerging black cultural movement in the United States, a musical extension of the Harlem Renaissance movement, which was an important outside influence on contemporary Haitian intellectuals. Price-Mars, for instance, called Harlem "the greatest black city in the world" (1932, 8). Roumain, too, wrote enthusiastically about Langston Hughes (who met with Roumain in 1931), calling him the "greatest black poet of America" (2003i, 635), and about Countee Cullen, who were two examples of what Roumain called the "flourishing black poetry" (2003c, 435) that Haitian intellectuals were beginning to read just as they were discovering jazz. Thus, if American economic power helped to popularize jazz during the occupation, Haitian jazz followers were to some extent "exploring an African-American musical kinship" and renewing a relationship between musics that shared "diasporic intimacy" (Averill 1997, 38–39).

Similarly, Cuban dance music forms became popular in Haitian clubs, especially in the later period of the occupation. Once again, patterns of migration and work helped circulate music among different locales. In this case, Haitian migrant cane cutters brought back with them from Cuba the guitar-based song tradition that creolized with Haitian traditions and became known as *twouba-dou* (troubadour) music (Averill 1997, 39). Nevertheless, the American-supported president Louis Borno sought to suppress popular culture, particularly Carnival, which he tried to recreate as an orderly, bourgeois festival, quite unlike the popular, spontaneous event that it had been and far removed, as the editors of the newspaper *L'Essor* put it in 1924, "from an African stage" (quoted in Corvington 1987, 308).

The relatively close formal and expressive qualities of music and poetry—the importance of sounds, melodies, meter, and rhythm—allowed for the easy appropriation of aspects of traditional Haitian music by indigenist poets. As the poet Normil Sylvain wrote in *La Revue indigène* in 1927, "It is the sound of the drums announcing the dance from one hillside to another, the call of the conch shell . . . it is the vibrant, sensual rhythm of a meringue with wanton melancholy, which must be incorporated in our poetry" (52). And as the many examples cited above show, the drum and rhythm were incorporated as never before into the elite's conceptualization of authentic, Africanized Haitian culture.

Somewhat ironically, once the Americans had left in 1934, indigenous Haitian music did not enjoy a new surge in popularity but was eclipsed by the craze for jazz and Cuban music. The most heard and requested tunes in the clubs and radio stations of the capital were Cuban-style *sones,* boleros, rumbas, and *guarachas* (Averill 1997, 52), a situation lamented by the Haitian violinist Velério Canez in 1942, when he complained that "the true rhythm of the Haitian *mereng* is no longer in fashion these days, to our misfortune. . . . Every day we hear Haitian melodies which are executed to the rhythm of the *bolero-son* or the Cuban *rumba*"(1). The indigenist movement did, however, continue to gather momentum in the post-occupation period as ideas of race and culture were developed and given scientific legitimacy by the nascent Haitian ethnographic movement. Yet, crucially, the loose alliance of anti-occupation intellectuals split along previously obscured ideological lines. Haitian Marxists such as Roumain tended to look outward and to leave their notions of race and culture loosely defined and indeterminate, whereas the Africanist Griot movement founded by Lorimer Denis,

Carl Brouard, and François Duvalier developed a narrower idea of black identity that was based on the essential, biological differences they believed existed between the races. During the occupation, indigenism had invoked Africanity and Haitian peasant culture in a loose, open-ended way, but after the Americans left the Griots sought to systematically define black identity and Haitian authenticity, and thereby they carefully laid out the intellectual justification for future black dictatorship (Dash 1981, 101).

Throughout the early twentieth century, music remained an important medium through which political ideas could be expressed and legitimized, which is perhaps not surprising in a nation with a notoriously high illiteracy rate. Even as Émile Lescot's government and the Catholic Church carried out its anti-superstition campaign in 1941–42, destroying Vodou temples and drums, Vodou music was being appropriated by elite art music composers such as Justin Elie, Ludovic Lamothe, and Werner Anton Jaegerhuber. Elie "classicized" Haitian music in that he suggested it had its origins in the ancient traditions of the exterminated Amerindian peoples of the Caribbean.[31] Lamothe "vulgarized" Haitian music by incorporating lower-class musical styles, notably Vodou rhythmic patterns and musical structure, into the classical repertoire (Largey 2006, 99–100, 114). For his part, Jaegerhuber placed great emphasis on reproducing the authentic rhythms of peasant music, the rhythm of the 5/8, which he considered "the only typical basis of the African music in Haiti," which contained the "Negro's highest emotional expressions," and in which the Haitian rediscovered "his spontaneity, his grandeur, and his liberty" (Maximilien 1952, 34–36). During the same period, folkloric choirs were formed, performing traditional repertoires that were officially sanctioned as "modern, sanitized expression[s] of heritage and local color," while the contemporary practice and belief system of Vodou was considered by the authorities as "archaic, barbaric, and threatening" (Averill 1997, 57). The group Jazz des Jeunes, formed in the early 1940s in the middle-class area of Moren-à-Tuf, was considered the first popular dance band to have incorporated the *noiriste* (or black-centered) ideology of the Griots, and it would mock other groups it considered to be less authentic, less *natif-natal*. Jazz des Jeunes's music, known as Vodou Jazz, drew on traditional folkloric rhythms, Vodou songs, and hybrid Haitian-Cuban styles, and it was received enthusiastically by the pronoiriste press for its expression of the "true soul" of Haiti (Averill 1997, 58–62).

BEATING BACK DARKNESS

Ultimately, however, the notion of Haiti's "true soul" was in many ways an artificial concept, strategically constructed and manipulated by the various post-indigenist factions, in particular the *noiristes*. Without the crisis and strife of the occupation, it is unlikely that the elite would have sought out indigenist culture with the same enthusiasm. The questions of identity that the occupation brought into sharp focus—what it meant to be a "black" nation newly subjugated by "white" foreigners—superseded for a time the elite's long-standing preoccupation with differentiating itself from the poor masses of Haiti and thereby with maintaining the rigid class divisions in the nation. New myths of blackness and Haitian identity were required to bolster the national resistance to the U.S. occupation, and it was peasant culture that provided the raw materials for these myths. In common with other "nativistic" movements, Haitian indigenism selected certain elements of culture that would mark Haiti's "unique character" in relation to the white, American occupier, and it objectified culture in ways that would make it easier in the future to intervene in and mold culture for political ends (Linton 1943, 231; Whisnant 1983, 13). As such, Haitian indigenism should be seen not as an open embrace by the Haitian elite of the Haitian peasantry but as a movement that selectively appropriated aspects of Africanized culture for its own ends, which did not truly ever include the elevation of the Haitian lower classes from their historically marginalized state. Elite nationalist rhetoric had two fundamental objectives: to differentiate "Afro-Latin" Haiti from the coarse and grasping Anglo-Saxon invaders, and to protect the elite's own privileged status in Haitian society. As one critic says, "By evoking the pèp ayisyen [Haitian people] as their symbol of an un-Americanized and hence unpolluted Haitian culture, Haitian elites embraced those aspects of lower-class culture that met their ideological goals while containing those features that challenged their control" (Largey 2006, 4).

If Haitian indigenism was to some extent an act of memory, it was selective in the memories it revived and in the aspects of Haitian culture—its "internal exotic" (Largey 2006, 19)—that it kept silenced and forgotten. Most notably, elite writers and musicians selectively appropriated popular rhythms, melodies, and language and labeled these aspects of culture as folklore, thereby allowing them to be manipulated for ideological and political ends. With a few honorable exceptions (such as Roumain and Price-Mars), these writers and musicians also neglected to deal with long-silenced elements of popular culture, such as Vodou belief itself, and with the material conditions of the Haitian rural poor, their economic marginalization, and indeed the relation between poverty and religious belief.

There is a tradition in Haiti that is typically invoked in times of particular hardship and insecurity; it involves the spontaneous rhythmic beating of spoons, metals, and other percussive materials. The cacophony is intensified in urban zones by the noise of car horns, pedestrians beating sticks against metal fences, people blowing into conch shells, banging on hubcaps, and merchants drumming on bottles with spoons (Averill 1997, 14). "In a daring and deafening act," as Beverly Bell says, the people of the slums "beat against metal to raise their voices against repression" and transform the rhythmic beating into "a mighty form of power" (2001, xiii). This act is called *bat tenèb,* or beating back darkness. It is suggestive of the way that rhythm and percussion have been used in Haiti to express working-class and peasant identity, and of the muted but insistent resistance of the lower classes to their ongoing marginalization. In fulfilling these functions, rhythm takes the place of words and constitutes its own opaque, indomitable discourse of resistance and survival. Moreover, the rhythms of the *bat tenèb* connect the contemporary Haitian poor to their historical past, to those who came before them and suffered under dictators, tyrants, and foreign occupiers and who perpetuated a close relation with rhythm, dance, drumming, and Vodou worship even as various bodies sought to repress these activities.

In a sense, Haitian leaders from Toussaint onward, often in collaboration with the Church and the social elite, have been beating back darkness too, in that they have sought to repress the dances and rhythms that are the most potent and persistent markers of poor black identity in Haiti. Until the early twentieth century, Haitian authors also tried to beat back darkness, to follow European forms and purge their work and sensibility of any tinges of the denigrated Africanized culture of the masses. Indigenism broadly sought to revalorize the culture of the masses, but it was always selective in which aspects of the culture it appropriated. In its own way, indigenism still beat back the black poor and did little if anything to improve their material conditions. It is tempting to conclude that the indigenists were the culmination of a long line of Haitian intellectuals who had slowly, often reluctantly, lent legitimacy to popular culture, to the drum, and to rhythm. In truth, however, the drum and rhythm had long been legitimized by the great mass of Haitian people. From the people's perspective, which few Haitian authors ever truly understood, the drum and rhythm required, and still require, no external sanction or validation.

2

Rhythm, Creolization, and Conflict in Trinidad

As Haiti was assuming its independence and moving into its uncertain post-colonial future, the rest of the colonial Caribbean remained firmly under the yoke of imperialism and slavery. The islands of the Anglophone Caribbean did not become independent until almost 160 years after Dessalines's declaration. One of the consequences of the Haitian Revolution was that the process of creolization in that country took on an idiosyncratic form: with the influx of Africans and Europeans largely arrested, and with relatively few other immigrant groups subsequently settling in Haiti, creolization there became largely a matter of further syncretizing the African and European elements of religion, music, dance, and language. In short, Haiti's postcolonial creolization was figured around a two-sided, French-African model inherited from colonial times. In much of the rest of the Caribbean, by contrast, creolization has taken on more complex, multidimensional shapes as colonialism and slavery continued, perpetuating the unpredictable play of cultures that characterizes the processes of creolization. When slavery ended in the mid-nineteenth century, creolization was accelerated and enriched as new waves of East Indian, Chinese, Portuguese, and later Syrian and Lebanese immigrants arrived in the region.

The island of Trinidad is one of the most ethnically diverse in all of the Caribbean, and the history of its music and its rhythms reflects and records the dynamic process of creolization that has shaped its culture and society. In this chapter, I present the history of creolized Trinidadian music as a classic case of colonial fear and repression of rhythm. Whereas in Haiti it was successive black and mulatto regimes that sought to silence rhythm, in Trinidad the conflict was more classically colonial, a struggle between the restrained, powerful, yet always edgy white (and brown) elite and the black masses. In contrast to Haitian anxieties about rhythmic peasant culture, Trinidad's rhythm-centered conflicts have been largely urban affairs. The streets of Port of Spain, in particular, have been the theater in which these conflicts have played out. The city creates an unavoidable intimacy among Trinidad's diverse, creolizing traditions, bringing them together inevitably and most strikingly in Carnival, the scene of virtually all the major conflicts concerning civilization, race, and rhythm that have shaped the development of Trinidadian culture and society. Unlike in Haiti (where rhythmic music has remained closely associated with sacred rites), but something like in Congo Square in New Orleans, Trinidad's Carnival largely secularized rhythm and thereby multiplied its possible meanings.[1] In the following pages, I focus on the history of Carnival and its associated musical forms from the early nineteenth to the mid-twentieth centuries, listening to their rhythms and the polemics that have surrounded them. What emerges is a cultural history shaped by evolving, contesting notions of race and civilization in which rhythm is a constant presence, an echo of the past but also a prescient force that carries intimations of times to come.

EARLY CONTACTS, EARLY RHYTHMS

Discord and disharmony are deeply inscribed in the history of transcultural contact in Trinidad, and music has often been the locus of this conflict. On July 31, 1498, after two months at sea on his third transatlantic voyage, Christopher Columbus and his crew caught sight of three hills on the southeastern coast of a large island; they reacted ecstatically, naming the island Trinidad and singing spontaneously the hymn *Salve Regina*. However, there was no indigenous audience for this first rendition of European music in Trinidad. It was not until August 2 that some contact was made with the island's people. On the southwest tip of the island, which Columbus named Point Arenal, his three ships anchored. At the same time, a large canoe containing twenty-five islanders left the shore, and when they came within ear shot they called out in a language that none of Columbus's crew understood. Columbus attempted to entice the islanders on board by showing them glittering trinkets and polished metal, but they were unimpressed and opted to stay in their canoe for two hours, gazing at the performance of the strangers. In a further attempt to demonstrate their good intentions, Columbus's men danced and played fife-and-drum music, but, to their dismay, the islanders reacted by paddling back to shore and raining arrows on the ship (Joseph 1970, 122–26; Manuel, Bilby, and Largey 1995, 183).

It has become commonplace to think of Caribbean cultures in terms of creolization and hybridization—the syncretic meeting of disparate, previously separated cultural fragments—but Columbus's initial experience in Trinidad reminds us that these processes do not take place in the absence of conflict, xenophobia, misunderstandings, and deadly struggles for power. Creolization does not *just happen,* and if we now conceive of Caribbean cultures in terms of a creative cultural synthesis, we should recognize that discord and disharmony are essential elements in the historical constitution of these cultures. The islanders' reflex to reject violently the foreign and the unknown prefigures the reactions of diverse groups in the subsequent development of musical culture in Trinidad, and it raises some of the questions that are of central importance to this chapter. What does music mean to different social groups? How does this meaning change according to context and to audience? What is music's role in the kinds of cultural negotiations that began awkwardly in 1498 and have since continued, becoming ever more complex as different groups—African peoples, Spanish, French, English, Irish, Scots, East Indians, Chinese, Portuguese, Syrians, Lebanese, and Venezuelans— settled in Trinidad?

A small community that calls itself Carib still exists in Arima in eastern Trinidad, but it is difficult to trace with any certainty the musical and cultural legacy of the Caribs and Arawaks on the island. As in other parts of the Americas, contact with Europeans led to the decimation of indigenous peoples. As a result of wars, deportations, slavery, disease, and flights to Venezuela and Guyana, Trinidad's pre-Columbian indigenous population—estimated at between 20,000 and 30,000—declined dramatically, to the extent that by 1612 only a few thousand remained, and by 1793 several hundred surviving Amerindians were gathered together in Toco, Savannah Grande, and Arima (Newson 1976, 30–33). The nineteenth century witnessed the further decimation of the Amerindian population: in Toco in northeastern Trinidad, the cholera epidemic of 1854 apparently killed all of the remaining indigenous people there, and a similar fate exterminated the Arima group, so that, by 1875, only a few pure-blooded Amerindians still lived on the island, with larger numbers of mixed bloods (of Amerindian-Spanish- African descent) living in the hills and valleys behind Arima.

Despite the long absence of the Amerindian people, the accounts (albeit rare) of their public and private dances, called *arietos,* introduce many of the aspects of music, rhythmicity, and dance that came to characterize Trinidadian culture. These dances brought together thousands of men and women who danced through the night, keeping time to the accompaniment of a drum and conch shells.[2] As one English historian later remarked, the dances were "licentious," adding that "the dances of all people in a low state of life are licentious or warlike" (Joseph 1970, 119). Music also had spiritual functions for the Amerindian peoples: the shaman, in a drug-induced trance, would summon his tutelary spirits, singing songs and shaking the sacred rattle, the *maraca* (Boomert 2000, 450). Once returned to consciousness, the shaman communicated the spirits' messages and instructions to the village, and positive messages from the deities would lead to the calling of an *arieto,* during which the singing, dancing, and chanting of the tribe communicated the "central cultural and religious repertory of the tribe" (Highfield 1997, 167). In a further prefiguration of modern Trinidadian culture, the events were accompanied by the beating of drums and the wearing of *guaizas,* or masks (Highfield 1997, 167).

The folklorist Mitto Sampson, in his investigation into the origins of modern calypso, argued that the topical, vitriolic songs or *carietos* sung in Trinidad by the figure "Surisima the Carib" in the nineteenth century were the "archetypes of calypso"—a claim dismissed by later musicologists such as Andrew Pearse and Jacob Elder.[3] However, even if Pearse and Elder were right to say that the cultural "cleansing" of Amerindian influence ran parallel to the drastic reduction in population, these cultural elements—the *arieto,* the shaking of the *maraca,* the topical *carietos*—have much in common with the most prominent manifestations of modern Trinidadian culture, and it is impossible to substantiate their claims that Amerindian cultural influence simply and completely disappeared from the island.[4] A more considered argument in this respect is suggested by Arnold Highfield, who proposes that traces of the Caribbean's original peoples and aspects of their cultures have survived the "catastrophe" of European colonialism by being assimilated and absorbed into the culture of the conquering power. Highfield argues that, although cultural transformation was most apparent and widespread within indigenous communities, a "partial transformation" of the conquerors also inevitably occurred (1997, 168). Biologically, the Amerindian bloodline mixed with African and European elements, creating new physical types. Culturally, too, as Highfield argues, certain aspects of Amerindian culture—words, place names, expressions, foods, dance, song—were transferred to and adopted by subsequent generations of hybrid Caribbean peoples (1997, 168).[5] No culture, language, or people remained "pure" in the Caribbean, and, although power relations dictated the relative prevalence of the various discrete, creolizing cultures, no culture has truly died there.[6]

HISPANIC ABSENCE AND PRESENCE

For almost three hundred years, the dominant culture in post-Columbian Trinidad was Spanish, even if the island was not permanently settled until 1592, when Antonio de Berrio founded the town of San José de Oruña, modern-day St. Joseph, and Trinidad's first capital. Concerned primarily with finding gold and silver, of which Trinidad had none, the Spaniards long used Trinidad as a staging post for expeditions into the South American mainland in search of El Dorado. This neglect of the island—one element of what V. S. Naipaul calls the "Spanish waste" (1982, 20)—meant that a large-scale plantation economy developed relatively late in Trinidad. It was not until the 1770s that the Spanish began to develop Trinidad, when two Cedulas (or royal decrees) of population were issued, inviting non-Spaniard Roman Catholics to settle in Trinidad and set up plantations, in what Eric Williams describes as a "confession of the total failure of Spanish colonialism" (1962, 43). The first new arrivals in Trinidad were colored and white French planters, enticed from the French islands and British Grenada by the promise of new lands and fresh opportunities. French immigration was given a new impetus after 1789, as planters and free coloreds of varying political persuasions fled the repercussions of the Revolution. At the time of the British conquest of Trinidad in 1797, the majority of the island's free population was of French origin and spoke French or French Creole. Trinidad's free coloreds at the turn of the century was unusually large: in 1802 they numbered 5,275 compared to 2,261 whites.

At the same time as the French Creole group was establishing itself as the dominant cultural class, immigrants from Venezuela—fleeing the revolutionary wars that began in 1810—brought further Hispanic influence to Trinidad. The more significant Venezuelan immigration later in the nineteenth century was of "peons," or laborers of mixed Spanish-Amerindian-African origin, who came to Trinidad for work and land and who reinforced the Hispanic culture of the island (Brereton 1979, 8). Later still, during the 1890s, Venezuelan musical influence impressed itself upon Trinidadian culture in the form of "Spanish" compositions, string orchestras, and general prevalence of flutes, violins, and guitars, instruments associated with Hispanic culture (Cowley 1996, 180). More recent contacts between Trinidad and Venezuela have been created by labor migration and in particular by the oil industry, the cornerstone of both countries' modern-day economies. Unofficial, temporary migrations, tourism, and linguistic exchanges—such as Venezuelans coming to Trinidad to learn English, or the Trinidadian government's promotion of Spanish as the preferred foreign language in schools—have perpetuated and diversified the Hispanic presence in Trinidad.

The longest and most significant Hispanic influence in terms of rhythm and music is *parang,* the Trinidadian form of the Spanish word *parranda,* which refers to a carousel, a spree, or a group of four or more people who, chiefly at Christmas time, sing at night to the accompaniment of traditional Spanish musical instruments (the bandola, cello, guitar, mandolin, tiple [a small guitar], and four-stringed cuatro mini-guitar) and to the rhythm of the Amerindian *maraca,* or chac-chac (Taylor 1977, 8, 33). Traditionally, the repertoire consisted of Spanish Christmas carols, or *aguinaldos,* songs that deal with seasonal Christian themes (Taylor 1977, 16). As the numbers of Spanish speakers in Trinidad have diminished, and as communications between and outside of the rural communities in which *parang* has traditionally thrived have improved, the nature of *parang* has changed. English is now often used in newer songs, and more secularized, hybrid musical forms such as *soca parang* have emerged.

The existing scholarly analyses of *parang*, albeit rather sparse, have put forward two general theories of its origins: first, that it came directly from Spain during the three hundred years of Spanish rule; and, second, that it came indirectly from Europe, via Venezuela, and has evolved through ongoing contacts with the latter. Whereas Daphne Taylor favors the first theory, Elder argues decisively for the second, saying that Latin-type folk music in Trinidad "may be deemed absolutely to have been contributed by Venezuelans" and that it is "part of the larger South American Latin musical cycle which stretches into Central America" (1969, 5). Indeed, Venezuelan influence is important to the development of calypso, both in instrumentation and in the "respectability" it brought to calypso to balance the less well regarded African elements.[7]

AFRO-CREOLE RHYTHMS

The influx of new planters—white and colored—and their slaves transformed not only Trinidad's society and economy but also its culture and its rhythms. The history of post-Cedula Trinidadian culture is remarkable in that its major conflicts, controversies, and victories have almost all been figured around rhythm, drumming, and percussion. To Gordon Rohlehr's argument that much of Trinidad's social history has involved a "dance of opposites" (abandon and responsibility; inhibition and censorship; scandal and respectability), we might add that the unending conflict and interplay between rhythm and melody has itself been the locus and figuration of the society's broader antagonisms (2001, 16). In Trinidad, the drum as the producer of rhythm, the inciter of "wild" dancing, has been at once the object of white repression and fear and an evolving, malleable symbol of black resistance and anti-authoritarianism. Subject to a series of bans and ordinances, the rhythm of the drum reappears in many different forms: from the tamboo-bamboo and biscuit tin bands to the steelbands that today are legitimized, sponsored by insurance or oil companies, and very much an accepted part of national culture. The post-Cedula cultural history of Trinidad is, in many crucial senses, the history of rhythm and percussion, elements that course through Trinidadian colonial and postcolonial history and that continue to shape ideas of race and nation.

In Trinidadian cultural history, different European groups reacted in their own diverse ways to the island's black culture. In this sense, cultural conflicts were seldom clearly two-sided; in fact, multiple positions and gradations of opinion can be traced in every major cultural controversy. The French Creole planters who first came to Trinidad in the 1770s and 1780s, encouraged by the issue of the two Cedulas, can be contrasted in this regard to the British, who conquered the island in 1797 and ruled it until independence in 1962. During the nineteenth century, these two groups—the British (including English Creoles) and the French Creoles—were often in conflict over social and cultural issues.

Tensions were created by religious and cultural differences between the two. The British generally espoused middle-class, Victorian values including the primary worth of industry and thrift, the belief in science and progress, the subordinate position of women, and, most important, the idea that Britain was the foremost example of a modern, enlightened, and civilized nation. Although the French Creoles certainly shared the British belief in white, European superiority, their outlook was more aristocratic, and many planters harked back to the France of the Ancien Régime, taking pride in their ancestors' loyalty to the royalist cause and their own claims to high birth and noble ancestry (Brereton 1979, 5).

These differences shaped the two groups' approaches to culture. In general terms, the French Creoles reinvigorated the Shrovetide festivities that their fellow Catholic Spanish predecessors had introduced to Trinidad, and they instigated the long Carnival season of fêtes and celebration that still runs from Twelfth Night to Shrove Tuesday. The Protestant British, more utilitarian in instinct, tended not to indulge in celebratory excesses and attempted to control and limit Carnival celebrations. The British approach to local culture was no doubt largely defined by prevailing Victorian attitudes toward lower-class entertainment. Just as in Britain, where there was a continuing struggle between "refinement and vulgarity" that was often figured around questions of noise, music, and the bourgeois desire for silence, in the colonies, too, the transplanted colonials sought to repress the carnivalesque "rough music" of the masses (Bailey 2004, 31). Moreover, there were clear parallels between popular contemporary street music in Britain and that in Trinidad. The sounds of the British streets, much like those in the colony, were "excessive, repetitive, and sustained noise," made up of laughter, shouts, obscenities, animal noises, and, most significantly, home-made percussion instruments such as kettles with stones rattling inside and pots and pans that were beaten (Bailey 2004, 26). Thus, the conflicts over noise and rhythm in both Trinidad and Britain were shaped by middle-class Victorian values. If there was an ontological division between "uncivilized" black culture and "civilized" white culture in colonial Trinidad, it was most systematically—though not exclusively—evoked and perpetuated by the British element in the white group.

RHYTHM AND REVOLT

The close relationship between music, dance, and (perceived or actual) slave rebellion was established early in Trinidad's relatively short time as a slave colony. Before the second Cedula in 1783, in the absence of a developed plantation economy, there had been only a few African slaves in Trinidad. With the arrival of the new, mainly French, planters, there were over 150 sugar plantations and 130 mills by 1797, and, by 1808, official figures put the slave population at 21,895 (cited in Elder 1969, 5). By the early 1800s, Trinidad's slaves, mirroring models found

in other, chiefly Francophone Caribbean islands, had already formed themselves
into dancing "societies," which later became known as *convois* or *regiments*, hier-
archical groups with their own leaders—kings, queens, and dauphins—and officials, including a prime minister, ambassadors, and generals. The main function
of these slave groups was to hold dances and feasts that marked the end of the
workweek, as a contemporary account suggests: "On Saturday evenings and on
Sundays after Mass, they gave vent to their passions for dancing and music. For
long hours and without rest they performed the dances called the 'calinda,' and
the 'jhouba,' which had come down from their ancestors, and also the dance 'bel
air' which was their own invention. All these were carried out to the sound of
their voices and the African drum" (Borde 1982, 2: 313).

The dances offered breaks in the repetitive routine of the plantation and chances
to breach temporarily the strict colonial authority. One of the earliest examples of
this kind of festive insurgency occurred at Christmas 1805, on the Shand Estate
in Carenage, west of Port of Spain. In his later summary of the incident, historian
Edward Lanzer Joseph writes of a conspiracy among some French and African
slaves, who, he says, "meditated on the destruction of all the white men, and the
dishonour of all the white women on the island" (1970,229). Convinced of the
authenticity of the plot, the governor and planters had the conspirators tried; found
guilty, four slaves were executed, more were flogged and banished, and more still
were "disgustingly mutilated." Although Joseph believes that the judges were convinced of the guilt of the slaves, he doubts there was any plot at all and proposes
that what was planned was a dance, organized by the slave societies (229–30).

The vigor and cruelty with which the so-called revolt was suppressed can be
partially explained with reference to contemporary events in the wider Caribbean.
Coming four years after a large-scale slave revolt in Tobago and barely a year after
the declaration of independence in Haiti, the Shand Revolt seems to have been
a product of the fevered imagination of the white elite. Despite the considerable
physical distance between Trinidad and Hispaniola, and despite the relatively
small numbers of Saint-Domingue refugees in Trinidad, all sectors of Trinidad's
society would have been well aware (through letters, newspapers, and oral
accounts) of the events of the Haitian Revolution. Although generally balanced
accounts of the events in Haiti—such as Marcus Rainsford's *An Historical Account
of the Black Empire of Hayti* and Pierre McCallum's *Travels in Trinidad During the
Months of February, March and April 1803*, both published in 1805—were probably widely read in Trinidad, Bryan Edwards's more lurid and sensationalist *An
Historical Survey of the French Colony in the Island of St Domingo* (1797) fed into
whites' long-standing conceptions and fears of black savagery and, as such, was
more influential in forming white opinion on Haiti and in fomenting the powerful
sentiment of "Haytian Fear" in the Anglophone Caribbean (Brereton 2006, 124).

Judged to be largely the consequence of the high concentration of African-born slaves in Saint-Domingue, the Haitian Revolution led the British administration to the conclusion that, in the interests of security, the mass importation of enslaved Africans should be halted. Prompted by the arguments of contemporary observers that the mass arrival of new African slaves would only expose Trinidad and the rest of the British colonies to the same perils that had besieged Saint-Domingue, the British prohibited the importation of slaves in 1806, and, as Bridget Brereton argues, the "Haytian Fear" had in effect prevented "the further development of Trinidad towards a classic slave society with a huge majority of enslaved persons" (2006, 125).

Although in the early years of the nineteenth century Trinidad's whites tended to think the colony's free coloreds were the most likely source of potential revolt, the events of Christmas 1805 demonstrated that the planters and politicians also had a deep, visceral fear of popular slave rebellion. It was suspected that the slave plotters had all come to Trinidad from the French colonies, including Saint-Domingue, and the new governor, Thomas Hislop, stated his conviction that the slaves intended "a general massacre" of both whites and coloreds on Christmas Day and that the swift repression of the suspects had "avoided a most Dreadful Event and such Diabolical Scenes as characterised the Outbreak in San Domingo" (quoted in Brereton 2006, 128). Significantly, in terms of the history of music, dance, and perceived or real rebellion in Trinidad, the most compelling evidence for a Haitian-style revolt at Christmas 1805 was said to exist in the words of a popular song, a "seditious ditty" that L. M. Fraser, in his *History of Trinidad* (1891), says was "in common use amongst the labourers for some months prior to the detection of the plot" (1971, 1: 268). Although there are apparently no written contemporary records of the words of the song, and thus they were probably passed to Fraser through the oral tradition, they do seem to confirm that awareness of events in Saint-Domingue was used to strike the "Haytian Fear" into nervous planters and administrators:

> Pain nous ka mange
> C'est viande beké
> Du vin ka boué
> C'est sang beké
> Hé St Domingo
> Songé St Domingo.
>
> The bread we eat
> Is the white man's flesh
> The wine we drink
> Is the white man's blood
> Hé St Domingo
> Remember St Domingo.
>   (Quoted in Fraser 1971, 1: 269)

This is the earliest song in the history of Trinidadian music that can be specifically dated (Cowley 1996, 14). Moreover, in its caricature of the Catholic Eucharist—Fraser talks of the plotters holding a "parody of the Christian Sacrament" with bread and wine being distributed before the singing (1971, 1: 269)—the song in many ways establishes the parodic tone and the subversive mode of subsequent popular Trinidadian music.

The three or four plotters who were hanged and then decapitated, their heads displayed on poles and their bodies hung in chains, the many others who were brutally flogged and mutilated, and the others still who were made to wear iron rings or chains provided material evidence of the potency of a simple song to send deep pulses of fear through the ruling classes. In this incident, music established itself as a cultural form that could penetrate the colonialists' rigidly erected and forcefully imposed authority. Music had emerged as a particularly slippery aspect of Trinidadian plantation society, one that seemed to evade control and censure and to be always one step ahead of, or at least to operate on different planes from, political and judicial restraints. Indeed, the history of Trinidadian culture since this episode has been characterized by the tension between official attempts to rein in music and musicians and the popular counter instinct to react to control and repression and to perpetuate revolutionary sentiment by inventing new modes, new instruments, new genres, and new rhythms.

REGULATING CULTURE

The British administration's fear and suspicion of dancing and music actually predated the Shand Revolt. Indeed, one of the administration's first acts after it took power in 1797 was to introduce new police regulations that placed strict controls on slave and free colored dances: slaves were forbidden to dance after eight o'clock at night, and free coloreds had to obtain permits to hold their dances after that hour. Blacks and coloreds were not, however, the only groups subjected to these kinds of controls. In 1800, martial law was declared at Christmas to curtail the excesses of white revelers. Under the British rule of the first three decades of the nineteenth century, Christmas was the year's "leading festival," a time of "rowdy merrymaking and licence" among the "urban apex" of Trinidadian society (Pearse 1956a, 179). Martial law—especially under Sir Ralph Woodford, who became governor in 1813—was effective in that by 1824 more sober and restrained white celebrations had been established, to the extent that the *Trinidad Gazette* commented that times had changed and that "the noise, the mirth, the inebriety are now found chiefly amongst the slaves and lower classes" (quoted in Cowley 1996, 16).

Despite all the fear and suspicion that separated the various groups in Trinidad's days as a slave colony, there was also, just as in colonial Saint-Domingue, mutual fascination and often-disavowed identification across race and class barriers. Role reversals and parodies—central aspects of post-Emancipation Carnival—demonstrate the complex exchange of conceptions and misconceptions that in turn destabilized fixed dualistic notions of identity, which were strategically promoted by the colonial administration and its various organs, including the Church. In the pre-Emancipation period, contemporary reports speak of slaves calling at the plantation house at Christmas, receiving their seasonal "allowances" and then flouring "each other's black faces and curly hair," crying out "look at he white face! And he white wig!" (quoted in Cowley 1996, 17). At these times of merriment and breaks in the routine of plantation work, such mutual parodies took place. Similarly, during Carnival season in the early to mid-nineteenth century, the white plantocracy themselves parodied the slaves' celebrations of Canboulay (from the French *cannes brulées,* or burnt canes), the feast that marked the end of one cycle of plantation work and that became associated with Carnival celebrations in Trinidad.[8] When a fire broke out on one estate, neighboring bands of *nègres jardins,* or field slaves, were called to put the fire out and to save what cane they could, working to the beat of their drums.[9] An anonymous correspondent to the *Port of Spain Gazette* on March 26, 1881, discussed the origins of Canboulay in the early part of the century and affirmed that the elite of the society "took an active part" in all aspects of Carnival. According to this correspondent, the upper-class white parody of Canboulay contained all of the essential elements of the slaves' celebration: the white women would dress up in *mulâtresse* (or mulatto woman) style, the men in *nègre jardin* mode, and together they would form separate bands "representing the camps of different Estates, and with torches and drums to represent what did actually take place on the estates when a fire occurred in a plantation" (quoted in Pearse 1956a, 182). The rhythmic aspects of the whites' parody are further suggested in an observer's recollection of this "take off" of slave life and his memory of whites dressed as "slaves stamping in time and singing a rude refrain, to a small negro-drum." In addition, the white elite mimicked the slaves' rhythmic drum dances, such as the *bamboula,* the *belair,* the *calenda,* and the *ghouba.*

In all, these transracial parodies indicate that, whereas work and social structures carefully delineated and perpetuated categories of race and class, those categories were far more fluid and far less "entrenched" than some observers suggest.[10] For all their purported disdain for "uncivilized" black culture, the white elites and especially the French Creoles reveled in this kind of interracial parody. If similar practices existed in colonial Saint-Domingue, they largely stopped with the revolution and the expulsion or extermination of the remaining whites. As slavery continued in other islands such as Trinidad, the processes of creolization grew ever more complex, and music, dance, and rhythm remained the most effective means of transgressing barriers of race and class.

EMANCIPATION AND PARTICIPATION

The culmination of long-standing debates on slavery, its economic viability, and its compatibility with the values of putatively Christian colonizing nations came in the 1830s, beginning with the Act of Emancipation in 1833. This legislation did not accord total freedom to emancipated slaves but engaged them in four to six additional years of "apprenticeship," an arrangement that essentially guaranteed the planter an extended period of unpaid labor.[11] Hundreds of apprentices protested the administration's refusal to grant "full free" status in Port of Spain on August 1, with the crowds chanting "point de six ans" (no six more years). Full emancipation was not finally granted until August 1838, a time that did not, of course, end white political and economic domination but that did seem to offer the newly freed black population certain cultural and social freedoms which would reshape and reinvigorate Trinidad's music and Carnival culture.

Black participation in Carnival predated Emancipation.[12] The diary of Frederick Urich, a merchant's clerk in the late 1820s and early 1830s, describes going to see "the negroes dance" and of following masked bands of black women and men, whose dancing "amuse us very much, for these dances are stupendous" (quoted in Verteuil 1973, 36). In 1832, the large-scale participation of blacks is attested in Urich's account of going to watch masqueraders, nearly all of whom he said "were coloured people" (36). The degree to which Carnival was becoming a vehicle for expressions of blacks' social frustrations is suggested in an account in the *Port of Spain Gazette* on January 22, 1833, which reports on an attempt by the assistant to the chief of police to break up a Sunday gathering of masqueraders "of the lower order of the population, who are accustomed about this time of the year to mask themselves and create disturbances on a Sunday" (quoted in Cowley 1996, 25). After arresting two masked people and having them incarcerated in a "cage"—a punishment that strongly suggests the interned were slaves—the officer's house was attacked the same evening by a "large concourse of rabble" who broke all his windows and "pelted, beat, and otherwise ill-treated" him (25). As a footnote to the event, the *Gazette* decried the practice of celebrating Carnival over several weeks, which, it said, is contrary to Spanish custom and law and had become "a great nuisance in the Island" (25).

Carnival had long been associated with violence, or at least with the potential to create various kinds of "nuisance." With the passing of the Act of Emancipation in August 1833, that year's Carnival was to be the last that the white elite could truly enjoy on its own. The following year's event, which was limited by police order to two days, saw a subdued participation of the plantocracy, who were no doubt apprehensive about the imminent loss of their slaves. Yet 1834 marked the moment when blacks participated in Carnival with a new confidence. Enthused and emboldened by their coming emancipation, black groups were most prominent in that year's celebrations. A report in the *Port of Spain Gazette* lamented the "deficiency of elegant bustle [of] olden times" and remarked that the only group of note was a "large crowd of idle negroes and little people" who accompanied a band that parodied the Trinidad militia, one of the island elite's most cherished institutions (quoted in Pearse 1956a, 183).

The early post-Emancipation period was marked by renewed official regulation of Carnival. Even if the 1834 festival had seen no major disturbances, the authorities maintained strict control of the duration of masquerading: six days in 1835, and only four days in 1836, 1837, and 1838. The growing official anxiety over the creeping "blackness" of Carnival is reflected in an ordinance issued in 1837 that restricted the playing of certain musical instruments, namely "any drum, gong, tambour, bangee, or chac-chac in any house, outhouse, building or yard."[13] With the increased participation of newly emancipated blacks, their musical culture and rhythms took on a new significance; the restrictions on percussive instruments suggests official wariness about black musical rhythm and its capacity to undermine order. Again, it seems that these anxieties were felt most acutely by the Protestant element of the white elite. In 1838, for instance, an outraged "Scotchman" wrote a letter to the *Port of Spain Gazette* complaining of the "desecration of the Sabbath" caused by a Carnival Sunday celebration attended by "hundreds of Negroes yelling out a savage Guinea song" that led to a "ferocious fight" between two of the black *regiments,* the "Damas" and the "Wartloos" (quoted in Pearse 1956a, 184). During the same period, however, a counter argument within white circles proposed that black participation in Carnival was unlikely to lead to any kind of serious disorder, far less any lasting political upheaval. This argument is echoed in one historian's comment that "Carnival as a whole served the function of an escape valve for the masses, whose lives were harshly limited, and desperately hard" (Brereton 1979, 174).[14]

This idea of Carnival as a means of containing and limiting potential black misconduct seems to have been borne out in the 1840s, when there were few reports of white anxiety over black participation in that festival. Similarly, concerns over the potency of percussive instruments and their repetitive rhythms to stir up seriously insurgent sentiment and action seem to have largely dissipated in this decade. A newspaper report from February 5, 1844, describes an orderly and harmoniously creolized event in which all classes and races, the "noble" and the "ignoble," participated "in every possible contortion and expression of 'the human face divine.'" (quoted in Cowley 1996, 35). The "nobles" march to the sound of "well-played" music—the violin, the guitar, the castinet, the drum, and the tambourine—while others, the reporter said, "delight themselves in the emission and production of sounds of the wildest, most barbarous, and most unearthly description imaginable, and their instruments are as extraordinary as the sounds they make" (35). Even if the description does retain suggestions of a dualistic elite view of high and low culture, this report is significant in that it seems to suggest an idea of Trinidadian culture as a hybrid amalgam of its disparate elements. The "graceful" upper-class masqueraders, the "Swiss peasant . . . accompanied by his fair Dulcima [and the] companies of Spanish, Italians and Brazilians" are brought together with the black groups of "goblins and ghosts, fiends, beasts and frightful birds . . . wild Indians and wilder Africans" (35–36).

The reporter in this case was no doubt a Catholic, as Protestant opposition to Carnival continued throughout the 1840s. Trinidad's white Protestants were also most likely to invoke the civilized/uncivilized dichotomy and use it to call for the control of black music, which became increasingly associated for some people with the most extreme excesses of carnivalesque revelry. Letters to the *Port of Spain Gazette* and the *Trinidad Spectator* in November and December 1845 renewed complaints about the desecration of the Sabbath and about scenes "anything but becoming of a civilised country" (quoted in Cowley 1996, 36). Significantly, the perceived lack of civilization is attributed in these letters to rhythmic sounds and to the omnipresent "wild banjee drum," which was accompanied by "sounds the most unmusical and grating" (36).

TRAVELING PERCEPTIONS

Although white Trinidadian conceptions of and participation in Carnival were divided, one further white category had its own particular take on the festival: the European travelers, worldly figures whose accounts of Trinidad Carnival were less concerned with questions of maintaining law and order than with interpreting the perceived oddities of the event in relation to the authors' experiences in other foreign lands. One such figure was Charles William Day, who witnessed Trinidad Carnival in 1847 and whose full description of it was preceded by his attendance of Carnival in Greece and Italy. Day seemed chiefly concerned with the aesthetic qualities of the masquerade; he described the "squalid splendour" of it, which he conceded "was not unamusing, cheapness being the grand requisite" (1852, 1: 313). He described grand processions of white masqueraders, "Indians of South America" portrayed by "Spanish peons" from mainland South America, near-naked "negroes" wearing chains and padlocks in a parody of slavery, and black men and women all wearing white flesh-colored masks. What each group had in common, according to Day, was the accompaniment of "bands of execrable music," which made "a tremendous uproar" (1: 315–16). Day used the same term—"execrable music"—to describe what he had heard on Christmas Eve 1846, another occasion for what he called "bacchanalian orgies" among the blacks who played fifes, fiddles, harmonicas, triangle, cow horns, and an "enormous *tambour*" that was "banged with a maniacal violence" (1: 288). In this description, Day took a more identifiably moral stance and was closer to local Protestant opponents of Catholic-approved bacchanalia in his criticism of the Catholic priests who, he said, encouraged the carnivalesque "as it serves to keep up their influence over their flock" (1: 289). For all his protestations, however, Day's writings also contain a sense of his fascination with the uncontrolled excesses of the Trinidadians and particularly of the blacks, who were the focus of his most vehement outrage but also, tellingly, of his most vivid and detailed descriptions.

A later visitor, the historian, cleric, and writer Charles Kingsley, visited Trinidad in late 1869 and early 1870, and he offered some valuable descriptions of popular black culture and music in his *At Last: A Christmas in the West Indies* (1889). Writing not of Carnival but of the races at the Savannah in Port of Spain, Kingsley described tensions between French Creole–speaking blacks and newly arrived Barbadian migrants, but he still grouped them together in his description of the "Negro, or the coloured man . . . in his glory" among the clamor of the day at the race track (369). Kingsley also wrote of the same evening's music and dance, of hearing "the weary din of the tom-tom which came from all sides of the Savannah" (369). The "coloured folk," he wrote, "would dance perpetually till ten o'clock to the music of the tom-tom and the chac-chac" (369). However, many would ignore the existing ordinances and "were too apt . . . to break out again with fresh din about one in the morning," using the excuse that the previous night's legislation could not apply to the new day (369). Showing a similar though markedly less disdainful fascination with popular culture to Day's, Kingsley described sitting with his host, the governor Arthur Gordon, on Belmont Hill, from where they watched "a dance in a Negro garden; a few couples, mostly of women, pousetting to each other with violent and ungainly stampings, to the music of tom-tom and chac-chac" (370). Given the location of this dance—east of the Savannah, near to the Dry River—Kingsley may well have witnessed not a Creole dance but a more directly and purely African celebration. More than 6,500 Africans freed from foreign slave ships had arrived in Trinidad from 1841 to 1861 and had settled largely in tribal groups—among them Yorubas, Radas, Mandingos, Ibos, and Congos—in which they were able to maintain their languages and customs. As one historian put it, these groups spoke no English and were "pagans retaining the full vigour of their tribal customs. . . . [T]hey were for the West Indies a throwback to those who had been transported to the British islands before . . . 1807" (Wood 1968, 74, 80). One of the most significant of these African settlements was in Belmont (the Dry River district was known as "Yarriba Village"), and, quite apart from the possibility that Kingsley could have been watching Africans rather than Creoles, the location of this settlement ensured that the growing Africanization of Carnival would have been given new momentum through the presence of these freed Africans.[15]

One particular element of Africanized culture may be related to the development of Carnival music and, later, of calypso. The *gayap*, or work song, had traveled the Atlantic and was essentially the musical accompaniment to African workers in Trinidad assisting each other in clearing their land. As in postrevolution Haiti, friends and neighbors would split into groups of two and help one man carry out his work. One group would call to the other, deriding their work, while the other would respond with its own commentary on the failings of the first group. A sense of community would be created and cemented through rhythmic interaction. Such collective call-and-response singing has been a characteristic of many of the diverse musical traditions of Trinidad and indeed of music across the African diaspora.[16] In addition, the Africans and the black Creoles had long-standing traditions of celebrating wakes, which would start off quietly enough with the singing of hymns and choruses but later in the evening would develop into unbridled drum dances, "orgies over the dead," with drums and "obscene songs."[17]

Further black diasporic influence to Trinidadian music came from the "Americans," descendants of freed American slaves who had fought for Britain in 1812 and had settled in seven villages in Savannah Grande, Trinidad, after 1815. Converted to Baptism by a U.S. Baptist Mission, the descendants of the first "Americans" adopted many of the musical practices—"shouter songs," chanted, repetitive refrains, and rhythmic movement—that were common in camp meetings in the American South (Brereton 1979, 138). By the late nineteenth century, Afro-Christian sects, variously called Shouter, Shaker, or Spiritual Baptists, had established themselves among the lower-class black population.[18] The rhythmic aspects of their worship are evoked by Brereton, who describes the events as "apocalyptic and noisy" and the great festival, the week-long camp-meeting, as a scene of "thunderous preaching and singing, and rhythmic movements by the congregation" (1979, 158).[19] These festivals, the rhythmic movements, and the repetitive chanting served much the same purpose as the drum dances—emotional release from the frustrations, humiliations, and deprivations of everyday life—with the major difference that these were sacred ceremonies, whereas the drum dances, like Carnival, were predominantly secular events.

The local elite seem not to have differentiated between the various black groups in their disparagement of lower-class Carnival music, further evidence of which exists in a report in the *Port of Spain Gazette* on February 20, 1849, which describes "bands of music *(soi disant),* including those 'elegant' instruments the tin kettle and salt box, the banjee and the schack-schack *[sic]*" that had paraded through the town at all hours of the day and night (quoted in Pearse 1956a, 184). Notwithstanding its disdain for the simple instruments, this report is significant in suggesting that, in the first decade after Emancipation, popular Carnival bands were organizing themselves musically around percussion and rhythm, and virtually anything that could be beaten to a rhythm was a viable instrument. The connection between black popular identity and rhythm—forged

earlier in the plantations and the dances of the slave *regiments*—was solidifying and diversifying through increased participation in Carnival and growing
experimentation with different percussive instruments. We can only imagine
the very real and recently inflicted psychological traumas that most, if not all, of
the black population had experienced and the troubled memory that was, and is,
one of slavery's most significant consequences. Slavery had cast the slaves into a
kind of abyss of identity; the much-theorized lack or absence of black Caribbean
identity must have been experienced in all its elemental rawness during the 1840s.
Rhythm, as a cultural remnant of Africa that had survived and yet began to
mutate into something new in the Caribbean, reflected the slaves' own experiences and functioned as a kind of compensation or palliative for the lacks and
absences that were the legacies of slavery. As something that was both intangible
yet real and truly present, rhythm was part of the post-Emancipation experience
that Trinidad's blacks could lay claim to. It was theirs, and it could not be easily
appropriated or subdued.

Evidence of the difficulties of containing rhythm and dance can be seen in
Day's descriptions of "negro balls" in the late 1840s. In one dance—most likely a
belair, a drum dance that originated in the Francophone Caribbean—Day identified five male drummers playing to the accompaniment of twenty women singing
the chorus, and another twelve women danced to the music (1852, 1: 294).[20] Even if
Day's distinctly Victorian prejudices and misconceptions necessitated statements
of disdain, he appears fascinated by the blacks' dances and (like Moreau de Saint-
Méry in Saint-Domingue) writes in great detail about that which he professes to
abhor. Notably, he describes the rhythmic elements of the dance, the "drumming
on the abominably monotonous tum-tum," and the "singing in chorus, accompanied by the simultaneous clapping of the hands" (1: 289).

SAME OLD SONG

Despite the difficulties of enforcing music-related legislation, the Trinidadian
authorities continued to update the dance and drum ordinances. The consol-
idation of the police laws in 1849 reconfirmed restrictions on "play[ing] and
danc[ing] . . . at any hour of the Sunday, or to assemble and dance to any drum,
gong, tambour, bangee, or chac-chac at any hour of the day not being Sunday,
after the hour of ten in the afternoon" (quoted in Cowley 1992, appendix 5, p. 3).
The same legislation also reaffirmed restrictions on masking (that is, wearing a
mask) at times not permitted by public notice, and it introduced a new clause that
banned the singing of "any profane or obscene song or ballad."

In adding songs to its list of restricted musical expressions, this ordinance
testified to the growing official unease about the capacity of popular music to
disrupt order and offend elite sensibilities. The power of popular song to unsettle

the white elite had effectively been established in 1805 with the "Hé St Domingo" refrain. However, by mid-century, with ever-increasing black participation in and indeed appropriation of Carnival, popular songs had new contexts in close proximity to the white elite in which to be heard and, as such, could be used to mock and attack whites, their scandals, and their manners in ways otherwise denied to the blacks by the strictures of colonial society. There is evidence that, by the early 1850s, ribald popular burlesques—precursors to the calypsos of the twentieth century and characterized by a Bakhtinian "festive laughter"—had begun to establish themselves in Trinidadian public life.[21]

Official tolerance of Carnival and its related music and dance fluctuated according to the attitudes of the incumbent governor. In the 1820s, under Woodford's governorship, Carnival—or at least the elite version of it—had flourished and had brought together disparate elements of the white group, creating a new social cohesion among the elite. In contrast, the appointment of Robert William Keate as governor in 1857 marked a period of increasing control of, and consequently tension over, Carnival. Keate was soon under the influence of the anti-Carnival elements in white Trinidadian society, and in 1858 a proclamation was issued forbidding the wearing of masks at Shrovetide. Nevertheless, the proclamation seems to have had little effect. Letters to the press subsequently complained of the usual "orgies," the "fearful howling of a parcel of semi-savages" who then used the mask "as a mere cloak for every species of barbarism and crime" (quoted in Pearse 1956a, 187). However, it was not just the black "masses" who disregarded the proclamation. An article on March 4 in the *Trinidad Sentinel* (a newspaper owned by blacks of French Creole sympathies) describes how a heterogeneous group of Carnival goers dropped their masks but still "betook themselves to fancy dresses, and in droll accoutrements led many processions through the streets." The writer questions the police actions that followed (arrests, prosecutions, and fines), wonders if they were not "provoking and mischievous," and strongly suggests that these actions were the sole cause of the "boisterous scenes" that followed (quoted in Cowley 1996, 54).

Keate's attempts to control masking once again opened up divisions between the French Creoles and the English. The *Trinidad Sentinel* published an editorial in February 1858 condemning the "absurdity" of Keate's apparent desire to "make this Colony English in its manners, habits and customs" (quoted in Cowley 1996, 54). The unforeseen yet predictable consequence of the governor's actions was, as the editorial said, "that new life and vigour was given to the almost defunct Carnival and in 1859 preparations were made to carrying it out on a more extended scale than had been the case for years" (55). This episode demonstrates the paradox that the best method of policing and controlling Carnival has often been to let it be, to give more or less full rein to the masqueraders. It also shows, in contrast to the colonial authorities' suspicion of and disdain for the festival, the strong identification with and protective instincts toward Carnival felt by indigenous Trinidadians, especially those of French Creole origins.

POETRY AND DEMOTION

In truth, however, the influence and prosperity of the French Creoles were waning, and Keate's attempts to anglicize Trinidad were but one more step in the gradual marginalization of the French group. By 1850, the educated French-speaking population numbered considerably less than 2,000 adults out of a total population of 69,000, and by 1900 a similar number out of 344,000 people (Verteuil 1978, 11). Just as the price of cocoa had fallen dramatically in the 1820s, the value of sugar in the 1860s had dropped drastically, and Trinidad's sugarcane planters struggled to compete with sugar grown in slave colonies and with the recent development of sugar beet in Europe. A revealing if little-known poem of the period, "La Canne à sucre—Chant du planteur trinidadien" (Sugar Cane—Song of the Trinidadian Planter), vaunts the attributes of island-grown sugarcane (Verteuil 1978, 54–57). Written by Sylvester Devenish, a French Creole government surveyor born in Nantes of an Irish Catholic family that first came to Trinidad at the time of the Cedulas, the poem can also be read as a kind of lament for a lifestyle and an ethic that was quickly being subsumed by the growing anglicization of Trinidad. The first stanza establishes the mixed celebratory and elegiac tone, and it introduces the theme of opposition to Europe and the "Old World":

> In our island with its sky like no other
> Where everything is gilded by the sun;
> Where nature is so fertile,
> What I lovingly admire
> Every minute of the day,
> Is this reed that the Old World
> Will always envy us for:
> The SUGAR CANE with its juice so sweet!

In contrast to the English, whose primary loyalties tended to be to England and the Crown, the French Creoles felt a very strong attachment to the islands and to their physical environment. Trinidad, to the French Creoles, was "our island," their primary place of belonging, and in many ways they distanced themselves from the "Old World" of Europe. The mocking of Europe continues in the second stanza, in which the speaker decries the attempts of "old jealous Europe" to "dethrone" king sugar and derides its vain attempts to find new sources of sugar such as sugar beet, imphee (African sugar cane), and, less plausibly, maple.

It is unlikely that those directly engaged in the arduous tasks of planting and harvesting sugarcane would have held the crop in such esteem. Indeed, it is remarkable in this poem that the black and Indian field-workers are never mentioned; it is as if they did not exist or were happily part of the felicitous French Creole plantation system. The final stanza indicates a further aspect of contemporary French Creole self-image, which was its apparent pride in producing sugar without slaves:

> May Europe, scornfully,
> Rejecting tainted sugars
> Poisoned still by slavery,
> Taste only, through humanity,
> The sugar of liberty! ...
> And repairing a longstanding outrage,
> Pay willingly and joyfully
> Double our own, with pride!

The call for Europe to reject sugar still "poisoned" by slavery—the Netherlands had just abolished slavery in its colonies (1863), and abolition did not come to Puerto Rico until 1873 or to Cuba until 1879—seems to indicate a kind of historical amnesia among the French Creole planters and a complacent view of themselves as somehow exempt from the moral and ethical taint of slavery. These aspects of French Creole self-image in fact conform to the well-known, though false, conception that slavery in Trinidad was a mild affair with well-treated slaves and paternalistic masters.[22] This idea was based on an impression that Spanish slave management was more humane than other systems. In reality, however, Spanish slavery legislation was never fully implemented in Trinidad, and it was the markedly more severe French (and Martinican) style that dominated the island's plantations from the 1780s until abolition. Combined with the ever-present fear of a "second Haiti," these traditions were far from benign and sanctioned all kinds of torture and mutilation as means of subjugating slaves (Brereton 2005, 1).[23] Yet, as the poem shows, French Creoles seemed to exempt themselves from any historical guilt, and by the 1860s they had already cultivated a celebratory and nostalgic image of their past in Trinidad. It seems that this nostalgia for a French Creole past was heightened by the accelerating anglicization of Trinidad (in terms of language, culture, even sports). The more the island lost its Creole ways, the more poignant the nostalgia became and the more the past could be neatly packaged into a series of myths and misconceptions.

JAMETTE CARNIVAL

Carnival was another element of the French Creole's threatened culture, and Keate's attempts to control masking had reinstated the festival as a major nexus of conflict between the British authorities and the French Creoles. Just as they felt compelled to protect and conserve their language, the French elite rallied round Carnival as the most public display of island Creole culture in Trinidad. In the 1860s, however, and especially after the serious skirmishes between black masquerade bands in 1860, even a pro-Carnival newspaper such as the *Trinidad Sentinel* expressed reservations about the way the festival was developing or, rather, degenerating into "savagism." A letter published in the *Trinidad Chronicle* on March 3, 1865, repeated familiar complaints of the "barbarous din" that had "disgraced the town" from midnight to five o'clock in the morning. In particular, the writer expressed distaste for the blacks' music, their "beating and playing of instruments" and their "filthy and obscene songs" (quoted in Cowley 1996, 58). Because the existing legislation did not control the playing of all music after midnight (only drums and other percussive instruments were prohibited), bands could lawfully play through the night, much to the frustration of urban respectable society. In 1868, Ordinance No. 6 was passed, further tightening control of the playing of music. Clause 53 prohibited playing of or dancing to "any drum, gong, tambour, bangee, chac-chac or other similar instrument at any time between the hour of ten o'clock in the evening of one day, and the hour of six o'clock in the morning of the next day" (quoted in Cowley 1992, appendix 5, p. 3). The official concern about Carnival and its growing appropriation by lower-class blacks is demonstrated in many of the other clauses of the ordinance: in addition to making it an offense to sing "any profane or obscene song or ballad," to appear masked or disguised outside permitted times, and to "blow any horn or use any other noisy instrument for the purpose of calling persons together," the ordinance included clauses that outlawed the practice of obeah and the "possession of articles used in obeah or witchcraft" (quoted in Cowley 1992, appendix 5, p. 3). Yet the ordinance suggests strongly that this increasing Africanization— again, a process generated by the disparate black Creole groups as well as the free Africans—of Carnival and, by extension, national culture had attained a momentum that would be impossible to arrest completely.[24] These were the early days of the *jamette* Carnival, a period in which the urban underworld came to run and define the festival.

The *jamettes*—from the French *diamètres*, "those living below the diameter of respectability," or underworld types (Pearse 1956a, 188)—were the urban slum-dwelling drummers, dancers, singers, stick fighters, prostitutes, and pimps; together they formed a subculture characterized by fighting, song, dance, wit, sexual prowess, and contempt for the church and the law. In short, the *jamettes* set themselves up as the opponents of everything that respectable colonial society promoted. Given the particularly stringent and morally repressive nature of Victorian British colonial society, it was relatively easy to parody dominant values in this dualistic way. In virtually every respect, *jamette* culture evolved as the opposite of British colonial culture: violent bacchanalia against restrained reason; drunken disorder against peaceful sobriety; and rhythmic, sexually charged music and dance against the polite respectability of society balls. In effect, the *jamettes* "reversed the canons of respectability, the norms of the superstructure" (Brereton 1979, 166). As a perceptive contemporary newspaper account put it, the bands of "immoral" men and women "base their right of existence on their power to outrage all that society holds most sacred, and all that religion imposes" (quoted in Brereton 1979, 166). In other words, and quite significantly, there was nothing innately shocking or immoral about *jamette* culture. These kinds of behavior were adopted or exaggerated by the lower-class blacks with the express intention of upsetting respectable society, and they were later imposed on and to some extent accepted as essential facets of black Trinidadian culture.

One interesting aspect of this dualistic, class-based cultural encounter is that, in terms of space, the two cultures and the two classes existed in close proximity to each other. Indeed, the carnivalesque practices of inter-band fighting, appropriating city spaces, squares, and streets and massing together in communities can be seen as "functions of cohabiting with others in a densely populated area" (Cozart Riggio 2004a, 20). The *jamettes* lived in the yards, which were the barrack ranges situated behind the upper- and middle-class homes and respectable shops that fronted each city street.[25] A barrack range was composed of long sheds split into up to a dozen or so rooms of ten or twelve square feet. Facilities were elementary and conditions squalid; living in close proximity to dilapidated cesspits and with limited access to water, as many as six or seven people would share the small rooms. Even the socially conservative *Port of Spain Gazette* recognized that the barracks' system was "a legacy of slavery, being nothing more than a modified form of the old slave barracoon and ought long ago to have been swept away as a social and moral plague spot" (quoted in Brereton 1979, 118).

As a result of the barracks' close proximity to the upper-class stores and homes, the urban poor constantly interacted with the higher class, especially, in the case of women, as household domestics and nannies. Sexual relations were not uncommon between middle-class men and *jamette* women; this was but one means whereby the barrier between the two groups was breached.[26] In effect, the dualistic cultural division between the *jamettes* and the upper classes was principally a question of rhetoric and ideology. In practice, both sides of the divide were "contaminated" by the other, not by any means equally but in ways that undermined and indeed parodied the rigidity of the social and cultural divisions.[27] A creative tension existed between the two discourses that superficially perpetuated them but that also transgressed the boundaries putatively separating them. The one drew its legitimacy from and fed off the other; each required the other to survive in order to ensure its own continued existence.[28]

The *jamettes* were essentially later manifestations of the *convois* and *regiments* that had appeared in the early years of the nineteenth century. Each region or district had its own particular group or band that protected its territory fiercely and would arrange fights with its rivals at Carnival time. *Jamette* identity evolved in the 1870s—a period marked by economic depression, immigration of poor blacks from Barbados and other islands, and the consequent rivalries over jobs, food, and money—into something more than the willingly degenerate counterpoint to respectable colonial society. In the absence of any official social welfare, the *jamette* bands, in their tight organization and in the sense of collective belonging and identity they offered, sustained Trinidad's poorest groups, who bore the full brunt of the difficult economic times. Drum dances were not mere entertainment but, again, a means of collective sustenance and of purging the pain and desperation that were the *jamettes'* historical legacy and that were exacerbated by the weak economy. This social function of the *jamette* bands reflects the similar roles carried out by the rhythmically organized collectives in Haiti. In both cases, rhythm, music, and dance were integral to social and moral well-being and constituted an alternative social structure to that laid down by the state or colonial authority.

Some of the names of the *jamette* bands of Port of Spain—the Bois d'Inde, the Peau de Canelle, the s'Amandes—referred to different trees or types of wood, which seem to have alluded to preferred weapons in one of their most important activities: stick-fighting, or *kalinda*. Both men and women participated in stick-fighting, and every band had its champions who would meet with rivals in the yards or in more public spaces on holidays. Music and rhythm were integral to the stick-fighting ceremony: fights were accompanied by *kalinda* songs that challenged rivals to fight, boasted of successes in previous battles, and were composed and sung for the occasion by the band's *chantwelles,* its folk artists and singers. These *kalindas* were usually sung in French Creole, with the *chantwelles* singing the verses and the rest of the band joining in the refrain. Sung in minor key, they were the precursors to calypso. The early *kalindas* were accompanied by drums; after the 1880s, the bands adopted tamboo-bamboo instruments (Brereton 1979, 166).

The reason for the switch from drums to the tamboo-bamboo bands lay in a series of new ordinances that were introduced in the 1880s in an attempt to control the *jamettes*.[29] Newspaper reports from throughout the decade indicate respectable society's alienation from Carnival and its disdain for what it interpreted to be an innate, lower-class, black propensity for obscenity and lewd exhibitionism. Few, if any, were able to see that the *jamette* masquerade, in its flamboyant violence and anti-conformist showiness, was in effect the reverse of the desperate lives the lower classes lived. The *jamette* Carnival did not actualize the urban poor's experience or sensibility; rather, it was a reaction to that experience, dressed up and masked as something else, according to the codes of

Carnival. What is remarkable in the newspaper reports from this period is their inability, or perhaps unwillingness, to interpret the masquerade for what it was: not another show of inborn depravity but a highly complex and indirect manifestation of togetherness (shown most obviously in the uniforms that band members wore) and an attempt to draw attention, without resorting to supplication, to an increasingly difficult social, economic, and existential situation. Where the middle classes saw only willful abandon and lasciviousness, the *jamettes* in reality were manifesting their dignified desperation and their impassioned desire for more concrete transformations and role-reversals through the only means open to them.[30] In this sense, the inter-band violence that accompanied virtually every Carnival of the 1870s can be read as a manifestation of the desire for something akin to its opposite: a peaceful, settled, dignified existence.[31] That the violence was largely inflicted on fellow *jamettes* was a sign of frustration and of an inability to damage in any decisive way the true source of their repression. Moreover, it constitutes a classic case of a repressed group turning on and damaging itself—purging its social and historical suffering through further hurting itself in a way that, for all the middle classes' purported outrage, suited the elite and the authorities perfectly.

THE CANBOULAY RIOT

Canboulay celebrations had been adopted as an integral part of the black masquerade in the 1840s, when Carnival became a two-day event. Canboulay began on Shrove Sunday at midnight and were announced by the beating of drums, the sounding of horns, and other musical signals. Canboulay seems to have been a symbolic commemoration of aspects of slavery in that, as discussed above, it represented the extinction of a fire by *nègres jardins*. Men and women carried flambeaux, and some masks depicted death and demons, material evocations of the recent past of slavery and of its disturbing presence in the collective memory. Canboulay was therefore both an act of black remembrance and a reminder to the white elite of the horrors it had inflicted on its slaves.[32] The stick-fighting bands were prominent in Canboulay, and violence between the different groups was a serious concern by the late 1870s. The appointment of a disciplinarian inspector commandant of police—Arthur Wybrow Baker, or "Baker of the Bobbies"—was greeted with some enthusiasm by the anti-Carnival elements. Baker was largely successful in containing and limiting the number of stick-fights from 1876 to 1879, but it was in 1880 that his hard-line policy had its greatest success. He followed a kind of "zero tolerance" approach: as fights broke out, his officers intervened, confiscating drums, flambeaux, and sticks from the band members. Although these tactics were predictably popular with the British authorities and most of the press, they were less so with other elements. The native black underclass's long-held antagonism toward the police was exacerbated by the presence of large numbers of Barbadians in the police ranks. French Creoles resented interference with what they still considered to be their particular culture. And merchants bemoaned the lost trade from restricted Carnival celebrations.[33]

The resentment engendered among the various pro-Carnival elements by Baker's successes in 1880 overflowed into the following year's festival. Word spread that Baker was determined to repeat and increase his control of Canboulay and that he planned to take on the stickbands without directly consulting the governor, Sir Sanford Freeling. Putting aside their own differences, the stickbands joined together to resist the expected police attacks. In what came to be known as the Canboulay Riot, Baker's forces ambushed the stickbands in the "French Shores" area as they began their processions at midnight, into the early morning of February 28, 1881. The three-hour battle that ensued inflicted many casualties on both sides, and once again Baker distinguished himself, at least in the estimation of the anti-Carnival lobby, who now labeled him "Brave Baker of the Bobbies." The fight dispersed around three o'clock in the morning, and the police claimed victory—even if they had sustained serious injuries—as they secured the streets and left a force there in reserve. The daytime Carnival continued much as normal, but, as the day progressed, Freeling took steps to avoid further nighttime disturbances. After meeting with the Executive Council, and piqued by Baker's unilateral action, Freeling decided to address the masqueraders directly (in response to which the police resigned en masse). It is not entirely clear what Freeling said to the masqueraders, but his decision to confine the police to barracks and to let the masqueraders regulate themselves seems to have averted any further serious violence. Baker's humiliation was compounded when the masqueraders marched past the barracks, deriding the police in their songs and staging a mock funeral for Baker (Cowley 1996, 84–88).

These events and their aftermath reveal some unexpected aspects of the nature of authority and resistance in colonial Trinidad. The black masqueraders reserved their fiercest indignation for the authority figures closest to them on the social scale, the regular police officers, who were themselves, in the main, recently arrived poor black Barbadians. In contrast, the upper echelons of colonial authority, and in particular the governor himself, seem to have been held in some esteem. Evidence of this lies in a reported—though later denied—visit by the stickbands to the governor's house on Carnival Monday evening. The *Trinidad Chronicle* reported that the notorious Maribones and other bands arrived at Queen's House, where the governor had them admitted and where the bands then played their drums, sung extempore songs in Creole, and gave demonstrations of stick-fighting. Enjoying the spectacle greatly, the governor served refreshments and threw money to the stickmen, who "vociferously cheered him on this evidence of his liberality and of their success in amusing him and party" (quoted in Cowley 1996, 89). As they finally retired, the report says, the stickmen were "pluming themselves inordinately on having, as one expressed himself, *'Nous halla baton douvant Gouvernour'*" (We did our stick-fighting before the Governor) (89). The good faith created by Freeling's conciliatory approach to the masqueraders ensured a relatively trouble-free Carnival the following year. Therefore, even if the governor was the supreme representative of white colonial authority, through his patronage and apparent good intentions he was held in greater esteem than the lower-class blacks of the police force, who were generally considered lackeys, the agents and enforcers of the authority that ultimately held the governor in his position.

If Freeling was respected by the *jamettes* and other pro-Carnival elements, the same could not be said of Henry Ludlow, who had been attorney general in Trinidad since 1874 and who in 1882 set before the Legislative Council his infamous Musical Ordinance. The proposed legislation not only would ban the drum and the chac-chac in places adjoining the public road but also sought to outlaw the playing of the piano after ten o'clock at night and to give police the power to enter any home and arrest those flouting the law (Verteuil 1978, 151). Such was the opposition to the ordinance that nobody was found to second it, and the proposal was dropped, at least until the following year, when Ludlow's hand was strengthened following violence during the Carnival of 1883.

A poem entitled "Sur le projet de loi contre la musique, le soir" (On the Proposed Law against Music in the Evening), written in 1882 by a writer using the pseudonym "Corde-à-violon," gives an idea of the hostility felt toward Ludlow and his ordinance among the French Creole group (Verteuil 1978, 88–92). The tone of the poem is at once indignant and ironic, qualities that are evident in the opening stanza:

> Poor people of Port of Spain
> They want to treat you like slaves,
> Run quickly to the country
> If you want to avoid it,
> For if you stay in town
> After such an offence,
> Nine hundred out of a thousand of you
> Will sin against the state
> It's Ludlow
> It's Ludlow
> Behind this new decree!

The poem, in the *picong* style of light banter that verges on insult, goes on to mock Ludlow's biliousness and to evoke the possibility of being arrested in one's home for whistling after eight o'clock in the evening, for piano playing, or for a teething baby crying in the night. The poem also plays on the old cultural opposition between the French Creoles and the English, notably in the seventh stanza, which foresees the reintroduction of more draconian legislation:

> Let us wait a little longer
> Here, we will perhaps see
> The proclamation of the "CURFEW"
> And a hundred old laws reborn . . .
> All of this because a fool
> Whose salary we pay
> Without him deserving a cent
> Is angry with us.

Moving into the realms of slander, the speaker suggests that the only harmony appreciated by the "musicophobe" Ludlow is that produced by the clinking of glasses, and he expresses his wish that Ludlow be kept awake at night by the "terrible serenade" provided by the "vilest instruments." This poem, like other obscure literary works of the French Creoles, provides an invaluable insight into the feelings of this group in relation to the British authorities and to the role of music in Trinidadian society. There is also a discernible trace of cultural elitism in the poem in its favoring of the melodies of the piano over the din of the no-doubt rhythmic and percussive "vile instruments" that it wishes on Ludlow like a curse. The poem implicitly indicates that upper-class elements in society retained their elitist view of music and perpetuated the idea that there was an inevitable connection between popular music, disturbance, and potential violence.

Thus, though Freeling's actions had led to a largely peaceful Carnival in 1882, many whites—French Creoles as well as English—remained concerned about the corrupting influence of music, drums, and rhythm. Indeed, the connection between drumming, rhythm, and violence was strongly suggested in a contemporary calypso composed by Beau Wulfe:

> The Canboulay fracas was a free-for-all battle,
> With lots of French Creoles, but mostly foreign people,
> Caused by drum-beating, and other instruments
> Said to be outlawed by the British Government.
> (Quoted in Leon 1988, 68)[34]

On March 9, 1882, a report for the newspaper *Fair Play* raised the question of the "*moral* aspect" of Carnival and identified rhythmic music and dance as the primary vehicles of moral degeneration: "The obscene songs and lewd dances of the Carnival are the same which are for months previously practiced in yards, open to the public, and where the rehearsals for the masked Bacchanalia hold sway. The young men and young women who are subsequently ruined are often the ones who, attracted by the sound of the drum, become the witnesses of the corrupting scenes enacted at these dances" (quoted in Cowley 1996, 93).

The connection between drumming, rhythm, and moral debasement was (and still is) constantly made by anti-Carnival elements in Trinidad.[35] As might be expected, the clergy was often the most vehement in its condemnation of drumming and dancing. After witnessing a celebration of Emancipation Day on August 1, 1882, a French Dominican priest wrote of the celebrants' "orgies without name, memories of the African way of life" and of the "horrible African drum" (quoted in Cowley 1996, 94). Like Day and other European chroniclers, this priest seems to have felt compelled to condemn the perceived corrupted morality of the former slaves, but, in his detailed descriptions, he betrays a fascination for the drumming, the rhythms, and the abandon of the dance.

The continued concerns over the incompatibility of rhythmic, Africanized music and dance and "civilized" morality, combined with the ever-present possibility of public disorder during Carnival, led to new, stringent ordinances in the early 1880s. The first of these was issued in 1882 to regulate the religious celebrations of East Indian immigrants, a growing area of concern for the authorities. In February 1883, in the midst of serious disturbances between the stick-fighting bands—a new band, the Newgates, had taken possession of the Maribones's drum, an act that demonstrated the potency of the drum as a marker of band, and therefore of black identity—Ludlow re-issued his Musical Ordinance, which now prohibited the unlicensed playing of all percussion instruments between six o'clock in the morning and ten o'clock at night and restricted the playing of "European" string and woodwind instruments. Notwithstanding the control of more "civilized" instruments, this law was generally seen even in conservative circles as a direct attack on lower-class black culture. Some newspapers welcomed it: in its March 1 editorial, *Fair Play* argued for the strict control of drum dances and presented a disdainful picture of the events and of black lower-class culture in general. The rhythmic, repetitive aspects of the drum dances drew particular scorn from the editorial: the songs were "generally a few foolish sentences" marked by the "sickening repetition of a refrain which gives the greatest possible amount of exercise to the lungs compatible with the least possible disturbance of the brain" (quoted in Cowley 1996, 97). In a similar vein, the editorial dismisses the dancing as "the most disgusting obscenity pure and simple, being an imitation more or less vigorous and lustful by the male and female performers of the motions of the respective sexes whilst in the act of coition" (97). The condemnatory editorial did, however, contain one interesting musicological observation in that it drew a distinction between the drum dances of African natives in Trinidad—who used far more advanced instruments, and whose dances were warlike—and those of the local Creole blacks, who by comparison used a crude drum, whose dances were apparently lewd and lascivious, and whose song melodies were more primitive (Brereton 1979, 160).

Other newspapers were less enthusiastic about the new law and less dismissive of black Creole culture. On February 10, 1883, for instance, the *Port of Spain Gazette* simultaneously criticized the ordinance and offered a reasoned and perceptive argument on the importance of music and rhythm to Trinidad's black Creoles:

> To European ears the tambour and the chac-chac produce nothing but the most discordant sounds, to Creoles, even of the higher classes, whose organs have been accustomed from their birth to this peculiar music, there is a cadence and a rough harmony in their accompaniment of native songs which is far from disagreeable; and on the lower classes their effect is magical. We have only to look at a round of Belair and note the peculiar undulating motions of all present, as they follow with their heads, their hands, their whole bodies the peculiar cadence of the music, to be convinced that, to their ears, there is more, in the sound produced, than the discordant noise which alone strikes the European. (Quoted in Cowley 1996, 96)

Four days later, the *Trinidad Chronicle* similarly attacked the legislation and published its own defense of rhythmic black Creole culture. The poor, it argued, had little in the way of recreation, and the attempt to deprive them of an "amusement both harmless and humanizing is running directly counter to the interests of civilization and the dictates of humanity" (quoted in Cowley 1996, 96). The new idea in this argument was that, far from being a force for social and moral degeneration (an old idea reiterated in the *Fair Play* editorial), rhythmic black Creole music and dance were something to be valued because they "humanized" the poor or, perhaps in other words, allowed them a means of escape from or of purging their significant everyday anxieties.

Despite these reasoned analyses of the importance of rhythmic music and dance to black Creole culture, the debates that followed the February legislation ended with a revised ordinance that applied specifically to the domains of the poor urban blacks. This new law forbade the owner or occupier of any house, building, or yard to permit or suffer any "Convicted Felons, Persons of Riot or Affray, Common Prostitutes, Rogues or Convicted Vagabonds, or Incorrigible Rogues to meet together and remain therein, and to play or sing or dance therein to any drum, gong, tambour, bangee, chac-chac or other instruments" (Cowley 1992, appendix 5, p. 4).

The fact that the named instruments are all percussion instruments underscores the authorities' concerns over rhythm and their conviction that it was rhythm—recall *Fair Play*'s dismissal of the "sickening repetitions" of black popular music—that created the conditions for moral abandon and legal transgressions. The ordinance makes a direct connection between rhythm and the various named transgressors. Clearly, the authorities felt that regulating rhythm was a means of controlling society's undesirables (and vice versa). The extent of the lower-class black population's attachment to drum dances and drumming in the face of such official attempts to control rhythm is suggested in the words of this contemporary calypso:

> Can't beat me drum
> In my own, my native land.
> Can't have we Carnival
> In my own, my native land. . . .
> In me own native land,
> Moen pasca dancer, comme moen viel [I cannot dance as I wish].
>   (Quoted in Espinet and Pitts 1944, 66)

This policy continued in 1884, when the Legislative Council met in mid-January to discuss its approach to Carnival. The legislation they drew up, the Peace Preservation Ordinance, stipulated that Carnival would not begin until six o'clock in the morning on Shrove Monday, a law that effectively banned Canboulay. A further act, the Torch Ordinance, sought to further suppress Canboulay, notably in its prohibition during specified periods of the "carrying of the lighted torch." Predictably, too, this ordinance restricted dancing, stick-fighting, and "the beating of any drums, the blowing of any horn or the use of any other noisy instrument" (quoted in Cowley 1992, appendix 5, p. 4).

Not surprisingly, the very elements targeted by the ordinances reacted to them violently. Throughout January 1884, in Belmont in particular, there was an almost constant series of confrontations between the police and "lawless bands" armed with stones. By the end of that month, the authorities issued a new proclamation that applied the Peace Preservation Ordinance to the period from seven o'clock in the morning on Saturday, February 23, to six o'clock in the morning on Wednesday, February 27. These acts of early 1884 were clearly attempts to divide the pro-Carnival elements in Trinidad. The Executive Council appealed to the white French Creoles by insisting that the legislation applied only to the predominantly black celebration of Canboulay and to the "rogues and vagabonds," who in its view were largely synonymous with the bands, drummers, dancers, and stick-fighters. Just as the *Trinidad Chronicle* and the *Port of Spain Gazette* had done the previous year, the *Trinidad Review* reacted critically to the legislation, which it believed bore "all the facts of class legislation" and was "a harsh enactment, the hastiness of which when resented, is attempted to be softened by the arbitrary limitation of its provisions to a particular class" (quoted in Cowley 1996, 101). As the *Review* realized, the authorities' appeal to the French Creoles was a more or less explicit call to commonalities of class and race: if the elusive solidarity between the diverse white elements could prevail over the more complex ties of culture, language, and history that bound the French Creoles to the poor blacks, then the blacks would be isolated and the *jamette* Carnival could be effectively controlled—or, better, ended altogether.[36]

THE HOSEIN MASSACRE

The divide-and-conquer policy of the colonial authority extended to and was complicated by the rapidly growing population of indentured Indian immigrants. Between 1845 and 1917, almost 150,000 East Indians arrived in Trinidad, and, by 1870, they constituted approximately one quarter of Trinidad's entire population. When indenture was ended in 1917, Indians constituted one third of the population, and today that figure has risen to around 40 percent. Set apart from the rest of colonial and Creole society by reason of their languages, religions, customs, clothing, and even food, the early Indian immigrants were long considered outsiders, an "exotic group, marginal to Trinidad society, insufficiently integrated to be considered part of it" (Brereton 1979, 177). Their alienation was exacerbated by the special conditions of their indentureship, their connection to a special government department, the separate social services they were provided with, and the legislation that applied specifically to them (Brereton 1979, 177). This separation was no doubt strategic. The basic three-tier structure of Creole society that was the heritage of slavery was fragile and volatile enough without the added presence of a new, non-European, and potentially rebellious group.

Significantly, the most viable and potent means of contact and collaboration between the Indians and the poor blacks—and therefore of the most concern to the authorities—were cultural: stick-fighting, carnivalesque parades, and rhythmic drumming. One critic argues that the strongest element among hybrid Carnival music traditions is that which emerges from the meeting of Afro- and Indo-Trinidadian rhythms: the East Indian tassa drum constantly intermingles, she says, with the "hybrid, indigenous Afro-based percussive rhythms" even as each group "maintains its own independent identity" (Cozart Riggio 2004b, 184).[37] In his accounts of Trinidad in the late 1840s, Day wrote of stick-fighting rivalries between black Creoles and Indians and of the "ludicrous spectacle" of a fight between the two races in which the physical inferiority of the "Hindoo" is compensated by his "superior strategy," which included an Indian accomplice "creep[ing] between the legs of his countryman and pull[ing] his antagonist down" (1852, 1: 250–51). The fight only ended, Day noted, with "white interference" (1: 251).

More congenial and creative contact between the two nonwhite groups existed in the blacks' participation in Hosein, the Indian festival that reenacted the events that led to the deaths of Mohammed's grandsons, Hassan and Hussain, and that—something like Canboulay—included parades by groups carrying torches and sticks through the main streets of the towns. Like Carnival, Hosein was ostensibly a religious (in this case Muslim) festival, which in its relocation to Trinidad had become somewhat secularized, and non-Muslims of Indian and Afro-Caribbean origin took part in it.[38] Again much like Carnival and Canboulay, Hosein parades were accompanied by the rhythmic drumming of the tassa (although East Indian drummers were predominant, black Creoles were paid to drum in the procession) and often by violent altercations between rival (East Indian) groups.[39]

The Hamilton Report on the 1881 Carnival disturbances had indicated the need for regulation of Hosein as well, in case it became a further vehicle for the violent expression of lower-class discontent. Moreover, there was a general concern among whites over the dangers of close collaboration between and integration of blacks and Indians. In an attempt to avert any kind of joint action or protest between the Indians and Afro-Creoles, and wary of the stick-fighting bands' growing participation in Hosein, the Executive Council issued an ordinance on July 30, 1884, that sought to prevent Hosein parades from entering Port of Spain and San Fernando, to confine the celebration of Hosein to the plantations, and thereby to ensure the segregation of the two nonwhite groups.

Much as the urban blacks had done in response to Carnival legislation, the East Indians reacted indignantly to the suppression of their celebrations, notably in the south and in San Fernando. Their protests were ignored, however, and the legislation stood. Defiant East Indians chose to parade regardless, and, as they marched on San Fernando in October 1884, police under the command of the notorious "Baker of the Bobbies" fired on the crowds, which resulted in 12 deaths and 104 injuries (Brereton 1979, 184). Despite, or indeed because of, the massacre, the authorities rigidly reapplied the ordinance for the following year's Hosein, which, as it did for the remainder of the century, passed off without major incident. Perhaps most significantly, the effect of these prohibitions was to reinforce the cultural and social divisions between East Indians and black Creoles, who gradually withdrew from the celebration.

FROM THE STREETS TO THE DRAWING ROOM

Elite attitudes toward Carnival and vernacular culture in general never quite solidified into generalized outright opposition or a desire to end the festival completely. As the century progressed, both the (French Creole) white and black middle classes seemed to take renewed interest and pride in Carnival and in local musical traditions. An important catalyst for this shift in attitudes was the popularity of black-American jubilee and minstrel music among Trinidad's whites, which in turn seems to have heightened their appreciation of their own forms of "black" music.[40]

Two tours by the Tennessee Jubilee Singers—one in 1888–89, the other in 1890–91—introduced a highly refined kind of black music (including formal arrangements of North American spirituals) to Trinidad's elite. Beginning its Caribbean tour in Kingston, Jamaica, on August 10, 1888, before subsequently working its way down the islands, the troupe arrived in Port of Spain on November 30. It was almost universally acclaimed among Trinidad's white establishment. Newspaper reactions reveal much of what attracted Trinidad's whites to this particular form of black music.

On December 5, 1888, the *Port of Spain Gazette* praised the Tennessee Jubilee Singers' vocal ability and its choruses, which had an "exhilarating and pleasing effect." More significantly, the *Gazette* expressed its particular appreciation for the troupe's distillation of "black" elements into a musical form that was more palatable to white tastes: "The happy expression of quaint, vigorous, original feeling [was] controlled, harmonized and refined under the powerful influences of civilised musical science. . . . In listening to and seeing the movements of the singers we find the spicy originality of negro-minstrelsy, made fit for the educated eyes and ears of the refined occupants of the drawing-room" (quoted in Cowley 1996, 115).

In this review, Trinidad's white elite seems to echo the reactions of contemporary white audiences in the United States to minstrel shows. Whites in both countries tended to view black culture with a mixture of disdain and envy: disdain for blacks' perceived crude manners and primitive culture, and envy of their supposed expressive and sexual freedom. As one critic has argued, it was the need to make sense of these mixed white feelings that lay behind the popularity of the minstrel shows, which "articulated with precision these attitudes, being a vehicle for caricature which served to render innocuous the fascinating but dangerous culture of the blacks" (Small 1987, 154). The Trinidad elite's enthusiastic appreciation of this distinctive style of black music also carried with it an implicit critique of Trinidad's own vernacular culture. Not averse to the "spicy originality" of black music but ever mindful of the perceived need to "civilize" African-derived cultures and peoples, the white elite saw in the Tennessee Jubilee Singers an ideal of a domesticated musical form performed by smiling, pious, reserved blacks, and this was reassuring in its apparent lack of historically or socially derived animosity.

The American group represented more or less the polar opposite of Trinidad's *jamettes* and their culture of fighting, drinking, lewd dancing, and generally "uncivilized" behavior. However, as has been discussed above, the *jamette* Carnival was more than just an annual round of bacchanalian excess. Its deliberately provocative acts and songs were also attempts to remind the elite of the past and of the continued failure to lift the social and economic status of Trinidad's underclass. The *jamettes*' Carnival behavior relayed every year to the elite that it was "white civilization" that made the *jamettes* the way they were: they were the creations of that which the elite promoted endlessly, but the contradictory history of which the whites were only too eager to forget. As such, the *jamette* Carnival was an act of memory, a reminder of the past and of how the past manifested itself in the present, which unsettled the elite in ways that the Tennessee Jubilee Singers—in their refined expression and outwardly reserved demeanor—did not. Yet, if the apparently civilized American group allowed the elite to forget, and if the uncivilized *jamettes* were constant historical reminders to Trinidad's whites, both were ultimately formed (or de-formed) by the same history that forced slaves and their descendants into false postures—exaggerated abandon or equally unnatural subservience—vis-à-vis a civilization that continued to demand compliance and adherence to its values even as historical reality exposed those values in their full hypocritical inadequacy.[41]

By the early 1890s, the strict enforcement of Carnival legislation and the increasing prevalence of Victorian ideals of morality and civilization had begun to change the nature of the festival. As the decade progressed, the *jamettes* gradually withdrew from Carnival. The final distinctive aspect of their celebrations— the *pisse en lit* cross-dressing masquerade—was subject to official legislation in 1895, and, at the same time, the evolving "Social Unions" were superseding the stick-fighting bands as the focus of black cultural organization.[42] The Social Unions retained many of the characteristics of the *regiments* and dancing societies of the early years of the century—for example, the satirical nomination of kings, queens, and other aristocrats, and inclusion of the *chantwelles*, who led the unions' chorus as they paraded in competition at Carnival—but they differed from their predecessors in that their members were primarily clerks and other lower-middle-class black Creoles and thus more likely to adhere to white middle-class notions of civilized behavior.[43] Indeed, educated blacks and coloreds went to great lengths to disassociate themselves from the *jamettes* and their rhythmic music. In particular, middleclass blacks and coloreds disparaged the drum as a "barbaric" instrument. One prominent member of this group, L. O. Innis, wrote later of his support for the drum ordinances and how, as a result of those laws, the "archaic instrument" of the drum "died a natural death, and quartos, bandolas, flutes, and clarinettes reigned in its stead, to the great comfort of the decent inhabitants" (1910, 97). An editorial in *Fair Play* called for stringent controls of the drum dances so that the colored middle class might not be categorized with the "scum" who participated in the drum dances (Brereton 1979, 104).

With the *jamettes* effectively marginalized, and with this new emphasis on respectability and good behavior, Carnival became a more subdued and (to the elite) acceptable event, so much so that the 1896 festival was reported with approval even by the *Port of Spain Gazette*, the most conservative and anti-Carnival of Trinidad's newspapers. The domestication of Carnival had apparently led to a greater participation from the "upper classes," which to the *Gazette* was one of that year's "pleasant features." Another agreeable aspect, at least to the *Gazette,* was the music: with drums being banned in parades, more sophisticated string bands had come to prominence, and, as the *Gazette* observed, "all the guitars in town seemed to be in use and there was lots of music" (quoted in Cowley 1996, 132). By this late stage of the nineteenth century, it seemed that the forces of respectability and order had finally taken control. But if Carnival had been tamed and rhythmic music replaced by genteel string playing, it was far from the end for the drum, rhythm, and percussion in Trinidadian culture. The *jamettes* may have been marginalized from Carnival, their drums and rhythms pushed aside in favor of more "civilized" European instrumentation, but rhythmic music would evolve, return, and reassert itself as a primary marker of Trinidadian black culture and identity.

EARLY CALYPSO

One effect of the drum and dance legislation was the renewed creolization of Trinidadian culture. The relative harmony that characterized Carnival by the end of the nineteenth century tended to weaken the long-held dualistic conception of race and culture, the idea that white European culture was the polar opposite of, and unquestionably superior to, black African culture. *Jamette* culture was altered in many important ways by the drum dance and Carnival legislation. Many aspects of *jamette* culture were appropriated by the new bands of socially mobile blacks, notably by the Fancy Bands, who held more elaborate singing and dancing events in the modified structures that previously housed the drum dances. These structures became known as tents and were the sites of Fancy Band events that incorporated and adapted the old traditions of electing kings and queens but whose music was based less on drumming and rhythm than on woodwind (clarinet, flute), strings (guitar, cuatro, stringbass, violin), and singing.

Linguistically, too, as the French Creoles were keenly aware, important changes occurred in this period. Throughout the nineteenth century, Creole had been the language of the black poor, both rural and urban, and of many planters. Because it was not understood by most policemen (a large proportion of whom were Barbadian Anglophones), magistrates, or other officials, Creole was a means of resistance, "a defensive and offensive weapon" (Brereton 1979, 164).[44] The drum dances had incorporated songs known as *caliso* or *cariso,* which were accompanied by the rhythms of drums and chac-chacs, though these were sung in French Creole and were fairly elementary in terms of structure and lyrics compared to the new English-language, rehearsed, topical songs of the tents (Cowley 1996, 135–38). It is significant that, during this period of relative cohesiveness in Trinidadian society, Creole was quickly discarded as the popular language, and English came to dominate in both society and culture. The first "calipso" in English to attain general popularity, "Governor Jerningham," was composed by Norman Le Blanc (known as Persecutor), sung at Carnival in 1898, and took its theme from the British decision to disband the Port of Spain Borough Council.

Carnival in 1898 also offered evidence of the increasing acceptability of the festival to the white British administrative class. Given official sanction to view Carnival, the British (and notably Chief of Police Sir Francis Scott and his staff) were reported to have been among the crowds driving around town taking in the spectacle. Even the *Port of Spain Gazette* gradually, and somewhat reluctantly, altered its long-held anti-Carnival stance. On January 20, 1900, it printed the words of a "calipso" that was to be sung in the approaching Carnival season, although it confessed to failing to see "either rhyme or reason in it." The enduring influence of the Tennessee Jubilee Singers was further suggested in the *Gazette*'s report seven days later that one band was "getting up a repertoire of Jubilee and Plantation songs" in preparation for Carnival. The switch from French Creole songs to "patriotic tunes in English" also met with the *Gazette*'s approval, as did the elaborate preparations of the Fancy Bands and their chosen themes of loyalty to the British Empire at the time of the Boer War. How the Social Unions had adopted and now celebrated Britishness is evident in the words to an eight-verse patriotic Carnival song printed in the *Gazette*, the final verse of which proclaims Trinidad's loyalty to Britain and the band's conviction that the island could help slay the Russian "white Bear":

> Then rule Britannia, Britannia must rule the waves
> Then the colonies will come in for a share of the pie
> The hip hip hurrah, for Great Britain pasca devera [is not turning back]
> Then Trinidad will claim the skin of the white Bear, sans humanité.
>   (Quoted in Cowley 1996, 150)

The Fancy Band that composed and sang this song, the White Rose Social Union, was far from alone in promoting the idea of empire: the Brigade Union, the Artillery Company, and the Cock of the North Highlanders are reported to have paraded, singing songs variously related to the Transvaal, Britannia, and Queen Victoria (Cowley 1996, 151). The following year, after Victoria's death on January 22, there was much debate over the propriety of holding Carnival at Shrovetide. When the festival did go ahead on February 18 and 19, the Fancy Bands appeared in their by-now customary elaborate costumes, accompanied by their string bands, much to the approval of the *Gazette*.[45] The transformation in Carnival since the 1880s was remarkable: the social tensions and official anxiety over the festival had largely dissipated as the Fancy Bands, imbibed with a strong dose of pro-British patriotism, introduced a more socially acceptable celebration. Crucially, the dominant Carnival music was now the patriotic calypso, accompanied by officially approved string and woodwind players. The drum had apparently disappeared, and with it the sense of menace and social conflict that it had evoked and perhaps also instigated. With the suppression of the rhythm of the drum and thereby of the memories it contained, it was perhaps easier to forget past conflicts and to live more fully in the imperial present.[46]

THE RETURN OF THE *JAMETTES*

This was, however, a short-lived period of social and cultural cohesion. The truce between the disparate groups in Trinidadian society was to be broken in 1903, when disaffection and disharmony again took hold. Sectors of the island elite—notably the French Creoles—became disenchanted with their lack of influence in key issues of policy (Hill 1993, 55). In early 1902 the colonial administration's decision to restrict the supply of water had increased local resentment over how the island was being governed, and it sparked a major disturbance on March 23 that became known as the Water Riot, during which sixteen people were killed and the seat of the Legislative Council, the Red House, was burned (Cowley 1996, 161).

The Water Riot marked the return of the *jamettes* to the foreground of Trinidadian society and consciousness; *jamette* women were particularly prominent in the assault on the Red House. Following a Royal Commission report, twenty-two people were indicted for riot, among them prominent drummers, dancers, and stickmen. The following year's Carnival was anticipated with some trepidation, as is made clear in a *Port of Spain Gazette* editorial of March 10, 1904, in which it expressed its concern over the content of Carnival songs and the possible return of more coarsely satirical and bitingly political lyrics. Fancy Bands still played in the 1904 Carnival, though, given the changing social mood, these were predictably losing their former prominence. Fights were reported between stickbands, and in general it seemed as if the *jamettes* had taken advantage of the split between the various elite factions. As John Cowley says, by 1904 the "stickmen and their entourages had re-established themselves as an antithesis of colonial propriety" (1996, 164). The return of the stickmen also meant the return of rhythm, in music and dance, as one observer noted: "As well as stickfighting, these men danced about the streets to the strains of this form of music ["Calenda" chants, "sung in patois," accompanied "by the beating of bamboos and bottles with a spoon"]. It was a kind of drill-dance, carried out with grace and symmetrical exactness" (quoted in Cowley 1996, 164, brackets in the original).[47]

Other contemporary reports corroborate the return of rhythm, not with drums but now with tamboo-bamboo and bottles and spoons, the improvised new instruments through which the same insistent rhythm returned and which accompanied the "calenda" songs, sung as ever in the "monstrous minor" (quoted in Cowley 1996, 164).[48] The tamboo-bamboo bands were sophisticated ensembles delivering a strongly rhythmic sound. The boom or bass bamboo was around 1.5 meters long and 12.5 centimeters wide, and it produced a deep, booming sound when it was hit in rhythm against the ground. The foulé or buller bamboo provided harmony, and the cutter bamboo introduced another beat into the poly-rhythmic performance. Further rhythmic variety was provided by the bottle and spoon players and the scraping in time of a file with another piece of metal (van Koningsbruggen 1997, 63). Although the tamboo-bamboo bands were able to produce a variety of tones, they did not play melodies; their sound was entirely rhythmic, or indeed polyrhythmic, an accompaniment to the call-and-response singing of a *chantwell* and chorus (Stuempfle 1995, 24).

The year 1907 marked the apogee of this revival in *jamette* Carnival culture. By that time, the number of arranged stick-fights had reached levels similar to those recorded at the end of the nineteenth century. The Fancy Bands had been displaced both in the streets and in the newspaper columns, which were full once again with anxious mentions of the stickbands: Corbeau Town, Rose Hill, St. James, New Town, Belmont. Faced with massed groups of stick-fighters, the police undertook an obvious but effective means of controlling the bands: they confiscated the sticks. The *Port of Spain Gazette* had by then reverted to its moral-izing, Victorian tone. Its disdain for the male stick-fighters was matched only by its disgust at the behavior of *jamette* women; together, according to the *Gazette*, the *jamettes* demonstrated how "the people have harked back to the same old thing," the "meaningless" songs and "monotonous music" (quoted in Cowley 1996, 172).

Repetitive, rhythmic, or "monotonous" music was similarly criticized by the *Gazette* the following year to the extent that it suggested that prizes be offered for "good part singing," which, it thought, should lead the people to "appreciate a better class of music than those who usually wind up with the hackneyed *sans humanité* refrain pitched in the minor key" (quoted in Cowley 1996, 173). In con-trast to preceding years, the 1908 Carnival passed off peacefully; the confiscation of sticks had apparently fulfilled its purpose. According to the prevailing elite, moralistic view of the festival, Carnival was once again on an upward spiral. The newspaper *Mirror* seemed to have a particular dislike of the more elementary percussion instruments; in 1909, it complained of the "usual hideous and dirty looking maskers making the greatest of noise on old tins, graters and other discordant instruments" (quoted in Cowley 1996, 175). In its account of the 1911 Carnival, the *Mirror* was pleased to note the diminishing numbers of *nègres jar-dins* and Pierrots and the further "pleasant feature" of the "decrease of tinpans, bamboo, graters and bottle and spoon bands" (quoted in Cowley 1996, 179). In general, the press pushed for a more ordered, regimented festival, structured by competitions that were essentially incentives to behave and dress well and to play acceptable music.

The extent to which the press, and by extension the colonial elite, failed to understand the importance of rhythm to black Trinidadian musical culture is suggested in the *Mirror's* Carnival report of February 4, 1913. The newspaper's expectations for a certain kind of order and form in music underlie its attack on black popular music, which continued to be determined by rhythms and repetitions. "All that is heard," said the *Mirror,* is the "twang of instruments or the beating of bamboos. In some isolated instances one gets a hint of something relating to Reform and another song which is extremely obscene but on the whole *the carnival refrains are songs without words*" (quoted in Cowley 1996, 188, emphasis added). In other words, "songs" in the accepted sense were far less important to the *jamettes* than the rhythms they beat out on virtually anything that came to hand. The "meaningless nonsense" of the words of their refrains masked the deep, unspoken meanings of their rhythms and the memories they contained.

RHYTHM ON RECORD

Carnival music in the twentieth century was further shaped by the coming of recorded music and the opportunities local artistes now had to release their work on records. The first Trinidadian band to record its own music was Lovey's Band, a prominent string band highly favored by the elite that went to New York in May 1913 and recorded titles for both the Victor Talking Company and the Columbia Phonograph Company. Predictably, the music and rhythms of these recordings were far removed from popular street music; they offered a more accurate reflection of what was acceptable musically in the upper-class dances. As Cowley notes, the rhythm descriptions indicate that titles expressed in Spanish were generally categorized as *vals* and *Spanish valse,* though the band also released Creole titles and folk melodies. A little local flavor was therefore considered acceptable as long as it was communicated through "proper" instruments and the songs were indeed songs, not the "meaningless" rhythms that were the true popular music of Trinidad. Lovey's Band was also the first musical group to encounter a foreign market; its Spanish titles were marketed through Columbia's popular Spanish-American series, not just in the United States (Cowley 1996, 183–86). Up to this point, Trinidadian music had largely been a local affair (even if its varied influences were distinctly cosmopolitan), its evolution and raison d'être shaped by insular concerns and tensions. Now, the advent of musical recording meant that Trinidad's music—or at least certain kinds of Trinidadian music—could be relayed to extra-Caribbean audiences. Developments in musical style were no longer to be shaped solely by local factors; from this period the dictates and tastes of foreign markets would play a prominent part in the evolution of Trinidadian music.

There is some uncertainty over whether or not Columbia Gramophone Company came to Trinidad to record Lovey's Band in 1914. It is certain, however, that the Victor Talking Machine Company came to the island in August 1914, with the express aim, as the *Port of Spain Gazette* put it, "of recording a complete repertoire of Trinidadian music including the Pasillos Spanish Waltz and Two steps by well known Bands; also Carnival and Patois songs and East Indian selections by local talent" (quoted in Cowley 1996, 191). Recordings were made of all of these various musical genres, though not all of the recordings were eventually released. Whereas the *pasillos* (or *paseos*), in their treatment of local issues—local reaction to Barbadian migrants, Trinidadian migration—and in their Spanish American rhythms, give some sense of how dynamic "respectable" band music had become, the "calipsos" and *kalindas* indicate how elements of street music were also being co-opted into the accepted repertoire. The "calipsos" had lyrics in French Creole whereas the *kalindas* were accompanied by the rhythms of the stamping tubes and the bottle and spoon, vernacular elements that now made their way into recorded sound and hence into the musical consciousnesses not only of the island but also of the larger listening audience abroad. Nevertheless, these recordings were somewhat sanitized versions of Trinidad street music, performed as they were by "J. Resigna," aka Henry Julian, formerly of the White Rose Fancy Band, who now restyled himself as the Iron Duke. His "calipso," titled "Iron Duke in the Land," is essentially a song of self-aggrandizement in which he vaunts his band and charts his rise to the position of bandleader. Perhaps the most telling lyric lies in the final verse, where Julian offers a vision of Carnival and its music as fundamentally enriching aspects of Trinidad life:

> It was a modern manifestation
> Of that elder civilisation
> That in the Carnival celebration
> Of the Social organisation
> Which causes the minds and extension
> Of all the population
> I Julian singing a Social recording
> With White Rose Union
> Sans humanité.
> (Quoted in Cowley 1996, 191)

The history of Carnival is presented here in terms that deny the social conflicts and tensions that have always underpinned and manifested themselves in the festival. Moreover, the song presents a linear version of the development of Carnival—which it claims has always enriched or "extended" the minds of the population—the apogee of which is the recording session, "I Julian singing a Social recording."

The commitment of Trinidadian music to disc seemed to increase its acceptability to the rich elite, those who could afford gramophones and records. Now not only domesticated but also commoditized, the music could be enjoyed without the presence of those who made it, and thus a subtle chasm was opened up between the people, who were always the source of innovation (and also the most reliable reminders of tradition), and the music.[49] The fact that only a certain class of musician—the talented but respectable band members—were invited to record indicates that recording brought with it a discreet appropriation of Trinidadian music from the *jamettes* to the more acceptable (and no doubt lighter-skinned) elements of society.

Just as it was doing in the United States, the advent of recorded music in Trinidad tempered the visual elements of music and disconnected the music from the people it came from. Recorded music allowed the commuted and sanitized sounds of blackness to permeate further into middle-class culture, and even as it democratized music, making it available to those who could afford it, it also had the effect of further consolidating notions of race and of maintaining Trinidad's class differences.[50]

JAZZ AND BAMBOO

The advent of World War I led to two years of strict Carnival regulations (1917–18). This bolstered the anti-Carnival elements to the extent that, in 1919, the *Port of Spain Gazette* and the *Trinidad Guardian* made renewed calls for the prohibitions to be implemented indefinitely. These appeals were countered by those of the *Argos,* Port of Spain's evening newspaper, whose editorial staff consisted of liberal black Creoles and which took its pro-Carnival case to the governor on January 29, 1919. The *Argos* campaign was successful in that it succeeded in persuading Governor Sir John Chancellor to remove the masking prohibition. However, this was not the end of the newspaper battle: the *Guardian* promoted a Carnival competition to be held in the neutral space of the Queen's Park Savannah, whereas the *Argos* stayed true to its slogan to "Keep the Carnival Down Town," the traditional site of the masquerade. Again, the *Argos* seemed to prevail, in that the *Guardian*'s competition was poorly attended while the downtown event received enthusiastic popular support (Cowley 1996, 208–9).

Despite this support for the *Argos,* its competition shared implicitly with the *Guardian* and the *Gazette* the desire to "improve" Carnival through encouraging competition and prizes, which were significant: monetary awards were offered for, among other things, the best patriotic song, the "Most Uniform and best dressed bands," and "Good Conduct." Moreover, the *Argos*'s views on Trinidadian music were tinged with middle-class ideas of the need to improve standards. Its alignment in this regard with the conservative newspapers is perhaps best shown by its prohibition in its competition of "bands using bamboos and bottles," the popular percussive instruments and receptacles of rhythm that had been adapted by the *jamettes* as substitutes for the banned drums. The *Argos*'s notice that there was "no need to wear expensive costumes" seems to have been an attempt to attract the poor or lower-middle-class urban blacks, to reassure them that they could move out of *jamette* Carnival and find a place in this improved festival. In addition, the *Argos* printed lyrics to songs, some patriotic, others celebrating its victory in reviving Carnival, for which the dance rhythms were either *paseo* or tango—in other words, nonindigenous and more "sophisticated" than the repetitive beats of the street bands.[51] Yet the *Argos* also printed the views of the well-known black musician Walter Merrick, who proposed that Trinidadian music should take its cues from contemporary British and North American popular music and should try to recreate their "catchy" quality, which was popular among local whites (Cowley 1996, 210–11).

The growing popularity of foreign, "catchy" tunes was evident in the *Guardian*'s San Fernando Carnival competition of 1919. In this event, musical content was strictly controlled, and, as they went down certain roads, bands had to play the popular contemporary songs "Good-by Broadway" and "Over There." In its post-Carnival assessment of the competition, the *Guardian* wrote of the "splendid fruit" borne by its "educational campaign" and reported with pleasure the encounter between a female band leader and a member of its committee, who enquired if the band was participating in the calypso competition, to which the woman replied "in a tone which showed her dignity was not a little wounded, 'we don't sing calypso, we sing rag-time'" (quoted in Cowley 1996, 215).

Even if, as Cowley suggests, the San Fernando committee members "appear to have believed they were in the process of engineering a complete break with tradition," there is strong evidence to suggest that such a break did not—indeed, could not—occur, because "catchy" could not supersede rhythmic as the dominant element in Trinidadian music (Cowley 1996, 215). This evidence emanates from the *Guardian*'s own report on its visits to seven tents in Port of Spain shortly before Carnival in 1919.[52] The report indicates that the spatial dynamics that had previously kept lowerclass blacks and middle-class whites in close proximity had been altered somewhat, and this had in turn enabled a cultural separation between the various groups. Beginning his report in the largely middle-class neighborhood of Woodbrook, the *Guardian*'s reporter wrote first of his visit to a well-attended tent in which he heard "Mr. E. Briggs and his musicians" play a "lively composition" on "violin, flute, quatro and guitar, their blending, soft and low, being very good indeed" (quoted in Hill 1993, 70). The reporter's appreciation was shared by the number of "prominent members of the community" present at the event who were enthused by the "principally patriotic" songs (70).

The evolving spatio-cultural contrast in Port of Spain and the continued popularity of traditional, rhythmic music are demonstrated in the details of the reporter's next visit, this time to an event in George Street, in the old "French Shores" part of the downtown area and one of the hotbeds of *jamette* culture. There, the reporter witnessed a "Bamboo Band" whose "musical paraphernalia were confined to the popular 'instruments' of the proletariat which consisted of lengths of hollow reeds of bamboo, a small grater operated by a musician with a stick, a 'schack-schack,' and the inevitable gin flask with a tin spoon as a beater" (quoted in Hill 1993, 70). In these and the other accounts of his visits around the pre-Carnival tents, the reporter suggests there was a proliferation of different musical styles that were closely identified with different areas of the city and thus with different social groups. This spatial division extended into Carnival itself, where only the more "respectable" bands paraded and where the bamboo bands remained in their own spaces, the tents where they played their own music. At this point in 1919, then, the social hierarchy was increasingly mirrored in a musical continuum that spanned from the rhythmic "proletarian" music of the poorer districts to the "catchy" patriotic tunes of the island and colonial elites. Despite the *Guardian*'s hope that competitions and prizes could engineer a break with tradition, the old musical styles persisted and were indeed strengthened and perpetuated by deep, long-standing social divisions.

Following social unrest in 1919—stoked by the anger of returning soldiers, who had experienced racial prejudice in Europe and who returned to Trinidad to face high unemployment—there was a fear that the bamboo bands would return to the streets for Carnival in 1920. As the *Guardian* reported, the police held a preparatory tamboo-bamboo session, ostensibly to familiarize their horses with the sounds of the traditional music. As it turned out, the police band was unusually adept at recreating the working-class music, which had firmly implanted itself in Trinidadian musical culture and which, as the music of the poor, resurfaced and regained new popularity in times of social and racial unrest. Whereas the war years had glossed over social divisions and brought a more restrained, respectable (that is, less rhythmic) Carnival, the postwar period saw the re-opening of racial wounds in Trinidad society, and the rhythms of the tamboo-bamboo consequently returned. This socially induced return of rhythm—not that it had ever completely vanished—is suggested in the *Port of Spain Gazette*'s report on Carnival on February 18, 1920: "In the matter of song, one was intensely bored with the meaningless ditties resurrected from the scrapbook of bygone years. . . . The weird reverberations of the 'bamboo' bands, with bottle accompaniment, monopolised the major part of the musical element, and it was welcome relief when a Yankee troupe came along with string band rendering of ever popular coon songs" (quoted in Cowley 1996, 225–26).

The "coon song," the catchy ditty, and the newly popular jazz tunes were no doubt attractive to the elite in that they were largely devoid of political and social commentary and thus provided an escape from the tensions of everyday Trinidadian life. Yet a new musical genre, the political calypso, was emerging, and it was to become an important means of expressing lower-class frustration and, indeed, antipathy. By this time, the most popular *chantwelles* had detached themselves from Carnival bands and only rarely sang at the front of band parades, preferring the new arenas of the improved tents (with seating and admission charges) and the competitions therein between individual calypsonians. The status and role of the calypsonian had therefore changed by 1920, and the new prominence given to individual singers allowed them to deal with political issues in a more direct and influential way than before. One of the first political calypsos was sung in 1920 by Patrick Jones, who performed under the name Oliver Cromwell or the Lord Protector. The words to his song "Class Legislation" indicate a new cynicism toward British rule and an underlying bitterness about continued black marginalization in Trinidad:

> Class legislation is the order of this land
> We are ruled with an iron hand
> Class legislation is the order of this land
> We are ruled with an iron hand
> Britain boasts of equality
> Brotherly love and fraternity
> But British coloured subjects must be in perpetual misery
> In this colony.
> (Quoted in Cowley 1996, 226)

The postwar period also saw the definitive rupture of the bond between the Carnival band and the calypsonian figure, the successor to the *chantwelles*. By the late 1920s and early 1930s, calypsonians were performing full-length programs in tents, the numbers of which had been reduced as the result of spreading commercialization and the growing rivalries between tent managers.[53] As of 1934, calypsonians traveled regularly to New York to record their work and to perform in concert halls and nightclubs. As Rohlehr points out, recordings of calypso music from the 1930s suggest the changes in style (and rhythm) that the music had undergone, reflecting the influence of "boogie-woogie piano, the rigidity of jazz-type bass lines, and New-Orleans-style instrumentation" (2004, 215). This international exposure brought with it not only obvious commercial gain but also a new-found dignity and respect for a tradition that had its roots in the most deprived elements of Trinidadian society (van Koningsbruggen 1997, 50). One of

the first calypsonians aired on NBC radio was Attila the Hun; the following song
written by him testifies to his pride in the evolution of calypso:

> Long ago you used to see
> Half-naked woman called "pissen-li"
> With chac-chac and vera held in the hand
> Twisting their body like electric fan
> You were not even safe in your own home
> With "negre jardin" and bottle and stone
> But today you can hear our kaiso
> On the American Radio.
> (Quevedo 1983, 52)[54]

Although calypso was gaining international respect, in Trinidad the British
colonial administration grew more anxious about the music. After all, the
calypsonians were unlikely to spread the spirit of "Rule Britannia," and the
administration sensed that its tight control on local culture was slipping (van
Koningsbruggen 1997, 51). Censorship of popular songs dated back to the law of
1868, which prohibited the singing in public of profane songs. In the 1930s, as
calypso continued to mock the scandals of white, upper-class Trinidadian society
and made increasingly pointed political commentaries, a more rigorous law, the
Theatre and Dance Halls Ordinance (1934), was introduced. It required calypsonians to submit their song lyrics for police inspection before being performed,
and it prohibited "profane, indecent or obscene songs or ballads" (Rohlehr 1990,
290).[55] In addition, licenses were now required for "any building, tent or other
erection open to the public, gratuitously or otherwise, where a stage play is performed, presented or held and includes Dance Hall" (quoted in Cowley 1992,
appendix 5 pp. 5–6).

The 1934 ordinance was part of an official program of censorship that extended
into film, literature, and calypso. During the Legislative Council's debates on
the ordinance, Captain A. A. Cipriani, a long-time defender of the lower classes,
had noted that the law already provided for individuals to act against "insulting"
songs, and he spoke against the government's "studied policy" of "shorten[ing]
the stride of the people of this country" (quoted in Rohlehr 1990, 291). The calypsonians and the lower class in general, Cipriani argued, had "an extraordinary
way . . . of amusing themselves and singing ballards [sic] and making references
to certain people highly or lowly placed" in Trinidadian society (291). The true
solution to the question of "insulting" song lyrics lay not in censoring culture
but, Cipriani argued, in the upper classes placing themselves "in a position not to
be insulted or sung about in carnival or other ballads" (291). As he stated, "if we
so-called decent people want to protect ourselves from the jibes of the barefooted
man let us give them proper example" (291).

From its introduction in 1934 to its amendment in 1951, the Theatre and Dance Halls Ordinance transformed the calypso tent scene. The safety dictates of the ordinance meant that the traditional-style tents—made of bamboo and palm fronds, and lit by flambeaux—were no longer usable and would need to be replaced by fewer, larger, more sophisticated venues. The ordinance would thus require more considered and elaborate management and would change irrevocably the relationship between managers and singers and between calypsonians and their audiences (Rohlehr 1990, 293).

RUM TIMES

World War I had been largely experienced vicariously in Trinidad, as a patriotic moment that united the society (until, that is, the soldiers came home with their tales of prejudice), but World War II came to Trinidad far more directly. In particular, the Lend-Lease Agreement of 1940, which leased strategically important territories in the British West Indies to the United States in exchange for fifty torpedo boats, brought significant changes to Trinidad. The peninsula of Chaguaramas to the west of Port of Spain was leased to the Americans for ninety-nine years, and there were immediate economic benefits for islanders as tens of thousands became involved in the construction of the base. By 1942, approximately 26,000 people were employed in the construction and maintenance of U.S. military and naval bases in Trinidad. Inflation soared as the average daily wage rose from forty cents to five dollars, and workers gladly left the plantations to take up the much more lucrative employment offered by the Americans. Less perceptibly but just as significantly, attitudes toward race changed: for the first time, Trinidadians saw whites engaged in hard labor and drinking and partying hard, the consequence of which was that the "automatic deference to a white face became a thing of the past" (Brereton 1981, 192).

Trinidad was experiencing boom times, a period of economic optimism that had significant effects on all sectors of the economy, including organized crime, prostitution, and the culture business. The presence of the big-spending American soldiers in the calypso tents reinvigorated the music and the commercial culture attached to it. Whereas World War I had provoked unequivocally patriotic songs, this time there was (at least initially) a more reserved, even indifferent reaction, as is suggested in the words of a calypso by a singer known as the Growling Tiger: "This war with England and Germany, going to mean more starvation and misery / but I going to plant provision and fix me affairs / and the white people could fight for a thousand years" (quoted in van Koningsbruggen 1997, 54). The memory of World War I was still fresh for many Trinidadians, in particular the racism and discrimination the Trinidadian recruits had faced in

Europe. Attila's calypso "The Horrors of War" (1938) expresses the disillusionment of the Trinidadian public and its general desire for peace:

> I heard an ex-soldier exclaim
> Never me go to fight again
> Why should I take a rifle in hand
> To shoot and murder my brother man?
> In fact, why the deuce should I go to war
> When I don't know what the devil I fighting for?
> (Quoted in Rohlehr 1990, 125)

Later, though, the patriotic impulse returned, and calypso became once again the "most powerful vehicle for the transmission of loyalist sentiments" (Rohlehr 1990, 125). Another calypsonian, Growler, wrote a piece that typified the patriotic calypso of the era:

> Britain will never
> Britain will never
> Surrender to Hitler
> We going to take the whole of his head next summer
> A million destroyers
> Commanding the waters
> Warm [sic] them Mr. Churchill
> Don't you venture to enter the English Channel.
> (Quoted in van Koningsbruggen 1997, 54)[56]

Carnival was celebrated in Trinidad from 1939 to 1941, but the governor, Sir Hubert Young, banned it in 1942. With German submarines attacking Allied possessions in the Caribbean, Trinidad, with its oil reserves and U.S. naval and military bases, had become a possible target. The ban did not extend to calypsonians nor to higher-class balls or American noncommissioned officers' festivities, which continued unabated. The calypsonian known as Invader expressed his disenchantment over these restrictions when he sang:

> The Governor stopped our festival
> But some say they'll still play their Carnival
> So the Lord Invader went out of town
> I was afraid they would shoot me down.
> (Quoted in Rohlehr 1990, 342)

For many calypsonians, however, the war years were seen as the greatest time of their careers, a period when the rise in their earnings was equaled only by the increase in prostitution and venereal diseases. Lord Kitchener recalls this era as "marvellous . . . the best time I think we ever had in Trinidad. . . . It seemed to me like a dream, when the Yankees was here" (quoted in Rohlehr 1990, 346). In the

popular imagination, the Americans quickly replaced the British as the paternalistic defenders and protectors of Trinidad. These years of easy money and loose
morality were most famously immortalized in the calypso "Rum and Coca Cola"
by Lord Invader and, later, by Mighty Sparrow's "Jean and Dinah." Invader's
infamous "mother and daughter/Working for the Yankee dollar" prefigured
Sparrow's girls lamenting the departure of the Americans, with "not a sailor in
town, the nightclub dry."[57] The period of American military presence in Trinidad
was a far more benign episode than the long U.S. occupation of Haiti from 1915
to 1934, and, though calypsonians such as Sparrow commented negatively on the
situation, their complaints were in truth less concerned with moral decline than
with losing their hold over Trinidadian women.[58] In "Jean and Dinah," an underlying misogyny relishes the new, mundane realities for Trinidadian women after
the American demobilization in 1945. Sparrow sang "Yankee's gone and Sparrow
take over now" and "Dorothy got to take what she get" for now it is "By the sweat
of thy crown [that] thou shall eat bread."[59] Kitchener's "My Wife Went Away with
a Yankee" (1946) is less misogynistic; sung in a slow, plaintive style, it is a lament
for the calypsonian's reduced status in the eyes of his woman:

> So I sat my wife on the sofa
> To see if I can influence her
> I told her, "Darling, remember
> That I am a romantic fellar."
> She say, "Kitch, that talk may be true
> But the Yankee boy is sweeter than you.
> So you can see clearly what I mean:
> With money and love I am like a queen."
> (Quoted in Rohlehr 1990, 361)

As Kitchener's and Sparrow's calypsos suggest, the American occupation in
Trinidad raised issues of masculinity based on access to women. This was also
a source of constant tension between the emerging steelbands. However, though
Sparrow and other calypsonians such as Invader, Spoiler, and Kitchener lamented
the prostitution and moral degeneration brought about by the American presence, they did not acknowledge their own pre-war celebrations of the exploitation
of women. Six years before the pseudo-moralistic commentary on Trinidadian
prostitution in "Rum and Coca Cola," Invader had boasted in "A Bachelor Life"
(1937) of the women he had working for him:

> I have got four women supporting me
> A Chinee and a Portuguese
> An Indian abstract and a Venezuelan
> So I don't want no Trinidadian woman.
> (Quoted in Rohlehr 1990, 364)

The difference during the war years was that the Trinidadian "sweet men" or "saga boys" were usurped by the American soldiers and sailors, who paid a better price and generally were "sweeter" than the local saga boys. The bitter misogyny of "Jean and Dinah" was echoed in many postwar calypsos, such as in Invader's "Yankee Dollar" (1946):

> Now the war is over
> Trinidad is getting harder
> Some of the young girls bawling for murder
> You should hear them how they gossiping
> No more Yankee dollars they spending, and thing
> Now they hustling for their usual shilling.
> (Quoted in Rohlehr 1990, 365)

The U.S. presence in Trinidad had undoubtedly "stripped the saga boy/calypsonian of his mask . . . leaving him naked in the cruel and public glare of the light" (Rohlehr 1990, 365). At the same time, however, and not surprising for a population well versed in carnivalesque mimicry, the Trinidadian saga boys imitated the Americans and adopted the perceived fashionable clothes and smooth manner of the soldiers. Dressing up in bell-bottomed or tight-bottomed pants, silk shirts, natty hats, and zoot suits, the saga boys used their clothes as a means of attracting women and of gaining respect, at once reacting against and expressing a kind of complicity with the American men.[60]

The occupation coincided with a watershed in Trinidadian politics: the island's intellectuals began to question the worth of ongoing imperial connections with Britain and to promote the idea of a discrete Trinidadian national identity. To young anti-colonial patriots like Albert Gomes, Ralph Mentor, Jean De Boissiere, Alfred Mendes, and Sylvia Chen, this challenge to Great Britain was more than a question of politics; much of their rhetoric was based on their conception and promotion of a distinctive Trinidadian culture. Put simply, politics and culture were "virtually inseparable" for these Creole patriots (Neptune 2007, 4).

In essence, this loosely arranged group was Trinidad's version of an indigenist movement. Although not nearly as well known as Haiti's indigenist movement, the Negritude movement of the French islands, or indeed the Afrocubanista movement in Cuba, Trinidad's anti-colonial patriots promoted a more or less similar idea of national culture as necessarily folksy, anti-modern, and anti-Western.[61] As in Haiti, previously neglected grassroots sectors of Trinidadian society were brought center stage by the middle-class, urban (and often non-black) intellectuals and recast as living embodiments of the island's distinctive, untainted, non-Western culture. Rallying round the calypso as the national art form, Trinidad's intellectuals, much like Haiti's, romanticized blackness in a way that "flirted troublingly" with metropolitan primitivism (Neptune 2007, 20).

Effectively "intoxicated" by the calypso, the nationalists ignored the truth of its evolution in the distinctly modern realms of mass entertainment and commerce, and they reinvented it as the single most important expression of Trinidad's exotic, timelessly African culture (Neptune 207, 44).[62] Just as in Haiti, too, rhythm was an integral part of this idea of authentic, traditional musical form.[63]

As the calypsonians tailored their art to the lucrative audiences of American troops, Trinidadian intellectuals were quick to point out the risks of diluting the putative authenticity and traditional rhythmicity of the song. After witnessing a calypso show in September 1943, Gomes wrote of how the music was deteriorating as the result of what he considered to be the excessive accommodations made to American tastes and expectations. Tellingly, Gomes's call for a return to a purer version of calypso invoked the importance of rhythm to the nationalist aesthetic. "The calypso," he wrote, "was losing its basic primitive rhythm," and "unless some new star appeared on the horizon, someone emphasizing the old forms with new vigor, the calypso as we know it is doomed" (quoted in Neptune 2007, 149). As it turned out, the "new star" that would reinvigorate Trinidadian music and its rhythms was far from the retrogressive, pre-modern entity that Gomes envisaged, and it was not so much a single artist as a new, modern instrument.

STEEL RHYTHMS

One of the fundamental aims of the Carnival Improvement Committee, founded in 1939 by the City Council of Port of Spain, was "to lift Calypso," which meant the promotion of heavier, more serious forms of calypso and, crucially, the "devaluation of rhythm, energy and verve" (Rohlehr 1990, 329). In truth, as Gomes lamented in 1943, calypso had been drifting away from its core rhythmic principle for some time, even though, as one observer later wrote, the only way to tell if a song is a calypso is to judge it "by the beat," for "this is what determines what is a calypso (not content, but the beat)" (Raymond 1978).[64] And yet, if by the 1930s calypso had broken away to some extent from its rhythmic past and incorporated less rhythm-driven influences such as swing and jazz (and instruments such as the trombone, clarinet, cornet, and saxophone), the urban black poor had remained faithful to rhythm and percussion, and indeed they had continued to innovate both in style and instrumentation.[65] Tamboo-bamboo had remained popular among the working classes, who had long been deprived of the right to drum and who had never taken to the stringbands because of those bands' "lack of rhythmic power" (van Koningsbruggen 1997, 63).[66] Tamboo-bamboo music had replaced the banned drum at stick-fights as well as at wakes, Christmas celebrations, and Carnival. Also, in Carnival *devil mas*, a tradition that is particularly strong in the mountain areas around Paramin, rhythmic accompaniment was provided first by tamboo-bamboo and then by a singular version of steel pan, biscuit tins slung around the neck and beaten with sticks, and also possibly some other iron percussion such as brake drums and whistles (Walsh 2004, 149). Well before the 1930s, of course, the connection between black working-class identity and rhythm had been firmly established, and the beats of the tamboo-bamboo bands constituted a direct connection with history, echoing (but also adapting and developing) the rhythms that had marked out the urban and rural poor's collective historical experience on the island.

Nevertheless, the relationship between rhythm and black identity had never been static, and by the mid- to late 1930s new innovations in instruments were again shaping and reflecting the black urban subjectivity. Around this time, tamboo-bamboo band players in the ghettos of east Port of Spain—including the areas of John John, East Dry River, Gonzales, and Laventille—began to experiment with metallic objects such as biscuit tins, dustbin lids, wheel hubs, and oil barrels, beating out their rhythms on these new instruments, which were all too obviously symbols of an increasingly industrialized, modernizing country and population.[67] There is some dispute and indeed a degree of romance surrounding the genesis of steel pan. Errol Hill cites this plausible version: "It all started in 1936 in Tanty Willie's yard about carnival time. The boys had gathered as usual to beat bamboo; one of them, Sousie Dean, picked up a dustbin and started beating it, there was an old motor-car in de yard and Arnim began to beat the gas tank. Realizing it was sounding sweet they discarded the bamboo. Rannie Taylor got hold of a paint pan, 'Killie' found a piece of iron, and my brother 'Mussell Rat' suggested the cutting down of a cement drum to be used as a kettle and so the first steelband was formed in time for carnival day" (1972, 48).[68]

These crude early experiments were soon refined in the backyards of east Port of Spain as rival bands embraced and adapted the new metal instruments, seeking to produce a melody from the different tones of the steel drum.[69] The trinity of steelband innovators credited with playing the first full melodies on the steel drum—Winston "Spree" Simon of the John-John band, Neville Jules from Hell Yard, and Ellie Mannette from the Oval Boys—have long passed into local lore as the inventors of the only new instrument created in the twentieth century (Brereton 1981, 226). The earliest steelbands were essentially rhythm bands that echoed the sounds and beats of the previous drum and tamboo-bamboo units; the bass was now made of a biscuit drum, struck with the hand or a ball.[70] The dudup or bass kettle, a two-note caustic-soda drum struck with a stick, overlaid the bass, while the lead was taken by the kettle, which was made out of a zinc can or paint can and had three notes. In addition, assorted iron instruments such as the brake drum of a car, the bottle and spoon, scrapers, and the omnipresent chac-chac reinforced the rhythmic drive of the band (Batson 2004, 197). In 1942, an article in the New York Times wrote of a band heard in a Port of Spain tent that "consisted only of percussion instruments: drums, biscuit pans of different sizes, bottles and spoons, which produced strange sounds and piercing rhythms" (quoted In Hill 1993, 207). Experiments with metal instruments continued in the early 1940s; new pitches were discovered as the metal was molded and hammered into different forms, and Mannette produced the first concave pan. As he said, affirming the fundamental importance of rhythm to black working-class culture in Trinidad, the steelband "was born from a very primitive form . . . rhythm, rhythm, rhythm" (quoted in Batson 2004, 198).

Like their predecessors the stickbands, the steelbands were the foci of neighborhood identity and, particularly in their early years, were involved in serious confrontations both with rival bands and with the police. Generally made up of Hollywood movie enthusiasts, the steelbands took their names from contemporary films—Carib Tokyo from the film *Destination Tokyo,* Boys Town from *Men of Boys Town*—and perpetuated the territorial disputes of the stickbands. Between 1942 and 1945, when Carnival was suspended, some of the steelbands came out onto the streets and clashed violently with the police. The ways in which the rhythms of the steelbands heightened the anticipation of violence and helped band members to brace themselves for the inevitable confrontation are suggested in the words of a calypsonian known as Lord Blaikie in his "Steelband Clash" (1954), which recalls the "Bacchanal Nineteen fifty Carnival," the "Fight fuh so with Invaders and Tokyo," and how his friend "run and left he hat / When dey hit him with ah baseball bat." As Blaikie narrates the moments prior to the clash, he pays particular attention to the two bands' rhythms:

> Invaders beating sweet
> Coming up Park Street
> Tokyo coming down beating very slow
> As soon as you see the two bands clash
> Mamayo if you see cutlass.
> (Quoted in Batson 2004, 200)

If steel pan was born in the backyards of east Port of Spain in the mid- to late 1930s, VE Day in 1945 marked a kind of second birth. The moment the news burst onto the city streets, it sparked an unprecedented release of rhythmic creativity—rhythm being, as ever, the musical accompaniment to the purgation of the masses' frustrations.[71] The *Evening News* of May 8, 1945, reported on "joyous thousands [who] dressed themselves appropriately and paraded in bands, dancing in the street to the crazy rhythm of improvised instruments." The celebrations for VJ Day on August 15, 1945, were all the more fevered as Trinidad's Chinese population celebrated the defeat of their historical adversaries and took to the streets on lorries adorned with banners carrying slogans such as "The Republic of China has won the War of resistance against Japanese aggression" (quoted in Rohlehr 1990, 354). It was steel pan that supplied the rhythms for the celebrations. Kitchener and the other leading calypsonians now wrote for the steelbands, and the general emphasis was on "the rhythm of the pans and the rhythms of the streets, not the contemplation of the tents" (Hill 1993, 209). It was Kitchener who first expressed, in his "The Beat of the Steelband," the calypsonians' reaction to the rhythms of the new bands:

> Yes I heard the beat of a steelband
> Friends, I couldn't understand
> It was hard to make a distinction
> Between Poland, Bar20 and John John.
>
> Zigilee, Pops and Battersby
> They coming with a semitone melody
> When they start this contrary beat
> They had people jumping wild in the street
>
> Port of Spain was catching afire
> When the steelband was crossing the Dry River
> Zigilee, the leader of the ping-pong
> Had people jumping wild in the town.
>   (Quoted in Rohlehr 1990, 355)

Kitchener was sensitive to the feelings and frustrations that, as ever, lay behind the rhythms and to the emotions that motivated the "contrary beat," which led to the violence on the streets. Despite the boom times that the American presence had brought, profound problems of poverty and deprivation remained, issues that were brought into sharp focus when the Americans left and the stark truth of Trinidad's social inequalities was unmasked anew. Rhythm was once again an agent and instigator of the cathartic (if ultimately self-destructive) violence of Trinidad's poor. The response from the authorities was itself a repetition of the legislation they had imposed since the early nineteenth century: an attempt to restore order through repressing rhythmic music. In December 1945, a Summary Offences Ordinance of December 1945 was introduced, which stipulated that: "No person shall, except during the Carnival without licence under (Ordinance No. 40 of 1945) the hand of a police officer not below the rank of a non commissioned officer in charge of a police station beat any drum or play any noisy instrument in any street or public place" (quoted in Cowley 1992, appendix 5, p. 6).

After VE Day, however, respectable society continued to view the steelbands with that familiar blend of contempt and suspicion. In the decade following the war, steelbands were disdained by the elite as a "resurrection of every horror that the society had for a century been trying to exorcise" and were referred to in newspapers as a "disgraceful and lawless hooligan element" (Rohlehr 1990, 370). Letters to the newspapers expressed middle-class outrage at the levels of "noise" (as opposed to music) that the steelbands created. In one letter to the *Guardian* on June 13, 1946, a reader drew a comparison between drumming in Africa and the steelbands' own rhythmic playing, arguing that the steelband was an inferior form of cultural expression: "There is a terrific amount of rot talked about 'culture' these days, and if steel bands are to fall into this category, I prefer to remain a savage and listen to Mozart" (quoted in Stuempfle 1995, 66). In interpreting the new steelband movement, therefore, certain members of the middle class resorted to their traditional distinction between high European "white" civilization and low African "black" culture. To be sure, the ongoing violence between the bands did little to allay middle-class fears, but few in society were able to identify the possibilities of using the steelbands as agents for social stability and for providing a focus for the creative energies of the urban poor (Brereton 1981, 65). It was not until 1949 and the creation of the Trinidad and Tobago Steelband Association that these energies began to be harnessed to a policy of social advancement and of reducing intra-ghetto violence. Conflicts between bands decreased in the 1950s, and attitudes toward the steelbands changed gradually as anti-colonial sentiment and a new racial consciousness took hold and the century and a half of British rule came to an end, thus radically altering the sociocultural dynamics of the island.[72] Long disdained and scorned, rhythm—chiefly through the rise to preeminence of the steelbands—could now be incorporated into the evolving national (and nationalist) aesthetic.[73]

Ultimately, Trinidad's post-Cedula history, sounded out, shaped, and prophesied by the changes in rhythmic music and developments in percussive instrumentation, is a history of popular improvisation. The apparently chaotic, unplanned shifts from one style of music and one kind of percussive instrument to another mask a deeper, irresistible purpose. Improvisation is usually understood as an act without foresight, prescriptive vision, or deep motivation, but in practice it is often a knowing, future-oriented performance that operates as a "kind of foreshadowing, if not prophetic, description" that carries "the prescription and extemporaneous formation and reformation of rules, rather than the following of them" (Moten 2003, 63). In the history of Trinidad, music and other kinds of performative improvisations are far from simple, naïve, nonhistorical acts. Instead, they foresee and embody what one critic calls "the very essence of the visionary, the spirit of the new, an organizational planning of and in free association that transforms the material" (Moten 2003, 64). Improvisation is also a matter of time and sight, a glance to the future, and, in Trinidad's case, the occasion to see the shape of that future. This vision has been communicated primarily through sound, through rhythm, and through the music without which the great transformations in Trinidadian society from the colonial era to today could never have taken place.

3

_____

Rhythm, Music, and Literature
in the French Caribbean

As the rhythm of the steelbands was being harnessed to a nascent form of black power in Trinidad, and as Haiti's musicians and intellectuals were incorporating rhythm as a primary feature of indigenist aesthetics, a similar conception of black rhythm was emerging as a defining aspect of another racial consciousness movement on the small French island of Martinique. During the 1940s, the Negritude movement developed an idea of black culture and black being that held rhythm to be an essential attribute of the black man. Whereas in Trinidad it was in popular music that blackness and rhythm were most extensively conjoined, in contemporary Martinique Negritude was a distinctly literary movement, and its explorations of race, culture, and rhythm were largely carried out through literature, chiefly poetry. This chapter charts the development of this discourse in the French Caribbean from the Negritude era to the 1980s, from the African-centered rhythmic poetics of Aimé Césaire through Léon-Gontran Damas's experiments with jazz rhythms and Frantz Fanon's denunciation of rhythm as an essential component of racialized Martinican identity. Moving into the post-Negritude era, my analysis shifts to canonic novels by Joseph Zobel, Édouard Glissant, and Daniel Maximin that have questioned and reworked many of Negritude's central ideas. At every stage, and in many different ways, rhythm has been reinterpreted and reasserted as a recurring element in French Caribbean history, culture, and everyday experience.[1]

Before Negritude, writing in Martinique consisted largely of minor works imitating French exoticist models of the nineteenth century. Antillean writers' imitation of the Romantics and Parnassians at once mimicked European form and echoed Eurocentric views of the islands as places of exotic escape. Such literary and cultural mimicry went largely unchallenged until the 1930s, when a new generation of young Antillean intellectuals emerged, not in the islands but in Paris. The initial products of this new sensibility were a series of student journals, the first of which, *La Revue du monde noir* (1931–32), adopted a broad, pan-African vision, stressing similarities and commonalities of purpose across the colonized world. Founded by the Martinican sisters Paulette and Jane Nardal, the Haitian Léo Sajous, and the Guadeloupean Henri Jean-Louis, *La Revue du monde noir* was an important landmark in the genesis of Negritude. The Parisian intelligentsia in the 1930s was enthralled by all things it considered primitive and other: exotic cultural artifacts, from jazz to Brazilian rhythms to *art nègre*, were lauded and consumed enthusiastically.[2] This French enthusiasm for non-European cultures emerged as Paris became a place of encounter for young students and authors from Africa, the Caribbean, and the United States. The Nardal sisters promoted such contacts and hosted a literary salon in Paris for some of the most prominent figures from the "black world": intellectuals such as Alain Locke, Jacques Roumain, and Jean Price-Mars attended the Nardals' salon, and all contributed to *La Revue du monde noir*.

The journal had three related objectives: to provide publishing opportunities for black artists and intellectuals; to study and promote African and black civilizations; and to create new links between previously isolated black thinkers from across the globe. The influence of Price-Mars, in particular, is apparent: the journal's promotion of African-derived culture in the New World echoed the principal interests of his own indigenist movement in Haiti. *La Revue du monde noir* differed, however, from Haitian indigenism in that the journal focused less on national particularities than on a pan-African idea of collective, racial identity. Paulette Nardal's article "Éveil de la conscience de race" (Awakening of Race Consciousness) prefigures Césaire in its reflection on Caribbean racial alienation and in the way it draws inspiration from Claude McKay, Langston Hughes, and the Harlem Renaissance movement to call for the rediscovery of racial identity as a means of countering French colonial assimilationism. It is chiefly in this call for racial reawakening that the journal set the terms for the later emergence of the Negritude movement. Indeed, Césaire became familiar with the authors of the Harlem Renaissance through reading *La Revue du monde noir* during his first year in Paris. He did not, however, attend the black literary salons because he considered them to be overly bourgeois, "mulatto," and Catholic in their outlook. Although *La Revue du monde noir* explicitly resisted French cultural assimilation, its editorial group did aspire to creating, "along with the elites of other Races[,] . . . the material, intellectual, and moral perfection of humanity in general," and as such it stopped short of the violently direct and angry challenge to "white civilization" that was to characterize Césaire's work ("Ce que nous voulons faire" 1931). Indeed, the elitist undercurrents of *La Revue du monde noir* were subsequently challenged in other pre-Negritude journals such as *Légitime Défense, L'Étudiant martiniquais,* and *L'Étudiant noir.* Césaire's own journal, *Tropiques,* would in the 1940s express his group's particular vision of black culture and Caribbean identity.

Césaire's most influential poem was also his first published work. In 1939, the first edition of *Cahier d'un retour au pays natal / Notebook of a Return to My Native Land* appeared, and it has remained one of the most forceful and complex expressions of anti-colonial revolt. All of the influences that he had absorbed in Paris fed into this long poem: there are touches of surrealist anti-rationalism, Frobenian valorization of Africanity, and Freudian moments of rediscovery of the "umbilical cord" between the Caribbean and Africa. Although it expresses a profound sense of disillusionment on returning to the "pays natal," the poem evolves into a powerful, indignant rebuke of colonially imposed identities. After *Cahier d'un retour au pays natal,* Césaire produced five more collections of poems—*Les Armes miraculeuses* (1946); *Soleil cou coupé* (1948); *Corps perdu* (1950); *Ferrements* (1950); and *Moi, Laminaire* (1982)—as well as important essays and plays. Césaire also pursued a remarkable and often controversial political career, the fundamental paradox of which was the apparent contradiction between his anti-colonial rhetoric and his unrelenting support for ongoing formal connections between Martinique and France.[3]

NEGRITUDE AND RHYTHM

How did rhythm figure aesthetically and philosophically in Negritude's vision of blackness? Rhythm was, in fact, fundamental both to Negritude's poetics and to its understanding of the basic differences between black and white cultures. Almost certainly Léopold Senghor, the only one of Negritude's three figureheads to be born in Africa, greatly influenced Césaire and Damas in their thinking about rhythm and blackness. Senghor's relationship to rhythm is quite understandably less forced and more "natural" than that of his Caribbean counterparts, for whom Africa and its culture were largely lost elements to be rediscovered and recuperated. Senghor's poetry incorporates rhythm in this unaffected way both as a technical feature and as a broader theme in African life. In his first collection, *Chants d'ombre* (1945), his poem "C'est le temps de partir" tells of an encounter with a lover with whom he finally rediscovers "the original rhythm" of love (1990, 39). In the same collection, the poem "Vacances" describes the movement between day and night as the cyclical "rhythm of the world" and relates it to other rhythms, such as the "crazy tom-tom" of his heart that is accompanied by the off-beat pounding of his lover's heart (43). In a later collection, *Éthiopiques* (1956), the poem "Congo" expresses a desire to be freed from a state of alienation and to be reconnected with the Congo itself, which is presented as a kind of matrix of his race, the "queen of subjugated Africa" (1990, 101–3). As the poem builds to its climax, rhythm plays an ever more dynamic role in the quest to reconnect with the proud Africa of his memory. Indeed, there is a sense of the speaker giving in to rhythm, for, as he says, "my strength builds up in abandon, my honor in submission" (102). His "science," or his knowledge and awareness, grows he says "in the instinct of your rhythm" (103). The final stanza of the poem sees the rhythm accelerate and swirl, leading the speaker into a trance-like state in which he is finally delivered from alienation and back into his natural, African consciousness:

> So beat then bells, beat tongues, beat out oars the dance of the Master of
>   the oars. . . .
> And I call twice two tom-tom hands, forty virgins to sing his deeds.
> So beat the shining arrow, the Sun's claw at midday
> Beat, cowrie-rattles, the rhythm of the Great Waters
> And death on the crest of exultation, to the indisputable call of the deep. (103)

In his essays, too, Senghor affirms the fundamental importance of rhythm to Africa. In "Lettre à trois poètes de l'Hexagone" (1979), he writes that the creative virtues of black poetry are its rhythm and melody, and of these two rhythm is primary because it creates not only melody but also the poetic image itself (1990, 394). Senghor develops this idea in his essay "Comme les lamantins vont boire à la source" (1956), which was written as an epilogue to *Éthiopiques*. Senghor's essay is essentially a response to European critics of Césaire and Damas and is a means of suggesting that diasporic blacks will return to "drink" at their African source, much like in the myth of the manatee to which his title alludes. According to Senghor, rhythm is a source of nourishment for the exiled black man in France, cut off from the tom-tom and from his "natural" connection with his authentic rhythms (1990, 156). What distinguishes the black man is that he comes from a world where, as soon as he feels his African authenticity, his words become rhythm and poetry (156). Words for the black subject are more than images or mere signifiers; the meaning appears as soon as an object is named, because for black people every being—everything including form, color, acts, tone, timbre, and rhythm—is sign and sense at the same time (159). In other words, the black man's relationship to the world and to phenomena is more immediate, natural, and instinctive than that of the European, who, having experienced centuries of rationalism, "has made a wall of what was previously a transparent veil" (159). In poetry, Senghor says, it is rhythm that frees up the analogical image, which provokes the "poetic short circuit" and gives words their deeper resonances (160).

Black poets, again in Africa and the diaspora, have for Senghor a kind of auditory memory that submits them to the tyranny of their "interior music" and in particular to rhythm. Drawing on memories of his own childhood, he recalls how the most "naïve" poets of his village could only compose their work in the rhythmic trance of the tom-tom drum (161). Turning to the French critic Henri Hell's denunciation of the "monotonous" rhythms and "gratuitous" imagery of Césaire's *Et les chiens se taisaient* (1956),[4] Senghor argues that, in Césaire's work, insistent, repetitive imagery is but a part of the rhythmic structure and therefore a sign of his blackness. Repetition of words, sounds, structures, and figures of speech such as alliteration, assonance, anaphora, parataxis, and apostrophe create, Senghor says, the overall rhythm in Césaire's work. To criticize Césaire and other black poets for their use of rhythm is ultimately, for Senghor, to reproach them for being black and for remaining true to themselves and their ancestral culture. As a diasporic black man, Césaire—like Louis Armstrong with his trumpet or a Vodou believer with his tom-tom—has, says Senghor, a profound need to "lose himself in the verbal dance, in the rhythm of the tom-tom, to rediscover himself in the Cosmos" (165). In effect, Senghor argues that there "exists an essentially black form of reason that is based on emotional ways of knowing" (Wilder 2005, 263).[5]

Such ideas were taken up enthusiastically by Damas and Césaire, two products of French colonialism, who had attended together the Lycée Schœlcher in Fort-de-France for a period in 1925–26 and who had gone to Paris and engaged with the great black commotion that was fermenting there in the 1920s and 1930s.[6] Although his legacy may have been eclipsed somewhat by the greater critical attention paid to Césaire, Damas's first published poetry actually preceded Césaire's by two years. Published in 1937, Damas's *Pigments* stands as a seminal collection in the literary history of the Caribbean. In contrast to Césaire's opaque surrealist poetics, Damas's work has a lyrical simplicity that makes it more readily accessible, something like the work of Haitian near-contemporaries such as Roumain and René Depestre. The importance of rhythm to Damas's conception of Negritude is signaled from the very first poem in the collection, "Ils sont venus ce soir," which is quite appropriately dedicated to Senghor. The poem's typography acts in conjunction with the words to create the rhythmic effects:

> They came that night when the
> tom
>   tom
>   rolled with
>   rhythm
>   upon
>   rhythm
>   the frenzy
>   of the eyes
>   the frenzy of the hands
>   the frenzy

```
of the feet of statues
SINCE
how many ME ME ME
have died
since they came that night when the
tom
      tom
         rolled with
                  rhythm
                        upon
                              rhythm
                                    the frenzy
of the eyes
the frenzy
of the hands
the frenzy
of the feet of statues.
      (Damas 1972, 13)
```

The plaintive tone of the poem is complemented by the rolling rhythm, which loops itself around the central theme of ancestral loss and death. The middle section seems to be fleetingly situated in the alienated present, while the rhythmic refrain is wrapped around this present time with its memory of a more racially authentic moment of frenetic dance and abandon. The rhythm appears to echo the African past and in general to act as a palliative for the torments of the present.

A similar conception of rhythm as a source of relief from the unsettling present is offered in Damas's poem "Trêve." The title suggests the idea of truce or respite from the "toadying," the "bootlicking," and the "attitude of the hyperassimilated" that the poem decries. The source of rhythmic relief in this case is not ancestral Africa but the contemporary black music of the United States:

```
Respite of the blues
of beating on the piano
of a muted trumpet
of madness stamping its feet
to the satisfaction of rhythm. (23)
```

This early salute to black America indicates Damas's preoccupation with the North American race question. A close acquaintance of Countee Cullen, Langston Hughes, and Richard Wright, Damas was markedly more concerned with the racial problem in the United States than were Césaire and Senghor. Indeed, Damas's poetry has something of the qualities of jazz and the blues: a lonely artist singing from the margins his songs of loss, love, and quiet revolt. His long poem

Black-Label (1956) typifies this prevalent strain in Damas's work. The exiled black man in Paris riffs around his melancholic isolation, his sadness soaked, though never dissolved, in alcohol. In one section he evokes an Africanized French capital, a "black Paris," the hub of mid-century pan-African culture:

> PARIS-Center-of-the World
> at the mercy of AFRICA
> of its soul
> of its joy
> its sadness
> its regrets. (51)

The following section develops the idea of Paris as an Africanized metropolis and introduces the figures of black music and rhythm:

> PARIS-Center-of-the World
> at the mercy of AFRICA
> at the mercy of its voice
> at the mercy of the fever of its rhythm
> of the dancefloor a pocket handkerchief
> of the invitation to the voyage to the wall
> of the muted trumpet. (51)

This black Paris is not, however, a site of felicitous cultural cross-fertilization. Rather, Africa and black culture sit at the heart of France as inviolable, immutable entities. The white man, the speaker says, will never be black (and vice versa), for beauty, wisdom, endurance, courage, patience, irony, charm, magic, and love are all black (52). Crucially, too, he affirms the blackness of music and rhythmicity (and conversely the rhythmicity and musicality of the black man):

> black is swaying the hips
> for dance is black
> and black is rhythm
> for art is black and black is movement. (52)

Published in the same year as Senghor's "Comme les lamantins vont boire à la source," Damas's *Black-Label* echoes his African comrade's idea that rhythm and black culture are synonymous, and he audaciously implants black rhythms and African diasporic music at the very heart of the colonial metropole. Just five years later, Césaire was to make his own most unequivocal statement on the black man's innate, instinctive connection to rhythm in a 1961 interview with the critic Jacqueline Sieger: "For me, the word, however essential it may be, is not as important as rhythm. . . . I wanted to bring into the French language an element that is foreign to it. *Rhythm is an essential element of the black man.* I believe, without having premeditated it, that it figures constantly in my poems. African people have told me something that makes me very happy; it seems that my poems are among the few that can be easily beaten on a tom-tom" (Sieger 1961, 65, emphasis added).

Rhythm does indeed figure constantly in Césaire's poems, and it is often explicitly linked to his idea of black culture.[7] From his first, classic work, rhythms and repetitions—of words, sounds, images, and structures—were a significant feature of his poetry.[8] There is a famous passage in *Cahier d'un retour au pays natal* in which the speaker evokes a previous encounter on a tram in Paris with a "hideous," "melancholy," "COMICAL AND UGLY" black man (2001, 30). The man is something of an epitome of the deracinated black in Paris, lost and alone, drifting and homeless. His alienation is presented in terms of a rupture with rhythm itself, as he is described as being "without rhythm [out of time]" (29). From his first work, therefore, Césaire suggests the close connection between rhythm and grounded, authentic black being.

His second collection, *Les Armes miraculeuses,* is particularly rich with rhythmically charged poems and Africanist imagery. Césaire's Africanism is, however, rarely presented in straightforward images or language. In most cases, the African element exists in a few words or symbols that appear among the surrealist swirl of images like lost fragments of the racial past but are repeated and reinvoked so that they echo rhythmically through the poem; they are thereby pulled through time and space to suggest a kind of presence and relevance in Césaire's Caribbean here and now. Perhaps Césaire's most compelling and powerful use of rhythm in this collection occurs in the poem "Batouque," the title of which denotes a Brazilian tom-tom drum rhythm (1983,146–53). The repetition of the word *batouque* throughout this poem creates at once a rhythmic intensity and an incantatory energy that are used to evoke lost memories and, in a sense, regurgitate the past onto the degraded Caribbean present. This process is not carried out systematically or in any easily decodable way; written during Césaire's most distinctly surrealist phase, the poem seems to accumulate a mass of jarring, discordant imagery. Yet there is ultimately a palpable sense of Césaire steering, driving, and structuring the poem, principally through imagery, rhythm, and repetition. One passage that exemplifies Césaire's use of rhythm and repetition to evoke memories of Africa and bring them into the Caribbean present occurs near the end of the poem, and it begins with the refrain "batouque":

> batouque
> once the world is a breeding pond where I angle for my eyes on the line of your eyes
> batouque
> once the world is the far-sailing latex drunk from the flesh of sleep
> batouque
> batouque of swells and hiccups

> batouque of sneered sobs
> batouque of startled buffaloes
> batouque of defiances of carmined wasp nests. (151)

Temporally, the first part of this section seems to project into the future and offer a surrealist prophecy of historical deliverance; the imagery of the breeding pond (and of seeing) contrasts with the more common Césairean water-related images of deathly swamps and murderous seas. The repetition of the batouque refrain seems to fortify the bold promises of the prophetic lines and to mark time. As the passage progresses, however, the repetition of the refrain becomes more insistent, and the rhythm quickens. This quickening of the rhythm coincides with an apparent temporal slip back into the past, or at least the past as it inhabits the present, and a lapse into more troubling imagery. In contrast to the new life of the breeding pond, the swells recall the movements of the ocean, the unsettling rhythms of the Middle Passage that repeat themselves and return with regularity—much like the liquid image of the "sneered sobs"—to inundate the consciousness of the present. The swells indicate the steady return of a disconcerting, unfinished past, and this historical rhythm effectively forms an internal rhythmic structure that clashes with the more prominent rhythmic pattern of repeated batouques. This rhythmic clash creates an effect something like two waves colliding.

Appropriately, this rhythmic collision produces a great surge of chaotically surrealist energy as the poem contends with the return of the never-forgotten past:

> batouque of hands
> batouque of breasts
> batouque of the seven behead[ed] sins
> batouque of the sex with a bird-like peck a fish-like flight
> batouque of a black princess in a diadem of melting sun
> batouque of the princess stoking up a thousand unknown guardians
> a thousand gardens forgotten under the sand and the rainbow
> batouque of the princess with thighs like the Congo
> like Borneo
> like Casamance. (151)

The first part of this section seems to evoke the rhythms of copulation, of bodies joining together rhythmically, liberated from Christian morality, and reaching their climax in the "fish-like flight" of ejaculation. The black princess appears in surrealist-mythical imagery as an ideal of black femininity who has the ability to "stoke up" the past, the forgotten guardians and gardens, which are symbols of security and perhaps, in the case of the latter, of racial genesis. Indeed, the idea of birth is further suggested in the image of the princess's thighs, which, like the Congo, are associated with the African matrix that Césaire often evokes to counter the sense of displacement expressed throughout his poetry.

At times for Césaire, the naming and evocation of the islands seems to be the most difficult and painful of all his poetic functions. Whereas he freely evokes African place names as soothing reminders of his lost ancestry, he rarely inscribes Caribbean places into his poetry, apparently because they remind him of the emptiness and exile that he feels are his historical legacy. The following passage is therefore all the more remarkable and significant in that it does name Caribbean, specifically Martinican, places:

> batouque of pregnant lands
> batouque of enwalled sea
> batouque of humped hamlets of rotten feet of deaths spelled out in the priceless
>   despair of memory
> Basse-Pointe Diamant Tartant and Caravelle
> gold shekels flotation planes assailed by [sprays and blights]
> sad brains crawled by orgasms
> smoky armadillos
> O the krumen teasers of my surf!
> the sun has leapt from the great marsupial pouches of the dormerless sea
> into the full algebra of false hair and tramwayless rails
> batouque the rivers fissure in the unlaced helmet of ravines
> the sugar cane capsizes in the rolling of the earth swollen with she-camel humps
> the coves smash at the ebbless bladders of stone with irresponsible lights. (153)

The rhythmic repetition of batouque in this passage seems more muted and less insistent, something like a death knell tolling balefully through the description of Césaire's Martinique. The pregnant lands of the first line seem not to suggest fertility or life but a swollen, physical deformity that is linked to the later images of the hunch-backed hamlets and the she-camel humps. The sea, instead of suggesting freedom and openness, is associated with imprisonment, and it appears as a liquid barrier that only reinforces the feeling of continued historical incarceration. The deformed, forgotten, and forgetting hamlets are named as Basse-Pointe, Diamant, Tartant, and Caravelle, Martinican villages that are evoked in unremittingly negative terms related to impermanency: floating on the ocean, their unsecured physical state reflects the indeterminacy of the people. The places (and the people) are assailed by blights and by the foam, the spray of the sea; their emptied-out, sad brains are encased like those of armadillos or are enwalled like the sea. The sun reappears and is now dramatically freed from the closed, restrictive sea, liberated into the totality of Martinican experience.

The final batouque in this passage signals an ultimate transformation, described in surrealist-apocalyptic terms as the cracking of rivers, the capsizing of the sugar cane (and all it symbolizes) into the earth, which is now like the ocean, rolling and swollen, and light smashes like the sea against the "bladders of stone," an image that can be related to the previous images of empty vessels. The transformation continues in the following movements with a sudden call to the sun and a return to more insistent, rapid rhythms:

> sun, go for their throats!
> black howler black butcher black corsair batouque bedecked with spices and flies
> Sleepy herd of mares under the bamboo thicket
> Bleed bleed herd of carambas. (153)

The object of the purgative violence of the sun is not entirely clear, but if the word black is here understood in terms of a typically Césairean racial reversal, or more simply as a means of designating sinister acts, then the object would appear to be the white butchers and corsairs of Caribbean history. The passage that follows confirms that the object of Césaire's ire is the historical oppressor, but it veers away quickly from violence into a more forgiving tone:

> Assassin I acquit you in the name of rape.
> I acquit you in the name of the Holy Ghost
> I acquit you with my salamander hands
> the day will pass like a wave with its bandoleer of cities
> in its beggar's sack of powder-swollen shells, (153)

The acquittal of the historically guilty echoes the better-known sections from *Cahier d'un retour au pays natal* in which the speaker accepts "totally, without reservation" all of the injustices and indignities that history has inflicted upon him (2001, 39). In both cases, the magnanimous gesture clears the way for a clearer vision of future freedom, and Césaire's prophetic voice foresees with certainty the passing of time and the coming of liberation. It is with this prophetic voice, and images of future reawakening, that "Batouque" concludes:

> Liberty my only pirate water of the New Year my only thirst
> love my only sampan
> we shall slip our calabash fingers of laughter
> between the icy teeth of the Sleeping Beauty. (1983, 153)

In many ways, this poem exemplifies Césaire's poetry as a whole: the deracinated, lost Caribbean subject is plunged into the nightmare of history and discovers solace and salvation in the memory of Africa, the rediscovery and reinstatement of which sets off an apocalyptic, violent transformation in consciousness, which in turn leads to a final state of acceptance and forgiveness and of apparent wholeness of being. The poem also reveals the dynamic role played by rhythm throughout these movements: the rhythms, as cosmic, sonorous figurations of Césaire's lost Africanity, at once echo and mirror the different phases of the movements, their peaks and troughs, their swells and lulls, and actually drive the transformations, bringing about the longed-for end of alienation and displacement. Moreover, there is something tangible and inextinguishable about the rhythms; they persist and live while almost every other sign of Césaire's African heritage seems lost, out of his grip.[9]

Rhythm therefore figured prominently in the aesthetics and vision of blackness of each of Negritude's three great figureheads. Although each of them, in different ways and to differing degrees, promoted rhythm as an essential element of black being and culture, they also ascribed other functions to rhythm. In Senghor's case, rhythm was more solidly grounded in lived African experience; it was a kind of social glue that unified communities and cultures. For Senghor, rhythm was a cultural marker that united him to his diasporic comrades and that set black cultures apart from white civilization. Damas, like Césaire, adopts uncritically Senghor's view of rhythm but also adapts it, in that he incorporates it in his work to make new connections between his Caribbean experience and that of North American blacks, chiefly through invoking the rhythms of jazz and the blues and by presenting himself as a kind of alienated jazzman, alone in his blackness in the white metropole. Perhaps most remarkably of all three poets, Césaire uses rhythm as a palliative force, a means of catharsis, and a dynamic way of sounding history and lost memory and of recovering from the depths of time the lost African-ness, the lack of which is seen as the fundamental cause of his (and his people's) neuroses. Rhythm in this sense is used by Césaire in ways that free it from the essentialist limitations that he and others have tended to impose on it. Rhythm appears in his work as a very real, potent force for disalienation and for effecting the psychological and mnemonic transformations that are the primary objectives of his entire poetic project.

POST-NEGRITUDE DISCORD

Unanimity apparently existed between Senghor, Damas, and Césaire on the essential connection between rhythm and black culture, but other contemporary figures were not so convinced. In his important collection of essays *Tracées* (1981), René Ménil—Césaire's close collaborator in the *Tropiques* group— questions the "credo" that "Césaire is black and therefore does not separate poetry and rhythm!" (173). Ménil also critiques the absolutist equation of black poetry with rhythm, calling it a "dogmatic affirmation" that, by being repeated, becomes an accepted truth (173). Even enthusiastically Africanist critics such as Georges Ngal hesitate to endorse Negritude's ideas on rhythm and black cultures. While affirming that rhythm is important in African cultures, Ngal rejects Negritude's apparent belief that rhythm occurs innately as the "internal dynamic" in black peoples (1994, 154). Rhythm's relative prominence in Africa is not down to biology but to culture; as a strictly cultural expression, it is, Ngal says, "one of the means the black has for acting on the world" (154). The African, according to Ngal, is not therefore subject to rhythm or helplessly "seized" by it, as in Negritude's Frobenius-influenced thought, but instead has a certain control or mastery of it (154).

Well before these later critiques, however, and even as the Negritude era reached its apogee in the mid- to late 1950s, newer, emerging authors, especially from the Caribbean, had already begun to question Negritude's vision of a monolithic, essentially rhythmic pan-African culture. Foremost among this newer generation was Frantz Fanon. Published in 1952, his *Peau noire, masques blancs* cast a skeptical eye over the mystical aspects of Negritude's Africanism and held it up to the everyday reality of Martinique, where Fanon believed that "the black man wants to be white" (7). Developing the psychoanalytical aspects of Césaire's work, yet abandoning the Césairean racial mysticism, Fanon grounds the analysis of Martinican subjectivity in more tersely scientific terms; his work, he states at the outset, "is a clinical study" (10).[10] Significantly, Fanon effects a turning away from pan-Africanism and looks inward to a specifically Martinican experience, insisting that because he is Caribbean his work can only apply to Caribbean people (11). From the outset, then, Fanon seeks to downplay the connections between Africa and Martinique and to debunk Negritude's vision of the Caribbean's essential, innate Africanity. Counter to Césaire's belief that the Martinican collective unconscious consists of images and memories of Africa, Fanon famously declares that the Caribbean identifies most fundamentally with and adopts subjectively the attitude of the European white man, developing "an attitude, a way of thinking and of seeing that are essentially white" (120).

Fanon's most sustained denunciation of Negritude takes place later in the essay, where he mocks the idea of rhythm as an essential part of his black being. Writing ironically of himself as an archetypal alienated Martinican intellectual, he moves through the recent history of Negritude and recalls how he decided first to call out his "black cry" and how he slowly "secreted a race" (98). This race staggered under the weight of its basic element: rhythm (98). Quoting Senghor at length—"[Rhythm] is the most tangible and least material thing. It is the vital element par excellence"—Fanon stops short and almost does a double take: "Had I read correctly? I read and re-read. From the other side of the white world, a magical black culture was calling me.... I began to redden with pride. Was that our salvation?" (98–99). Having rationalized the world, and then having been rejected by the (white) world in the name of racial prejudice, he then threw himself back toward the irrational, a way of thinking from which emanated or "vibrated" his rhythmic voice, which he then illustrates by quoting a repetitive passage from Césaire's *Cahier d'un retour au pays natal* (99). Fanon's mockery of his great predecessor—and of himself as the former editor of a student journal called, significantly, *Tam-tam*—continues in a passage where he invokes classic

Césairean imagery and vocabulary: "Eia! The tom-tom jabbers the cosmic message. Only the black man is able to transmit it, to decode its meaning, its import. Astride the world, my vigorous heels against the flanks of the world, I luster the neck of the world" (100).[11] Altering briefly his ironic tone, Fanon makes his point that "we should be wary of rhythm, of the Earth-Mother bond, this mystical, carnal marriage of the group and the cosmos" (101).

Fanon is keenly aware that the idea of innate black rhythmicity, along with Negritude's other related conceptions of blackness, did not come directly from an untainted African source but were, to a considerable extent, products of European thinkers, from Schœlcher through Frobenius, Westermann, and Delafosse (105). Disillusioned with what they considered to be a soulless European industrial civilization, such thinkers turned to Africa as a source of what had apparently been lost during centuries of rationalism and capitalism in Europe. What they saw in Africa were elements more or less the same as those promoted by Negritude: the black man as instinctive, mystical, poetic, artistic, musical, and rhythmic, in sum a means of reconnecting the Europeans with their irrational selves (107).

Although he dismisses this strain of European Africanism (which extends into the surrealism of the 1920s and 1930s) as almost naïve romanticism, Fanon is more trenchant in his denunciation of his contemporary, Jean-Paul Sartre, who had published his famous essay "Orphée noir" in 1948, four years before *Peau noire, masques blancs*. What Fanon finds particularly damaging in Sartre's essay is that Negritude is interpreted in Hegelian terms as the antithesis to the thesis of white supremacy—"an anti-racist racism" in Sartre's famous phrase, a step toward the synthesis of the universal and the "human." Fanon also critiques Sartre's argument that Negritude's raison d'être is to finally destroy itself, being only a passage and not a final destination, the means and not the end (107–8).[12] As Fanon sees it, all that this supposed "friend of the blacks" achieved in "Orphée noir" was to incorporate the great postwar generation of black poets into his broader universalist scheme and to "relativize" Negritude, as if it could only mean something in relation to the "white world" and Europe. To truly discover and understand one's consciousness, Fanon argues, one must be able to "lose oneself in the absolute," and in a key phrase he affirms that "consciousness engaged in experience ignores, must ignore the essences and the determinations of its being" (108). This phrase, which indicates the philosophical influence of Maurice Merleau-Ponty and phenomenology, is important because it indicates something of the difficult path that Fanon's work had to negotiate: a route somewhere between the relativist, assimilating impulses of rationalist European thought and the no less alienating "unfortunate romanticism" of Negritude (109).[13]

For Fanon, a true understanding of Caribbean consciousness must be firmly grounded in the analysis of experience, in the study of what *is*, not of what is putatively missing or lost. When laying out the conditions for valid inquiry into the Caribbean, Fanon not only marks a break with the racial essentialism of Negritude but also, inadvertently perhaps, maps out the future shape and direction of French Caribbean writing, which would soon make a decisive turn toward the recording and interpretation of lived experience. As a key aspect of Negritude's mystical version of blackness, one might have thought that rhythm would have been discredited completely and disappeared as a valid cultural concept in the post-Negritude era. In truth, though it has rarely been associated again with innate racial qualities, rhythm did not simply vanish but has returned in various forms and contexts, demonstrating its remarkable resilience as a cultural concept.

POST-NEGRITUDE RHYTHMS

It is not accurate to think of the movement from the Negritude to post-Negritude eras in the French Caribbean in terms of a clean break. A temporal and thematic overlap quite naturally exists between Césaire and his immediate successors in particular, notably Fanon and Glissant, who in their different ways took up Césaire's interest in psychoanalysis as a means of "curing" the neurotic black Antillean subject. Glissant's take on psychoanalysis and race is different from Césaire's, and particularly Fanon's in this respect, because Glissant is less concerned with racial politics or the quest for equality than with the problem of identity in a country like Martinique, with its very singular colonial condition as a department of France. The fundamental flaw of psychoanalysis for Glissant is its reductive universalism, which tends to ignore or have little consideration for questions of race, far less the specific situation of Martinicans. Much like Fanon, Glissant argues that the scope of psychoanalysis is simply too limited to address the contradictory and unresolved questions of identity that he feels characterize Martinican subjectivity (Britton 2002, 61–63).

Just as he takes up and modifies the terms of Césaire's and Fanon's interest in race, identity, and history, so Glissant evokes and manipulates the figure of rhythm. One of the fundamental aspects of the Martinican's alienation is his relationship with his island space, or "antispace" as Glissant terms it in *Caribbean Discourse* (1989, 160). The land is unloved and abandoned, and the freed slave prefers to live marginalized in the urban areas than take possession of the land, because the land has historically been associated with the white other and with alienating, forced work. This history has created a distorted relationship with the land and a poetics of excess, the scream, the cry (most likely of Negritude) where all "is exhausted immediately" (160). The Martinican land becomes a site on which the various kinds of historically inherited madness and neurosis—the impossibility of belonging, the compensatory urge for excess and exhaustion—

are projected. This drive for excess and exhaustion, Glissant says, denaturalizes it in the sense that it interrupts and wears out the "rhythms of the land" (160).

This rather obscure idea of an arrhythmic, out-of-step relationship with Martinican space perhaps becomes clearer in relation to Glissant's idea of a distorted Antillean experience of time. The loss of collective memory and the careful erasure of the past have made of time and history little more than a series of natural disasters, so that Martinicans have no real sense of a linear progression through time, which instead "keeps turning around in us" (161). The rhythms of time and history, like those of the land, have therefore been ruptured and denaturalized by the effects of slavery, colonialism, and departmentalization. Time turns in cycles, not in any kind of salutarily natural process but in a way that perpetuates the neurosis and alienation. This idea is developed when Glissant considers the virtually unchanging pattern of the seasons in the Tropics, which he calls the "rhythmic plainsong" that denies Martinicans the pattern of seasonal change that influences and to some degree shapes European consciousness. Glissant says that the absence of such a shifting pattern of seasons allows Martinicans to live according to "another rhythm . . . another notion of time" (161).

This other rhythm, the residue of troubled consciousness, further influences Martinicans' structures of speech. Here, too, Glissant finds a taste for excess; rhythms of language are continuously repeated because of the "peculiar sense of time" (162). These repetitive rhythms of speech are related to the key Glissantian concept of detour: the trope of resistance through indirection. Detour results, Glissant says, from a situation of domination in which there is no direct confrontation but rather an opaque set of hidden, indirect acts of resistance. In contrast to Césaire's blunt, black/white model of resistance, Glissant's detour is a means of resisting the very particular oppression that is occulted by Martinique's status as a French department and the notional equality that it enjoys with the metropole.[14] As such, detour is "the ultimate resort of a population whose domination by an Other is concealed" (19). The dominated group must look *elsewhere* for the source of its domination, which "is not directly tangible" (19). Detour, says Glissant, "is the parallactic displacement of this [search]" (20). Glissant's counterpoetics of indirect resistance does not emanate spontaneously or innocently from everyday communication; it is instead the "unconscious rhythm" of daily communication, an "instinctive denial" that has not been (and perhaps will not be) "structured into a conscious and collective denial" (163). Glissant therefore takes up many of the themes and tropes of Césaire (and Fanon) and reworks them according to his own vision of Martinique as a uniquely equal-but-repressed place, an "antispace" that perpetuates the slaves' sentiment of exile and of a distorted relationship with time. Rhythm is refigured by Glissant as a polyvalent sign of alienation and resistance—and, conversely, alienation and resistance are interpreted as polyrhythmic facets of Martinican experience. Glissant's case demonstrates that, in the post-Negritude period, rhythm has been released from the reductive racial essentialism that attracted Césaire, Senghor, and Damas. Instead of simply disappearing, rhythm persists and reappears in subsequent theorizations of Caribbean culture and identity. In this sense, post-Negritude rhythm has become less a fixed, closed marker of black identity than a floating, malleable signifier of lived Caribbean experience.

THE TRUTH OF FICTION

Although there was no clean break with Negritude's central preoccupations in Martinican writing in the 1950s and 1960s, what is striking in this period is the shift from poetry to prose narrative, a move so decisive that poetry became and remains a "relatively minor" genre in contemporary French Caribbean literature (Gallagher 2004, 451). Like Fanon and Glissant, Césaire stresses the importance of human experience, but his conception of that experience and of the role of the poet is heavily imbued with the surrealist-Frobenian-Negritudist view of existence and poetry as a means of attaining the lost African past through the poet's abandoning himself to the "vital movement" of the universe (1945, 163). The poet speaks and his words take language back to its pure state; the poet enounces the "primitive phrase" that plays with and draws on the timeless and the universal (164). Therefore, in setting out in theory and practice the role of poetry and the poet, Césaire not only fixes a conception of poetic functions but also sets a certain tenor and register for poetry that few of his literary successors in the French Caribbean have even attempted to replicate, far less develop. His elevated ideal of the poet and poetry has proved to be enduringly influential among contemporary prose writers such as Patrick Chamoiseau, Daniel Maximin, Raphaël Confiant, and Glissant, all of whom have included intertextual references to Césaire in their works even as they have challenged many of his political and cultural arguments.[15] Many of these authors have also developed prose styles that seem to capture some of the density and opacity that characterizes Césaire's poetry, and they tend to refer to their writing practices in terms of "poetics" (Gallagher 2004, 451). Yet only Glissant and, more recently, Maximin have published poetry. Glissant's *Les Indes* (1965) remains perhaps the most successful post-Césaire attempt to write in the epic poetic mode. This instance apart, it is almost as if Césaire and his view of the poet are untouchable, incontrovertible elements of French Caribbean literature.[16]

The radical shift to prose—chiefly novels, memoirs, and short stories—in the post-Negritude era can also be attributed in part to the increasing emphasis on lived experience in that period. With poetry firmly fixed in the literary imagination as a mystical means of reconnecting with the mythical African past, prose has become the favored means of investigating the "real," the everyday, and the personal (which is always nevertheless closely related with the collective). Possibly the key novel of the early post-Negritude period and a fine example of this turn to the real is Joseph Zobel's *La Rue Cases-Nègres*, a work that was published in 1950 and that represents retrospectively the Martinique of the 1930s. The novel demonstrates, among other things, Zobel's interest in music, rhythm, and dance, which was already apparent in his earlier collection of short stories, *Laghia de la mort* (1946), in which the *laghia* dance in particular is presented as a means of communicating unspoken issues of sexuality and masculinity.[17]

RHYTHM AND LIVED EXPERIENCE
IN *LA RUE CASES-NÈGRES*

A predominantly autobiographical novel, *La Rue Cases-Nègres* revisits the childhood and adolescence of a black peasant boy, José Hassam, who is raised by his grandmother on a sugar plantation in interwar Martinique and who moves through different schools (and different locations) to finally reach the very apogee of French colonial education on the island: the Lycée Schœlcher in Fort-de-France. The novel therefore has clear echoes of a classic Bildungsroman, even if, by the end, the protagonist has become distinctly ambivalent about the road he has taken and the social and cultural distance it has created between him and his original rural community. As in many post-Negritude novels, the plantation is presented as a complex, rhythmic "cradle of Creole society and culture," and, as Mary Gallagher says, the writing of the plantation experience, here and in many other Caribbean works of fiction, recalls and reproduces the rhythms of the plantation (2002, 146).

The journey taken by José from the plantation to the town is symbolic of a wider societal movement from apolitical post-slavery subjugation to the more politicized, urbanized modernity of the mid- to late twentieth century.[18] Indeed, the opening descriptions of the plantation depict a world in which little has apparently changed since the time of slavery, with virtually all adults engaged from morning until night in the demanding work in the sugarcane fields. This feeling of unfinished time is compounded by the sense that the plantation is cut off spatially from the rest of Martinique. Early in the novel, José remarks that, at the age of five years, he had never left the plantation, and when he does venture further into the hinterland with his band of friends he feels he has crossed "infinite distances" and is markedly disorientated, losing completely his "notion of place" in this "distant, unknown" location (Zobel 1950, 21). In a very real sense, therefore, José's closed, restrictive world is a place that has barely changed in the ninety years since the abolition of slavery; the plantation is a site isolated in time, a living memory of the unfinished past. The novel provides an opportunity to visualize, and equally to listen to, a world that has now disappeared but that was then largely unchanged from the time of slavery.

It is important to note that the rhythms of slavery, in terms of patterns of work and rest, sowing and reaping, are still in place on the plantation in this novel. The young José's experience of time is marked by nameless weekdays that lead up to the days whose names he knows—Saturday, Sunday, and Monday (47)—and by the ripening of seasonal fruits such as mangoes and breadfruit. For the adult workers, however, it is the less felicitously natural seasons of planting and harvesting that mark out existence (63). For the children, harvest seems like a festival, a time to suck on the plentiful sweet sugarcane, whereas the parents accompany and give rhythm to their work by singing songs that give "vigor and grace" to their actions (64). To the watching (and listening) José, the scene is entirely admirable: everything from the glowing, sweaty black and brown bodies to the glistening cutlasses and the endless songs creates, he says, "a vast music" that includes the trotting of the mules, the curses of the cart and mule drivers, the dense songs, and the never-ending, repetitive chants (64). The multifaceted music of the plantation, he says, bewitched him and cast an oppressive spell on him that he could only alleviate by joining in the rhythmic singing. The act of repeating the same words and the same tune over and again, however, has an unexpected effect: "It ended up by sinking down to the deepest part of me and weighed me down like a vague sadness. I stopped." Thus, while the rest of the field workers continue to labor obstinately "to an accelerated rhythm," José stops short, invaded by this indistinct, oppressive feeling of sorrow (65).

His narration does not explain the unexpected sensation any further, but it seems that the enchanting, rhythmic music of the plantation harvest communicates to him something of the tragedy of his people's situation; the rhythm and repetition seem to draw him into the adults' world in a way that lets him touch the deeper sadness of their lives, which again are scarcely distinguishable from those of their slave forefathers. This is rhythm as a marker and reminder of subjugation: the rhythms of the planting season, of repetitive work, and of the workers' songs that only partially numb the pain of their subjugated status.[19] These rhythms are, moreover, atemporal; it is as if their repetitions reverberate endlessly into time, which is essentially unchanging—emancipation has not radically altered poor black experience—or as if time itself has been "cancelled" (Gallagher 2002, 76). This scene is remarkable in that it provides an example of a receptive character listening to and feeling the past that is not yet over but that still swirls around him and has a tangible effect on him, invading his consciousness of the present and reminding him of the unfinished nature of history.

The notion of rhythm as a palliative force also appears in another scene. The field workers have just been paid their weekly wages, the meagerness of which only seems to compound their sense of desperation (50). For the children, the return to Rue Cases-Nègres marks the start of a party; for the adults, too, Saturday night offers a rare chance to escape the demanding world of the plantation through drumming, dancing, and drinking rum. Long after he is sent to bed, the young José—ever the attentive listener—hears above the noise, beyond the torches, out of the stink of disease and sweat the "somber pounding" of the "diabolical, irresistible" tom-tom drum (50). The rhythmic, rapid prose captures the rhythms of the dance and also some of the great energy built up in the cathartic dance: "And all of that, those purulent feet, those agitated breasts, those manly shoulders and those frenetic hips, those glazed eyes, and those rainbow smiles, all of that, gorged, drunk, and oblivious, sang in a voice burning and intrusive like a forest fire, and all of that had to dance, dance, dance" (51).

Such moments of rhythmic escape, however, offer only a temporary catharsis; they constitute one end of a cycle that will begin once more and repeat itself each Monday. In Zobel's novel, the only way to escape definitively the oppressive rhythms of work and history is through education, and José's grandmother, M'man Tine, pushes him relentlessly along that path. José is given another kind of education from Mr. Médouze, the transmitter of oral knowledge and a father figure for José, whose own father never returned to Martinique from World War I (35–36). The evenings spent at Médouze's hut initiate José into the world of the *griot,* the storyteller figure who not only shares Creole riddles and folktales but also opens up to José the past of slavery and the memory of Africa. Significantly, as Médouze goes through the ritual of lighting his pipe with a burning twig, José says that the light applies to his face "a hallucinating mask—Mr. Médouze's real face" (42). This is Médouze's "black mask," his true look that he only takes on at night, in the play of light and shadow, and not in the daytime, which is associated with the alienating rhythms and routines of work. Médouze's tales and riddles broaden José's perspective on the world, which "expands, multiplies, swims dizzyingly" around him (43).

At the same time, however, Médouze and his knowledge are involved in a struggle with M'man Tine and her belief in formal education. It is significant in this respect that José's interactions with Médouze are interrupted each night by M'man Tine calling him home. José is never allowed to hear a tale to its conclusion, and he is tellingly unsure whether M'man Tine called him too early or Médouze took too long to tell his story, whether the one is too efficient and perfunctory or the other too loquacious and rambling. Every night when he leaves Médouze, his heart is unappeased, his thirst for the *griot*'s knowledge unquenched (45).[20] In this sense, M'man Tine's priorities and dictates prevail, and these are based on quite different values from those of Médouze. It is M'man Tine who opens up to José the broader contexts of Martinique, the capital Fort-de-France, and even France, the "very distant" country that she nevertheless introduces into his imagination as a land of plenty, "where they make all kinds of nice things" (45). Importantly, then, France is related to the maternal figure, whereas it is the father figure, Médouze, who evokes Africa. In this situation of lost, absent, half-heard fathers, it is almost inevitable the maternal—M'man Tine and France—that will prevail, at least at this stage in José's development. France is also closely related to formal education, and, in her determination to save José from the "little bands" in which his friends are already employed, M'man Tine decides to send him to school to get "a bit of learning" (69). At virtually the same moment that this announcement is made, Médouze goes missing, only to be found dead, alone among the sugarcanes. Even if the men who carry his frail body say it "weighs a ton," thereby suggesting something of his weightiness and significance beyond his physical body, Médouze's death also signifies the diminishing influence of his folkloric knowledge (77). Unable to decide whether Médouze's death was a sad event or something banal, with little meaning (77), José witnesses the wake, which is also a kind of wake for his own passing childhood and is fittingly carried out in the traditional way, with rhythmic, repetitive chanting and folktales that create for José a "magical domain" of folk culture that he will never fully recuperate. In another sense, too, Médouze's death and his difficulty in completing his stories suggest the impossibility of ever fully reintegrating the fading African heritage into the Martinican present. As such, his passing represents an implicit commentary on Césaire's Negritude, which was still in the early 1950s promoting the myth of Africa and the hope of disalienation through rediscovery of the racial collective unconscious.[21]

José consoles himself over Médouze's death with the "great event" of going to school in Petit-Bourg, a small community that, though close to the plantation, José has never previously seen (83). The rhythms of the plantation are replaced by those of the daily routines of school, which bring each day "a new emotion" for José (86).[22] Perhaps ironically, the rote learning style—repeating words and sounds to mimic exactly the school mistress—recalls Médouze's Krik? Krak! storytelling style, only now he has been superseded by the female and the French. The movement from oral into written learning is represented in the way the mistress "moulds implacably" on the black background of the board the white signs of the written language. The young José does not object to this cultural "whitening," to the movement from oral to written culture; on the contrary, he delights in taking part in the repetitive "chorus" that echoes the voice of the mistress (95).

After José and M'man Tine move to Petit-Bourg, he becomes "a child of the village" (107) and has no reason or wish to return to the plantation. However, he slowly comes to realize that the village, in its social structures and race and class hierarchies, largely mirrors the plantation world. The apparently inescapable strictures and systems of the plantation reappear rhythmically, repeating themselves in their essential patterns across José's various locations. Living in the Cour Fusil, a modest row of barrack houses, José is again drawn to a father figure, in this case Mr. Assionis who, much like Médouze, is a storyteller, singer, and drummer (109). Assionis stands apart from the other men in that he does not work in the factory or on the plantation; he earns his living through playing and singing at wakes and at the Saturday night plantation parties (110). Médouze's absence is further compensated by José's schoolfriend Vireil, who shares his supernatural, folkloric tales with the class and who confirms what Médouze had told José: all the white *békés* and all the rich are *gens gagés,* people possessed by the devil who come out in various animal forms in the night (113). Vireil's warning about whites indicates a growing awareness on José's part of the internal class and race dynamics of his society, an awareness that grows through his friendship with another child, Georges Roc, "Jojo," the melancholic, illegitimate son of a well-to-do mulatto and Mam'zelle Gracieuse, a "dirty and vulgar nigger woman" (120). The political message of the novel slowly develops through investigations of such characters and the presentation of the intricate hierarchies of Martinican society.

José's new repetitive routine of school and chores in Petit-Bourg is dramatically altered and enlivened by the arrival of a traveling fair. Initially dismayed by his lack of money, José is receptive once more to the sounds of recreation and becomes enchanted by the rhythms of the carousel. Indeed, as he says, the whole village is "enthralled" by the orchestra that accompanies the carousel. From a distance, all he can hear of the music is the beat of the tom-tom that scans the waltz to which the carousel rhythmically turns. But the beat has an entrancing effect on him and his senses—he simultaneously listens to and "feels" the rhythm—and he is drawn irresistibly to its source: "It was like so many beats of a gong inviting us to its joy, so many beats struck in my guts and which, to the pain of my alarming, almost desperate, penniless situation, and which at any moment, like a coaxing, seducing voice and an irresistible and perverse force, drew us all to the market square" (150).

Just as it did on Saturday nights for the plantation workers, rhythm works as a palliative for José's despair. What is interesting is that the rhythm does not work against the pain but with and to it, almost as if it were on a common frequency that does not deny the pain but finds its beat and falls into its rhythm. Similarly, too, discrete personal subjectivity collapses—the "we" subsumes the "I"—and the collective supersedes the individual. The carousel's rhythmic music has a visceral, bodily effect that only intensifies as José is drawn closer to it: "As we approached the rhythmic drumsticks, the *shasha,* appeared and at the very moment the revolving, banner-trimmed roof appeared, the sound of the clarinet burst in my head, in my stomach, took me, pulled me ever more quickly" (150). The rhythmic sounds of the carousel are complemented and emphasized by the swirling movements of the carousel so that José, in a distinctly filmic scene, feels at once the aural and visual effects in one irresistible rhythmic ensemble. This polyrhythmic effect is narrated in prose that omits periods and gradually reduces the length of clauses to form one long, rhythmic sentence: "Then, seeing the women who, under the effect of the music walked rolling their shoulders and shaking their behinds, the men whose hips rolled strangely, seeing up close the carousel horses turning with children in white dresses and red bows, children in new suits, children in polished shoes, black children, laughing clearly and passionately, and feeling in the very depths of me the convulsion of the tom-tom beats, hard and soft like a thick blood, I remained in a kind of trance that lasted for a long time" (150).

From José's perspective as a spectator, the carousel swirls and entrances in color and sound until the identity of the children on the horses becomes indistinct, lost, at least for the duration of the ride. Similarly, the rhythmic sounds and motions seem to alter the experience of time: the children are transported to a state of being outside or, perhaps, *inside* time and space. The penniless José is desperate, however, to switch from spectator to participant, to be the one with the blurred identity. He realizes that, from the perspective of the participant on the horses, turning at great speed to the beat of the tom-tom, it is impossible to see the spectator, while on the outside the crowd "could not distinguish those who turned" (151). In other words, only from the seat on the horses is identity completely, albeit momentarily, lost—or indeed that it is found, released from the gaze of the community and from its strictures and hardships. It is significant in this regard that what prevents José from pushing onto the carousel like some of the other boys do for a free ride is the thought of M'man Tine and her presence on his conscience, which even when she is physically absent keeps him on the path of respectable, nondeviant behavior and away from total surrender to the swirling, rhythmic world of escape and liberty (151). Much as she had done with Médouze, therefore, M'man Tine directs José away from the popular and the Creole. The image of him standing on the outside in his school uniform, on the threshold of the absolute liberty and surrender of identity that the carousel offers, is a poignant one, suggesting something of the split subjectivity of José and the difficulty he has and will have of reconciling the world of education and respectability with his instincts for escape and rhythmic release.[23]

This remarkable sequence presents a striking example of rhythm as a very real force that invites and seduces the poorest, in particular, into an intimate relationship with it and a different state of consciousness that offers a kind of escape and healing. In a sense, Zobel comes close to suggesting, like Césaire, that rhythm is an essential aspect of the black man, something innate, "hard and soft like a thick blood" as José says (150). And yet, however much the people are drawn irresistibly to the rhythm, in placing the event in the everyday existence of the village Zobel is able to avoid the questionable mysticism of Césaire's poetry and to present the phenomenon in more ethnographic, phenomenological terms. If the people do have a visceral connection to rhythm, it is grounded in everyday existence and therefore has a function that can be partially explained with reference to the hardships of that existence and to the way that rhythm has historically offered escape and healing to the Martinican poor. Moreover, Zobel's fairground rhythms are creolized in that they mix the African tom-toms with the beats and melodies of the carousel orchestra's European instruments, creating a hybrid musicality that reflects the broader cultural fusions that are truer legacies and reflections of Martinique's complex history than Césaire's more monolithic drumming. Zobel also suggests a more sophisticated understanding of rhythm than is found in Fanon's *Peau noire, masques blancs,* in which rhythm is mockingly derided as a remnant of Negritude's mysticism with no apparent role in Fanon's own attempt to represent Martinican sensibility. Zobel seems to hit on precisely the right track between Césaire's essentialism and Fanon's sweeping denunciations, thereby suggesting a new, potentially valuable model for future analyses of Martinican rhythm.

Such examples of close intimacy with Martinican popular culture are, however, rare in the novel. More common is José's growing sentiment of educationally induced assimilation and alienation. In the classroom, he learns the names of French rivers and mountains and the dates of military victories, and he practices dictation, the art of reinscribing faithfully the words of the master (155–56). His education also brings him into new social contexts that in turn further sensitize him to the complexities of his society. This slow process of political awakening gathers momentum in the third and final section of the story, in which José, having won a quarter-scholarship, moves to Fort-de-France to attend the Lycée Schœlcher. On his first visit, the city appears to José to be bigger and noisier than the most monstrous factories or plantations he could have imagined (162). Later, though, when he relocates with his mother to the new district of Sainte-Thérèse, he is immediately moved by the energy of the place and of the newly arrived population of black urban workers whom he considers to be "pioneers" (194). In a sense, these people represent an urbanized version of his own country folk: singing, shouting, and working but with a new vitality born of the freedom that the city offers. Away from the new popular districts, however, and particularly on the Route Didier where his mother works as a housekeeper for a wealthy *béké,* José remarks how subservient blacks are and how they try to live invisible, "erased" existences in the white neighborhood (196).

It is on Route Didier that José meets Carmen, a character who recalls Médouze with his storytelling and singing but who is closer to José in age and thus more of an older brother than a father figure (197). Having been born on a plantation and followed the "natural stages" in the destiny of a plantation child—cattle and mule driver in the fields, then military service in Fort-de-France—Carmen represents, to some extent, José's own alternative destiny, had he not "branched off" down his own path (198). Carmen's life serves as a reminder of the hardships of the plantation and thus helps José to avoid any nostalgic romanticization of the world he has left, however ambivalent he is about the one he has entered. Significantly, the only salutary aspect of the plantation that Carmen invokes concerns rhythm: on certain evenings, he would tap the rhythms of plantation songs with his fingers on the side of the table (201). José recognizes the songs through their beats, even if the words Carmen sings are unfamiliar. José explains this by saying that the plantation blacks are so keen to sing the songs that pass from one location to another that they care little for the words, adapting them to reflect local concerns and events. What remains constant is the beat, which thus acts as a kind of social glue and a metalanguage that is the most consistent and unchanging—yet also dynamic and energizing—aspect of poor black culture. The simple beats of Carmen's fingers, accompanied by his singing and whistling, have the capacity to transport José back to some of the most memorable rhythm-induced moments of his childhood: "Carmen continued, singing and whistling, beating softly tom-tom rhythms with such an intensity of inspiration, so much joy and sensual vigor that I stayed there for a long time listening to him, mute, almost in a trance" (201). The sensual, joyful, inspiring rhythms form a mnemonic link to José's previous experiences on the plantation and at the fairground, those entrancing moments when he is taken out of the material conditions of his existence and enters into a trance-like state in which, once again, he finds identity through losing himself. He is absent yet present and living intensely, as he never is in the everyday run of things.

In each of these rhythmic experiences, José is the spectator and the listener rather than the producer of the rhythm, which seems to be the preserve of the truly popular and unschooled. Caught somewhere between a complex set of dichotomous worlds—urban and rural, educated and uneducated, French- and Creole-speaking, black and white, rich and poor, traditional and modern, rhythmic and arrhythmic—José is typically cast in the novel as an outsider and observer, a passive spectator rather than an active participant. At this stage, he perhaps suggests something of the awkwardness of the bookish Antillean author vis-à-vis rhythm and the difficulty the author figure has of truly engaging with the popular. José's final movement out of this passive state, after the death of M'man Tine, seems to purge this awkwardness and is signaled by discordant sounds that assail him with a visceral violence: the ringing and chiming that pierce his ears, the beating of his heart, and the uncontrollable growling in his chest (238). These sounds mark the beginning of José's grieving for M'man Tine and also of his metamorphosis from passive child into active writer and chronicler of his life and of the existence of his people. Whereas rhythmic sounds had previously brought on a privileged, trance-like and blissful state, these violent, discordant sounds seem to purge him of his passivity and reticence (and also of his trauma) and act cathartically, heralding a new purposeful and engaged rebirth for José. Lying in his bed, surrounded by the muted Carmen and Jojo, it is José who realizes that he must now take the initiative, tell them a story, his story, which is also their collective story and which will, he says, be shouted to those who do not see and do not listen (240). The writer will therefore retain an important connection to oral storytelling and to bearing testimony for the collectivity. And rhythm, as an enduring aspect of the popular tradition, will continue to feature in the French Caribbean novel as a historical, political, and cultural theme and as a structuring device, creating circles and waves of narrative rather than linear, progressive movements. As José concludes the novel, he also in a sense starts it, or starts it again, by indicating that the novel we have just read is the one he will write.[24] In this way, Zobel casts his novel in the kind of circular pattern that typifies oral narrative, thus inscribing repetitive rhythmicity into the very structure of his work in a way that prefigures similar structures in the French Caribbean fiction that was to follow.[25]

RHYTHMS, HISTORY, AND MEMORY
IN *LE QUATRIÈME SIÈCLE*

Zobel's tentative inclination toward repetitive, rhythmic narrative structure is taken up and developed in all its complexity in Glissant's fiction, which is notoriously and willfully nonlinear in its structure and in its presentation of time and history. Glissant's *Le Quatrième siècle* (1964) is a classic of Caribbean fiction that has the historical sweep of epic narrative. It traverses more than 150 years of Martinican history, from 1788 to 1946, through the retelling of the story of the Longoué and the Béluse families, who are descended from two Africans, one a maroon, the other a plantation slave, both of whom arrived in Martinique on the same ship in 1788. However, Glissant's narrative is far removed from conventional historical fiction; its interest lies less in reordering time and events than in the mechanics of the telling of the history, in recording a Martinican notion and experience of history, and in showing how, for him, time is a slippery, elusive concept that contracts and expands and loses itself now and again in the swirling, rhythmic historical movements around which the book is shaped.[26]

Much like Zobel does with Médouze and José, Glissant juxtaposes a *griot* storyteller figure, Papa Longoué, with a young boy, Mathieu Béluse, and structures his historical and existential investigation around their exchanges.[27] In both cases, the boys have been to French colonial schools, but, whereas *La Rue Cases-Nègres* largely follows the movement of a classical Bildungsroman, Glissant's Mathieu refuses to finish secondary school (260) and can only recall from his time there sparse fragments that come to him intermittently (257). In both novels, the storyteller figures are virtually destitute: Médouze is "the oldest, the poorest, the most abandoned" person on the whole plantation (41); Papa Longoué, in his ragged trousers and dirty vest, resembles a "black mummy half stripped of his clothes" (13–14). Both are resolutely men of the hinterland: Médouze lives and dies around the plantation; Papa Longoué never goes to town (256) and sees it as "the unnamable thing" that, with its "spluttering," discordant music, is not only arrhythmic but also ahistoric, "the closed vase where the history of the land and the knowledge of the past gets stuck down and loses itself" (221). Papa Longoué, like Médouze, is presented as the last in the line of storytellers, a fading "not very good" *quimboiseur* whose knowledge is incomplete and failing (17). In both stories, the juxtaposition of the old man and the young boy stresses the fundamental questions of history and memory: the boy places himself before the man, demands to know more about history, and implicitly asks in what ways the old man's knowledge is relevant to the young boy; the old man sounds out history, which comes back to him in irregular movements and fragments that confuse and frustrate almost as much as they clarify and respond to the child's need to know. In the two novels, these exchanges are characterized by pauses, interruptions, and discontinuities.

Glissant's Mathieu often comes to see Papa Longoué early in the morning, but at irregular intervals that make his intentions unclear. On each visit he stays until night, waiting with a "savage indifference" for the rare moments when the old man will finally continue with his story of the ancestors (13). The *griot*'s storytelling style is marked by diversions and detours, circular repetitive movements that do not advance the story as such but turn it around and cast it into different shapes. The point of the story is not so much to reveal the past—Papa Longoué says Mathieu wants "to know a story that [he] knows already" (13)—as to ponder the nature of the past and of pastness and to reflect on the possibility of truly knowing the past.[28] "How can this little boy know the end and the beginning," Papa Longoué wonders, when nobody remembers yesterday, and when yesterday is "defunct" (13). Like Papa Longoué, Mathieu is aware of the oblivion in which the Martinican people live and, moreover, of the alienating effects of this ignorance of the past, which leads them to reach out to Europe (and Africa), to the "manners of an other, whose voice and ways they would never be able to imitate" (31).[29] Even before meeting Papa Longoué, Mathieu is gripped by the realization that there is "another past," which is described as a land of "extinguished or forbidden truths" (261).[30] In a sense, Mathieu does not live or grow in the present; rather, he is a "young plant" who "grows in yesterday," whose trajectory points toward the past and to the impenetrable shadows of the night, even as the old man, paradoxically, looks toward the future and the imminence of his death (13). Indeed, Papa Longoué's status as a *quimboiseur* indicates that he is the "master" of the future (14). It is out of this complexity of temporal imperatives—the young man who only wants to know about history, the old man who possesses in a sense the future but who, feeling time constricting around him, is compelled to speak of the past—that history is conjured up in the novel.

In comparison to Zobel's Médouze, who fades away quickly, unable to truly dredge up the past, Papa Longoué persists and relentlessly digs into, chips away at, and sounds the depths of the past. Significantly, José only ever sees a tiny slit of Médouze's eyes, which remain almost shut (42), whereas Papa Longoué's eyes are wide open and alive, difficult to look into for any length of time because they have seen all the "subterfuges of the present and the heavy mysteries of the past" (14). Papa Longoué's relative effectiveness as a *griot* lies in part in this ability to see the sweep of time, in relating the obscure depths of the past to the deceptions of the present. His art is not, however, simply a question of seeing; it is a complex system of remembrance that involves his other senses, notably hearing, his skill for listening to and gauging the "weight of the silence, this accumulation of lightning flashes, this mass of heat piled up in the heat itself by the slow power of the two men, by their motionless patient confrontation" (14). Later, he says he can smell the odor of vomit, blood, and death from the slave ship the *Rose-Marie;* his mother Stéfanise, he says, taught him it (23).

History, much like the monotonous present, is itself largely characterized by repetitions and returns. At one point, in an image that recalls José's fairground scene in *La Rue Cases-Nègres,* the recurrent slave revolts are almost banalized; they are described as a fact of the "*merry-go-round* of suffering," the constant, recurring movement of history (101).[31] Appropriately, then, rhythm plays an important part in Papa Longoué's sensual evocation of the past. Mathieu's patience is finally, inevitably rewarded with a rhythmic flow of words from the *quimboiseur* "in that imperceptible language, full of mannerisms and repetitions, which nevertheless led surely towards a knowledge that existed beyond words, that only Papa Longoué could fathom" (14). The repetitions and returns are indeed the single key element in these evocations, as Papa Longoué has no idea of what he will say but is guided by the "capricious flow of words; yes, by that way of speaking that was so well attuned to the density of the day, to the weight of the heat, to the slow memory" (14). Thus, it is the "way of speaking," the rhythm, and the repetition that is primary and that precedes revelation and knowledge, which are implicitly not relics of the past but are living and dynamic, ready to be reformed and reunderstood according to the flow of the words.

Glissant emphasizes the rhythmic aspects of memory and history, but he seems to neglect or abandon the drum as a more straightforward repository and producer of collective rhythmicity. In *La Rue Cases-Nègres,* the two wakes— first for Médouze, then for M'man Tine—are carried out to the rhythms of the drums and the traditional songs in a way that, to some extent, reconnects the Martinican present to the African past. In Glissant's novel there is also a wake with rhythmic beating of drums, but it is a quite different occasion, with quite different connotations. First, there is no actual death in Glissant's wake; the father of Papa Longoué's lover Edmée, embittered by her departure five years previously, decides to hold a wake for her. The father insists on following in every detail the rituals of the wake: lighting candles, procuring holy water, and preparing food and drink for the mourners. A tom-tom is played, and the heavy beating hangs over the surrounding hills, above the trees, and along the barely traced paths. The rhythm is imperfect, however; the drumming occasionally "sputters," missing a beat (216). Indeed, the whole event seems out of step and is paradoxically more deathly and somber than a conventional wake: "This tom-tom flowed gloomily over the Touffaille district, where all that gives light and movement to a wake (the thick-voiced storytellers, the lewd dancers, the trembling children, the food, and the familiarity with the deceased) was that night as absent as the presumed dead person" (216).

The imperfect, gloomy rhythms of the tom-tom complement the deathly atmosphere; its beats "die in the black hole of the room where the lamp gave less light than a candle" (216). Moreover, the sound of the tom-toms "came from too far away," which perhaps suggests that the temporal and spatial distance between Martinique and the drums' origins in Africa distorts and weakens their sound and consequently their ability to bring life and a sense of continuity to a dying place.[32] As the wake progresses, the true object of mourning becomes the Touffaille district itself. The father, forgetting Edmée, lays out the spirit of the Touffaille on the death bed, the sons respond ritually to the father's chants, and the daughters bring to the lifeless litany the "weight of their silence" and are gradually enveloped in the "long hymn of abandon," a silent lament for the ills of their district (217). The drums themselves die as the deathly parody marks the death of the Touffaille, an inevitable demise that is apparently signaled in the very name of the district, which seems a corruption of "Tout faillit" or "everything fails."

Glissant seems similarly ambivalent about the practice of rhythmic, call-and-response chanting and the figure of the cantor, the chorus leader who has much in common with the *chantwelles* of the early Trinidad *kalinda* bands. In Glissant's version of Martinican history, the cantor figure appeared not so much at a certain time but rather in the space, the clearing that opened up between the wild humus and the domestic compost, therefore out of decomposition and decay. The singers came out of the nothingness, "born from their own beatitude" to praise beauty, and, in a country where to sing is to "become free," the coming of the singers was inevitable. Glissant's ambivalence toward the singers is first suggested in his quoting of one of their songs that depicts a harmonious, rhythmic life on the plantation: "How fine it was, in ordered lines, to the rhythm of the tom-tom, and in the joyful assurance of work, to cut the cane: while far away the trade winds caressed the softness of the flowers, the fruits, the leaves, and the branches" (222).

Rhythm functions in this instance palliatively but also as a phenomenon that entrances, lulls, and finally deadens the senses, distorting reality. Thus, in lauding the fragile beauty of the place and of plantation work, the singers are unaware of the "robe of death" that envelops this beauty (222). The rhythmic singing is an amnesiac act, a way of forgetting the everyday horrors of the plantation. The singer feigns voluptuous pleasure and pursues sources of joy without knowing that they will finally fall away from his outstretched hand. But he will not be able to forget the "obscure lack" that will be a permanent reminder of "the man who stirs in the forgotten depths of his soul" (222). There will remain, therefore, an ineradicable memory of the singer's situation, a core of truth that his delusive rhythms will not be able to penetrate.

The singer is also implicated in the amnesia that develops between the field workers and the white masters, perpetuating the entire plantation system. Glissant suggests this rather obliquely in a passage where he first presents Mathieu Béluse (the young boy's father) in a kind of temporal impasse, where he is stuck in an unending past, with no present, and with a future that is only attainable by crossing a precipice in which the "emasculated singers, men of refinement and good will" dance their elegant dance, stamping beneath their feet the discolored bones that sometimes jut out of the earth, on the terrain where the anonymous heroes of the past cry out still (224). These heroes—maroons and other rebels— will never be resuscitated, never be raised up from the earth; they will remain buried by the popular conception that their struggle was in vain, because the post-Emancipation period had leveled the differences between the maroons and the slaves, between resistance and compliance. Instead of digging up these heroes and reinstating them in popular memory, the people during this period turn to the sea and to Africa, trying to "dry up the ocean" not to return to Africa but to "run across the miry sea bottom," entangled in the past and still separated from the land. At the same time, they enter into a complicit amnesia with the master, Lapointe, helping him to draw up his latest report, which seems to take the place of collective memory and to be a metaphor for the official recording and transmission of events on the plantation. And because this report will tell stories that are difficult to bear, the words will be light and flowery, with honeyed turns of phrase that will suppress in language the "incongruous horror" of the account (225). It is this tacitly agreed-on amnesia, wrapped in the sugary phrases of the Creole language—a "language of complicity"—that creates what Glissant calls the "mania for languid folklore," which in turn creates a kind of false commonality between the whites and the blacks (225).

These examples—the wake without a deceased, the joyful yet joyless singer complicit in perpetuating the plantation system—indicate most obviously that Glissant does not see an easy connection or continuity between African tradition and Caribbean experience.[33] In the first case, the distorted, at times arrhythmic drums of the wake seem powerless to bring life back to a dying community and instead act as apposite accompaniments to a disjointed, out-of-step existence. In the second instance, the rhythmic call-and-response singing creates only a superficial, delusory sense of bliss that is ultimately incapable of eradicating the miserable and brutal truth of plantation life and that is easily co-opted by the white planter to perpetuate the system. Thus, Glissant has no nostalgic vision of Africa as an eternally enriching motherland. The slave ship—something like in Césaire's poem "Batouque"—is a kind of matrix for Glissant's characters: the first of the Longoués does not forget Africa, but the sea journey, the whippings, and the other (Béluse) with whom he shared the journey "had already made him a Longoué"—that is, something new, unforeseen, and idiosyncratic (46). For Papa Longoué, the day of his ancestor's arrival in Martinique in July 1788 is the beginning, "the first day, the first cry, the sun and the first moon and the first century of the country" (74). The country does not, therefore, precede the first of the Longoués; rather, the day of his arrival marks the beginning of the country, which is itself transformed or born anew at the moment of arrival. Personal history thus takes precedence over and instigates collective historical experience. Also, Glissant's emphasis on the personal and the intimate marks a radical shift from Negritude's attempts to evoke the past: for Césaire, the key to individual subjectivity lay in the collective identity; for Glissant, it is conversely in the individual and idiosyncratic that any investigation of wider group identity must begin.[34] And to make a final distinction with Zobel's Médouze, who sought out an order, a teleology of the past—who was born after whom and so on—Glissant's storyteller lays his trust in sounding the rhythms and pulses of the past, in letting them invade his sensibility and feeling them come to him in their own movements and their own time, a process that confounds the notion of an easily understandable historical teleology.[35]

Papa Longoué's rhythmic sounding of the past is not a search for lucidity. As Mathieu realizes, in contrast to his own desire to "advance the story, put the events in order" (30), the *quimboiseur* is repelled by logic and clarity (14). The two, however, share a fear of words (and implicitly the way words tend to fix meaning), and they only advance with care *in* (not toward) knowledge, which is itself a concept that relates more to feeling and sensing the nature of the impenetrable and unknowable than to knowing with any kind of certainty what is not known or lost. Mathieu's apparently innocent request and question—"Tell me the past, Papa Longoué! What is the past?" (15)—indicate in fact the most fundamental interests of the book: the need to tell the past, whatever the difficulties involved in such a narration, and the equally pressing need to know the nature of the past, to know whether it is over or comes back in cycles, and whether indeed it is knowable in any real sense. As Papa Longoué realizes, the "childlike" form of the question is deceptive in that it raises some of the most basic yet difficult issues of memory, history, and narrative, issues that, as he recognizes, are to "completely engage him" in the ten years over which his exchanges with Mathieu develop (15). Typically, too, the response to Mathieu's question does not come immediately but is deferred and comes quite unpredictably in a dense narrative passage in the middle of the novel. Speaking specifically about the violence between the scions of the original patriarchs Anne and Liberté, Papa Longoué's deferred reply reveals much about his notion of the past and how it conflicts with the more rational view of Mathieu, who regularly interrupts the narrative, doubting the veracity of certain events and questioning the *quimboiseur*'s ability to tell the past: "When you say: 'the past,' how can you expect to know if there even is a past, when you do not see the violence without cause planted in [Anne's] heart like a figuier-maudit tree?" (146). The key aspect of this initial response is the fact that the past—Anne's violence—is "without cause"; in other words, there is no reason for it and no basis for the kind of rational, cause-and-effect explanation that Mathieu often requests. Consequently, the past is not, or not solely, made up of explicable events and acts. Certain episodes occur for obscure reasons or for no reason at all, and Papa Longoué insists that his retelling of the past must take these aspects into account: "Because the past is not in what you know with certainty, it is also in all that passes like the wind and which nobody grasps within their closed hands" (146). Moreover, Papa Longoué insists, Mathieu's desire for closed certainties excludes the unknown and the never-known, which are parts of the past that the rational, "scientific" historical narrative does not incorporate.[36] Science, Papa Longoué says, does not "give the thing," because, as he observes, Mathieu sits shaking feverishly before him, "without even having a cutlass in sight" (147). Nor, Papa Longoué says, can the literate Mathieu understand that which is not found in books (40). Mathieu reads, Papa Longoué says, in order to forget the small details, the odors, and the facts of everyday life that are crucial to a full explanation. His young companion will never know, the *quimboiseur* says, how much he has lost in reading his books, in "spelling them out from a to z" (121). The past, Papa Longoué says, is not like a palm kernel, straight and smooth with the tuft at the bottom, but begins with the first root, which then spreads, sprouting endlessly to the clouds (147). Crucially, then, the past is not the seed of the present; there is no kernel or irreducible core to be conceived of and held in one's hand. Rather, it has unseen, subterranean beginnings that then grow in unpredictable, unsystematic ways, endlessly, vertically, through space itself.[37]

The rhythmic aspects of history are further suggested in the way the novel relates the past and memory to the movement of the wind. The first instance of this phenomenon (in the story if not in the sequence of the narrative) occurs when the fugitive slave Longoué runs to the hills and feels the wind, not around him or all over his body, but which "followed like a river the tracks of the whip" on his back, as if the wind were traveling a road on his back, which is like the land itself, scarred and bloody (44–45). This is the wind insinuating itself into the very real and raw primary scars of history: it has a presence and a timelessness that brings it (and history) back, rhythmically, as the maroon soon realizes, in "wave after wave, endlessly" (45). Papa Longoué is at all times sensitive to the movement of the wind and its relationship to historical changes. Described as a figure alone in his family lineage, who has "never been able to link anything to anything, nor his father to his son, nor consequently the past to the future" (19), Papa Longoué insists there is no chain of history, with each link in its correct, ordered place. Instead, history is like the wind, a force that rushes into the deepest part of the *quimboiseur,* and it has a vertical movement that begins at the bottom of the trees and rises right up to the sun (19). Papa Longoué is not truly incorporated into this historical movement but is merely "the caressing surface of the wind" (19).

This idea of history as a rhythmic wind movement is developed as Papa Longoué and Mathieu sit around their fire and the wind rises, stoking up the embers in "rhythmic bursts" that burn out quickly, "consumed in the violence of the air" (19). The cauldron vacillates between the three black stones on which it sits; the earth itself moves like "waves of clay reeling towards the shack," and the wind, which had not yet reached the height of a man, "rose up with regularity" (19). There is something in this scene that acts as a metaphor for the rhythmic processes of history and memory: the rising, regular movements of the wind momentarily vivify the fire on which sits the pot, just as the unpredictable force of memory brings to life the past, heating up the soup or stew of historical narrative. The pot itself, the narrative, sits precariously on its stone base, while the earth, the land, moves in rhythmic waves that seem to threaten Papa Longoué's shack. The wind, Papa Longoué confirms, is the past, is what Mathieu "has been asking about" (19). At times, too, the wind in all its upward movement seems to mock the two men, who are "run to earth by uncertainty, oblivion, by memory itself when it did not respond to hope" (38).[38]

Unwilling to accept this rhythmic, wind-like conception of history, Mathieu often interjects Papa Longoué's narrative with his demands for a more ordered retelling. These demands are consistently frustrated: seeking to "sweep away the wind from his temples," he is impotent against the rising breeze, which "can never be chased" (34). Somewhat paradoxically, therefore, in terms of syntax and style, Papa Longoué's narrative is relatively well ordered and coherent, whereas the most rhythmic, repetitive parts of the narrative itself relate to Mathieu's own thoughts and expectations. Mathieu's rage for order is narrated in the most disordered, rhythmic, and repetitive prose in the whole novel, as in the following passage where Mathieu imagines the first Longoué coming ashore from the slave ship: "For he would have preferred oh rowing boat me rowing boat and he me on the stomach the powder me boat and hit on the back the current and the water each foot me rope slide for and die the harbor country and so far far away and nothing me nothing nothing to end fall the salty, salty, salty water on the back and blood and fish and food oh country the country . . . me the end without hope and faces faces of beasts shouts holes hair but without eyes without look me the wind and leave in the whip delirium delirium delirium" (35).

These rhythms are quite different in form and function from those of the wind and the wider historical and temporal movement. Mathieu's rhythms are born of his desire for irrevocable truths—"the certainty that it was all finished, unable to return" (35)—and in this sense he is out of step with the wind-like, rhythmic shape of history that Papa Longoué offers, which returns in waves, unpredictably, with a force of its own. Mathieu's mania for order leads to a breakdown of syntax and to a staccato rhythmicity that is, in this instance, related to his delirium. Thus, somewhat paradoxically, the need for rational, closed interpretations creates a disordered, manically repetitive narrative, whereas Papa Longoué's vision of rhythmic, unknowable history is narrated in relatively ordered, coherent prose, with its own rhythms and repetitions that function more as structural features, shaping the narrative, turning it back upon itself, than as primary elements of language and syntax.[39]

There is a constant struggle in the novel between the two modes of historical narration: Mathieu's ordered, sequential mode, and Papa Longoué's more disordered, rhythmic, repetitive style, which originates in his first ancestor, who "had not tried to think nor to put in order," for "order and thought are for today" (47). Papa Longoué's narrative allows for and incorporates doubt and imperfect memory, and his recollections are often preceded by "perhaps" (55), presented as hypotheses and guesswork rather than as undoubted truths, or else are pure acts of invention and imagination (72). At times, Mathieu's preference for logic and reason prevails, and Papa Longoué is forced to "follow the path of 'the most logical'" and to explain "in *that*, in *therefore*, in *after* and *before*, with knots of *why* in his head, drowned in a tempest of *because*" (47). At other points, however, Mathieu's resistance to Papa Longoué's narrative weakens, and he finds the frequency, the rhythm of the *quimboiseur*'s evocations. One instance of this occurs, significantly, just as the wind rises above the shack, climbing toward the clouds, leaving the two figures below silent amid the "swift, motionless time" in a privileged situation that seems out of time and yet intimately connected to the rhythms of history (41). In a kind of epiphany, Mathieu glimpses quite suddenly the slave ship and its narrow cabin, smells its odor, sees the rifles and pistols nailed to the wall, and notices the empty rum flasks and the box with red marbles to count the number of dead among the cargo (41). This is the first time that Mathieu finds himself completely "surrounded by the power of the *quimboiseur*, without the time to study what is true" (41). In another epiphanic moment, Mathieu realizes that the *quimboiseur* is revealing the "real truth" of the past (220). Quite significantly, too, Papa Longoué's mnemonic process involves connecting with the rhythms of planting, harvesting, and production that shape plantation life. It is not, therefore, that Mathieu is unable to find or tune into the rhythm of history; rather, it is that, in favoring the rational and the scientific, he diminishes his chances of finding, seeing, smelling, hearing, and touching history in the way that Papa Longoué does. Nor is it that the *quimboiseur* is the exclusive defender or guardian of this history, because it is apparently accessible to others if they abandon the need to know things with certainty, which in turn may allow them to sense the fluctuating, unpredictable rhythms of the past.

Indeed, toward the end of the novel there is a more definite sense of Mathieu finding the rhythm of history. Railing against those in Martinique who claim Amerindian ancestry, even though all of the island's Caribs were exterminated, Mathieu identifies a general urge to forget the Middle Passage, to erase forever and by any means the "furrow in the sea" (268). The mania for the (European and African) other and elsewhere will only be cured, he realizes, by digging into the "contiguous land," an act that finally creates a bodily felt sensation of the past, "the shaking that passes into your eyes, which sings to you" (269). The land becomes a "reality torn from the past" but also the "past unearthed from the real"—in other words, the primary site on which this temporal, spatial, and historical reordering is effected (279). Mathieu finally adopts and repeats Papa Longoué's words, teaching the old man "timeless truths" just as the *quimboiseur* reaches the end of his life (269) and as the Longoué family line dies out (287). Papa Longoué therefore succeeds in passing on to Mathieu his understanding of the past, which is a kind of dehumanized and troubling experience of history, the "bodyless, faceless anxiety that was his lot" (273). Mathieu inherits this notion of the past as a form of knowledge that "stiffens," hardens the individual in the land and pushes the individual and the collectivity forward into tomorrow (280). But as his old collaborator and future wife Mycéa insists, this knowledge, once gained, this past, once remembered, must be forgotten and left behind if Mathieu and Martinique are to exist more concretely in the present and to contemplate more clearly the future (285).[40] For the first time, the land is "tied up with Time" (279). Mathieu grasps a sense of the future and sees that the "light is in front," that he has found a way out of the past through finding the elusive yet insistent rhythm of Martinican history (269).[41]

PAN-CARIBBEAN AND PAN-AMERICAN RHYTHMS
IN *L'ISOLÉ SOLEIL*

Glissant's influence ripples across subsequent French Caribbean fiction so rhythmically and insistently that it is possible to trace Glissantian themes and figures in the great majority of Antillean novels from the 1970s to the present. Perhaps nowhere is this influence so apparent and so ably incorporated and developed than in the novels of Daniel Maximin. Much like Glissant's novels, Maximin's are characterized by self-referential narrative structures that question history in a way that "puts in question our ability to know the past" (Nesbitt 2003, 148).[42] Maximin's *L'Isolé soleil* (1981) largely introduces the themes and characters that he revisits in his subsequent two novels, *Soufrières* (1987) and *L'île et une nuit* (1995), and is a sprawling historical epic in the Glissantian vein, traversing five generations of Guadeloupean history from slavery to the contemporary period and tracing the evolution of a discourse of resistance to colonial domination and assimilation. As in Glissant's work, the past in *L'Isolé soleil* is not a static, closed entity, and Maximin's writing is informed by his conviction that any people creates for itself multiple, shifting conceptions of the past, that "the present always invents a past for itself out of its own desire" (quoted in Zimra 1989, xxvii). The ancestral past and the predominantly masculinist identity that are typically associated with Guadeloupean history are, for Maximin, little more than "inventions generated out of desire, a rhetorical *inventio*" (Bongie 1998, 358).

Maximin's characters, again like Glissant's, are obsessed with the past, with reinventing history, and with various modes of remembrance, including personal letters, private diaries, intertextual references to Césaire and the *Tropiques* group, the historical memory of Guadeloupean rebel Louis Delgrès ("incinerated in our memories" [Maximin 1981, 19]), and writing fiction itself. The central figure, Marie-Gabriel, is primarily preoccupied with reconstructing the lost notebook of her father, Louis-Gabriel, who died in a 1962 plane crash in Guadeloupe. Louis-Gabriel had written a history of the Caribbean, and Marie-Gabriel's narrative becomes in part a "simulacrum of her father's journal" as she invents a new history that also incorporates the rediscovered writings of her ancestor Jonathan, her mother Siméa's journal, and the notebook of her friend Adrien (Murdoch 2001, 109). An important aspect of Marie-Gabriel's project is the shift she effects from the male-centered stories of the past to a narrative that incorporates and validates women's histories. More generally, Marie-Gabriel is charged with unlocking and repossessing the past: "You will open the drawers of our confiscated history, the heroic and the cowardly parts, those of hunger, fear, and love; you will refresh the memory of testimonies and stories, you will make truth work for the imagination, and not vice versa" (Maximin 1981, 18). This distinction, which prioritizes imagination over truth, recalls the way Glissant, in *Le Quatrième siècle*, favors a remembrance evoked from the senses and the imagination over the memories contained in facts, dates, and incontrovertible truths.

There is also a similar dialogic construction of history, a swirl of narrative voices both past and present, figured around the two central voices of Marie-Gabriel and Adrien. The "drawers" of memory in Maximin's novel are related to three key moments in the growth of Guadeloupean consciousness: first, and most fundamentally, to 1802, when the French army landed in Guadeloupe to bolster

Napoleon's reintroduction of slavery after eight years of abolition, and when the mulatto army officer Delgrès led a popular revolt, which ended with his and his soldiers' mass suicide at Fort Matouba. The second key moment was World War II, when Guadeloupe was controlled by the Vichy government and resistance inhered in indirect satire and parodies. Third, the crash of a Boeing aircraft carrying the leaders of the Guadeloupean independence movement in the 1960s is evoked as a traumatic moment and related to the wider global maelstrom of racial militantism and to the American Black Power movement in particular. Each of these moments is linked to various periods when island history clashed or meshed with broader historical developments, when events on the small island resonated directly with the outside world. This more outward-looking perspective marks another distinction from Glissant's *Le Quatrième siècle,* which, relatively speaking, is more resolutely focused inward, toward the specificity and idiosyncrasies of Martinique and its history.

Consequently, and again in specific relation to Glissant's novel, Maximin's work tends to incorporate outside (black, diasporic) influences more freely and with more conviction. Although Glissant's novel is firmly grounded in the specifics of the French Antilles, and though Glissant believes that in many crucial aspects the Caribbean has a shared history, Maximin's idea of a common Caribbean (and black Atlantic) culture suggests more directly a fundamental bond between different islands that generally transcends the local and the particular and that encompasses "an archipelagic history, attentive to our four races, our seven languages and our dozens of bloods" (9).[43] In the words of the character Louis-Gabriel, to speak simply of Martinique or Guadeloupe in isolation (and especially in the case of Césaire and the *Tropiques* group, who apply European ethnography, psychoanalysis, Marxism, and surrealism in their conception of Martinican identity) is a kind of "mania" (192). Identification with Europe (and Africa) is, to Louis-Gabriel, "the enemy of identity," and he proposes that all Caribbean people form a single, essentially coherent civilization: "I am necessarily Caribbean, and Guadeloupean only by chance" (193). The single most important means by which this common black Caribbean (and black Atlantic) culture is transmitted is rhythmic music. *L'Isolé soleil* is a novel that quite literally moves to the beat of black musics, from calypso and steel drum to bolero, merengue, and jazz.

Although he does not incorporate music into his work as extensively as Maximin does, Glissant is nevertheless keenly aware of the importance of rhythm and music to French Caribbean culture. In *Caribbean Discourse,* he states plainly his view that music is a "constituent part" of Martinican historical and everyday existence, and that this is "because of rhythm" (1989, 110). Just as he tends to look toward Faulkner's American South for literary models of the plantation, so he compares the history of Martinican music to the "prestigious history" of jazz

(110). He traces the history of black American music back to the plantation and to the collapse of the plantation system and the subsequent migrations, first to New Orleans, then to northern cities like Chicago and New York. At each historical stage, Glissant says, black music was reborn—gospel, blues from New Orleans and Chicago, Count Basie's big band, bebop, and free jazz—so that the music records the history of the community, "its confrontation with reality, the gaps into which it inserts itself, the walls which it too often comes up against" (110). And if jazz has become a universal form, he argues, it is because it is never an "abstract music" but "the expression of a specific situation" (110).

When he compares the great musical triumphs of North American blacks to the history of the Creole song in Martinique and the beguine in Guadeloupe, Glissant sees a historical rupture between music and the evolution of the people in the islands. After the collapse of the island plantations, he says, nothing—neither large-scale urbanization nor industrialization—came to replace them, and the Martinican people remained "in a state of suspension." The consequences for Martinican music are that it became cut off from work and the "imperatives of reality," ceased to evolve, and thus became folkloric "in the worst sense" (110). Even if, he says, the beguine was in the past the "true voice" of the French islands, it ceased to be so in Martinique in 1902 (the year of the great St. Pierre volcano) and in Guadeloupe in 1940 (presumably due to the effects of the war, the Vichy government, and then departmentalization). No longer tied to collective experience, Martinican music has become an empty, folkloric form. Although Glissant does not say so, the apparent emptiness and stagnation of the music could be viewed as a direct expression of a society rendered apathetic by the collapse of all productivity and creativity and by the "sustained oblivion" that is the consequence of departmentalization. By contrast, Glissant looks to independent Jamaica and to reggae's emergence as a necessary creation born out of relentless struggle and resistance (111).[44] Fittingly, Glissant sees the salvation of Martinican music in its adoption of outside influences—the jazz stylings of the 1930s and the hybrid contemporary Caribbean forms that mixed salsa, reggae, and jazz and that cross the Atlantic to Africa—and in the possibilities of cultural syncretism (112). It is this exposure to outside influences that, in Glissant's view, offers the greatest hope for renewal and could allow "the creativity and solidarity that will make rootlessness more tolerable, make the present void more negotiable" (112).

Maximin's *L'Isolé soleil* enacts and recounts just such a project of French Antillean renewal through creative engagement with diverse diasporic musical styles. The novel is replete with musical references and with characters that, like the narrator Adrien, are "fans of all black American musics" (1981, 25). In the short epilogue, Maximin introduces the idea of the French Caribbean islands as broken and bloody fragments, with the ruins of plantations on every hillside, and yet the islands continue to exist and are alive to the "rhythm of the *gros-*

ka drum" (9). It is Marie-Gabriel's father, Louis-Gabriel, the rootless musician figure, who weaves Guadeloupean music into the broader patterns of New World black diasporic music. A multi-instrumentalist who plays jazz, beguine, and Afro-Cuban music, Louis-Gabriel leaves Vichy Guadeloupe in 1943 and shifts with apparent ease between New York, Cuba, London, Paris, and Haiti, the places where he can play "the music of his heart" (17). His aim, akin to Maximin's, is to write a history of the Antilles through music (16), and, as Maximin himself has said, *L'Isolé soleil* is a novel "which shows from beginning to end the memory of music and song" (1986, 50). Yet, by incorporating music so extensively into the fabric and structure of his writing, Maximin implicitly calls for a new way of reading, one that is attuned to the sounds of the novel and that listens as it reads.

Much as this history seeks to connect Guadeloupe through music to the wider diasporic world, it also involves a fundamental inquiry into the functions of the local and the Creole. At one point, Adrien proposes a long list of axiomatic truths, among them the belief that "we must speak Creole: the Creole of the drummers/ the Creole of the *ka*-drums" (1981, 103)—in other words, a language that is closely associated with rhythm and music, key aspects of Maximin's Creole culture. In a party scene that recalls similar episodes in Roumain's short fiction, a current Haitian hit is followed by a Cuban bolero (a "sacred" music and dance form). During an intermission, a record of Antillean "slow numbers" is played, a "local specialty" based on Creole rhythms and bland lyrics sung in French rich rhymes. It is, the narrator says, as if emotional pain or declarations of love were too serious or too derisory for the Creole language, which at the time was used only for lascivious allusions and virile boasts (24). The tacit general acceptance of this linguistic and cultural distinction is suggested in the observation that the music drifts over the partygoers without their listening to it (24); the "message" of the separate roles of French and Creole language and culture is almost subliminally communicated and accepted.

This misconception of Creole culture as something childlike or banal is, according to Adrien, similarly prevalent in popular literature, which favors childhood memoirs over the more engaged writing (specifically that of Césaire and the *Tropiques* group) that Maximin's narrators draw on and cite with the intertextual zeal of the true disciple. As Adrien says, the danger in endlessly retelling tales of childhood is that hearts "be put to sleep" and that Caribbean people will be seen as children seeking solace and comfort in the memories of childhood, whereas in reality they are "sleeping volcanoes that we must awaken with our stories of zombies, macaques, bamboo, white rum, music, and cutlasses" (24). The model for cultural renewal through diasporic engagement is once again provided by the example of Louis-Gabriel, the musician who plays the North American music, jazz, but whose "fine, silvery" clarinet notes raise the music far above its foundations in the "grave rhythms of the bluesmen," like a "rosary of islands flying above a continent. Like a revolt that penetrates hearts in little spoonfuls to linger more deeply" (25). The musician's aim is not, therefore, simply to imitate but to transform, transcend, penetrate, and finally to create something new that reflects the shape and character of the islands—in one critic's terms, a "composite whole" made up of the novel's many "disparate voices" (Herbeck 2005, 173, 174).[45]

The past that Maximin evokes is in fact characterized by the close association between art and what Glissant calls "the imperatives of reality" (1989, 110). In *L'Isolé soleil,* the slave Georges, at age eighteen one of the best violinists in Guadeloupe, teaches fellow slaves to read and thereafter goes to play his violin, "improvising melodies to the unison of the peasants' high-pitched voices, to the rhythm of the *gros-ka* drum" (Maximin 1981, 34). In its fusion of the "civilized" European violin melodies, popular voice, and Africanized rhythmicity, this scene evokes the plantation as a matrix of creolized culture, the site of a new and nameless form emerging from disparate elements. Significantly, music is presented as a malleable form that, in the spontaneous jamming of the melodic violinist, the singers, and the rhythmic drummers, creates almost immediately something new and unforeseen (and unheard). Music is a means of attaining the creative freedom and personal identity that was denied by the institutions of colonialism and slavery but that was nevertheless an important aspect of the "imperatives of the reality" of slave life. It is an indirect, almost subliminal means of inventing and affirming black Creole identity in a situation that, as Georges writes, seeks to render slaves "beings without heritage and paternity" (41). This idea of music as an invisible force that insinuates itself into the dominant discourse is reinforced by Georges's description of his search for liberty "beneath the water" (41). In contrast to Jonathan, his twin and a maroon who lives amid the trees and near the volcano, Georges says he has chosen to be a "child of time, water, and the night," preferring to live by "water and the shore," slowly forming the "precious stone of our liberty" (41).[46] The destiny of water, he says, is always to flow to the lowest point, the spatial opposite of the volcano, which is associated with the sun and its more fixed, dualistic day-and-night movements; moreover, sunlight is unable to reach the depths of the water or the deepest forests (41). Georges's attachment to water is therefore also a commitment to the patient molding of a more profound freedom. Just as the water moves inexorably, weaving its way toward the lowest, deepest parts of the island, so his music permeates the dominant ideology, slowly eroding it and touching finally the deepest parts of the new creolized Antillean reality.

As Glissant often does in his work, Maximin tends to blur the dichotomy between the mountain and the plain, between the slave and the maroon. Georges calls for the concerted action of the maroons and the island's recently emancipated blacks against the combined forces of the planters, proprietors, militarists, mulattoes, and lower-class whites in order to truly liberate themselves from the treacherous elements and to protect themselves from the revenge of the French (43). In Georges's case, education, music, and revolution are interconnected: he spends all of his time teaching black soldiers in Pointe-à-Pitre yet takes time to play music and to compose songs that comment indirectly on the political situation. Music is presented as a primary bonding force between Caribbean blacks, more so than language, which in this context is inevitably connected to loss and alienation and is subject to control and compromise.

Music is also the one true inheritance that is passed on to and modified by each generation. The character Carole is a repository of old Creole songs, and she plays the banjo and the saxophone at balls while her sons Ignace and Louis—named after their famous rebel predecessors Joseph Ignace and Louis Delgrès—spend all of their leisure time playing music with their orchestra. Ignace plays drums, and Louis plays the violin in a way that recalls Georges's earlier fusions of melody and rhythm. Later, too, Louis-Gabriel, named by his mother in honor of Georges (in their shared initial G), himself becomes a musician under circumstances that invoke destiny and fate. His mother, father, and twin brother Jean-Louis (named in honor of Jonathan) are killed in the hurricane of 1928, which devastated the whole of the island. In the novel, hurricanes have their own rhythmicity, returning regularly and approaching the island slowly, inevitably "to the rhythm of the old folks' rosaries" (94). The 1928 disaster leads to the modernization and "civilization" of the island through the construction of new concrete and stone buildings. Louis-Gabriel escapes the hurricane by playing truant from school to listen to the practice sessions of a Haitian orchestra, which took place by chance in the cellars of the Royal Hotel, an effective shelter from the ravages of the hurricane. None of the musicians or their young admirers were killed in the hurricane, and Louis-Gabriel, the orphan "having played musically with destiny" became a musician, a "great specialist of improvisation" (81). Again, music survives disaster and adapts to new circumstances. In this case, Louis-Gabriel emerges quite literally from the rubble of the past as a great master of the modern mode of improvisational jazz.

Of all the diasporic musical modes evoked in L'Isolé soleil, it is jazz—principally bebop, its precursors, and the free jazz of the 1960s and 1970s—that is most tellingly represented and incorporated textually as a dynamic means of refiguring and transcending history and culture. As Nick Nesbitt says, "Jazz is thoroughly linked to L'Isolé soleil's production of meaning, a driving force in its historiographic machine that formulates and generates constructions and critiques in ever-new combinations of once-buried memories" (2003, 148).[47] Jazz, for Maximin, is more than mere musical practice; it contains, as Nesbitt suggests, "encryptions of the social reality out of which it arose" (2003, 157–58). In this sense, Maximin prefigures Paul Gilroy's project of "taking the music seriously," and he presents music in terms that echo Gilroy's view of how it has developed from the "grudging gift" that supposedly compensated slaves for their exclusion from modern political society into a refined form of expression, "an enhanced mode of communication beyond the petty power of words—spoken or written" (Gilroy 1993, 76). It is true more generally that music in *L'Isolé soleil* is privileged as the most dynamic, searching, and profound expression of black Atlantic experience. It is significant that Maximin, unlike his predecessors Zobel and Glissant or the later *Créolité* writers, does not evoke storyteller figures as repositories of history, language, and culture. Maximin substitutes the storyteller with musicians who, much as in Gilroy's formulation, transcend the "petty power" of words in their creative, often improvised modes of communication.

In *L'Isolé soleil*, Louis-Gabriel's movement out of the rubble into the modern, essentially jazz mode is complemented by the broadening of the political frame of reference to include extra-Caribbean influences. These influences come principally from North America and only partially from Africa, which, it is suggested, fades in the memory over time and loses its cultural and political relevance to the Caribbean. As Adrien says, by the mid-twentieth century the peasants' *gros-ka* drum had long ceased to stir up a memory of Africa; by then it only stoked the imagination (92). Just as the new music flows between various points on the diasporic map, so political ideas travel and are incorporated into island thinking. At one point, Adrien talks about hearing the Black Power militant Stokely Carmichael—born in Trinidad yet most closely associated with North American radicalism, thus himself something of a free-flowing diasporic militant—speaking in London. Carmichael's argument was that the only true revolutionaries he had ever encountered were jazz musicians playing in a cellar. For his part, Adrien is less convinced about the political function of music, which, he says, "never plays revolution." In his view, revolution and music "may dance together sometimes, like two loving bodies improvising their movements to the rhythmic diapason, when the revolution has a moment of freedom" (90).

When Adrien moves to Paris, the metropole becomes for him a kind of stage on which he plays out the dramas and tensions that are the legacies of centuries of colonial distortion of relationships between "blacks" and "whites" and the hypostatization of the notions of blackness and whiteness. Music and rhythm are, of course, primary elements in this unequal exchange of (mis)conceptions of the other. The reception of "black music" in Europe is often far from innocent or neutral, and it tends to solidify distorted images of the other, as Adrien realizes when he visits a record shop in Paris and finds a secondhand album of live steelband music from Trinidad. The record sleeve contains a short text in three languages that is intended as an introduction to the music, culture, and character of the Caribbean: "The calypso is the original music of the Caribbean. It has been able to capture all of the magic and mystery of these islands, and it reflects admirably the happy and carefree temperament of the island people of the Caribbean

Sea. It is comforting to think that Caribbean people in Europe remain faithful to the music of their native land. The remarkably joyous harmonies of a calypso reflect the very character of the Caribbean person: happy, carefree, but also very sensitive. In spite of the numerous and constant obstacles he encounters, the Caribbean man does not become discouraged: he remains courteous" (99).

These sleeve notes effectively express the commonly held European conception of the Caribbean as a "magical" place, peopled by smiling, insouciant characters who are never anything less than polite and courteous. History and ongoing hardship—"the numerous and constant obstacles"—are mentioned only obliquely and remain conveniently unspecified and forgotten by Europe and by the Caribbean man, who in any case is at all times blithely deferential. Presented at a time when Europe was losing its empires, such images of the Caribbean seem to have served as reassuring myths that helped erase the unsettling truths of island history. The easy-going rhythms of steelband calypso music similarly reinforce the image and in this way lull the senses, creating, as the notes say, an ultimately "comforting" misconception of a musical form that in truth—as is made clear in chapter 2 on Trinidad—is firmly rooted in class and race struggle. In its travels to Europe, therefore, this kind of music is translated into another discourse that falsifies its original forms and functions. The fact that Adrien finds the record in the secondhand section of the record shop seems to suggest that the idea is already worn, used, but is still passed around invisibly and discreetly in the metropole.

Highly sensitive to this kind of stereotyping and, indeed, compelled to act out the image of the courteous black, Adrien writes his own acerbic note to the white people of London and Paris, imploring them to have trust in their Caribbean bus conductors and hospital orderlies and to preserve their elemental racism while feigning to appreciate "the rhythm of their reggae, their beguines, their cadence-rampas and their calypsos" (100). Continuing in this caustic vein, Adrien asks that the whites limit their thresholds of tolerance, be sensitive to the quality of blacks' service and devotion (which are guaranteed by three centuries of practice), and disperse the blacks into little pockets among the vast greyness of the suburbs. Striking a more openly defiant, even prophetic tone, Adrien asserts that in this case it will not be so easy to effect the sweet and happy colonization of these "new Caribbean islands that you wanted to create yourself for your own gain in London and Paris" (100). It will therefore be more difficult to perpetuate the myth of the joyfully obliging black man when these new islands (or indeed ghettoes) grow up in the heart or even on the margins of the metropole. Implicitly, too, the music that will come out of the new islands will challenge the easy yet insincere appreciation of traditional, rhythmic Caribbean musical forms. Adrien's prophecy implies the development of more grating, confrontational rhythms that will better reflect the new urban reality of displaced Caribbean communities.[48]

Adrien's Parisian exile is preceded by the earlier migration of Siméa, Marie-Gabriel's mother, to the metropole. Her narrative is dated 1939 and seems to express her own turmoil and trauma in a world that is being turned upside down by impending war and by the emerging generation of black intellectuals affirming a new idea of blackness and calling into question the legitimacy of colonial values and practices. The year is also significant in that it marks the publication of Césaire's epic *Cahier d'un retour au pays natal,* just one of the many literary intertexts that permeate and, to a significant extent, constitute Siméa's narrative in *L'Isolé soleil.* In many ways, Siméa is the antithesis of the smiling, courteous black person; she opens by evoking the pain and devastation of abortion, and she sees this act as the repetitive, displaced return of the 1928 hurricane. "All of my land is devastated," she says to her aborted child, "my vagina burning. Your cadaver torn from my rubble" (113). In her own way, like Adrien but in far more traumatic circumstances, Siméa's self is doubled in Paris, split into two different parts that are born of exile and the distorted class and race values that travel the ocean and, in Siméa's case, give life to a kind of displaced urban blues, a black Atlantic mode far removed from the compliant calypso on Adrien's second-hand record. Siméa's aborted child is associated with deeper and wider historical themes: the bourgeois mulatto and white values that compelled her not to give birth to the child are related to the long-standing and deeply embedded fear and hatred of blackness and to the murderous history of the Caribbean. It is perhaps most fundamentally the Caribbean colored bourgeoisie that Siméa critiques as the social group that embodies and perpetuates the debilitating psycho-racial complexes of which she and her child are victims.

An extended passage describes these complexes in terms of music and rhythm: the bourgeoisie take their afternoon tea to the accompaniment of the violin, but when the night falls it is the sound of the "black drums" that dominates (124). The price to pay for this generation's revolt is suicide—Siméa talks of many "pieces of ebony wood" floating down the Seine (126)—alcoholism and madness, the folly of "rhythms that escape the beat" (124). This notion of a rhythm that runs free, that is out of step yet remains a rhythm, seems an apposite way of conceptualizing Siméa's narrative in both its form and its content. For example, Siméa talks of her inner thoughts in terms of rhythm. She translates the work of male poets, a practice that to some extent is a sign of her female alienation: "I have put so much faith in men that I have never composed a single sentence of my own" (129). At the same time, though, she says she can only translate works that she has learned by heart and that then "drift in my memory, and to their own rhythm attach themselves to the French, English, and Spanish words" (129). Her prose itself is bluesy and melancholic but with its own improvised rhythms born of her revolt and her necessary madness, which are essentially means of challenging the values that led her to abort her child. Indeed, she evokes the idea of black rhythm and dance as a means of subterfuge against the trickery of whites, who, she says, always have "adolescent . . . strategies in their heads and innocent faces" (127). However, she adds, "our dances and chants work to knock them off their stride" (127–28).

The connection between rhythm and black Caribbean identity is further emphasized when Siméa goes to a Cuban club in Paris, which offers her a refuge and some respite from her sleepless nights. The smiling black doorman opens for her the "door of fraternal rhythms," the entrance to the black underworld of blues and bolero that beats beneath Paris (132–33). The visit to the club is also an initiation for her unborn child into black music; Siméa wishes the singer could "make it a bit blacker" or indeed that the club itself could be even darker so that the music could settle into the child's body more comfortably (133). Although she says she never dances, Siméa aligns herself symbolically with rhythm and percussion by sitting at her favorite table, beside the drummer (133). Just as significantly, she comes this time to the club alone, without her "maroon-chaperones," her usual company of poets and musicians, and is free in particular from her poet friends' mistrust of or disdain for rhythmic music. Flashing back to a previous April evening at the same club, Siméa recalls how, after seeing her watch his hands working incessantly, the drummer Oscar gave up his place to her at the drums during a bolero. As Oscar sang his plaintive song, Siméa played in rhythmic harmony with the double bass on her two tumbas and her single bass congo drum, which she says is the "true heart" of the rhythm section, indifferent to the more feverish beats of the bongos and maracas, and which resonates, again like a heart, between the "lungs of the bass" and the rhythmic call-and-response singing. That evening, however, she drummed under the disapproving gaze of Léon-Gontran Damas, who could not accept that his "little translator could give up her composure to the sweetness of rhythm" (133). Poets, she says, mistrust the energy of "naked music" and, like jealous lovers, prefer to dress music up in clothes (133).[49]

The memory of that joyful April evening serves as a counterpoint to Siméa's current traumatized state. This evening, Oscar sings a contemporary Cuban love song, which lauds a woman's beauty and her rhythmicity, but, far from being moved by the song, Siméa tries to erase the words from the music.[50] The song reminds her of André Breton's *Union libre* but to an Afro-Cuban rhythm. She sees, therefore, a connection between the Cuban love song, which sings of the woman's forehead and hair, and the French surrealist poet's glorification of female beauty, both of which indicate a universal male desire to "dismember" women. The words of the Cuban singers and Antillean poets now make her ill, and she sees their male bodies trapped in words that are but "amorous strategies" (134–35). It is only the recently published *Cahier d'un retour au pays natal* that offers hope and serenity, in that Siméa finds nothing in it that sings "the splendor of our land, the beauty of our women, the exploits of our ancestors" (140).[51]

If she must, Siméa says, she will tear up all of her (pre-Césaire) books, but, in a further sign of how she privileges music over literature, she says she could never without dying give up singing or dancing (134). The principal aspect of music, she says, is rhythm because it, and in particular the rhythms of improvisational jazz (and the rhythm of the "sweet or furious madness of words"), can shatter the tacit strategies of female dismemberment and control that are expressed in Caribbean songs and poems (135). This kind of improvisational jazz is seen in positive terms as "uncivilized" and "black maroon music" (189). Fittingly, then, Siméa says her farewell to her white lover Ariel, dancing with him to Coleman Hawkins's *Body and Soul*, which, like Césaire's epic poem, is a contemporary work of art that breaks free from regular, predictable rhythmicity and implicitly from the misogynistic impulses of the past. Maximin's choice of Hawkins's work is significant in that they share similar approaches to form, incorporating African vernacular elements into European models.[52] Both Maximin and Hawkins also reject male revolutionary iconoclasm and search through narrative and musical improvisation for "an elegant resolution to the social contradictions they objectify in their musical and poetic texts" (Nesbitt 2003, 163). Significantly, Siméa's attempts to dance in time to Ariel's regular steps are impeded by her simultaneous effort to try and follow the thread of Hawkins's melody "in the labyrinth of his improvisation" (Maximin 1981, 143). This evening, she understands clearly the role of the kettledrum and the bongo, which upset and destabilize the "grave, measured regularity" of Cuban peasant songs and Creole waltzes.

The evening leads her to an epiphany of how in the past she lived by and had complete faith in (male) poets and musicians, and of how her idea of the future was formed around "the drums and chants of the Negro, the hawker of revolts" (135–36). Closing her ears to the words of Oscar's bolero, she hears, or rather feels, only the vibrations of the conga drum and the double bass. Rhythm is another form of salvation for Siméa; it contains and expresses an elemental truth that beats through Caribbean poetry and music, which, as the female Cuban singer Malhia asserts, are conventionally considered the "private property" of men (136). It is Malhia's song that opens Siméa's ears again and whose voice takes what is left of Siméa's body to somewhere different, "far out of the reach of men" (136). Yet, though Malhia's song re-awakens Siméa, it is Hawkins's *Body and Soul* that finally helps her to "restore" her body, to feel "full and complete"; the image of the jazzman alone, playing for himself in the darkness, complete and yet obscure, acts as a representation of how Siméa now conceptualizes her future self (144).[53]

This episode also exemplifies Gilroy's later claim that the "characteristic syncopations" of black music and its "unique conjunction of body and music" still animate the black subject's basic desires—"to be free and to be oneself" (Gilroy 1993, 76). Siméa's own attempts to be free *and* to be herself will, she suggests, be effected by two principal means: her return to Guadeloupe, and her playing once again the clarinet of her father Gabriel (Maximin 1981, 144). What is ultimately fascinating and original in this episode is the identification of rhythm—so often associated in black poetry and music as a fundamentally male aspect—as a female principle, a force that works against the male drive to control and figuratively dismember women, reducing them to the classic roles of inspiration or caregiver. Siméa says later that, since returning to Guadeloupe, she has tried to learn to play the conga drum and the double bass, "those instruments that are supposed to belong to men" (173). Siméa therefore feels a strong urge to reappropriate rhythmic instruments for herself and, by implication, for women, and through the act of drumming, in particular, she touches truths and a depth of experience that she is unable to feel in male poetry and music, which, she realizes, effectively debar her from existing as any kind of full person. Later, Siméa's daughter Marie-Gabriel will charge herself with a similar task, not in music but in writing: "You will write . . . to liberate yourself from paternalism, from the law of the return of prodigal fathers and sons, and of all that tries to go back to the same" (19).[54]

Hawkins's *Body and Soul,* the soundtrack to Siméa's farewell to Ariel, remains with her as a reminder of the traumatic time of the abortion and of her bodily and spiritual restoration. Spending the carnival of 1943 back in Guadeloupe, Siméa sees and hears the prestigious Fairness Jazz Junior Orchestra of Pointe-à-Pitre. To thank the people of Saint-Claude for their hospitality, some of the musicians take out their instruments and play a mixture of Afro-Caribbean musics (mazurka, beguine, meringue, bolero), and the community is delighted to hear the orchestra and feel "the power of its rhythmicity in the very heart of the old town" (167–68). The music soon fades, however, the instruments are put away, and out of this silence comes discreetly and surely "like a shortcut, a goodbye without farewell" the sound of a clarinet playing the tune that Siméa recognizes immediately as *Body and Soul,* "the blues of [her] farewell at the Cuban Cabana" (168). Once again, it is the improvisational aspect of the song, the way the clarinet "escapes in solo beyond the appearance of melody" that attracts and enthralls Siméa (168). The unpredictable, spontaneous movements of the song, "like a sail escaped from coasts and maps, drifting from rhythm to surprises, caring only for the fundamental harmonies, far from the pretty bits and variations for lazy ears," are again connected to Siméa's own ideal, rhythmically liberated trajectory (168).

Siméa's mnemonic connection to *Body and Soul* is further demonstrated as she discusses the track with Louis-Gabriel and runs her left hand slowly up her right arm "in an act of memory" that simultaneously makes her heart beat "to the rhythm of . . . serenity" that comes with her natural, easy communication with Louis-Gabriel (171). The continued importance of rhythm to Siméa is symbolized in the presence of the conga drum, which sits "in the place of honor" by her bed (171) and upon which are laid copies of *Tropiques* (172). Similarly, the trope of improvisation is revalorized and newly theorized in her exchanges with Louis-

Gabriel, who first evokes the common prejudice that improvised music is little more than an invention of lazy players incapable of delivering the melody that the record player or the dancefloor demands (172). In his own case, he says, he always thinks of freedom when he plays, not so much political liberty but what music would sound like if it were free. The great shortcoming in Caribbean music, he says, is that it is excessively dictated by the capricious tastes of the dancers. In contrast, what he appreciates in contemporary North American music is the belief in playing music for music's sake. Far from being a trivial matter on an island occupied for four years by Pétainist troops, music is seen by both Louis-Gabriel and Siméa as a primary means of true liberation, as Siméa suggests in her improvised slogan "First article: The liberation will be musical or will not be" (172). There is no irony in Siméa's proclamation; she believes deeply that music has always been closely connected to resistance and affirmation in the Caribbean, that it is "the only freedom that we have conquered to date, during the three centuries of our oppression" (172). In this scene and more generally in the novel, Maximin presents music as a phenomenon that offers transcendence of social and historical limitations as a means in itself of achieving freedom.

As if to infuse Caribbean music with some of the improvisational élan of jazz, a party scene in L'Isolé soleil brings together the Guadeloupean gros-ka drum, a peasant singer, and Louis-Gabriel's clarinet. The music begins spontaneously, with drumming solos and impromptu call-and-response singing, which is quickly augmented by an old peasant woman who stands up to sing a song, and in turn by a young boy who throws a series of intense, violent dance moves in perfect time with the rhythm of the drum. This spontaneous, polyrhythmic manifestation seems to enact what one jazz theorist calls "the rhythmic disruption that animates swing, out of which swing emerges, before meaning" (Moten 2003, 27), in that it is presented as a surging forth of a deeper, more authentic Guadeloupean music that "came from the heart of the island, buried deep, covered up under the call of the beaches and the intoxicating vistas of the volcano. Music of drums and shouts, dance of pounding feet, supported by the nourishing earth" (Maximin 1981, 211). In other words, this music is often silenced and neglected under the weight of touristic and exoticist images of the island, music that connects the people to the land in a natural, organic bond. Improvisation is asserted as an integral part of this repressed music, and each beat of the gros-ka is a "burst of improvised freedom, which climbs to the high pitches then falls again exhausted like the voice of the singer, into the serious, assured, and firm fraternity of the boula drummers and the call-and-response singers" (211). Improvisation is therefore primarily an act of individual expression but always reconnects ultimately with the collective feeling, reinforcing the common bond. The gros-ka drum is valorized as the means of attaining this individual and collective freedom; its constitution as both plant and animal, united by skin, rope, and wood, gives it a double quality: "solid and hard like the trunk of a tree, vigorous and emotive like a forest animal" (211).[55]

Hearing this pure, rootsy music is an act of rediscovery for both Siméa and Louis-Gabriel, whose "civilized childhoods" alienated them from Creole music and language and from the forest, the "terrain of *marronnage*" (212). Louis-Gabriel, in particular, is moved to take up an alto saxophone and, standing alone, begin to improvise to the beat of the drums, which "came from the very heart of the earth": "A dizzying series of cries . . . like a bird in flight above a forest, exploring each trail, charging into the entries that emerged breathlessly from the exits, hesitating at the crossroads, climbing the trees, falling down the ravines, walking without knowing its music in your open throat and body, penetrating like a hurricane, yes, like a hurricane that's what [Siméa] felt, but a hurricane that would reduce to nothing all in its path that was not emotion, love, and communion" (212).

The improvised saxophone thus has a similar and complementary function to the drum. In both cases the improvisation cuts a solitary path that ultimately rejoins the collective body in fraternal communion. In both cases, too, the spontaneous music connects with the hidden contours and depths of the land, which are in turn linked to repressed or forgotten rhythmic, improvisational collective culture. As Siméa later reflects on Louis-Gabriel's playing, this improvisational music has no regressively nostalgic or compensatory function but expresses the "most naked, the most simple, the most generous desire to create" (227). And, as the character Toussaint affirms, whereas he translates Damas into Creole, and Siméa translates him into English, Louis-Gabriel plays Damas on the saxophone, and there is nothing "more revolutionary than that music, which goes beyond language" (227). For all that it is grounded in history and experience, therefore, improvisational music is far removed from the recuperative impulses of more conventionally folkloric music, and it is more creative and liberating than the standard, rhythmic dance music that Louis-Gabriel criticizes. In his presentation of the improvising drummer and saxophonist, Maximin seems to suggest something of what Ralph Ellison calls the "cruel contradiction" that is at the heart of jazz production. True jazz, to Ellison (and in Maximin's novel), is "an art of individual assertion within and against the group. . . . [E]ach solo flight, or improvisation, represents (like the canvasses of a painter) a definition of his identity; as individual, as member of the collectivity and as a link in the chain of tradition. Thus because jazz finds its very life in improvisation upon traditional material, the jazz man must lose his identity even as he finds it" (1964, 234).

Ultimately, Maximin's evocation and exploration of improvised rhythms is an attempt to break free from reductive (and essentially male) interpretations of black culture, history, and identity. The criticism of Negritude's and indigenism's emphasis on recovering black alienation through images of "work, sweat, and earth regenerated by great spurts of pure slave blood" is complemented by the idea that the slaves in this romantic narrative are themselves "well-rhythmed" (Maximin 1981, 243). What this latter idea seems to suggest is the theme found in Césaire, Zobel, and Glissant of slaves trapped and deadened by the rhythms of work. It also seems to hint at the stereotypical popular image of the rhythmic black man, which constitutes a kind of bondage of identity. Moreover, music in the novel is a means of bypassing nationalism, of not having to belong to one single country. The character Antoine, a friend of Marie Gabriel, seems to express this fundamental point when he writes "no land, no dream, no style, has ever been the property of one person. Works circulate, free from their fiction and equal to their reality" (273). Also, as Siméa says of Louis-Gabriel, he lives *in* (not *for*) music, and his country, his nation, is music (246). This idea of a transnational community of musicians, singers, and dancers is one of the most profound and original features of *L'Isolé soleil*. In exploring improvisational rhythm and by dissociating rhythm from an exclusively male aesthetic, Maximin indicates a way out of the traps of Negritude and narrow nationalism and into a creative, liberating (and feminized) future, one in which music will continue to be a primary conduit for the most inventive and revolutionary theorizations of black culture and black existence.

4

James Brown, Rhythm, and Black Power

Despite its particular colonial history and the ways in which that history has encouraged a lingering fascination with its former European metropoles, the Caribbean does not exist in isolation from the rest of the Americas. As Daniel Maximin's *L'Isolé soleil* shows, there are intricate, sometimes hidden, but nonetheless profound and enduring links between the Caribbean and North America, in particular. Rhythm and music offer some of the most fluid and effective means of connecting the islands with other New World diasporic communities, but politics is another domain in which crosscurrents of influence have shaped history and society in the Caribbean and North America. From the Haitian Revolution to Black Power, the impact of diverse political movements has reverberated across national frontiers, offering examples and ideas that have been enthusiastically greeted by thinkers and activists across the Americas. Frantz Fanon may have written first of his experiences in Martinique and then of Algeria, but he was still one of the most influential theorists for American Black Power militants, being one of Stokely Carmichael's "patron saints" and being so widely read in the United States that Eldridge Cleaver claimed "every brother on a rooftop" could quote him (quoted in Macey 2000, 24). In *L'Isolé soleil,* Maximin demonstrates that this dynamic of pan-American political influence and dialogue works in both directions, with ideas and images (and sounds) rebounding from one place to the other. Near the end of the novel, he writes of the stopover made by Angela Davis in Guadeloupe in 1969 and of the complementarity between U.S. Black Power and the ongoing political-cultural struggles in the Francophone Caribbean (1981, 277). Also, the character Adrien recognizes the tendency for Caribbean intellectuals to "desert" to other zones (Fanon to

Algeria, Marcus Garvey and Claude McKay to Harlem, Jacques Roumain to Spain) before affirming the importance of contemporary U.S. black radicalism for Guadeloupeans in the 1970s: "We are discovering America with Black Power," he states (279).

In Maximin's novel and in historical reality, music and rhythm are inextricably linked to politics. The sounds and images of black America in the 1960s, in particular, resonated across the Caribbean. Even where there was no overt political message in the music, the very images of blacks apparently making it big in a "white" country and the innovative soundtracks that jazz, soul, and R&B provided were highly potent markers of the growing liberty and increasing economic influence of fellow New World blacks that could only have had political connotations for Caribbean people. Black American music thus blew in images and sounds of Black Power, just as almost two hundred years before in New Orleans the drums and rhythms of migrant Saint-Domingue slaves had carried the idea of revolution to the plantation world of North America.

Indeed, the plantation is a kind of common matrix for the diverse nations and territories of the circum-Caribbean. The basic configuration of the plantation, in terms of its physical layout and the social relations it created, was essentially the same from northeastern Brazil to the American South. When Édouard Glissant visited Mississippi and Louisiana, he found himself explaining to Americans the ways in which their world mirrored and echoed his own homeland of Martinique and of how the families that fled the French and Haitian revolutions brought a distinctive culture that persists in various forms: in cooking, in architecture, and in music, which are "principally the same in the culture of this whole area" (2000, 29). The African trace, Glissant says, was kept alive and reconfigured according to the "inspiration" of particular places in this circum-Caribbean world, a zone shaped by a common, interconnected history that "travels with the seas" (29).

This chapter effects a similar transmarine movement by shifting the primary focus from the Caribbean to the United States, in particular to a case where rhythmic invention by an artist born in the South was seized on by Black Power militants and incorporated into a notion of black aesthetics that served a politicized notion of African American culture as a largely homogeneous, untainted entity. Although the main focus will be on the United States, my analysis will demonstrate some of the ways in which the Black Power interpretation of rhythm in African American music compares and contrasts with the Caribbean examples evoked in the previous chapters. What emerges is a sense of the ongoing, though often obscured and seldom acknowledged, connections between African American and Caribbean cultural politics and the ways in which, across the New World, rhythm has been at the heart of conceptions of race, culture, and subjectivity.

OUT OF SIGHT

In March 1964, James Brown released his first single on the Smash label, a division of Mercury based in Chicago. A big-band version of Louis Jordan's standard "Caldonia," it was an uncharacteristically safe choice for an artist who had routinely pushed the boundaries of rhythm and blues and who had just walked out on his previous label, King Records, in search of greater commercial and artistic autonomy. Brown's next single was another artistically conservative release, a cover of "The Things That I Used to Do," the Guitar Slim blues that had originally featured Ray Charles on piano. Like its predecessor, it failed to chart. It seemed for an instant that the number-one R&B singer in the United States, the highest-selling artist in the history of the King label, was faltering, caught in a kind of artistic limbo, turning back toward the traditions from which he had emerged. Listening to the B side of his next single, "Maybe the Last Time," one of Brown's most convincing pure gospel performances, the impression of an artist hesitating, marking time, appears all the stronger. This track, along with other previous gospel-soaked Brown songs like "Lost Someone" and "Oh Baby Don't You Weep," seemed to encapsulate the essence of Southern soul music to that point. The title itself, "Maybe the Last Time," suggested that Brown felt that he had come to the end of an era (it was his final studio appearance with his band the Famous Flames) and that he was on the verge of something new. Indeed, if the B side represented the past, the A side of the same release, "Out of Sight," announced itself as a bold step into a new mode, as the first hint of the sound of the future. And that future was built on and composed of rhythm (Guralnick 2002, 239). How was this new rhythmic direction in his music interpreted by critics and fans? How was it used by contemporary civil rights and Black Power activists to promote the idea of a distinctive African American culture and way of being?

RHYTHM, ROOTS, AND AFRICANISM

Much as in the Caribbean, the notion of rhythm as the defining feature of black American music has a long history. Indeed, long before James Brown, from the earliest days of slavery, rhythm had influenced the white reception of the music. During slavery in the British colonies of North America (as in the British Caribbean colonies), slave owners were deeply suspicious of slave music, in particular the drum and its rhythmic language. In 1740, for instance, one year after the Stono slave rebellion, the South Carolina legislature outlawed the "using and keeping [of] drums, horns or other loud instruments which may call together or give sign or notice to one another" (White and White 2005, 47). A half-century later, a similar law was passed in North Carolina, and in 1839 Louisiana restricted the use of drums (White and White 2005, 47). And, much as in Trinidad and

other Caribbean islands, American slaves reacted to such legislation by inventing new makeshift instruments: jugs, bottles, pans, even their own bodies, upon
which they could continue to strike out their rhythms (White and White 2005,
48).

In the first half of the nineteenth century, this improvisational impulse found
further expression in urban centers such as New York, Philadelphia, and Boston.
During this time, urban slaves began to create a new music and dance form
that was judged by whites to be wild and unruly and that evolved dynamically with the changing environment (White and White 2005, 159). Visiting one
of New York's dance cellars on a Saturday night in the late 1840s, journalist
George Foster was struck by the strangeness of the noise produced by familiar
instruments such as the fiddle, the bass drum, and the trumpet. Most striking to
him were the music's rhythm and the playing of the drummer, whose "frightful
mechanical contortions" seemed to be "in all violation of the laws of rhythm,
like a man beating a baulky mule and showering his blows upon the unfortunate
animal, now on this side, now on that" (Blumin 1990, 142–43). This was "the
relentless beat to which black New York moved," and its rhythmic echoes have
reverberated throughout the development of modern African American music
(White and White 2005, 160).

In the postbellum period, rhythm has remained for many people the defining
element of African American music. Indeed, in one of the founding moments of
the blues, rhythm and repetition were identified as the primary distinguishing
features of the music. When, in 1904, the formally trained black musician W. C.
Handy was forced to spend several hours waiting for a delayed train in Tutwiler
railway station, deep in the Mississippi Delta, he was shaken from his slum-
ber by the sounds of an evidently poor black man, "plucking a guitar" (Handy
1991, 74). The man played by pressing a knife against the strings and created
a sound that was "unforgettable" (74). He sang three times the refrain "Goin'
where the Southern cross' the Dog" while "accompanying himself on the guitar
with the weirdest music" Handy had ever heard (74). The music remained deeply
imprinted in Handy's consciousness, not for its words, he says, but for its "distinctive and repetitive sound" (74). One of the myths of the origin of the blues,
this incident brings together the sophisticated and formally trained Handy and
the untrained, rhythmically adept music of poor African Mississippians in a
way that heralded the coming of the commercial form of the blues (White and
White 2005, xviii). Perhaps most significantly, it was the repetitive rhythm that
struck and stayed with Handy and that drew him to the music, much as it would
do later for countless others as African American music developed and evolved
throughout the century.[1]

During the same time—the early twentieth century—African American music
became more prevalent in the public sphere, and this seemed to make more urgent

the need for clearly defined ideas of black (and white) culture. The interpretation of black culture became closely associated with what Ronald Radano calls "the dialectics of modern racial ideology," and rhythm was seen increasingly as a natural, "primitive," and African musical element, the single most important feature of black music (2003, 247–55). This moment was, for Radano, a "veritable watershed in the formation of black modern music" (272) in that black music was reinvented in its new public sphere essentially as rhythm music. As black performers came to prominence throughout the twentieth century, they entered into a complex, commercialized, racialized play of self-definition in which their identity as rhythmic blacks was already cast, compelled as they were to work within the parameters that defined rhythm or "race music" (271). The association of rhythm with specific African origins and with the past is termed by Radano as "descent" (233–34). He also identifies a further concept of blackness, "displacement" (233–34), which emerged as African Americans moved more freely around the postbellum United States, expanding the boundaries that had long restricted them socially and physically. This internal displacement brought black music into new spheres and complicated whites' conceptions of their American others. Blackness in America could no longer be thought of as a static, unchanging category but became a fractured, multiple, unpredictable phenomenon.

Rhythm, too, was displaced in these migrations and was interpreted as an uncanny, almost mystical force that was irresistible to all who heard (or felt) it. White susceptibility to rhythm was often seen in terms of bodily infection, so that when "hot rhythm" reached its apogee in the 1920s it was interpreted as a kind of epidemic, "get[ting] into the blood of some of our young folks, and I might add older folks, too" (quoted in Radano 2003, 237). With roots in New Orleans honkey-tonks and brothels, displaced jazz rhythms were seen as threats to the more sober mores of the North. On January 21, 1923, for instance, Reverend Richard Yarrow of the Illinois Vigilance Association warned in a report that "moral disaster is coming to hundreds of American girls through the nerve-irritating, sex-inciting music of jazz orchestras." Yarrow's emphasis on female morality belied an older white male anxiety over the putative sexual potency of black men, only this time it was the rhythm (of the black musicians) that was inciting female moral abandon. The reverend and his association had attributed the moral "fall" of more than a thousand girls over the previous two years in Chicago alone to jazz and rhythm. Yarrow's description of the depravities in the dancehalls highlights the effects of rhythm on white dancers: "Amid the distracting notes of the saxophone, and the weird beat of the tom-tom was witnessed conduct not hitherto seen outside the old red-light district. . . . Couples on the floor gave way to almost every form of indecency. Dancers violently threw their arms about each other, frequently assuming immoral postures."

Yarrow's judgment of jazz was determined by the conventional, "primitivist" contrast drawn between white and black dance forms at the time. White forms tended to control body movements and thereby restricted sexuality with "formal rhythms and innocuous tunes," whereas black music expressed the body and sexuality with a "directly physical beat and an intense, emotional sound" that were "felt" rather than interpreted via a set of societal and moral conventions (Frith 1983, 19). Writing in the 1960s, Eldridge Cleaver echoed this idea that the primary attraction of black music to whites lay in its eroticized rhythms. According to Cleaver, young whites' enthusiasm for the "potent erotic rhythms" of R&B gave them access to the "communication between the listener's own Mind and Body," which he believed was one of the distinguishing features of black culture (1968, 185–87). By that time, the invention of the electric bass guitar had further established rhythm as the single most important element of modern music. As Nelson George says, the electric bass "forever altered the relationship between the rhythm section, the horns, and other melodic instruments" (1988, 38). Quincy Jones, too, recognizes the ways in which the electric bass imprinted itself on the sound of the 1950s: "Before the electric bass and the electric guitar, the rhythm section was the support section, backing up the horns and piano. But when they were introduced, everything upstairs had to take a back seat. The rhythm section became the stars" (quoted in George 1988, 38–39). Although it was to some extent new technology that made rhythm the "star" of the new sound, for many whites rhythm retained its unequivocal connection with black primitivism. Simon Frith has critiqued the persistent primitivism of white discourse on black music, and he is no doubt right to say that the close association of rhythm and sex is a "product of high cultural ideology rather than of African popular music practice" (1996, 141). Frith, like Radano, addresses the complexities of receiving rhythmic music as it is displaced in various, predominantly white contexts and as the meanings attached to it are fractured into new configurations and solidified as a manifestation of the immoral, primitivist, internal black other to white America.

Notwithstanding these historically grounded critiques and the complex history of rhythm and African American music they set out, a persistent strain remains in black music criticism that interprets the music and its rhythms as direct, unmediated echoes of Africa. Olly Wilson, for instance, promotes the idea that all black American music is essentially rooted in an "African conceptual approach" (quoted in Vincent 1996, 34). The fundamental qualities of black American music that Wilson attributes to the African approach relate essentially to rhythm: the tendency in blues, jazz, boogie-woogie, and funk to approach musical structure with a primarily rhythmic principle; the way that singers and players of any instrument perform percussively; the prevalence of antiphonal structures that emphasize audience participation; the tendency to create a high density of musical events within a short time frame; and the way that physical body movements are often incorporated into the music making process (Vincent 1996, 35–36). Picking up on Wilson's Africanist cues, Rickey Vincent further argues that the practice of making musical instruments sound like human voices—such as Louis Armstrong's "wicked and wild atonal scales" in his *Hot Five* in the 1920s—were meant to "drive past the conscious mind and hit the soul in a language all its own," thereby continuing African musical tradition (1996, 36).

Although there is undoubted validity in the Africanist interpretation, it needs to be read in conjunction with the more historically and critically engaged approach of Radano, who underscores the role played by internal displacement, audience expectation, and even commercial considerations in the construction of what we know as black American or rhythm music. The Africanist interpretation should also incorporate the truth that rhythm is not a static element of black music but a dynamic, evolving force for innovation that projects forward into the future, imagining new functions for the beat and inventing new musical styles. No artist better harnessed rhythm in these ways than Brown himself.

NEW THING

As its title boldly promised, "Out of Sight" propelled James Brown into a new mode, almost a new dimension of music that was far removed from that of any of his peers. The song retained something of a basic blues structure, but its staccato bass lead, sharp horns, and most of all its driving, irresistible rhythm marked a departure from the gospel roots of much of Brown's previous work and from the conventional melodic structures of Western music. This new thing was the rhythm as song, the song as rhythm. In his autobiography, *I Feel Good*, Brown stresses that "Out of Sight" marked a new direction for his music: "Everything about it was new," he says, "the rhythm, the arrangement, the lyrics, and the way the beat kept on jerking up and hitting" (2005, 124–25). Equally innovative was his use of breaks, the sections where horns, voices, or guitars are heard unaccompanied; this technique would be taken up by disco deejays more than a decade later (George 1988, 102).[2] In truth, however, traces and suggestions of this new direction can be heard in his 1962 releases "I Don't Care" and "I Found You," tracks that harnessed rhythmic drive and insistent repetition to smoother melodies reminiscent of the more polished sound of artists like Louis Jordan and Lucky Millinder.[3] Also, Brown's live performances had long involved him slowly working his audience into frenzied states through rhythmic improvisations and repetitions of simple phrases.[4] His early performances with the Famous Flames often climaxed with "Please, Please, Please," a track based on repeated, rhythmic harmonies that "pointed established doo-wop tradition in the direction of call-and-response antiphony" (Rose 1990, 27). Even at this stage, Cynthia Rose says, it was clear that Brown's basic interest was "commanded more by the beats than the sentiment" (1990, 28).[5]

Brown's landmark LP *Live at the Apollo* bears testimony to his purposeful, preacherly ability to move the audience slowly through rhythm and repetition to a state of consciousness that is close to trance and that nobody can (or even wants to) resist.[6] The extended, slow-burning version of "Lost Someone," which begins on side 1 and continues on side 2, is a fine example of Brown's penchant for repetition—he repeats insistently simple phrases like "Come on home to me," "I'm so weak," and "I'll love you tomorrow"—that draws responses from the audience and that, in harmony with the steady, ever intensifying beat, slowly builds to its climax as the rhythm speeds up and the band segues into the following numbers. That track is the centerpiece of the album, and it stands as the embodiment of "the whole history of soul music, the teaching, the preaching, the endless assortment of gospel effects, above all the groove that was at the music's core" (Guralnick 2002, 236). In *Live at the Apollo,* we hear Brown as R&B shouter, but we also get a sense of the future, of him stripping away song form and clearing the way for his works to come, the "records built from rhythm" (Wolk 2004, 104).[7]

More generally, too, repetition was crucial to all live soul performances. It served a communalizing function, "reinforcing phatic contact between performer and audience" (Ward 1998, 202). Repetition was used to build suspense and anticipation, which skilled performers like Brown could manipulate, delay, renew, and finally shatter with ecstatic screams. Performers like Brown, Solomon Burke, Wilson Pickett, and Aretha Franklin would adapt the "house-wrecking" tactics of black preachers, and their shows functioned in much the same way as black religious events in that both performer and audience became immersed in the music, arriving together at an ecstatic state that allowed them to feel a deep intensity of experience and, more specifically, to sense their blackness, which was the "celebratory core" of many soul songs (Ward 1998, 202).

What "Out of Sight" announced was a new groove, a new function for rhythm other than as a regular, predictable complement to melody. The rhythmic core of the James Brown band had been bolstered by the arrival in 1964 of a succession of fresh, innovative players: musical director Nat Jones on alto saxophone; Melvin Parker on drums; and Maceo Parker on alto and baritone saxophone (White and Weinger 1991, 24). From that point on, rhythm virtually replaced melody as the single structuring device in a Brown song.[8] The typical Brown track now moved less in linear, melody-driven movements than in looping rhythmic shapes that blurred the distinction between beginning, middle, and end and that gave the impression of an infinitely turning sound, a rhythm that would not stop. The words of the song now "meant" less in a conventional way and had their own rhythms, inhering as they did in repeated short phrases ("Get on up," "Get into it") or else grunts, groans, and screams, which became some of Brown's aural signatures.[9] This new prominence of rhythm in Brown's music has been recognized by the musicologist Robert Palmer, who points out that, because there were few or no chord changes but many rhythmic interludes and suspensions, "the rhythmic elements *became* the song" (1992, 167). Palmer also details how Brown's band fell in with the new groove and how every instrument was played as if it were a generator of rhythm:

> Brown and his musicians began to treat every instrument and voice in the group as if each were a drum. The horns played single-note bursts that were often sprung against the downbeats. The bass lines were broken up into choppy two- or three-note patterns, a procedure common in Latin music since the Forties but unusual in R&B. Brown's rhythm guitarist choked his guitar strings against the instrument's neck so hard that his playing began to sound like a jagged tin can being scraped with a pocket knife. Only occasionally were the horns, organ or backing vocalists allowed to provide a harmonic continuum by holding a chord. (167–68)[10]

One of the fascinating elements of Palmer's analysis is his description of how the rhythm guitar sounded like metal being struck, which, along with the overall impression evoked by Palmer of Brown's music, recall the sound of a Trinidadian steelband, another rhythmic ensemble that was itself coming to ever greater prominence in the contemporary Caribbean. Thus if, as the critic Cliff White says, Brown's new music was in several crucial ways completely unique and "divorced from other forms of popular music" (quoted in Guralnick 2002, 242), its rhythms found an echo (albeit distorted and somewhat commuted) in music that was coming out of other diasporic traditions.[11]

"FIGHTIN' THE FUTURE"

Brown's revolution stalled for a year after "Out of Sight" as he worked out his business problems. He finally returned to King with virtually all of the concessions he had requested now granted, and with greater artistic control. The hiatus seemed only to foment the revolution, and, when he came back in July 1965, the new rhythmic sound kicked on in spectacular fashion with the release of "Papa's Got a Brand New Bag." Recorded in typical, improvisatory James Brown style— in less than an hour on the way to a gig—at the post-production stage the track had its introduction spliced off and its entire performance sped up for release (White and Weinger 1991, 27). Announcing itself with an unexpected light, early accent on an expected strong beat, the rhythm is set with a short toot from the horns, "a marked attack played as if it were a little early in relation to the basic pulse implied by the rest of the rhythmic fabric" (Danielsen 2006, 73). The guitar sections, played on beats two and four, are marked by the same "snappy phrasing of each stroke," and then at the end of every blues sequence (on the first beat of bar ten), the bass and the guitar make an off-stroke gesture in unison, just before the vocal line "Papa's got a brand new bag" and the distinctive "shangalang" riff on the guitar (Danielsen 2006, 73). In Brown's own words, this track "had its own sound: the music on one-and-three, the downbeat, in anticipation" (1991, 3). He soon adopted "rhythm on One" as a personal slogan, and the technique itself of playing the One on top—or, as he put it, a downbeat in anticipation—later became central to the funk sound of the 1970s.[12] He had discovered, he said, "the power of the percussive upbeat, using the rhythm in an untraditional way. . . . I didn't need 'melody' to make music. That was, to me, old-fashioned and out of step. I now realized that I could compose and sing a song that used one chord or at the most two" (2005, 80).

For Brown, "Papa's Got a Brand New Bag" was a statement of black musical independence, "something that would give us a place in the business" (1991, 3). It was a new idiom, "a slang that would relate to the man on the street . . . that represents the man in the street" (3). Despite—or indeed because of—its atypical, jarringly rhythmic sound, "Papa's Got a Brand New Bag" was Brown's first Top 10 hit; moreover, as Dave Marsh says, it declared a "new order of rhythm and himself as its avatar" (1989, 4). Both the success of the song and its sound took Brown by surprise: as it hit the charts, he told disc jockey Alan Leeds that "it's a little beyond me right now. . . . If you're thinking, 'well, maybe this guy is crazy,' take any record off your stack and put it on your box, even a James Brown record, and you won't find one that sounds like this one. It's a new bag, just like I sang" (quoted in White and Weinger 1991, 27). Perhaps most tellingly, Brown suggests that the new phenomenon is something almost strange to him and his time, a prophecy of music to come that has an unnerving effect even on him: "It's—it's—it's just *out there*," he says, "I'm actually fightin' the future" (quoted in White and Weinger 1991, 27). In the mid-1960s, Brown said he was not seeking to reproduce "some known sound" but was "aimin' for what I could *hear*. 'James Brown Anticipation' I'd call it. You see, the thing was *ahead*" (Rose 1990, 59). "Papa's Got a Brand New Bag" retains that portentous quality, the sense of a rhythmic prophecy that is still being played out, still "fightin' the future." As Marsh says, in 1965 James Brown "invented the rhythmic future in which we live today" (1989, 5).[13]

Brown's future-oriented impulse may be related to a fundamental aspect of broader African American music discussed by the founder of Atlantic Records, Ahmet Ertegun, when he said that "black people tend to think about the future more. Black musicians don't like to play in an old style; they prefer to play in today's or tomorrow's style" (quoted in George 1988, 93). This idea is echoed by Nelson George in the distinction he draws between the European tendency to preserve form for the sake of tradition and the "consumerism and restlessness" of black listeners, who demand endless invention. But black musical invention does not, George says, involve the complete destruction or rejection of previous forms; the essences and textures of established forms are filtered into the new music, to create styles that are "in the tradition yet singular from it" (1988, 108).

Brown's rhythmic inventions form an idiosyncratic part of this process, with the added twist that, as he developed his style, he was largely signifyin(g) on himself. Brown's comments on his mid-1960s' work suggest that his project—his prioritizing of rhythm above all—was not conceived consciously but emerged more from his instincts, primarily musical, as well as his impulse to create something new, even if he was unsure of the form it would take. In terms of rhythm, his producer Brad Shapiro stated in 1979 that he was "mesmerized" by Brown's "raw sense of rhythm," which suggests that Brown possessed a gift for rhythm that was to some extent "natural" (quoted in White and Weinger 1991, 43). At the same time, the rawness of Brown's rhythmic sense was cultivated and honed throughout his long, demanding career, and it was shaped by, among other things, his own musical instincts, his collaborators and players, commercial considerations, external musical developments, and the expectations of his audience.

NO SWEAT

By the fall of 1965, when he released "I Got You (I Feel Good)," which reached number 3 on the pop charts, James Brown was assuredly into the new mode. Chart success followed for his subsequent releases, too, all in the new rhythmic style. "Ain't That a Groove," "Money Won't Change You," "Bring It Up," "Let Yourself Go," and "Cold Sweat" were all big hits and demonstrated the way Brown was pushing the new mode to its limits, further dismantling traditional song structures, virtually dispensing with melody, crying out, moaning lyrics in repetitive fragments, and bringing two or even three drummers in live shows to accentuate the percussive beats that had largely become the music (Guralnick 2002, 242). Brown had figured out how to orchestrate a drum set and to make every element of his band work around a rhythm, a "groove, rather than a melody" (Vincent 1996, 73). He had made an important discovery, as he later reflected: "I had discovered that my strength was not in the horns, it was in the rhythm. I was hearing everything, even the guitars, like they were drums. I had found out how to make it happen. On playbacks, when I saw the speakers jumping, vibrating a certain way, I knew that was it: deliverance. I could tell from looking at the speakers that the rhythm was right" (quoted in Vincent 1996, 74).

These songs took music, as Vincent says, "to a whole new rhythmic dimension," where the downbeats were replaced by horns and drums, the bass played in competition—confrontation, almost—with the drums, guitars, or keyboards, and the guitar was played "in percussive spurts like a drum" (1996, 61). The movement over two years from "Papa's Got a Brand New Bag" to "Cold Sweat" demonstrated Brown's unrelenting step toward consolidating rhythm as the single, defining element of his music. Whereas the former has identifiable elements of a song (a melodic line, a chord sequence spreading across the rhythm), the latter has only fragments of conventional song structure: "It was just rhythm," Cliff White and Harry Weinger say of "Cold Sweat," "barely any chord changes—with jazz intervals in the horn section" (1991, 31). The rhythm in "Cold Sweat" becomes an intricately woven fabric of percussive sounds in which the texture of the music has changed from "horizontally divided layers of sound to a rhythmic patchwork" (Danielsen 2006, 40). In technical terms, the rolling quarters of "Papa's Got a Brand New Bag" are replaced in "Cold Sweat" by a vertical swing: the basic 4/4 meter is overlaid with an asymmetrical counter rhythm, which ends on the first beat of bar two, which in turn makes up the third main beat of a "virtual cross-rhythmic pulse" (Danielsen 2006, 63). The differences between the two tracks are further accentuated in their respective drumming styles: the floating rhythm of "Papa's Got" is created by the laid-back drumming style of Melvin Parker, whereas in "Cold Sweat" Clyde Stubblefield's style is choppier, cut up into different accents, syncopations, and ghost strokes that create a more fragmented sound (Danielsen 2006, 74). "Cold Sweat" is also the first of many tunes by Brown in a Dorian mode, which creates a less linear, more circular temporal movement. In general, once again, Brown's music increasingly weakened the traditional formal divisions of a song and arrived at a point where "the groove becomes what everything turns upon" (Danielsen 2006, 41).[14]

By the time "Cold Sweat" hit number 7 in 1967, Brown had established this new, modern sound as distinctly and uniquely his own, something never heard before that would soon metamorphose into funk—itself "a distillation of repetitive rhythm" and seen as "blackness in its purest [musical] form" (Danielsen 2006, 28)—which would serve as a crucial point of reference for future generations of hip-hop and dance music acts.[15] If there was such a thing as pure blackness in music, it was not something to be recuperated from the past but a new thing to be created and re-created endlessly into the future.

Brown and his new, future-oriented music were also being lauded as expressions of a broader, African-derived collective identity and aesthetic. Peter Guralnick considers Brown's new rhythmic style, along with his repetitive grunts and screams to be "intimations of African roots, declarations of black pride" (2002, 240). From the mid-1960s to the early 1970s, Brown was to George "so defiantly African in America" (1991, 7). For the *Village Voice* reporter Thulani Davis, Brown was more than a unique act that made her want to go to the Apollo; he was proof, she says, that "black people were different" (1980, 148). And rhythm was one of the fundamental elements that differentiated black people from whites: "Rhythmically and tonally blacks had to be from somewhere else," she says, and in Brown's music she found "proof that Africa was really over there for those of us who had never seen it—it was in that voice" (148). More recently, Sarah Brown and John Mortland write in the sleeve notes to their 1994 compilation *Roots of Funk* of how James Brown used his entire band as a drum kit, "creating polyrhythms that took the music back to Africa."[16] And though Brian Ward is generally cautious about excessively Africanizing black American music, he does agree that "James Brown succeeded more brilliantly than any other artist in 'blackening' the sound of his soul in the mid-to-late 1960s" (1998, 350). Finally, Cynthia Rose argues that the classic James Brown tropes of repetition and circularity are born not of "personal eccentricity" but "denote a black culture with Afrocentric values, values distinctly separate from white European systems of thought about the physical world" (1990, 120). Again, like the history of the critical reception of rhythm in African American music, there is undoubted validity in relating Brown's music to African practice. The problem is that, in projecting racialized, often primitivist notions of culture onto his music, we risk trapping the music in a deadeningly limited conception of black culture that always looks back in time for its lost purity. Instead, in many ways the music seems to free itself from the shackles of the past and envision a freer, unpredictable, yet always rhythmic future.[17]

The Africanization of James Brown in the late 1960s was largely brought about by the demands of the contemporary political context. As social and civil rights activists began to acknowledge and promote the political functions of black music, they also started to seek the support of soul stars. The campaign to recruit prominent black musicians to the cause began in the mid-1960s. In January 1965, the special steering committee of the Council of Racial Equality (CORE) met to discuss whether it should concentrate more of its fundraising efforts in the black community and on music stars in particular. Ten months later, it was announced that Brown would do a benefit for the CORE chapter in Queens. This benefit marked Brown's belated involvement in the political sphere (Ward 1998, 389). In the late 1960s, Brown pronounced widely on issues of poverty and race, and political groups continued to seek his support. His Africanization continued in 1968 when he changed hairstyles from his carefully managed process to a natural. As a contemporary editorial in *Soul* magazine observed, this change was seen as a further act of liberation and won the approval of black radicals: "The King's been a slave for years," the editorial stated, "James Brown's been putting up with the painful and time-consuming process hair do for as long as anyone can remember . . . until last month that is. Now the King's got a natural. Everyone, including the Black Panthers and SNCC, think it's fine, just fine" (quoted in Guralnick 2002, 244).

According to Brown's sideman Hank Ballard, "machine gun toting Black Panthers" forced Brown into addressing more radical political issues in his work in 1968, shortly before he released three socially conscious works, "Blackenized,"

"How You Gonna Get Respect (When You Haven't Cut Your Process Yet)," and the era-defining, crossover hit "Say It Loud (I'm Black and I'm Proud)" (Vincent 1996, 78).[18] For the Black Panthers, Brown was a "one-man demonstration of how deep the codes and meaning of music run in black America, how they evoke an historic continuum, how they can move to unite" (Rose 1990, 56). Brown's "blackening" was repeated across the spectrum of R&B as the music's iconography changed markedly: on stage, television, and album covers, tuxedos and processed pompadours were exchanged for dashikis, ghetto chic, and natural hair. The cover of the Last Poets' 1970 album *Niggers Are Scared of Revolution* demonstrates this Afro-urban turn in black music's iconography: it presents three of the band's members sporting dashikis and natural hair, one wearing sandals, set against a grim urban backdrop of overflowing trash cans and a run-down apartment block. Significantly, too, one of the group members stands behind a tall African drum, his hands poised as if ready to play, an image that seems to assert the central importance of earthy, African rhythms to this new, black, urban music. In effect, the various strands of the Black Power movement were something like an urban indigenist movement, a late echo of the Africanist movement in twentieth-century Black Atlantic cultures that stretched back across time and space to the French Caribbean of the 1940s and to Harlem and Haiti of the 1920s and 1930s.

On the one hand, therefore, James Brown had essentially invented a new, modern musical style that had never been heard before and that was recognizably his own, personal sound. On the other hand, his critical reception, both among white critics like Guralnick and black observers like Davis, stressed how his sound was an echo of a collective, ancestral past and a means of reconnecting with Africa and blackness. Although he insisted he was pushing toward the future, critics (to varying degrees) sought to situate him and his work within a regressive notion of black culture as irrevocably earthy, unique, and untainted. This apparent paradox can be better understood by considering how contemporary ideas of black culture shaped critics' interpretations of Brown and other prominent black musicians of the period. It is important, therefore, to understand the intellectual and cultural context into which Brown and his dynamically rhythmic sound were introduced. The key black American intellectual of the period, and one who took a keen interest in Brown and his new rhythms, was LeRoi Jones, later known as Amiri Baraka.

BARAKA, THE BLACK AESTHETIC, AND JAMES BROWN

For many young black intellectuals, the death of Malcolm X in 1965 brought into sharp focus the unrelentingly racist nature of American society and the futility of holding out for true and equitable integration. Prominent figures such as Larry Neal, Haki R. Madhubuti (Don L. Lee), and Ron Karenga began to develop and define in clearer terms the meaning of black cultural nationalism and the "Black Aesthetic." The central figure of the movement was Amiri Baraka who, following Malcolm's death, left behind his bohemian set (and his white wife) in Greenwich Village, moved to Harlem, declared himself a cultural nationalist, and committed himself to black people as "a race, a culture, a nation" (Baraka 1966, 9). Breaking with white liberal ideology, Baraka now believed that race was the single most important factor in the life of a black person. Art, for him, was the best means of awakening and embedding a sense of self-consciousness across the black American population. Accordingly, he set up the Black Arts Repertory School in Harlem, a model of black theater that inspired other similar developments in cities across the country, including Detroit, Philadelphia, Jersey City, New Orleans, and Washington, D.C. (Harris 1985, 9). Another key figure in the Black Arts movement, Julian Mayfield, set out with the general objective of discovering and explaining the Black Aesthetic, which was to him something essential, something beyond outward signs of black style such as hip talk, African dress, and natural hair. The Black Aesthetic, Mayfield suggests, is "lost and buried deep in our African past" (1972, 27) and exists now in the collective "racial memory, and the unshakable knowledge of who we are, where we have been, and, springing from this, where we are going" (26). Just as it had been in the various Caribbean nationalist-indigenist movements, art was assigned a clear political function. As Addison Gayle, Jr. writes in the introduction to his anthology *The Black Aesthetic,* what became important in black culture was less its intrinsic aesthetic value than the degree to which culture improves the social and psychological status of the people: "How far," he asks, "has the work gone in transforming an American Negro into an African American or black man?" (xxii).[19] Again, much like in the Caribbean, the Black Arts movement signaled what Samuel A. Floyd calls "a return to myth" whereby "it became acceptable, respectable, even expected, for African Americans to seek out, believe in, and display their mythological roots" (1995, 185).

The impulse to distinguish black aesthetics from white culture can be seen in Baraka's poetry as he distanced himself from the Beats and declared poetry to be "what white men did" (1966, 10). Baraka sought to create verse that better communicated his own black voice, and rhythm was an important element of this authentic expression. "I have my own language," he declared, adding that "we can use our own language and rhythms to recreate [our] experiences" (quoted in Harris 1985, 58). He rejected what he termed "White Christian Poetry" in general, since it followed "academic rhythms" that were "passed across desks like canceled stamps" (Baraka 1971, 18, 19). Although he had earlier considered the possibility of using "Southern Baptist church rhythms" (Baraka 1963b, 81) in his poetry, by the mid-1960s the rhythms he sought to reproduce were those of the streets and of black urban life, and these were part of his wider move toward black oral modes, the dozens, scatting, shouts, chants, blues, and jazz rhythms (Benston 1978a, 13). Unlike James Brown's use of rhythm, therefore, Baraka's was largely premeditated and made to fit in with his preconceived ideas of what constitutes authentic black culture.

With this renewed emphasis on the auditory aspects of African American culture, black poets placed an increasing importance on oral performance and on addressing an audience that would not normally read poetry. Poets aligned themselves more closely with musicians and sought to capture the immediacy and directness of musical performance. Thus, the poets diverged from the rhetoric of the Black Panther party, which tended to downplay the political potential of music. The advertisement for *Seize the Time,* a Panther-produced album from 1969 by Elaine Brown, expressed the party's belief that songs expressed the emotions, desires, and hopes of a people, but, it added, "they are no more than that. A song cannot change a situation, because a song does not live and breathe. People do" (quoted in Ward 1998, 413).

As black poets began to listen to R&B and soul, the "big hero" was James Brown, whom they thought to be a "magnificent poet," according to Larry Neal (quoted in Vincent 1996, 79). Crucially, Neal identified the performances of Brown as the model for black poets to follow; the poet, he said, must become a performer, "the way James Brown is a performer—loud, gaudy and racy" (quoted in Baraka and Neal 1968, 655). Neal's emphasis on the gritty, raucous elements of black popular culture is echoed in Baraka's own declaration in *The Dead Lecturer* that "the poor have become our creators. / The black. The thoroughly ignorant" (1964, 29). In this sense, black radical poets like Neal and Baraka shared the implicit objective of Brown's music, which was, as Brown's childhood friend Leon Austin said, to "[make] the ugly man *somebody*" (quoted in Guralnick 2002, 233).[20] Yet Baraka was wary of associating rhythm too closely with black people and with his idea of black culture. In "A Poem for Willie Best," he reflects on the popular film character actor Best, who was presented in various Hollywood productions as a black buffoon, a stereotype created in the white American mind who is:

> Lazy
> Frightened
> Thieving
> Very potent sexually
> Scars
> Generally inferior
> (but natural)
> rhythms. (1964, 26)

Baraka's impulse was to play on and invert these misconceptions, something like John Coltrane, whom Baraka lauded for taking a "weak Western form" and infusing it with discordant rhythms and aggressive sounds "to attack and destroy the melody line." Coltrane's aesthetic was interpreted by Baraka and his fellow black radicals as the epitome of their own artistic and political struggle: in Coltrane's splintering of chords and playing notes backward or upside down in order to break out of established forms and structures, Baraka heard "our own search and travails, our own reaching for new definition. Trane was our flag" (1974, 176). Musically, therefore, Baraka took his cues less from R&B than from jazz and, to a lesser extent, blues. The more predictable, repetitive rhythms of R&B were perhaps too close approximations of the "natural" black rhythmicity that he critiqued as part of the negative stereotype of the black. In jazz there was more aesthetic and rhythmic freedom, more scope to destroy the white forms that Baraka came to abhor. Imitating Coltrane, Baraka's poetry played on white models and replaced them with black jazz forms, specifically supplanting the "quiet rhythms" of his Beat poetry with the "more frantic rhythms of bop" (Harris 1985, 100). For both Baraka and Coltrane, the play on established forms and styles is a kind of signifyin(g), in that they set up expectations for the listener or reader only to destabilize those expectations by repeating "with a difference" the original text, and thereby implying through indirection a critique of the original and, to some extent, of the social or racial milieu from which it emerged.[21] The great attraction of jazz (and implicitly its great advantage over more fixed, regular modes such as R&B and soul) to Baraka was its improvisational quality, the way it created itself in unpredictable forms as it came into being, and how it simultaneously was a highly personal expression and captured a collective feeling.

JAZZY JAMES

Even if James Brown came out of the R&B tradition and defined himself as a soul artist, his new rhythms, his new style, were in fact not too far removed from jazz or from Baraka's concept of the jazz aesthetic. This in turn helps explain Baraka's enthusiasm for Brown.[22] In general terms, much of Brown's music, like jazz, was heavily orchestrated. Sammy Lowe and Alfred "Pee Wee" Ellis, the writers of many of the charts for the James Brown band, functioned similarly to jazz arrangers like Duke Ellington and Charles Mingus in that they translated Brown's ideas into flexible but highly structured arrangements (Ward 1998, 265). By the early 1960s, Brown was beginning to arrange his music into recognizably jazz-like forms, bringing instruments in and out where they had not been before and emphasizing the importance of the jam session and improvisation in his creative processes.[23] Once again, Brown's live shows in particular had long been loosely structured, raw affairs that, far from being polished and predictable, had relied on improvisation. As he recalled, he would play "Please, Please, Please" for thirty-five or forty minutes, getting "real happy" and singing the same tune until "the "spirit came up" and the audience "took [him] off again" (quoted in Guralnick 2002, 232). Brown's recollection of his performance in fact echoes the descriptions of nascent swing music in New Orleans cited in chapter 1, in particular the observations on how the rhythmic movement of bodies and objects in ritual ceremonies became secularized elements of jazz music. In early swing, as in Haitian Vodou, performers or participants sought to balance or swing ritual objects and bodies back and forth, the aim of which was to heat things up in the dance, to "activate or enliven" the ritual (K. Brown 1995, 222). By making the "spirit [come] up" through insistent, rhythmic repetitions, James Brown suggests his affinity at once with the gospel tradition, with "gettin' the spirit," and with the earliest roots of jazz (and by extension with the rhythms of the Saint-Domingue slave migrants).[24]

In his recordings, too, Brown often captured an improvisational, unpredictable quality that related his work to the modern jazz aesthetic. Classic tracks such as "Get Up Offa That Thing" and "Sex Machine" have a raw feel that turns around rhythms and repetitions interspersed with impromptu shouts, whistles, and screams. In "Sex Machine," Brown uses his voice as an instrument and as a means of providing cues for the various sections of the song, such as the bridge and the piano riff (Danielsen 2006, 82). In terms of rhythm, the voice in this song provides the down beats in anticipation, invokes traditional antiphonal elements—Brown's "Get up" answered over and again by Bobby Byrd's "Get on up"—and generally gives the track its distinctive sense of controlled, tight improvisation.[25] Furthermore, just as Coltrane signified on European or "white" musical forms, there is a sense in many of Brown's funk tunes that he was playing on the demands of the white listener. Commercially, Brown's music had to communicate on different levels to different publics; they had to work both as pop songs and as grooves. In tracks like "Sex Machine," therefore, are some (albeit limited) elements of melody, chorus, and recognizable form that would draw in the *listener* as well as the rhythmic, repetitive parts that communicate directly to the dancer, the *participant* in the creation of the groove. The track thus engages the body by way of rhythms, "processual deviations and ambiguous phrasing," and appeals to the "head" (or the ear) with its suggestions of conventional "phrase-based form" (Danielsen 2006, 178). As Anne Danielsen puts it, though the funk track does not have the traditional form of a song, "it is not experienced as *not* having such a form either, even though this is nearer the truth" (2006, 179).[26] Apart from this jazz-like, self-referential, improvisatory impulse, the paradox that Brown's music was unquestionably his own, modern creation yet received by many as an Africanized, collective expression reflected the similar paradox for jazz musicians like Coltrane, who produced the most idiosyncratic works that were nonetheless interpreted by critics and fans like Baraka as intimations of broader racial cultural identity.[27]

It is significant in this regard that, in Baraka's music criticism, James Brown is one of the few non-jazz (or non-blues) musicians who is evoked and lauded.[28] Baraka incorporates Brown into a long tradition of African American music, which is grounded in the rhythmic call-and-response form of Africa and which Baraka says "has never left us" (1979, 158). The rhythm quartets of the mid-twentieth century were, for Baraka, a continuation of the earliest black vocal traditions, and the large choirs were initially composed of dancers and singers whose purpose was always religious or ritual. This tradition is therefore rooted in religious worship, in summoning spirits, as Brown's own description of his performance indicates above. Baraka lauds Brown for being part of the "national genius" of the black man and the black nation and for being the "direct, no monkey business expression of urban and rural... Black America" (160). For Baraka, Brown's "hard, driving shouting" is an auditory marker of African American experience: "JB is straight out, open," Baraka says, "speaking from the most deeply religious people on this continent" (160). Moreover, Brown speaks from and to the most disadvantaged of all America's people, the "most alien" group, Baraka says, in the white American social order. Therefore, Brown's milieu is "the Blackest and potentially the strongest" in the United States (161). Also, because it comes from the "blackest" elements in American culture and because it is "straight on and from straight back out of traditional Black spirit feeling," Brown's music is more resistant to "whitening" than the contemporary jazz of Cecil Taylor and the "New Black Music," according to Baraka (171). In their unadulterated blackness, Brown's screams and shouts are more radical, "Blacker... further out" than most jazz music (176). When, Baraka says, a "whitened Negro" or white man listen to Brown, they are taken by the lyrics, the rhythm, and the sound to another place, "where black people live" and move "in almost absolute openness and strength" (quoted in Vincent 1996, 75).[29]

From the early 1970s, Baraka followed Neal's instruction for black poets to be performers like Brown: "loud, gaudy, and racy." As William Harris notes, Baraka became a great performer; his poetry readings were often accompanied by a live jazz group and "rival[led] James Brown's performances" (1985, 103–4). Reviewing a later performance by Baraka, the *New York Times* music critic Jon Pareles wrote of how the poet "preached and sang a poetic history of African-Americans," how he incorporated scat-singing and talking drum language into the performance, and of how rhythm had become a predominant feature of the show: "The poems were incantations," Pareles wrote. "They centered on a handful of resonant images that were repeated in different rhythms and tones of voice" (quoted in Harris 1985, 104). Rhythms, Baraka notes in *Black Music,* "carry to the body," particularly in Brown's work, because the form of this music "definitely includes the body as a high register of the love one seeks" (1967, 200).

BARAKA AND CARIBBEAN RHYTHMS

Baraka consciously drew on the rhythms of African American speech and music, but he was also aware of broader New World diasporic traditions and of the importance of rhythm to them. When he went to Cuba in 1960 (the year following the revolution) as part of a group of black intellectuals and writers, he met Nicolás Guillén, the Afro-Cuban revolutionary poet, who, much like the Haitian indigenists, had used indigenous speech and music in his work and had moved away from peninsular Spanish influence to create a more distinctively Cuban style. Baraka praised Guillén's 1930 work *Motivos de Son* for its incorporation of elements of Cuban *son* (song) and, in particular, its use of "Afro-Cuban dance-song rhythms" that infused the work with traces of "African (slave) forms" (1984, 184). In his own way, Baraka sought to forge a new poetry in which the music, rhythms, and sounds that had evolved from slave forms were integral, indispensable elements.

Baraka's consciousness of non-U.S. diasporic poetry and music and of the rhythmic bases of many of these forms was not limited to Guillén and Cuba; he also engaged with the work of the Francophone Negritude poets Léopold Senghor and Aimé Césaire. Baraka was particularly drawn to Césaire as an exemplar of a post-slavery New World poet who had engaged with the European avant-garde and had sought in his poetry not only to reorder established ways of thinking and being but also to destroy and go beyond them. The radical black artist, Baraka wrote in *Daggers and Javelins*, seeks more than a mere "rearrangement of reality" and reaches for the "creation of a new reality after the destruction of the old" (1984, 200). Therefore, in Baraka's view, Césaire's (and Senghor's) surrealism differed from European surrealism in that they sought to dismantle and turn European rationalism around in order to open up a space and indeed to create a new language in which they could begin to express their own experiences. In short, as Baraka says, the Negritude poets were finally a lot more than "merely thin replicas of Breton or Tzara" (1966, 131).

In seeking to break away artistically from white poetics, Baraka had been looking for "something more essential, more rooted in my deepest experience," and he compares his poetry to Césaire's *Cahier d'un retour au pays natal*, which was, for Baraka, an exemplary case of a diasporic artist overturning the received norms of European poetry (1974, 166). Baraka also stresses the importance of rhythm in this process and lauds Césaire for "showing how even the French language could be transformed by the Afro-Caribbean rhythms and perceptions" (1974, 166). In both cases, surrealism was an important source of inspiration for the nonwhite artist. For Baraka, surrealism was compatible with jazz in that the two movements shared the fundamental belief that "the shit had to be turned upside down" (1974, 33).

In his 1960s cultural nationalist phase, Baraka shared with Césaire and the Negritude poets (and certain earlier Trinidadian intellectuals and Haitian indigenists) a belief in the biological bases of black culture. There are, for example, suggestions of biological determinism in Baraka's view that blues was necessarily and essentially music that could be played only by black Americans, because the "materials of blues" were not available to whites but were "secret and obscure" aspects of the music that was itself a kind of "ethno-historic rite as basic as blood" (1979, 57–58). Also, in *Black Music*, Baraka writes of blues in terms of an innate, primal impulse that is transferred through black musicians (1967, 12). In his essay "New Black Music," he further insists on the innate differences between black and white cultures and on the impenetrability of black art for nonblacks: "The expressive and instinctive (natural) reflection that characterizes black art and culture," Baraka says, "transcends any emotional state (human realization) the white man knows. I said elsewhere, 'Feeling predicts intelligence'" (1967, 175). For Baraka, therefore, as for Césaire, black culture is often related to a quasi-mystical conception of race, and rhythm and music are seen as hidden, secret elements of an enduring racial cultural memory.

In Baraka's drama, in particular, music and rhythm are constant features, both thematically and as structuring devices. His most extensive exploration and use of music and rhythm occurs in *Slave Ship* (1965), a work that was published at the same time as James Brown was releasing his own rhythms onto the American public. In *Slave Ship*, Baraka incorporates music fully into the structure and content of the play, bringing his theories on music and African American experience to the theater and creating a work that demands to be *listened to* as much as viewed. Music in the play is a marker of strength and a source of memory, resistance, affirmation, and survival. In short, it reflects "the entire historical and mythical process of Afro-American being" (Benston 1978b, 183).

Ultimately, Baraka's mystical cultural nationalism was a reflection of broader intellectual trends among New World black intellectuals. There are telling connections between Baraka, Negritude, Haitian indigenism, and Trinidadian cultural nationalism of the 1930s that express a common conception of black culture as something hidden, mystical, premodern, and uncontaminated by contact with other cultures. These movements sought to mobilize culture for political ends; indeed, culture was the primary conduit for the expression of political arguments. In each case, intellectuals turned to the folksy, grassroots elements of their culture and interpreted these neglected sectors in starkly primitivist terms. And for each movement, rhythm was a central aspect of this putatively untainted black culture. This in turn heavily influenced the reception that African American critics in the 1960s gave to black music in general and to the rhythm-driven work of Brown in particular. Given the charged cultural and intellectual context into which Brown launched his new rhythms, it was almost inevitable that they would be incorporated into, or perhaps consumed by, the prevailing ideas of cultural nationalism and the Black Aesthetic.

CRITICS/CRITIQUES OF BARAKA

For all of their impassioned, often perceptive analyses of American society and black culture, Baraka's writings, again like those of his Caribbean counterparts, are not always founded on sound theoretical bases, and this flaw erodes the durability of his ideas beyond their immediate context in 1960s America. By extension, too, his black nationalist reading of African American music and rhythm in general and James Brown in particular is useful up to a point, but it is compromised by its own inherent theoretical weaknesses. In 2003, Fred Moten's adept post-structuralist criticism laid bare the faults in Baraka's essentialist thought. Already in the 1960s, however, Ralph Ellison had offered his own penetrating critique in his review of Baraka's *Blues People*. In both cases, the critique of Baraka implicitly opens up new interpretative possibilities for James Brown's rhythms and offers a way out of the critical dead end to which Baraka's (and others') primitivist thought threatened to condemn them.

Ellison takes issue in particular with Baraka's racial absolutism and with his schematic understanding of race, color, and class. Where Baraka sees everywhere rigid categories of race, class, and culture, Ellison sees nuanced gradations, a more fluid system governed to some extent by human agency, personal whim, and circumstance. Ellison questions the rigid correlation in Baraka's thought between color, education, income, and personal preference in music—the assumption that poor, dark-skinned blacks would necessarily appreciate country blues while middle-class, lighter-skinned blacks would be drawn inevitably to the more sanitized forms of the music played in urban night clubs or theaters. Wondering how a blues-loving, light-skinned, wealthy, Republican-voting black born of a light-skinned mother and darker father would fit into Baraka's scheme, Ellison finds that Baraka's theory "flounders before that complex of human motives which makes human history, and which is so characteristic of the American Negro" (1978, 58–59). For Ellison, black American culture could not be considered an abstraction, completely separated from broader American culture. Any consideration of black American music must, he says, reflect also on the role of the music in shaping what Baraka calls the "mainstream" of American music. Moreover, black American music is not, for Ellison, an untainted, pure form but has evolved through processes of borrowing and incorporation of aspects of European music, and as such it bears testimony to the historically pluralistic nature of American culture (61). This process (which in the Caribbean is termed creolization) works unpredictably and in various directions, not only from white to black or European to African, so that, as Ellison says, American whites have been walking "Negro walks, talking Negro flavored talk . . . , dancing Negro dances and singing Negro melodies" so long that it is impossible to talk of a mainstream American culture from which blacks are irrevocably excluded (61). Ultimately, Ellison's objection to Baraka's politically engaged interpretation of black music is that it flattens and simplifies black American experience, that in "impos[ing] an ideology" on black cultural complexity, it does it a disservice, distorting its history for narrow political ends (61).

It follows that Baraka's Afro-centered interpretation of black music in general and James Brown in particular tells only part of the story. If strong African elements remain in the music, then these have inevitably been creolized throughout American history and have adapted to different times and places to create new hybrid forms. Indeed, it is difficult to find any evidence from the 1960s that Brown attributed his rhythms to African influence, and, when he promoted blackness, it was primarily with reference to the United States.[30] Even as his "Say It Loud (I'm Black and I'm Proud)" became an anthem for the Black Power movement, and even as he inspired the subsequent racially conscious work of, for instance, the Temptations, Sly Stone, Curtis Mayfield, the Last Poets, and Gil Scott-Heron, Brown's own political impulses were distinctly conservative. He promoted good-sense ideas such as staying in school (on "Don't Be a Dropout" [1966], he sings "Without an education, you might as well be dead"), working hard, and making the system work for black people rather than destroying it.[31] Thus, in June 1968, two months before the release of "Say It Loud," Brown brought out the patriotic and conciliatory "America Is My Home" and shortly after went on a government-sponsored tour of Vietnam to boost troop morale. Tellingly, Baraka criticized this release for its lack of "black spirit"; the track, he argued, bore the musical stamp of R&B "but it did not have the consciousness of Black, so it could not be called Black. To sing lies about America is not beneficial to the Black Nation, therefore it's not conscious of Blackness" (1971, 132). Brown was similarly criticized by the Black Panther party for exploiting his singular status within the black community to make money for himself and for the capitalist system. "You hear James Brown talking about Black and Proud," complained Emory Douglas, the party's minister of culture, "then you hear him on the radio saying, 'Why don't you buy this beer?'" (quoted in Ward 1998, 412).

IN THE BREAK

Moten's more recent critique of the notion of "black spirit" further exposes the theoretical weaknesses of Baraka's analyses, and it helps to re-situate the rhythms of Brown and soul music within their immediate spatial (American) and temporal (postmodern) contexts. Far from being simply a matter of changing intellectual trends, the differences between Baraka's and Moten's theories of black culture indicate developing notions of blackness that also offer new means of conceptualizing Brown's rhythmic inventions of the 1960s and 1970s. Moten challenges most fundamentally Baraka's notion that black culture is experienced primarily in terms of deeply felt instincts, an idea similar to Césaire's and to some extent Jean Price-Mars's previous conceptions of blackness in Martinique and Haiti, respectively. Faced with the hypermodern "white" world, Baraka, like his earlier counterparts in the Caribbean, retreated into a vision of black culture as an organic though static and unchanging phenomenon, a state of being and feeling that existed outside the orbit of white experience.

Juxtaposing Baraka's thinking with Martin Heidegger's argument that everything essential and important in human history and experience has occurred only because man had a (single) home and was rooted in a (unique) tradition, Moten argues that both Heidegger and Baraka search ceaselessly for "the unique word, the essence, the meaning, the essential quality of 'being'" (2003, 128, 144). Drawing on Jacques Derrida, Moten questions the notion of "being" as a static, knowable condition, proposes that there is no one word for being, and argues that all we can know or investigate in regard to being is "the complex origin of quantification, differences, formalizations" (144). In the absence of a single word for being, Moten argues, Baraka reinfuses being with spirit and *anima*—in Jungian psychology, the true inner self (144). Moten further interprets Baraka's conceptions of race and culture in terms of a Heideggerian confusion of *humanitas* with *animalitas*—that is, the human with the animal, the biological (145). It is as if, for Baraka, human nature is programmed biologically and racial differences are fixed and inherited inevitably. Moten's skepticism over Baraka's racialized notion of culture leads him to the question of rhythm and blackness, and he asks pointedly, "What, then, is the connection between *animalitas* and rhythm?" (145). This question recurs in various forms throughout the history of rhythm in the New World. In this specific case—Moten's deconstruction of Baraka's racialized critique of the white jazz player Burton Greene—the contradictions of Baraka's theories are laid bare. "Baraka uses the discourse of animality to dehumanize Greene," Moten says, "a discourse marked by race and rhythm, though he criticizes that discourse as it applies to blacks in the very same essay" (145).

Black performance for Baraka is not just or not primarily the sound; it is, Moten says, "the unmediated performance of essential blackness (and whiteness) that is made apparent in the difference between sounds" (145). In and on this space of racial difference is where rhythm acts as a primary racial differentiator and where Baraka erects his barrier between earthy, authentic black culture and alienated, rootless white culture. In effect, Baraka adheres to the view of "an immutable black musical essence that survives apart from the contingencies of social and cultural change" (Radano 2003, 3). Baraka's case also seems to illustrate Georgina Born and David Hesmondhalgh's argument that, though music is often seen as a means of imagining "emergent and labile identities," it is equally at times used as a medium for "marking and reinforcing" existing sociocultural categorizations (2000, 32).

An important sexual element also exists in Baraka's discourse of race, rhythm, and music. His blackness is hyper-masculine and self-consciously opposes itself to what Moten calls an "aestheticized Euro-cultural effeteness that is alienated, commodified, artifactualized, necessarily homosexual" (2003, 150). Baraka's black, male "earthiness" functions as a corrective to this feminized white aesthetic by deploying a "purely and necessarily heterosexual, socially realistic (if not naturalistic), lyric masculinity" (151). This extreme masculinism, as Moten recognizes, is a product of history, a response to and repudiation (and, he says, repetition) of the historical violation of black maternity (215). It is, he says, a masculinist radicalism born of the severance of filial ties, "the aesthetic and political assertion of motherless children and impossible motherhood" (215). Therefore, it is a defensive, compensatory masculinism that responds to very real historical traumas but that tends to trap itself by reducing and limiting its own potential meaning. As perhaps the single most important aesthetic aspect of this male assertion, rhythm acts like mother and father (or stands in place of them in their absence) and is jealously guarded by Baraka and others, who assert their earthy, grounded, authentic cultural attachments even as this assertion implies their historical lack of attachment and their ongoing social and political emasculation.

Although Moten recognizes the historical reasons that lead to such hypermasculinism, he seeks to free himself and black radical art from the emotionalist, essentialist conceptions of black music and rhythm that entrap Baraka. Criticizing Ekkehard Jost's argument in *Free Jazz* that the new jazz of the 1960s is "easily connected to a kind of expression of emotionalism" (quoted in Moten 2003, 129), Moten takes issue with a long-standing critical perspective through which, he says, black art and thinking have been obscured (2003, 129). The new black music of the 1960s, Moten contends, was characterized less by retrogressive, essentialist gestures than by an effective dismantling of traditional binary categories. In this period, he says, a new kind of black art and thought emerged in which emotion and structure, preparation and spontaneity, and individuality and collectivity can no longer be understood in opposition to one another. Rather, the art itself resists any interpretation in which these elements are opposed; it resists any designation, even those of the artists themselves, that depends on such oppositions (129).

These oppositions are derived from and act as props for the black/white opposition that underpins Baraka's interpretations of American music and that belies the true advances in music and thought in the 1960s. Brown's musical practice never relied on such oppositions; his emotion was always part of the structure, his spontaneity was part of his preparation, and his individuality was connected to broader collectivities, be they the band, the people, or his listeners. The question, put rhetorically by Moten, is whether the discourse that surrounds the music "gets to the liberatory space the music opens" (129). Baraka's black, Heideggerian nationalism is a response to the white, Western world's apparent loss of "spirit and origin," and as such it is caught in a self-nullifying circular movement, driven by the dream of an "impossible return" (130). The music, however, manifests a quite different reaction to the white other, adapting, inventing, and renewing itself in a future-oriented movement ("fightin' the future," as Brown said) that makes black identity more of an evolving, unpredictable, phenomenon that, according to Moten, "effectively obliterates the ethical, ontological, and epistemological conceptual apparatuses" on which Baraka's racialized complexes depend (131). Put simply, the music—of James Brown and others—would not do what Baraka wanted it to do (131).[32]

Baraka's impulsive movement toward what Moten calls the "impossible return" again links his vision of race and culture to that of Césaire, and in many ways Moten's critique of Baraka functions like Glissant's own questioning of Césaire's Negritude. In his post-Negritude theories, Glissant recognizes the inevitable impulse of any transplanted group to return, to deny the voyage in a sense, and to attempt to reconnect with what was lost in the movement to the new place. Return *(retour)*, Glissant says, is the "obsession with the One"—a unified conception of self, race, and culture (1981, 44). This kind of return for Glissant, as for Moten, is always impossible because it denies the changes that the journey has inevitably effected, culturally, and in terms of the group's relationship with different times and spaces. To return, Glissant says, is to consecrate permanency and "non-relation" (1981, 44). The unpredictable, unfixed, impermanent formations of identity that occur when one relinquishes the impulse to return and enters into "relation" are for Glissant (and implicitly for Moten) the paradoxical chance that the Middle Passage offers to New World blacks.

In general, Glissant and Moten share a conception of black New World identity and culture that is based less on laws, fixed categorizations, and dogma than on the realities of diasporic relation. Identity evolves inevitably, as Glissant and his fellow Martinican author Patrick Chamoiseau have argued, but it cannot establish itself where rules, edicts, or laws draw on nature as their authority and justification. People, individually and collectively, may be aware of how their identity is evolving, but they cannot decide the movement of this evolution in advance by fixed precepts or postulations. Identity is a "being-in-the-world," something born out of living, relating, and changing, not a fixed category decided in advance. If it is not so, say Glissant and Chamoiseau, then collectivity would become mechanical, "its future sterilized, rendered infertile by fixed systems, as if in a laboratory experiment" (2007, 2).

Therefore, if Baraka and other black cultural nationalists of the 1960s were right—that blackness was a fixed, immutable category, more or less completely divorced from whiteness—then the future of black music would have been sterile and lifeless, and the music would have died, taking James Brown with it. As Moten argues, however, Brown's music, as much as it is haunted by history and as much as the repetitive screams and moans echo the earliest experiences of African Americans, is not concerned with solidifying blackness into unchanging impregnability but with singing the uncertainties and making the music itself the vehicle of change and renewal. In this regard, Moten hears at the fractured climax of Brown's "Cold Sweat" a notion of revolution embedded in a set of questions: "What is the edge of this event? What am I, the object? What is the music? What is manhood? What is the feminine? What is the beautiful? What will blackness be?" (2003, 22).

THE RHYTHM REVOLUTION

The evolution of Brown and his band supplies some of the answers to Moten's questions. In March 1970, ever the strict disciplinarian and money-conscious capitalist, Brown fired his band after a dispute over pay and conditions. He called as replacements a group of studio musicians from Cincinnati called the Pacesetters, led by their eighteen-year-old bass player, William "Bootsy" Collins, and his twenty-five-year-old brother Phelps or "Catfish," a guitarist. Bootsy fell in quickly with the rhythm, extending its limits, and "stretching out Brown's sound" (Vincent 1996, 80). "When he started playing," drummer Stubblefield said of Collins, "when you set in the groove, *everything* moved" (quoted in Vincent 1996, 81). With trombonist, arranger, and bandleader Fred Wesley gone for nine months and the Collins brothers pushing the James Brown sound to its limits, the band's music turned ever more insistently around rhythm. As Vincent says, Bootsy and Catfish maintained the all-powerful James Brown funk groove and "turn[ed] it inside out," much as they would do to George Clinton's band a few years later (1996, 81). Brown had taught Bootsy, in particular, the importance of the one-beat, the down-beat at the beginning of every bar, and by the time Bootsy left with his brother in March 1971, he had picked up and confirmed "the orgiastic primacy of the rhythmically placed bass note" (Vincent 1996, 82).

In the meantime, Brown and his band had effected and inspired what Vincent calls "the rhythm revolution" in black American music. From the hit machines of Detroit, Memphis, and the Fame recording studio in Muscle Shoals, Alabama, to the New Orleans sound of the Meters and the pared-back, Afrocentric beats of the Last Poets, a rhythm revolution was indeed taking place. Brown had made the breakthrough, first with "Out of Sight," then more spectacularly with "Papa's Got a Brand New Bag" and its previously unheard percussive ensemble of guitar, brass, drum, and voice. From Otis Redding to Stevie Wonder and Junior Walker and the Allstars, the "rhythm in rhythm and blues was getting a shakedown" (Vincent 1996, 61). The standard structure of R&B drumming had, since World War II, been a double-timed, skipping shuffle rhythm that came from the swing rhythms of jazz. With the advent of James Brown, the shuffle was replaced by the "even" hi-hat pattern that extended "the rhythmic tension on every beat" (Vincent 1996, 61).[33] The demise of the shuffle rhythm and its dance corollary, the shuffle step, was in itself a sign of the new confidence of African Americans. The shuffle step had originated during slavery as a caricature of skipping, hopping African dance styles. In the minstrel shows of the nineteenth century, blackface characters would exaggerate the shuffle in their parody of black popular dance. Symbolically, the shuffle had connotations of brow-beaten blacks, never looking whites in the eye, but, as black confidence grew through the 1960s and as the new rhythmic patterns asserted themselves in music and dance, as in broader society, the feeling grew that people were "gonna shuffle no more" (Vincent 1996, 62).[34]

Which came first—the rhythm revolution or the social revolution? Can rhythm bring about social change? In his extensive discussions of the links between R&B and the Civil Rights movement, Ward—like other historians in the field—asserts that the various forms of R&B contained and expressed the hopes, dreams, fears, and frustrations of "ordinary blacks" (1998, 290).[35] Moreover, as black music and dance spread across America by means of tours, dances, records, and television, they helped to "nationalize" the new black pride and consciousness, which, Ward says, was "inextricably linked, cause and effect, to the emergence of a viable mass campaign for black civil and voting rights" (290). And yet, Ward is more cautious about the general perception that R&B artists were constant commentators on and agitators for the Civil Rights movement. Most writing on the ties between black music and the movement in the 1960s simplifies the relationship, either by pointing to song lyrics that underscore black pride and black economic and political struggle, or else by exaggerating the extent of personal involvement in the struggle by major soul artists. Typically, commentators have cited Brown's "Say It Loud (I'm Black and I'm Proud)" as proof of soul music's political engagement and sensitivity to race consciousness. As Ward argues, however, this song was not released until 1968, by which time the movement was more than twelve years old. Although there had been some notable exceptions—such as Sam Cooke's "A Change Is Gonna Come" in 1964—soul music, like its immediate predecessors R&B, rock and roll, and black pop, had become the primary musical expression of popular black consciousness "while paying relatively little explicit attention to the ongoing freedom struggle" (290).[36] More generally, too, commercial concerns often stifled the instinct to protest, especially in the early 1960s and before the situation was reversed later in the decade, when it became commercially expedient to emphasize blackness, to pronounce on issues of race, to hold benefit concerts, and donate to civil rights causes.[37] The prominent activist Harry Belafonte bemoaned the diffidence of the leading R&B artists—Brown, Cooke, the Motown acts—toward the civil rights struggle: "All of these people distanced themselves from the Movement," he told Ward, "not only once removed from it, but sometimes twenty times removed from it" (quoted in Ward 1998, 324). Therefore, in terms of the musicians themselves and what they did, there was generally a lapse between the progress the movement was making and the translation of that progress into the form of overtly political lyrics and extra-musical activities for the cause. Vincent implicitly agrees with Ward by arguing that it was the social revolution that preceded and inspired the rhythm revolution: desegregation had increased the mobility of black performers, and the general air of optimism had given black musicians confidence in their diverse traditions and encouraged creativity (1996, 62).

Perhaps, then, the prophetic aspects of music and rhythm, if they exist at all, function differently and on more subliminal, affective levels. Theorists of sound such as Murray Schafer read (or hear) the "acoustic environment" of a society as an indicator of social conditions and of the ways in which a particular society is evolving (2004, 6). The French economist Jacques Attali is even more forthright in asserting the prophetic qualities of music. Music, for Attali, heralds change and carries the essence of times to come (2004, 10). Music is prophetic, he says, in that it allows the exploration of the whole range of social and behavioral possibilities in a given code much more rapidly than material reality can; moreover, every major social rupture has been preceded by a radical mutation in musical codes (15). We could perhaps argue against Ward and Vincent by stating that music and the musical "mutations" of the 1950s and 1960s played no small part in creating the conditions for desegregation and that the rhythm revolution did not necessarily look back or reflect the contemporary in the ways Vincent suggests but projected forward, pulling the movement with it, pushing the notion of liberty to its limits, just as it pushed rhythm as the defining element of black music to its extreme.[38] Also, as Brown stated, the music was not just *about* rebellion, "it was the rebellion itself" (2005, 65). To recall Brown's own phrase, the music held in itself the portent of the future, and he, acting as a kind of conduit for the music, experienced it almost unnervingly as a prophecy: the music was "just *out there*," he said, and he was "actually fightin' the future" (quoted in White and Weinger 1991, 27).

In some senses, the freer, rhythmic music of the 1960s heralded the further progress made by (at least some) African Americans in the 1970s, such as in the further growth of the black middle class, the movements into white neighborhoods, and the tripling of interracial marriage rates.[39] This greater freedom and increased black self-confidence expressed in the music also perhaps anticipated, somewhat ironically, the demise of the black music industry in the late 1970s. By that time, the market had become more extensively desegregated, and the need for a separate black music industry became less urgent. Increasing numbers of black artists, hoping for crossover sales, left black record companies to sign with the majors. However, only a very few managed sustained crossover success, and many were caught in a kind of limbo between the white market that wanted pop hits and the black listening public from which many artists had become disconnected.[40] In a way, the music had come full circle: its characteristically "black" features, its heterogeneous sound, its tendency to use every instrument (including the voice) as percussion, and the primary importance of textured rhythms and counter-rhythms were "too bound up with connotations of black America" to sit well in the new, secularized context in which black music found itself (Danielsen 2006, 111).[41] This was a musical manifestation of what Cornel West calls "the bitter irony of integration," the fact that, in attaining their longed-for civil freedoms, African Americans also lost something, namely the "cultural structures that once sustained black life in America" but are no longer capable of resisting what he terms "the nihilistic threat" of the post–civil rights era (1994, 24). In another way, too, perhaps the focus, at least in Brown's project, on black capitalism and on making the system work for the people prophesied the depoliticized future of much of the music and the emphasis in certain forms of contemporary hip-hop on material gain and materialist showiness. Yet, even as black music apparently lost its way in the 1970s, it is significant that the most important counter to black nihilism situated itself in the rhythmic tradition and reworked Brown's rhythm revolution in its attempt to consolidate black identity as it fragmented into class divisions.[42] The band Parliament, featuring George Clinton and James Brown's former collaborators the Collins brothers, had an appeal that went beyond class division, as West recognizes: "Black technofunk articulated black middle-class anxieties toward yet fascination with U.S. 'hi-tech' capitalist society, black working class frustration of marginal inclusion within and ineffective protest against this society, and black underclass self-destructive dispositions owing to outright exclusion from this society" (1994, 182–83). Musically, Parliament reconfigured Brown's rhythmic textures, placing increasing emphasis on the One, slowing the beats down, and reinventing them into a new, heavier, deeper, funkier sound. Political renewal and black self-affirmation once again coincided with rhythmic reinvention and reappropriation of the beat.

Even after the departure of the Collins brothers in 1971, Brown and his band continued to innovate, and, with Fred Wesley, Jimmy Nolen, and Fred Thomas back onboard, they produced a series of albums that defined the funk sound and would later provide rich pickings for hip-hop samplers. Rhythm remained the essential element of the music even as the band experimented with funk horn solos and choppy, melodic interludes. "Get on the Good Foot" from 1972 remains the foremost example of the polyrhythmic funk of this period, and it was, Wesley said, the James Brown formula in its purest form. Wesley indicated a fascinating aspect of the music in general and this song in particular in his remark that what made the song quintessentially James Brown was that "none of those parts really go together" (quoted in Vincent 1996, 82). The music, a phenomenon comprising often jarring, discordant parts, should not work, should not hold together the way it does. What holds it together is the rhythm, the ever-present beats that inspired artists as diverse as Kool & the Gang, Earth, Wind and Fire, Mick Jagger, Elvis Presley, and, perhaps most significantly, the great African bandleaders Fela Kuti, Manu Dibango, Mongo Santamaria, and Hugh Masakela.

Appropriately, perhaps, the rhythm that many had attributed to African sources re-traversed the Atlantic in the early 1970s, transforming African popular music just as it had done in the United States and indeed the whole of the Western world. Manu Dibango mixed a funky rhythm guitar with conga drums on his important 1972 track "Soul Makossa," a work that opened up African music to American soul enthusiasts. Fela Kuti met Brown on the latter's tour of Africa in 1970 and soon incorporated Brown-style horns and guitars into his Afro-beat workouts (Vincent 1996, 70). African music fans demanded that their own artists play Brown tunes, and, as Fela Kuti says, the artists had little choice but to play some funk among their own innovative works, as they "had to eat" (quoted in Werner 2006, 139).[43] The music's recrossing of the Atlantic back to Africa, though suggesting complementarity between black American and African styles, also confirmed, ironically perhaps, that this was not African music but something new that had grown up in a different place and under different circumstances.[44] The African musicians embraced it as a new and fresh phenomenon, something they had never heard before but wished to incorporate into their own music.

However much, therefore, its rhythms could be traced back to Africa via New Orleans, Saint-Domingue, and the Middle Passage, James Brown's music and the rhythm revolution it inspired are quintessentially New World creations. Although Vincent insists that funk is deeply rooted in African cosmology—that is, in a harmonic relationship with the rhythms of nature (1996, 4)—he also recognizes that there is ultimately "something about The Funk that remains uniquely American" (70).[45] Indeed, without displacement, modernization, commercial concerns, and contact with other groups, the music would never have been what it is. These are fundamental, constitutive aspects of the music, not factors that somehow taint it. Many critics look backward in the sense that they seek to affirm where the music came from and, in some cases, assert the oneness of the culture it emerged from. But others, like Moten, turn things around by thinking primarily of where the music might *go*, where it might take people and societies. Ultimately, it is less important where the rhythms come from than what they do, where they take the music, and who listens to and participates in it. If, as Moten argues, the climax of James Brown's "Cold Sweat" had posed the question "What will blackness be?" then the subsequent evolution of Brown's band and of funk, dance music, and hip-hop suggests that blackness would be, will be, proud, new, future-oriented, confident, unbound, and rhythmic.

Conclusion

Listening to New World History

In a 2006 book on the intellectual history of the Caribbean, author Silvio Torres-Saillant writes critically about the region's music and questions whether music and musicians, despite their commercial success, actually bring any "discernible benefit" to the region (33). Evoking the historic Peace concert in Jamaica in 1978 when Bob Marley famously summoned political foes Michael Manley and Edward Seaga to the stage to shake hands, Torres-Saillant argues that this was one of the few examples of music and musicians having any significant, albeit short-lived, effect on the sociopolitical reality of a Caribbean country. Taking issue with the general perception that music can influence the material existence of Caribbean people, he argues that there is an "apparent incongruity between the power that writers and cultural critics ascribe to Caribbean music and the power that the rhythms and their performers have actually exhibited in the modern history of the region" (33). Moreover, he says, the "insertion of rhythms" from the region into the global music market has led to the "diminished relevance of Caribbean literature and thought production" (33) and has coincided with a regrettable but decisive "shrinking of the space" of the Caribbean "intellectual arena" (40).

While Torres-Saillant is no doubt right to question the assumption that there is a straightforward connection between music and social progress, he makes the error of dismissing music almost entirely, as if it were an aspect of culture whose worth, import, and influence could only be measured by tangible social change. In turning away more or less completely from music and rhythm, Torres-Saillant closes down an area of inquiry that has only been partially investigated and that requires the formulation of new questions, new approaches, and new theoretical paradigms to bring to light its deeper significance. In effect, Torres-Saillant closes his ears to a cacophonous history, one that, as this book has shown, has been shaped to a significant extent by music, rhythms, and sounds. What is required now is not the silencing of Caribbean and New World history but a new awareness and understanding of all its auditory aspects. We need, in short, to open our ears and listen to history.

THE SOUND AND THE THEORY

We may think we know—from old images, paintings, and even films—what slavery *looked* like, but how did it *sound?* We can perhaps conjure up images of the slave ship, the plantation, slave revolts, and slave dances, but can we put a soundtrack to those images, or do they run muted in our imaginations like silent movies? Were the sounds of slavery similar across the plantations of the New World, from Brazil to Virginia? Do these sounds die with the passage of time and the institution of plantation slavery, or do they survive, mutate, and evolve so that they may be heard even today in their commuted forms? If sounds do not die completely, what particular sounds have persisted through time and can still be heard today, and do these sounds constitute living ties with the past, parts of history that have outlived slavery and yet still bear witness to the lived experience of bondage? How can we listen to the past when sound is, by its nature, evanescent, when it fades as quickly as it comes, and when the ability to record sounds is historically a new development?

The task of tuning in and listening to the past, of "hearing history," is not a new undertaking. From classical antiquity to the nineteenth century, thinkers have reflected on the nature of hearing, listening, and aurality.[1] In the mid-twentieth century, too, historians of the French *Annales* school and theorists such as Marshall McLuhan and Walter Ong wrote influential works on the history of the senses in general, including the history of aurality and listening. In the 1970s, with the prominence of the study of social history, interest in aural history continued to grow and was complemented by related work on intellectual history and the history of seeing, notably Martin Jay's *Downcast Eyes*.[2] Thus, interest in the history of sound is not new, but modern historians, wary of and skeptical about the "hypervisual" (Bailey 2004, 23) nature of the modern world and the neglect of the other senses, are now listening to the past with greater intensity. They have extended the history of aurality beyond the boundaries of music and musicology and are considering sound in all its varieties, from, for example, the sounds of religious ceremonies to those of church bells, television, radios, telephones, and urban living. One of the most prominent of these tuned-in historians is Mark Smith, who sees (or hears) in this new historiography the hope of redirecting the "visually oriented discipline of history," a discipline that often places emphasis on the search for "perspective" and "focus" through the "lens" of evidence, an approach heavily "indebted to the visualism of 'Enlightenment' thinking and ways of understanding the world" (2004a, ix).[3]

This radical readjustment of historical inquiry away from the visual and toward the aural highlights the importance of any and all sounds that form what the Canadian composer R. Murray Schafer calls "soundscapes." In Europe, Schafer argues, the ear was superseded by the eye as the primary bodily gatherer of information around the time of the Renaissance as the result of developments in the printing press and perspective painting.[4] It was not until the Renaissance that, for example, God became visualized in portraiture. Previously, the divinity had been conceived of and invoked through sound —songs and chants—which were often accompanied by dancing (Schafer 2004, 8). The rise of European modernity and gentility subordinated some senses, such as smell and touch, and privileged others, particularly sight. In the seventeenth century, René Descartes had "declared war on the senses," salvaging only sight as necessary for science and technology (Bailey 2004, 28). Descartes's pursuit of cerebral purity was to limit drastically intellectual interest in broader sensory consciousness (Bailey 2004, 28). With industrialization came noise, which Peter Bailey defines as "sound out of place" and which included a great cacophony of human and mechanical sounds that disrupted the cherished bourgeois Victorian state of silence; this was and is the perennial "sound of authority" inscribed in the regimes of church and state (2004, 23, 26).

In the United States, as Americans pushed farther westward, the ordered, regular, and rhythmic sounds of progress (the steam engine, the axe falling, wheels turning, even church hymns) drowned out the less predictable, unsettling sounds of the frontier such as the calls of unfamiliar animals and the "yell of the savage" (M. Smith 2004b, 366). Bells marked out newly tamed spaces and provided regular and reassuring auditory reminders of the reign of order.[5] During the same period in France, music came to be appreciated in new ways that reflected the evolving class system there, in particular the rise of the bourgeoisie and its impulse to define itself by excluding its social others, principally the rowdy working classes. The bourgeoisie developed a new way of listening that involved a greater sensitivity to emotions and sentiments in the music. The effect of this new mode of listening was to "turn inward to feel the passions the music evoked," and, though this created a new level of musical appreciation and judgment that "exhibited a sensibility toward egalitarianism," the coming of this new type of silent, introverted listener also defined bourgeois sensibilities and confirmed social identity through setting a norm for manners and politeness, which excluded the uncouth, the boisterous, and the outwardly expressive (J. Johnson 2004, 172, 176).

The nature of music (and indeed the nature of societies) changes over time, however. Treating the world as a "macrocosmic musical composition," Schafer observes that the definition of music in the contemporary era has been fundamentally revised: today all sounds may be considered to be music, and musicians are now "anyone and anything that sounds" (2004, 4–5).[6] Schafer also argues that music, in history and in the contemporary age, bears a close relation to the social and political conditions of the time. Mozart's "grace and balance," he says, reflected the "egalitarian and enlightened" reign of Maria Theresa, whereas Strauss's "sentimental vagaries" echo the decline of the same Austro-Hungarian empire (6). More generally, the broader "acoustic environment" of a society may be read, Schafer says, as "an indicator of social conditions which produce it and may tell us much about the trending and evolution of that society" (6). Music is also a tool of power that can be manipulated for various ends, including bringing people together under a collective banner (race, nation, class, gender, age), making people forget about social or political ills (wars, economic depression), and conversely reminding them constantly of expected norms (of behavior, conduct, limits). At the same time, however, sound, noise, and music are almost impossible to control and silence completely; anyone with a voice can sing or make sounds, whether or not anyone hears them.

SOUNDS OF YOUNG AMERICAS

It is in the Americas that some of modernity's most intense conflicts over sound and music have occurred. As this book has shown, the historic, often violent, chaotic, and disordered coming together of disparate peoples, cultures, musics, and sounds in the Americas has engendered (historically one-sided) debates over the nature of civilization, humanity, and culture, and these debates have often had prominent auditory elements. In early modern England, sounds such as the whoops and hollers of country folk and lower-class craftsmen were heard by educated listeners as markers of their social inferiority and of the boundary between civility and barbarity. With colonial expansion and voyages of conquest, this boundary was extended into ever more remote geographical spaces, and notions of civility and barbarity came to turn less on differences of class than of color and "race" (B. Smith 2003, 134).

Historians of early America have established the ways in which colonial Americans managed sounds in meetinghouses and churches to add "layers of meaning that enriched and reinforced deeply held beliefs" (Rath 2004, 207). The "acoustical spaces" of early Quaker halls were square, hexagonal, or octagonal, the acoustic effect of which was to make sound equally audible from any point in the building, which in turn reflected Quaker notions of egalitarianism (Rath 2004, 216). The management of aurality and sound remained of prime importance to religious thought in America both during and after the eighteenth century. In particular, the evangelical movement was marked by its opponents as offensively noisy, an emitter of the uncontrolled sounds of the saved and the cries of the distressed that undercut the more general reverence for silence. Yet, whereas the boisterous sounds of the evangelicals were for some discordant and disruptive, the very same sounds attracted others (both black and white) to the movement (Schmidt 2004, 236).

The social or racial other always "offends the senses," be it through the supposed stench of the working class or the loud, jarring, at times frightening sounds of the immigrant or the racial other (Schmidt 2004, 236). In the United States, the revulsion of the Anglican hierarchy toward noisy evangelicalism was compounded (and further charged with a sense of moral and racial superiority) when the sources of religious noise were black Americans. To the ears of antebellum whites, the sounds of African American churches—the preachers' flowery, elaborate phrasing, the noisy interjections of worshippers, the yelling, the rhythmic stamping of feet, the hand-clapping, the vigorous singing—seemed out of place, a chaotic noise ill suited to a place of worship. Traditional white congregations were more familiar with the careful regulation of sound in churches: the preacher spoke while the worshippers listened; hymns were chosen beforehand, not launched into at random; and those hymns were closed, fixed compositions that were not embellished or added to by the faithful. As one Presbyterian minister, criticizing the "inappropriate" nature of black worship, stated in 1847, "Public worship should be conducted *with reverence and stillness on the part of the congregation*" (quoted in White and White 2004, 248).

For black slaves, however, the noisy, interactive mode of worship was a rare means of expressing themselves with any kind of autonomy. It was also an integral part of their broader, African-inherited cultural performances, both secular and religious. The interjections of the black congregation were related to the antiphonal, call-and-response modes of expression that slaves had held onto from their African pasts. And preachers fed off the responses of the congregation, which helped them attain the emotional peaks that were another aspect of black worship heard as curious and unnecessarily noisy by many white ears. Although black preachers were often considered by whites to be effective orators, the intellectual content of their sermons was frequently dismissed as "nonsensical" or absurd, lacking in meaning (White and White 2004, 257). Yet blacks would respond enthusiastically and expressively to these preachers, much to the bemusement of white observers. It seems that what black worshippers responded to was less the meanings of the words than their sounds, the rising and falling intonation of the preacher, the communal singing, and the various, swaying rhythms of the service. As Shane White and Graham White say, "The presence or absence of intellectual content played no part in this reaction" (2004, 258). And, as author James Weldon Johnson wrote, the typical "old-time Negro preacher loved the sonorous mouth-filling, ear-filling phrase because it gratified a highly developed sense of sound and rhythm in himself and his hearers" (1929, 19). In gospel music (something like in James Brown's work), plaintive sounds and moans take the place to some extent of words; the essence of the style, Anthony Heilbut writes in *The Gospel Sound*, "is a wordless moan [that] renders the indescribable, implying, 'Words can't begin to tell you, but maybe moaning will'" (quoted in Moten 2003, 194).[7] Thus, what was inappropriate, ungodly noise to white listeners was part of a broader African American aesthetic that favored, among other things, the *sounds* of a performance—its tones, repetitions, and rhythms—over the dry intellectual sermonizing of white preachers. The noise itself was meaningful and contained a memory, a code that transmitted its own messages on a frequency that few whites could quite tune into.

In the South, masters cherished quietude and experienced the plantation as a site of organic, controlled noises that reflected and reinforced the "natural" hierarchies of slavery. For slaves, however, the plantation was a place of unnatural, bustling, slashing, whipping sounds that they often resisted through song and music, or conversely by holding their silence, refusing to speak and thereby appropriating the masters' ideal of quietude. The slaves' silence was feared by planters, who could not control the inaudible resistance, could not quite catch the murmurings of planned escapes, and were perennially susceptible to revolts plotted in silence and darkness (M. Smith, 2004b, 373).[8] Silence may be etymologically derived from the Latin verb *to obey*, but, in the American South and elsewhere in the New World, slaves used silence as a means of resisting, of saying something while remaining wordless. In this and other ways, sounds (or the lack of them) came to be pivotal markers of African American identity. As White and White argue, "Much of what was distinctive about black culture was to be found in the realm of sound" (2005, ix). Although silence was sometimes used as an impenetrable means of resistance, slave culture was ultimately distinguished by sounds "made to be heard" (White and White 2004, ix) and was inherently polyphonic.

HEARD WORLDS AND THIRD WORLDS

The field of aural history is expanding rapidly, but much of the work done so far has focused on the United States and Europe, and, as Mark Smith recognizes, the history of listening, sound, and noise in developing regions "begs for detailed attention and investigation" (2004a, x). There has been no extended (circum-)Caribbean auditory historiography to date and therefore no specifically Caribbean theoretical tools, though many of the concepts and arguments of American and European auditory historiography are potentially applicable to this region. The debates that have been simmering among auditory historians (particularly those dealing with slave cultures) have put forth conceptual and theoretical tools that are applicable not only to Europe and the United States but also, with some careful interpretation, to further research in the field in the Caribbean. Indeed, some of the more general concepts and arguments seem all the more valid when applied to the Caribbean.[9]

Perhaps the most fundamental point made by auditory historians is that sound and subjectivity are closely linked: the "heard world" serves as "an index for identity" (M. Smith 2004b, 368). In a region shaped by the historical genocide (and thereby silencing) of one group of people, by the brutal displacement and enslavement (and attempted silencing) of another, and by the complete (and univocal) mastery of another, the control of sounds, voices, and languages has long been associated with defining and circumscribing identity. To adapt one critic's argument (on the nature of noise in Victorian England), sounds in the Caribbean have long been expressive and communicative resources that have registered, manipulated, distorted, and created collective and individual identities. In Caribbean history, noise (of carnivals, revolts, dancehalls, protests) has been and remains a potent form of social energy with the capacity to "appropriate, reconfigure or transgress boundaries" and to convert space into territory (Bailey 2004, 34).

The modern, European conception of the self, epistemized and cognitive, constitutes itself in terms of perception and seeing. As several theorists of auditory history have argued, European thought since the Renaissance has experienced the "epistemological regime of the eye" (Connor 2004, 54). As such, the rise of scientific and technological rationality was enabled by what Heidegger called the *Gestell,* or the visual objectification and enframing of the world. This modern, Western emphasis on the visual—conceived, tellingly, at the time of early European colonialist expansion—allowed the world to be treated as an object, differentiated from the self, and thereby liable to be controlled, dominated, and manipulated. The control that modernity exercises over the world is dependent on an understanding of the seen world as separate from the self, and, as Steven Connor states, "Where knowing is associated so overwhelmingly with seeing, then the will-to-self-knowing of the epistemized self has unavoidably taken a scopic form" (2004, 54). In the Caribbean, the Europeans' visualized conception of nature allowed for the framing and separation of the land as an object to be mapped, dominated, and exploited. Similarly, non-Europeans, because they were visually different, could be thought of as distinct beings or different "races." Thus, having identified non-Europeans as irrevocably other, Western colonials could feel a degree of justification in dominating and exploiting them.[10]

Racism is indeed a discourse of power "that thinks with its eyes," and race itself is a product of history and not nature that sets human difference in visual terms (Bull and Back 2003, 14).[11] In effect, these processes of visual-racial differentiation were repeated across the plantation societies of the New World and created a culture that stretched from Virginia to Brazil. That culture persists today in various forms, chiefly in music and dance, across this broad post-plantation world. Appropriately, therefore, this book has focused primarily on the Caribbean but has also situated the Caribbean within a broader New World frame and, in dedicating one chapter to the United States, has recognized and explored some of the often hidden connections between African American and Caribbean experience. Not surprisingly, of all the work done by established historians of aurality, it is the research on the American South and the experience of American slavery that is potentially the most useful critical bridge in beginning to listen to Caribbean history. In its music, its work sounds, its religious sounds, and its obstinate silences, the heard world of the American South echoes across the plantation world to the Caribbean, communicating with it in ways that require us to tune into the sounds of the past and to listen attentively for their reverberations in the present.

In the colonial Caribbean, the control of sounds and noises was a similarly important condition for the definition and demarcation of space and, thus, of identity. The sounds of slave experience were primary elements in converting the alienating spaces of the Caribbean into new territories. Of importance in this regard are the sounds of language, particularly the various Creole tongues that evolved out of cross-cultural contact. For Édouard Glissant, language, sounds, and silences defined and shaped slave experience. The alienated body of the slave was, says Glissant, deprived of speech; self-expression was not only forbidden but "impossible to envisage" (1989, 122). All pleasure for the slave was silenced, repressed, and denied, and in such a situation expression is necessarily "cautious, reticent, whispered, spun thread by thread in the dark" (122–23). From the beginning of slave-master contact, when Creole language came into being, the spoken form imposed on the slave its "particular syntax" (123). For the Caribbean person, Glissant says, the word is first and foremost not written but sound and noise. As Glissant argues, the pitch of sounds—screams, shouts, cries—conveyed meanings that escaped the comprehension of the master, and slaves in this way "camouflaged the word" in the varying intensity of their sounds. This, Glissant says, is how the alienated slave organized his or her speech, by "weaving it into the apparently meaningless texture of extreme noise" (124). This historical speech tendency translates itself into Creole language in the speed of popular conversation, a seamless stream of language that makes speech into "one impenetrable block of sound" (124). The meaning of a sentence is again hidden in the sounds and pitch of the popular language, and in this sense Creole was a "kind of conspiracy" that concealed meaning and thought (124). Crucially, Glissant sees (or hears) in these linguistic practices, and particularly in the speed of Creole speech, echoes of music—the "embryonic rhythm of the drum" (124). The rhythm of the speech, like the rhythm of the drum, carries meaning, and this meaning is occulted, only available to those attuned to the varying sounds, pitches, and rhythms of the language.[12]

Therefore, in focusing on four circum-Caribbean contexts and on one element of sound that even auditory historians have tended to ignore—rhythm—this book has responded to some extent to Mark Smith's call to listen to history more carefully and to consider the ways in which sounds have shaped history, identities, and cultures. In each of the times and places studied in this book, rhythms, repetitions, and cyclical notions of time were not initially associated with Africa and blackness but were integral parts of the vernacular culture of European settlers. Indeed, only with the arrival en masse of millions of Africans (speaking many different languages and with their own diverse, heterogeneous cultural traditions) did the notion of a distinct black and white culture begin to solidify into the dualistic models that we live with today. This process of racial and cultural differentiation, shaped and supported by the racial thinking of European philosophers such as Hegel and Artur de Gobineau, came to attribute rhythmic music and dance exclusively to Africans and to the state of savage, pre-modern humanity that the Africans were supposed to exemplify. The Africans brought with them a particular affinity to rhythm, which was never biologically inherited but was an acquired aspect of music and everyday life, social interaction, speech, recreation, and work.[13] These rhythms clashed with the industrial rhythms of the plantation system, the unnatural, dehumanizing, profit-driven cycles of work that radically interrupted natural rhythms of life, birth, and death. African rhythms adapted themselves to this alienating environment in the antiphonal work songs that accompanied field labor and in the slave dances that were sometimes sacred, sometimes secular gatherings that purged (to some extent) the suffering endured in working to the machine-like rhythms of the plantation.

In each place and time, too, vernacular culture—dances, music, religion, storytelling, language—acted as a repository of rhythm, and, as the three-tiered social structure typical of Creole societies developed, the brown-skinned middle class often as much as the white elite distanced itself from rhythm and "black culture" in general. Rhythm therefore became associated not only with a certain "race" of people but also with the lower class. As such, especially in the Caribbean, middle-class intellectuals of color often aligned themselves with the putatively superior, arrhythmic literary and musical culture of Europe. In the nineteenth century, with a few exceptions, rhythm remained for many mulatto intellectuals a marker of Africa and thus of social and cultural inferiority. The poetry and art music of this period rarely evoked rhythmic, vernacular culture in anything but derogatory, disdainful terms. Yet rhythm has also been a primary means through which lower-class Caribbean and New World black peoples have asserted and enacted their historical and political agency.

As the twentieth century began and as various pan-African movements gathered momentum, rhythm was slowly recuperated into the emerging middle-class, nationalist consciousness as a potent sign of racial difference and a primary element of the lost, devalorized parts of national culture. The terms in which rhythm was evoked—as something irrevocably pre-modern, primitive, and anti-rational—were virtually the same as before, but now these qualities were seen positively as means of uniting separated diasporic peoples and of further solidifying the notion of black culture as radically, incontrovertibly different to white culture. Rhythm flooded into all areas of middle-class, mulatto culture and became, for the first time, a prominent, distinguishing feature of poetry, art music, and choreography. "Primitive sources" were now raided in the quest to recast national culture in primordial, anti-European (and often anti-colonial) terms. The putatively authentic culture of the previously neglected masses became seen as the single most important marker of national difference, a great, supposedly uncorrupted resource to be plundered and appropriated as the middle classes slowly shed their mimetic impulses and embraced cultural nationalism. In the great political, cultural, and social maelstroms of the New World in the twentieth century, rhythm was thrown center stage, and it played a dynamic role in Haitian indigenism, Negritude, and Black Power, movements that harnessed rhythm to their notions of black culture and black difference.

There are remarkable similarities in the history of rhythm and the discourse that has developed around it between the different times and places studied in these four chapters, but there are also, inevitably, important differences created by the particular historical and social realities of each situation. Perhaps most strikingly, in post-revolution Haiti, rhythm was suppressed and associated with cultural and intellectual backwardness by black leaders who largely echoed the prejudices and fears of the colonial regime they had fought so hard to dislodge. The particular development of Haitian society—the deep class and color divides, the divisions between rural and urban communities—led rhythm to be considered an aspect of vernacular culture that had little place in the elite's conception of Haiti as a modern, westernized nation. It was only with the American occupation that these elite attitudes began to change and that rhythmic peasant culture was seen (and heard) in different, less-derisive ways. Paradoxically, the elite rejection of rhythmic non-urban culture had allowed it to become deeply embedded in popular expressive culture, most notably in Vodou, its dances, and music. The extended schism between the Haitian state and the Catholic Church only reinforced the Vodou religion, allowing it to develop, creolize, and further integrate rhythm into its rites and rituals.

By contrast, in Trinidad, the more classically colonial situation meant that rhythmic popular culture was under constant attack from the white establishment, particularly the Protestant British. Although it remained an important aspect of suppressed African-derived religions, rhythm in Trinidad could not retain its sacred functions to the same extent as in Haiti. Carnival became the focus of dualistic debates over culture and rhythm, and, throughout the nineteenth century, the colonial authorities in Trinidad systematically repressed the rhythmic music of the masses. Slowly evolving from a mainly white celebration, Carnival was gradually appropriated by the black lower classes, who translated their rhythmic culture and music into the secularized space of the festival, spreading fear among the whites who saw (and heard) constantly in black expressive culture intimations of revolt. The many ordinances that banned drum playing only further strengthened the connection between black identity and rhythm. At every point, rhythm did not disappear but returned in new forms, by means of new instruments. The racial dualism of debates over rhythm and Carnival was complicated by the divisions between the British administration and the French Creoles; the latter were generally more receptive to rhythmic culture and contributed to its creolization through participating in Carnival and its associated dances and celebrations. Something like in Haiti, but in a more muted way, in the early to mid-twentieth century Trinidad's rising class of largely nonwhite intellectuals turned to popular culture as an untainted repository of authentic, rhythmic black culture. As the pro-independence movement gathered momentum in Trinidad, rhythmic music was slowly rehabilitated into nationalist discourse. The final step of this evolution was the promotion of the steel pan, which had emerged from the long-neglected culture of the urban poor as the national instrument of independent Trinidad.

The fact that Martinique and Guadeloupe are not independent but remain departments of France has had important repercussions in the history of rhythm there. The Negritude movement did allow for—indeed, relied on—the elaboration of dualistic, racialized notions of culture in which rhythm was recuperated as a marker of pan-African blackness. Negritude did not, however, lead to political independence for the French Caribbean territories, and as such rhythm was not incorporated into a triumphalist idea of national culture and blackness. Instead, the notion that a natural bond existed between black peoples and rhythm was quickly rejected and subjected to the most rigorous intellectual examination of all the contexts discussed in this book. The piercing critiques of Frantz Fanon and René Ménil effectively cut short the essentialist discourse on blackness and rhythm, and they cleared the intellectual ground for a less racially oriented, more phenomenologically based engagement with rhythm. In Joseph Zobel's fiction, we find some of the earliest post-Negritude reinterpretations of rhythmic popular culture. His presentation of the various dance and carnival scenes demonstrates his interest in and acute sensitivity to the ways in which rhythm acts as a release from daily hardships but also carries within itself something of the painful experience of those hardships and memories of the living past of slavery. Glissant takes up and develops Zobel's interest in history and memory and the ways in which they are transmitted through rhythm and recurring sounds. Glissant radically undermines the idea that the rhythm of the drum carries comforting memories of Africa, and he uses repetitive, rhythmic structures as means of working around and toward history, of sounding the past and trying to decode its meanings through listening to its continued reverberations in the present. Daniel Maximin, in turn, uses Glissantian techniques in his investigation of circum-Caribbean history. Rhythms and repetitions are at once integral elements of narrative structure and cultural tropes that unite the Caribbean with the broader New World, in particular with the great musical traditions of North America.

Perhaps Maximin's interest in and affinity with African American experience is the result of the fact that, in the United States as in the French Caribbean, black nationalism did not lead to liberation and the black culture there has had to negotiate its terms and its place vis-à-vis a politically and economically dominant white establishment. Since the early twentieth century, however, African American music has benefited from worldwide exposure and corporate backing in ways that music from the other New World sites has not. When James Brown turned decisively to rhythm in the mid-1960s, the repercussions of that move were always going to be more significant than those of the similar rhythmic turns in the other places. Although black nationalists such as Amiri Baraka sought to racialize Brown's rhythms and limit their potential meanings, the rhythms of seminal tracks such as "Cold Sweat" and "The Payback" escaped this potential prison and spread across the globe—to Africa, where they were enthusiastically greeted as new creations, and to Europe, where everyday Europeans began to rediscover the exhilaration of finding the beat and getting with "the One." This process of rhythmic globalization had actually begun in the 1920s with the spread of swing, boogie-woogie, and other forms of African American music. The global proliferation of rhythm—so often viewed as a marker of cultural primitivism—has coincided, paradoxically, with the expansion of modernity, urbanization, and industrial development.[14] In a sense, too, the history of popular music from the 1960s to the present has seen the partial deracialization of rhythm, particularly since the late 1980s and the emergence of hybrid forms of dance music such as Chicago house and its various offshoots.[15]

It may seem that rhythm has been secularized to a significant extent, that it has lost almost all of the religious functions it had both in pre-modern Europe and in the rituals of the New World slaves. Yet rhythmic dance music continues to function in the ways it has always done, creating trance-like states that are often experienced as spiritual happenings by its participants.[16] In particular, the rave scene that grew out of unofficial, illegal parties often held in secret, rural locations in England in the late 1980s has spread across the Western world and attracted young participants who, in many cases, talk of the scene in religious terms. For one commentator, dance parties have transmuted the role that religion once played in lifting people to the "sacramental and supramental plane" (Ray Castle, quoted in St. John 2003, 3).[17] The description of the rave scene as a "savage trance" (Gauthier 2003, 79) takes us back to the terminology of the white colonial order in the New World, only now the term is intended to commend rave as a post-Christian resurgence of the festival that provides "new avenues for the experience of the sacred in atomized societies" (St. John 2003, 9). Rave also functions like religious dance ceremonies in that it involves the abandonment of individual subjectivity to a broader collective sense of being, the "dissolution of the individual in sharing, the union of the separate" (Gauthier 2003, 80).[18]

Rhythm is, once again, the primary factor in bringing about these spiritual experiences, which often have little to do with established religion but which create new, noninstitutional notions of what religious experience is.[19] Moreover, rhythm is still perceived by political authorities as a threat to the established order. Faced with media-instigated panic over the supposed dangers of the rave scene, for example, the British government in 1994 issued the Criminal Justice and Public Order Act, which tellingly defined a rave as a gathering of people playing amplified music, "characterized by the emission of a succession of repetitive beats" (quoted in Reynolds 1999, 173). Rhythm has returned to Western public consciousness as a figure of potential subversion, creating panic among some while offering access to a new, if ancient, experience of time and subjectivity for others. Rhythm thereby completes one of its own looping, circular movements through history, movements that will continue to return and repeat themselves, turning to their own rhythms and to the beat of new and different drummers.

NOTES

INTRODUCTION

1. Paul Gilroy's well-known Black Atlantic critical framework is potentially useful here, too, in that the places and cultures discussed belong to a loose, still under-theorized "non-traditional tradition, an irreducibly modern, ex-centric, unstable, and asymmetrical cultural ensemble that cannot be apprehended through the manichean logic of binary coding" (1993, 198). For this study, I use the terms *American, New World,* or *circum-Caribbean* rather than Black Atlantic, as my interest lies more in this hemisphere than on the dynamics of transatlantic cultural exchange. For more on cultural affinities between the Caribbean and the American South, see Adams, Bibler, and Accilien (2007).

2. Rhythm is being increasingly used in the treatment of a variety of disorders such as Parkinson's disease and Alzheimer's disease. Rhythm-based music therapy is also being used to treat posttraumatic stress disorder and various psychological conditions. See, e.g., Thaut (2005) and Friedman (2000). For a general introduction to neuroscientific approaches to musical appreciation, see Levitin (2007).

3. See Layne Redmond's idea that "through rhythmic repetition of ritual sounds, the body, brain, and the nervous system are energized and transformed. When a group of people play a rhythm for an extended period of time, their brain waves become entrained to the rhythm and they have a shared brain wave state. The longer the drumming goes on, the more powerful the entrainment becomes. It's really the oldest holy communion" (quoted in Friedman 2000, 44).

4. Henri Lefebvre similarly argues that the study of rhythm involves both quantitative and qualitative aspects, and that "the multiple natural rhythms of the body (respiration, heart, hunger, and thirst, etc.) are superimposed and modified by *rational,* numerical, quantitative, and qualitative rhythms" (1992, 17–18).

5. The residual importance of Amerindian music and dance in the Caribbean will be discussed in chapter 2.

6. In this section, I am indebted to Anne Danielsen's excellent analysis (2006, 150–71) of temporality in Western musical theory.

7. Nevertheless, European classical composers did place a value on the importance of keeping time. See, e.g., Mozart's declaration that "accompanists who can't keep to a regular beat are vulgar and amateurish" (cited in Klingfors 1991, 347).

8. Even if scholars such as Susan McClary have revealed the ideological foundations of classical European theories of music and debunked the notion that teleologically driven European music is the ideal type for all musical forms, similar expectations still persist in European musical culture concerning music, time, tension, release, and closure. Listeners to Anglo-American popular music still largely expect a "song," constructed primarily of melody and chords, as opposed to a "groove," a more rhythmically driven, less teleologically directed track (Danielsen 2006, 153–54). Yet with the global popularity of various African American and Afro-Caribbean musical forms, and particularly since at least the late 1960s and early 1970s and the rise of James Brown and the funk movement, music with rhythm as its defining element has brought a different set of expectations and disrupted the linear model of musical structure. The rhythms and repetitions of these traditions have created nonlinear forms that have implicitly and explicitly questioned the putatively normative classical model and the ideas and assumptions behind them.

9. In the mid-seventeenth century, the missionary priest Jean-Baptiste Du Tertre expressed his opposition to selling young white men in the French islands "as slaves" into indentured labor, which he termed a "detestable" and "hateful commerce." At the same time, he approved of the sale of Africans into slavery (Du Tertre 1973, 2: 464–65, 525). See also Miller (2008, 17, 21).

10. In Danielsen's words, "The mind-centered Western tradition of religion and thought has resulted in a culture hostile to, scared by, and deeply fascinated with both bodily pleasure and the possibility of losing control" (2006, 107). See also Shane White and Graham White's argument that, though there were (and to some extent still are) stark differences in the production of European and African music, it seems also that European and African listeners were listening for and to (and to some extent still listen for and to) different things. Where the traditional white listener might listen for intelligible lyrics, accurate pitch, and purity of tone, blacks "needed to hear the complex rhythmic patterns, inflected pitches, and timbral diversity that delighted them" (2005, 32).

11. See Malik (1996, 39–61). See also, e.g., Mosse (1978) and Goldberg (1993).

12. Hegel also wrote famously in *The Phenomenology of Spirit* (1977) on the master-slave bond. In her well-known article "Hegel and Haiti" (2000), Susan Buck-Morss argues that the events of the Haitian Revolution were foremost in Hegel's mind as he wrote this work. See also Buck-Morss 2009.

13. For more on the links between European philosophy and racism, see, e.g., Popkin (1973) and Bracken (1978).

14. See the discussions of works by Jean Price-Mars in chapter 1 and Aimé Césaire in chapter 3.

15. This is not to suggest that non-Europeans were or are by nature attracted to drum-

ming and dancing. In Trinidad, for instance, calypsonians at times have shown their contempt for the rhythmic, African aspects of Trinidadian culture, as for example in Caresser's calypso about the African-derived religion Shango, in which he sings of how "The beating of the drums send the spirit to the head / And give them power to wake up any dead" (see Rohlehr 1990, 152–77).

16. For Christopher L. Miller, the Atlantic slave was someone who had "been translated and who had to, as a consequence, translate. His or her translation thus begat others—all the linguistic and cultural transfers that flowed from the huge infusion of Africans into the Americas" (2008, 101).

17. See Julie Ann Huntington's study (2005, 68–129) of the importance of rhythm in the work of Ousmane Sembene and Ahmadou Kourouma.

18. See David Brackett's argument that "rhythm as a separate field of inquiry in Western music did not develop until the nineteenth century. Until then, treatises had regarded rhythm largely as a function of pitch" (1995, 137). As a consequence of this, Brackett says, rhythmic analysis in Western music "has not developed to nearly the same extent as the analysis of pitch" (137).

19. For an excellent, detailed discussion of "African rhythm," see Danielsen (2006, 43–60).

20. Steven Connor suggests that "clapping and stamping may have provided the first systematic music produced by human beings" (2003, 67).

21. For more on the role of drumming in African societies, see Huntington (2005, 56–67).

22. See Christopher L. Miller's nuanced discussion (2008, 58–60) of the slave trade and its contribution to the enrichment of pre-revolutionary France.

23. See also Miller (2008, 48–49).

24. See also Tolstoy's remark to Gorki that "where you want to have slaves, there you should have as much music as possible" (quoted in Schafer 2003, 30).

25. Sara E. Johnson makes a similar point about the particularities of Caribbean rhythmic music, and she argues that Caribbean musical forms like the Cuban *tumba francesa,* the Puerto Rican *bomba,* and the Martinican *bèlè* do not have "direct corollaries in Africa" (2005, 42).

26. Antonio Benítez-Rojo argues that Caribbean rhythm is more than percussion; it is, he says, "a metarhythm which can be arrived at through any system of signs, whether it be dance, music, language, text, or body language, etc." (1992, 18).

27. See Moten (2003, 69). See also Lefebvre (1992, 90) on the differences between cyclical (cosmic) repetitions and linear (mechanical) repetitions.

28. See also M. Smith (1997).

29. On the way that bells marked out time, see, e.g., this anonymous contemporary account of plantation life: "At sunset I heard the bell ring, and noticed from all directions the workers retired gaily to rest from their labor until the following morning" (Popkin 2007, 71).

30. Laurent Dubois remarks that, to Saint-Domingue plantation owners and managers, the slaves were "laboring machines, cogs in a system meant to produce as much sugar or coffee as possible" (2004, 45).

31. See also McLellan (1992).

32. See also Miller (2008, 30).

33. Paul Gilroy talks of how slaves were equipped with "the living traces of an African onto-theology" and, as such, "neither sought nor anticipated the mode of dominating the external world that had provided Europeans with the essential preconditions for developing consciousness of freedom" (2001, 200). Also, as Gilroy says, "the plantation system made that way of dominating nature part of the slaves' experience of unfreedom" (200).

34. Milla Cozart Riggio sees a similar function in modern-day Carnival, in that it "privileg[es] leisure over work [and] recalls pre-industrial social rhythms," thereby "affirming the power of imagination and fantasy against the logic of reason and . . . resisting the tyranny of clock time in favor of an organic and seasonal temporal flow" (2004a, 19).

35. This submission of individual identity is still apparent in modern-day Carnival, which relies less on expressions of individuality than on the yielding of discrete subjectivity to the broader body of collective masqueraders, dancing more or less uniformly to fixed, repetitive rhythms.

36. This interpretation of early Caribbean rhythms seems to echo Allesandro Falassi's theory of festival representation, which argues that carnivalesque social commentary cannot be properly achieved by simple role reversals but only by "the simultaneous presence in the same festival of all the basic behavioral modalities of daily social life, all modified—by distortion, inversion, stylization, or disguise. . . . In sum, festival presents a complete range of behavioral modalities, *each one related to the modalities of normal daily life*" (1987, 3, emphasis added). See also Gordon Rohlehr's argument that slave dances "provided therapy for the enslaved trapped in the tedious ménage of plantation labour" (1990, 3).

37. Petro is the branch of Vodou that evolved largely in the New World (with some retained Congolese elements), and as such it carries "the marks of slavery and resistance" (Deren 1953, 62). The other branch of Haitian Vodou is called Rada and is thought to have evolved more directly from West African, "Yoruba" tradition (see Desmangles 1992, 36).

1. BEATING BACK DARKNESS

1. Yanick Lahens cites Toussaint's decree in her novel *Dans la maison du père* (2000, 82), a work in which the narrator uses dance as a means of escaping the strictures of Haitian life in the mid-twentieth century.

2. For detailed discussions of the Bois-Caïman ceremony, see Geggus (2002, 81–92), and Fick (1990, appendix B). See also Léon-François Hoffmann's controversial essay (1993), which questions whether the ceremony took place at all.

3. The term *bossale* is from the Spanish "bozal," meaning "muzzled," and as such referred principally to Africans who did not yet speak a European language.

4. See also the anonymous contemporary description of the rebel leader Jeannot's troop and how "their musicians made a hideous din beating cauldrons—all this as an accompaniment to the accustomed shriekings of warring Africans" (Popkin 2007, 77).

5. See also Laguerre (1993). It was only in 1913 that Haiti had its first civilian president, Michel Oreste.

6. McNeill (1995) develops this argument.

7. This instrument is essentially the same as the "banjo" described in other contexts.

8. For a further contemporary description of a *calenda* dance, see the anonymous "Mon Odyssée" (Popkin 2007, 71–73).

9. Doris Garraway argues that Moreau's description of the ceremony and the whites' enthusiasm for it betrayed their desire to "participate in and acculturate to black Creole rituals and dance forms" (2005, 255). It was, she says, as if the campaign to wipe out slave culture was "really about appropriating it" (255).

10. It is worth noting here that enslaved musicians played important roles in the theaters of colonial Saint-Domingue. See Fouchard (1955).

11. See also Roumain (2003g, 1132–34).

12. On the anti-superstition campaign, see Roumain (2003a). Roumain argues that the Haitian people are not any more or less superstitious than any other (745) and that the fundamental problem in Haitian society is not superstitions but lack of economic and social development (750–51). Ultimately, he argues, the campaign exposed the pro-Vichy, pro-fascist inclinations of the Catholic Church (752).

13. For an ethnomusicological interpretation of Vodou rhythmic music, see Dauphin (1986).

14. See Nesbitt (2005).

15. On the influence of Saint-Domingue refugees in New Orleans, see also Sublette (2008).

16. On the history of the various orthographic forms of voodoo, Vodou, etc. and their specific connotations, see Pettinger (2004).

17. Again, it is important to state that there were other important sources of influence for New Orleans music in the nineteenth century, including Cuban and Mexican forms.

18. Leslie G. Desmangles describes this process as a "symbiosis of identity" according to which African deities are "doubled" with Catholic saints (1992, 10–11).

19. On the ways in which rhythm structured rural community life and law, see Barthélemy (2000).

20. As Nick Nesbitt says, "Two of the processes that came to distinguish the Twentieth Century were invented in Haiti: decolonization and neo-colonialism" (2005, 6).

21. See Johnson (1989). On the links between music and free verse in poetry, see Holmes (2008).

22. For an analysis of how these ideas apply to Aimé Césaire's poetry, see Munro (2000, 112–18). See also Dessons and Meschonnic (1998, 188–89) on the rhythmic analysis of written texts, which is characterized as a creative, open-ended practice, an "intersubjective reality" between a "text-subject" and a "reader-subject."

23. J. Michael Dash says of Durand that "his evocation of voodoo rituals may appear stylized today but is unprecedented in its treatment of this sensitive area of Haitian culture" (1981, 19).

24. Durand's poem seems to have been inspired to some extent by his contemporary Alcibiade Fleury-Battier's work "Le Bamboula," which describes a similar scene of a peasant dance, the most significant aspects of which, for the poet, are the movements of the

women dancers and their grace and beauty "whether they have golden or ebony-colored skin" (quoted in Vaval 1971, 64–65).

25. As Hans Schmidt writes, "During this period the United States made a determined effort to indoctrinate Haitians with American concepts of political morality, pragmatism, and efficiency, and to teach Haitians modern agricultural and industrial skills through manual-technical education programs." These efforts failed, Schmidt says, because of racial and cultural prejudices. Instead of adopting the Americans' ways and values, many Haitians "came to despise them" (1971, 135).

26. Jean Price-Mars's lapse into biologically determinist racial thinking is all the more surprising given his well-known encounter in Paris with the French sociologist and anthropologist Gustave Le Bon, whose work divided the human races according to their innate moral and intellectual attributes, with the Indo-Europeans, predictably, at the top of the scale. "I revolted," Price-Mars wrote later of Le Bon's work, "against the injustice and insolence of such a judgment and I swore to take part in the glorious battle for the triumph of scientific truth, for the exaltation of human truth, for the shining truth, nothing more" (1929, 10).

27. The "white" misconception of blacks' natural inclination toward art, music, and dance predates Gobineau. See, e.g., the description of Saint-Domingue in the 1790s in the anonymous text "Mon Odyssée" and the argument that "all the Negroes are by nature poets and musicians" (Popkin 2007, 73).

28. This enthusiasm for "African" cultural elements was a pan-Caribbean phenomenon. On similar developments in Cuba, see, e.g., Moore (1997).

29. On the relationship between work and rhythm, see Lefebvre (1992, 100).

30. Lyonel Trouillot identifies in Roumain's prose a rhythmic quality that has been replicated by many subsequent Haitian authors. Speaking of Edwidge Danticat, Trouillot says that what connects her with the Haitian novel since indigenism is "the poetic rhythm of her phrasing, her visual metaphors and the rhythm that gives the prose a beat, a cadence. Since Gouverneurs de la rosée . . . the phrasing of certain Haitian novelists has had hips, an almost carnal swinging quality" (2010).

31. The Haitian historian Émile Nau's work Histoire des caciques d'Haïti (1894) is the best-known example of Haitian intellectuals' attempts to reincorporate an awareness of Haiti's original Amerindian inhabitants into the national consciousness.

2. RHYTHM, CREOLIZATION, AND CONFLICT IN TRINIDAD

1. For an analysis of the residual African, sacred aspects of Trinidadian music, see Saba Saakana (2005).

2. See also Médéric-Louis-Élie Moreau de Saint-Méry on the rhythmic dances of Saint Vincent "Caribs" and his suggestion that "perhaps the Caribbeans and the [African] originators of the Chica had a love of the dance and the effects of climate in common" (quoted in Reiss 2005, 4).

3. See Pearse (1956b, 252–53, 256).

4. Mitto Sampson asserted that, when the African slaves came to Trinidad, they "found a form of [Amerindian] singing. They took up the local songs and of course they

sang their own songs too. They introduced more pep, more vigour, more liveliness and more animation. . . . Consequently the negro enriched the calypso but did not originate it" (Pearse 1956b, 257).

5. On place names, see Naipaul (1982, 13–14).

6. There may be an attenuated Amerindian influence in the "Red Indian" Carnival masquerade. See Bellour and Kinser (2004).

7. As Gordon Rohlehr points out, Latin American song forms were so popular in Trinidad in the 1920s and 1930s that Ralph Perez, the agent for the Decca record label who recorded most of the local calypsos between 1937 and 1939, "viewed calypso as an extension of Latin music in the Caribbean and a variation on the songs he had already included in Decca's Latin American collection" (2004, 214). See also Charles Espinet and Harry Pitts's early study of calypso, which concludes that "the rhythm of the Calypso was African, the lyrics were African with possibly a little French embellishment and . . . the melody was Spanish on an African base" (1944, 30).

8. As John Cowley points out (1996, 233), there were direct equivalents of Canboulay in Carriacou and St. Lucia, and possibly also in Martinique and Guadeloupe.

9. Jacob Elder argues that Canboulay can be examined in four basic ways: as a "Black resistance ceremony"; a "recreational pageantry of Africans"; an "anti-Catholic celebration of freedom from slavery and the origin of the present Carnival"; and a "popular street theatre, exhibiting African-style dance, theatre, and music" (2004, 49).

10. See Cowley (1996, 21). Stuempfle (1995, 14) also emphasizes "intercultural exchange" as a salient aspect of early Trinidadian culture.

11. For discussions of the reasons and motivations for the abolition of slavery, see Carrington (2000) and Drescher (2000).

12. Andrew Pearse identifies three key stages in the development of Carnival: after Emancipation the whites withdrew and the previously excluded blacks "joined in tentatively and experimentally"; in the 1860s, the *jamettes* [the poor urban blacks] were the "moving spirits" of the festival, and Canboulay was established as the "midnight overture to Carnival"; and, toward the end of the century, Carnival became "acceptable to and practiced by all the main sections of the community" with the exception of some older Protestants and less integrated East Indians (1956a, 190).

13. I am very grateful to John Cowley for providing details of the various dance and drum ordinances in Trinidad.

14. See also A. M. Alonso for a theoretically engaged assessment of the subversive potential of *jamette* Carnival (1990, 117), in which she argues that the carnivalesque cannot lead to true revolutionary change.

15. Maureen Warner-Lewis has written on the importance of these African groups and their religious chants in the genesis of calypso (1995).

16. Rohlehr identifies the call and response structure as "the cornerstone of African music," which is "replicated in the scores of 'party songs' that are composed each year" in Trinidad (2001, 2).

17. See Brereton (1979, 156–57), which also discusses All Saints' Night and Christmas as occasions for similar festivities.

18. For a detailed account of the history of the various Baptist groups in Trinidad, see Rommen (2007, 12–18).

19. For an ethnographic analysis of a Shouter group in Toco, Trinidad, see Herskovits and Herskovits (1976, 190–223). In their summary of musical influences on this remote part of Trinidad, the Herskovitses conclude that African influences predominate. These African characteristics include "the emphasis on rhythm, the tendency, in rhythmic accompaniment of the melodic line[,] to introduce and maintain polyrhythms, the antiphony between leader and chorus in singing, and the employment of intervals characteristic of African music" (1976, 316).

20. Pamela Franco argues that the *belair* was "black women's premier performative domain" and that these women "constituted the major and majority participants; they were the dancers and singers, and men were often the drummers" (2004, 70).

21. In Mikhail Bakhtin's classic analysis, "festive laughter" is distinguished from the more cynical, individual laughter of satire and is instead "the laughter of all the people ... universal in scope; it is directed at all and everyone, including the carnival's participants. . . . [T]his laughter is ambivalent: it is gay, triumphant, and at the same time mocking, deriding, it buries and revives" (1984, 12).

22. In her history of Trinidad and Tobago, Gertrude Carmichael states that Trinidad's slave owners "had always prided themselves on their good treatment of slaves under the law originally laid down by the Spanish Government" (1961, 164).

23. In the view of the prominent French Creole P. G. L. Borde, the slaves were "like big children who were entrusted to the supervision of their masters; and this comparison is far from being wholly imaginary, because they were to some extent a part of their families" (1982, 2: 274–75). See also Anthony de Verteuil's argument that, because of the legacy of "reasonable treatment from Spanish times" and the relative shortage of slaves in Trinidad, they became "precious piece[s] of property" whose lives "differed very much from their unfortunate lot in some of the other colonies" (1975, 5).

24. As Rohlehr says, *jamette* Carnival and its characteristic conflict between the various Afro-Caribbean communities were "the result of the phenomenal inflow of immigrants from the southern and eastern Caribbean into both rural and urban spaces in Trinidad" (2001, 2).

25. The yard was the center of activity both in the urban barracks and in the pre- and post-Emancipation rural habitations. See Hill (1993, 22–24).

26. As Pearse says, the barrack yard dwellers were well aware of the distance between them and their upper-class neighbors but were also "paradoxically closely associated with them, especially through the women who were servants and often the predominant influences in the lives of the [white] children" (1956a, 192).

27. Pearse makes a similar point in his appraisal of hybrid nineteenth-century Trinidadian culture and society: "Law and custom, the African drum and the fiddle, the country doctor and the bush healer, the Catholic liturgy and the cults of Yorubaland and Dahomey, school English and Patois, lived side by side ... and a dual acculturation process took its course—creolisation, and accommodation to the institutions and standards of the super-structure" (1956a, 191).

28. As Richard Schechner asserts in relation to modern-day Carnival, "Some scholars argue that a 'real' carnival is no longer possible because there are no coherent communities to stage the carnivals or to rebel against" (2004, 5).

29. Peter van Koningsbruggen rightly states that official restrictions on lower-class culture helped stimulate *jamette* creativity: "The ban on the African drum provided a challenge to seek assiduously for new forms for the rhythmic accompaniment of song and dance . . . eventually leading to the birth of the steel band," and the verbal jousts associated with stickfighting mutated into modern calypso (1997, 34).

30. See Don Handelman and David Shulman's argument that this kind of "bottom-up play" and the intrusion of the "ludic into routine living is often *a battle for presence,* a struggle over space and time devoted to their practices, and a *confrontation over legitimacy*" (1991, 44–45, emphasis added).

31. This interpretation challenges or modifies the traditional interpretation of *jamette* culture as a straightforward denial of the dominant culture, "the reversal of the values of the respectability and a flamboyant rejection of the norms of the superstructure" (Pearse 1956a, 551).

32. In Rawle Gibbons's interpretation, Canboulay was a "symbolic action" that "both represented and actualized the refusal of ex-Africans and the whole agglomeration of peoples that made up the jamet class to submit to white norms of respectability and white control of their labor" (2007, 153).

33. For more on black working-class resentment of the police, see Brereton (1979, 127–28).

34. Although he does not say he has done so, Rafael de Leon must have translated from the original Creole, the language of calypso at the time.

35. Donald Wood is no doubt correct to argue that white attitudes toward black Trinidadian culture in the nineteenth century were influenced by a range of related factors: "Behind it lay the whole intricate experience of the Afro-European encounter since the Renaissance, the stereotypes formed by slavery, the legacy of the master and servant relationship, and, equally importantly, the growing dogma of the superiority of European culture and technology" (1968, 248).

36. As Stephen Stuempfle notes, drumming continued to be an integral part of black Trinidadian culture, particularly, he says, at "more private sacred and secular occasions such as *Orisha (Shango)* feasts and beles" (1995, 23).

37. The tassa drum rhythm is seen by some commentators as a primary influence on soca music and as the distinguishing factor between soca and calypso. See Dudley (1996, 286–87, 294), and Rommen (2007, 132–34).

38. As Burton Sankeralli says, Hosein or Hosay is the product of the "cultural confluences of Persia, Arabia, India, Africa, and Europe: the fusion of sacred and secular, of funeral and fete" (2004, 78).

39. As Donald Wood says, the joint celebration of Hosein was and is a "ray of hope in race relations when members of one group go to the public festivities of another, not to disrupt them, but to join in the fun" (1968, 153). Kelvin Singh writes, it was probable "that the Negroes found tassa drumming not very different from their own ancestral drumming and were naturally drawn to it. The stick-wielding 'combats' of the Muharram

[Hosein] celebrants were not very dissimilar from that of the 'jamet' bands that had come to dominate the creole carnival" (1988, 7).

40. Paul Gilroy interprets the contemporary world-wide tours of the Fisk Jubilee Singers as a seminal moment in black music's entry into the "public domain of late-nineteenth-century mass entertainment" (1993, 88).

41. On minstrelsy and "commodified blackness" in the United States, see Gitelman (2004, 285).

42. Daniel Crowley describes the *pisse en lit* masque as one played exclusively by men dressed as women and characterized by "sexual horseplay including the use of a poui stick protruding between the legs, or a skirt gathered in front in the manner of the Chiffoné dance of Carriacou" (1956, 196).

43. As Bridget Brereton points out, the essential aspect of this black and colored middle class was not individual wealth but an aspiration to European culture: "In fact it was their boast that they were more 'cultured' than the whites, whom they dismissed as being for the most part crassly materialistic and commercially minded" (1979, 5). Barbara Powrie adds that the colored middle class "copied the manners and behaviour of the whites, education became *de rigueur,* and 'respectability' was the aim of all concerned" (1956, 224). C. L. R. James caustically criticized the colored middle class and its color and class prejudices: "There are the nearly whites hanging on tooth and nail to the fringes of white society, and these . . . hate contact with the darker skin far more than some of the broader minded whites. Then there are the browns, the intermediates, who cannot by any stretch of the imagination pass as white, but who will not go one inch towards mixing with people darker than themselves" (1932, 15).

44. Rohlehr makes a similar point about language in colonial Trinidad: words, he says, "were a barrier behind which the enslaved person protected himself while acting out the role which he thought was expected of him" (1990, 57).

45. Crowley describes the elaborate costume of Julian White Rose: "He wore a long cloak of green velvet edged in white swansdown and decorated with mirrors, an 'Admiral's hat' bearing a long white ostrich plume, and he carried a long, gilded wooden sword" (1956, 197).

46. For an excellent analysis of calypso's rise to prominence as the emblematic music of Trinidad, see Guilbault (2007).

47. Similarities exist between the stickfighting bands and the contemporary New Orleans tribes or gangs, who sang war songs and performed war dances, and whose Creole and African-American songs were sung to the improvised percussion of sticks, bottles, tambourines, and hand-clapping in rhythmic, trance-like dances. See Turner (2003, 135).

48. As Stuempfle points out (1995, 23), the use of bamboo percussion occurs in Africa and in other parts of the Caribbean, such as Venezuela, Jamaica, and Haiti.

49. Donald Hill makes a similar point about the effects of recording music on calypso. The greatest effect, he says, "was in the separation of the performer and his audience from the performance. Once a record was produced and thousands of copies made, the singer could hear the result as if he were an audience. The audience was no longer bounded by a culture of knowing peers; anyone, anywhere a record player could be found, could hear that record" (1993, 115).

50. For an excellent analysis of contemporaneous developments in music and the recording industry in the United States, see Gitelman (2004).

51. The *Argos* was effectively calling for the "de-Africanization of the music, the final abolition of its percussive *Jamette* elements" (Rohlehr 1990, 96).

52. The tent was "originally an informal arena set up in a masquerade camp or calinda yard for practicing a Carnival band's songs" and was effectively "the center to the calypso wheel" (Hill 1993, 64).

53. For a more detailed analysis of calypso in the 1930s, see Rohlehr (1990, 125–212).

54. For an engaging analysis of the later "Calypso Craze" in 1950s America, see Eldridge (2005). As Michael Eldridge points out, contemporary U.S. pop-culture publications such as *Real: The Exciting Magazine for Men* highlighted the rhythmic aspects of calypso and how its "animalistic" beats were "throbbing" across the country (2005, 4). Interestingly, Eldridge's argument that white Americans' mimicry of calypso expresses "both a deep-seated loathing and a twisted longing, equal parts ridicule and desire, for their object" reflects my own reading of early white planters' transracial parody of Canboulay in Trinidad.

55. As Rohlehr writes (1990, 125), the 1930s were a decade of "political and social ferment" that culminated in the 1937 labor riots.

56. For a more detailed analysis of calypso, patriotism, and empire, see Rohlehr (1990, 182–86).

57. Sparrow's "Jean and Dinah" was composed fully ten years after the theme of the postwar situation of Trinidadian women had been explored by, among other calypsonians, Kitchener, Invader, Lion, Growler, and Beginner. Rohlehr suggests that Sparrow was able to resuscitate the theme partly because the bitterness among Trinidadian men had not subsided but mainly because of the force of Sparrow's youthful personality, vigor, and confidence (1990, 526–27).

58. As Harvey Neptune says, occupied Trinidad resembled "neither the utopias nor the dystopias of epic fame" and "yielded no clear-cut narratives," being "neither paradise on earth nor hell incarnate" (2007, 1). See also Neptune's challenge to interpretations of contemporary calypsos as unambiguous expressions of anti-Americanism (145–48).

59. By 1947, only 5,300 people were employed on the American bases; by 1951, only 1,053 worked there (Rohlehr 1990, 357). Rohlehr has written extensively on Sparrow, and he stresses "rhythm, life-pulse, celebration, excess, self-assertiveness, [and] the boasting rhetoric of the traditional warrior-hero" as that calypsonian's essential attributes (2001, 10).

60. Crowley identifies the *jamette* male masque, with its silk shirts, Panama hats, and detailed attention to accessorizing, as a predecessor to the sharply dressed saga boys of the 1940s (1956, 197). Neptune discusses at length the saga boys phenomenon, and he interprets them as figures that challenged Anglocentric ideas of taste and manhood by adapting the clothes, talk, and attitude of the American jazz dance scene (2007, 104–28). Gibbons argues that it was the saga boys of the 1940s who invented the "sailor" dances in Trinidad Carnival (2007, 158).

61. On the Afrocubanista movement, see Arnedo-Gomez (2006). See also Alejo Carpentier's discussion of the Cuban intellectual elite's "discovery" of the rhythms of

Havana's black neighborhoods: "Those who already knew the music of 'The Rite of Spring' were beginning to realize that, in the neighborhood of Regla, across the bay, one could find rhythms as complex and interesting as those Stravinski had invented to recreate the primitive games of pagan Russia. Everyone's eyes and ears turned toward that which was living and nearby" (1961, 171).

62. Espinet and Pitts (1944) provided a contemporary challenge to the rigidly African-ist interpretation of the form's roots, and it stressed the importance of acculturation and creolization.

63. On a similar tendency in post-independence Jamaica, see Rohlehr (2005, 155–58).

64. For a precise, musicological analysis of the way rhythms function in calypso (and soca), see Dudley (1996).

65. By the 1930s, as Rohlehr puts it, a "jazz straitjacket was forcibly imposed on the fluid prosody of calypso which, with its history of Latin-style syncopation and its roots in calinda, belair and bamboula, had only recently sorted out the transition from French Creole to English prosody" (2004, 215).

66. Earl Lovelace writes of contemporary middle-class Trinidadian tastes in music and of how they remained "frozen in the mode of European classics, the melodic line emphasized at the expense of the rhythmic" (2004, 192).

67. "These pots and pans produced only noisy rhythms, but there was something about it—perhaps its harsh volume, its virile metallic tones—that seemed appropriate to modern times" (Bellour, Riggio, and Johnson 2002, 26). Metallic percussion instruments, such as the tin kettle, the salt box, the biscuit tin, and the *marli-doundoun* (made from an olive oil container), have featured in Trinidad Carnival since at least the mid-nineteenth century (Stuempfle 1995, 26–27).

68. Stuempfle (1995, 32–37) discusses other similar "legends" of the origin of steelband, most of which include elements of improvisation and chance discoveries of metal objects.

69. Metal percussion is widespread in African and African diasporic music: in Africa, iron bells, cymbals, and hoe blades are used; African-style bells have been used in Haiti, Cuba, and Brazil; old canisters and pieces of metal were used in eighteenth-century *John Canoe* masquerades in Jamaica; and, during the nineteenth century, metal containers were beaten in street processions in Cuba and at dances in Louisiana (Stuempfle 1995, 26).

70. Andrew Prospect argues that *kalinda* and *orisha* (or *shango*) rhythms were repro-duced by the tamboo-bamboo bands and then adopted by the steelbands (see Stuempfle 1995, 39).

71. As Jacob Elder puts it, steel pan can be understood as "the objectivation of man's psychological tendency to react with hostility to psychic dissatisfaction and social status deprivation. . . . [I]t is a deliberate invasion of an area of artistic activity from which in Trinidad the unprivileged were traditionally debarred through social and economic dis-ability" (1969, 16).

72. Donald Hill makes a direct connection between the steelbands' "re-afrocreoliza-tion" of Trinidadian culture and the societal move toward independence (1993, 203).

73. On the postwar incorporation of popular culture into the politicized aesthetic of the emerging Creole middle class, see van Koningsbruggen (1997, 89–126): "After World War II, middle-class groups annexed [Carnival], above all at the level of organization,

for political and nationalistic reasons" (91). Powrie writes of the increasing participation of the colored middle class in postwar Carnival, which she attributes to the increased number of competitions, the "breakdown of middle-class reluctance to be seen openly joining the street parades," and to the new acceptability of female participation, which, in turn, is interpreted as a direct result of the altered gender relations brought about by the war (1956, 230). See also Stuempfle's argument (1995, 1, 76–124) that the patterns of conflict and consensus that have characterized postwar nation building were also played out in the tensions and dramas of the steelband movement. Even as steel pan has developed into a melodic instrument, rhythm remains, as Kim Johnson says, the "gravitational force that attracts and musically synchronizes so many players" (2004, 207).

3. RHYTHM, MUSIC, AND LITERATURE
IN THE FRENCH CARIBBEAN

1. As Paul Miller says, music is one of the most important structuring and metaphorical devices in Caribbean literature: Caribbean authors "introduce specific rhythms and cadences into the 'musicality' of their language . . . [and] music is often an indispensable cultural referent in their narration" (2005, 59).

2. See James Clifford's discussion of Parisian "Negrophilia": "In the 1920s Paris was flooded with things nègre, an expansive category that included North American jazz, syncretic Brazilian rhythms, African, Oceanian, and Alaskan carvings, ritual 'poetry' from south of the Sahara and from the Australian outback, [and] the literature of the Harlem Renaissance. . . . The writings of the anthropologist-collector Leo Frobenius . . . proposed East Africa as the cradle of civilization. Lucien Lévy-Bruhl's *La Mentalité primitive* . . . gave scholarly credence to a common image of black societies as 'mystical', 'affective', and 'prelogical'" (1989, 901).

3. Aimé Césaire's most far-reaching and perhaps most controversial political act was to promote the 1946 departmentalization bill, which effectively made Martinique an integrated part of France and which has perpetuated and strengthened connections with the former colonial power. After 1945, when Césaire was first elected mayor of Fort-de-France, his political activities took precedence over his literary work, and, as new generations of French Antillean authors have emerged, his ideas have been increasingly challenged.

4. Henri Hell argues that "the poem that contents itself with adding list upon list, cry upon cry, is no longer a poem. This work, with no rhythm other than the regular return of certain incantatory words comes apart, all too slowly." From Hell's "*Poètes de ce temps: Pierre-Jean Jouve, René Char, Aimé Césaire, Jacques Prévert,*" *Fontaine* 57 (n.d.), quoted in Senghor (1964, 162).

5. See Gary Wilder's excellent analyses of Senghor's thought, in particular the idea that blacks have an organic, rhythmic connection to the natural world (2005, 262–64).

6. Césaire was also influenced later by the work of the German journalist Janheinz Jahn, who proposed his vision of a common "Neo-African literature," at the heart of which was the idea that "all Neo-African writers shared a vision and, indeed, a rhythmic sense, that proceeded from their African roots" (Arnold 2008, 269).

7. For a full discussion of Césaire's conception of poetry and "cosmological human-ism," see Wilder (2005, 265–67).

8. Although he does not overtly acknowledge it, Césaire's understanding of rhythm, particularly with regard to poetry, also has some European sources, notably surrealism and the great avant-garde tradition of post-Romantic French poetry. The most influential of this latter group was Stéphane Mallarmé, who wrote on the importance of "incantatory rhythms" to his project of addressing the insufficiencies of language (1976, 252). See also René Ménil's article (1943, 52) in which Césaire's close collaborator talks of the "incanta-tory, magical" effects of Mallarmé's rhythms. On European sources of Césaire's rhythms, see Munro (2000, 112–18).

9. Nick Nesbitt makes a similar point about the singular durability and emancipatory potential of rhythm in Césaire's work. Writing about *Cahier d'un retour au pays natal,* Nesbitt argues that "the poem brings a newly liberated black subject into contact with a repressive totality that would annihilate all traces of resistant subjectivity through the element of its form that holds out the greatest promise of freedom: rhythm" (2003, 89). See also Nesbitt's discussion (2003, 90–91) of anaphora and parataxis in *Cahier d'un retour au pays natal,* and A. James Arnold's argument (2008, 264) that Césaire's use of anaphora is modeled on similar techniques in the work of the French poet Charles Péguy.

10. As Celia Britton says of the difference between Césaire's and Fanon's psychoanaly-sis, Fanon approaches Freud "not as a surrealist poet and proponent of Negritude, but as a psychiatrist and, eventually, revolutionary fighter" (2002, 28).

11. On Fanon's earliest writings, see Macey (2000, 127–28).

12. The vision of a "society without races" also appears in Sartre's *Réflexions sur la question juive* and again in Simone de Beauvoir's *Le Deuxième sexe.* In each case, the work looks to a "classless-raceless society in which neither the Jewish question, the 'woman question' nor the black question will have any meaning" (Macey 2000, 186).

13. On the influence of phenomenology and Merleau-Ponty on Fanon, see Macey (2000, 163–77). On Fanon's later meeting with Sartre and the influence of Sartre's *Critique de la raison dialectique* on Fanon's *Les Damnés de la terre,* see Macey (2000, 452–69).

14. The situation of the French Antillean people is put succinctly by Daniel Maximin as that of being "the most alienated from Europe, and the least hungry in the third world" (1981, 262).

15. For more on these intertexts, see Gallagher (2002, 110–44).

16. It is also important to recognize the influence of Saint-John Perse, the Guadelou-pean-born Nobel laureate about whom Glissant has written (1969, 1981, 1997) and whose *Éloges* is alluded to and quoted in Chamoiseau (1993) and Confiant (1993).

17. For an analysis of Zobel's use of music and dance in this text, see Hardwick (2008).

18. As Mary Gallagher argues, the expectation that José's move from rural to urban space will effect an improvement in his socioeconomic status is never fulfilled in the novel. The lack of upward mobility is signaled in the names of the three places he moves between: Petit-Morne, Petit-Bourg, and Petit-Fond. "The prefix 'petit' characterizes each one of these locations as lowly or inferior, its fateful recurrence denying hopes of social advance-ment and working against any notion of deep metamorphosis" (Gallagher 2002, 184).

19. This section seems to echo Henri Lefebvre's idea that pleasure, joy, and pain have

their own interrelated rhythms. He says that pain returns because "the repetition of pleasure gives rise to pain(s)" and adds that "joy and pleasure have a presence, whereas pain results from an absence (that of a function, an organ, a person, an object, a *being*)" (1992, 12).

20. A further example of interrupted narrative occurs when Médouze recalls how his father would try to retell the story of his life but, once he reached a certain point, "would suddenly fall silent" (Zobel 1950, 46). See also Gallagher (2002, 64–65).

21. As Colette Maximin observes, at this point in the novel the inaccessible dream of Africa is replaced by the image of France, which is "equally mythical but significantly more present" (1996, 41).

22. Jacques André argues (1981, 65) that José is quickly drawn from the cyclical, repetitive time of the plantation and subsumed into the alienating order of linear, historical time. Although this is true to some extent, the repetitions and cycles of the plantation are far from benevolent and organic. Rather, they are closely aligned with the desperate life of working the sugarcane and thus, in turn, with the alienating historical rhythms of slavery. Also, if José narrates his childhood experience of time as "simply an alternation of days and nights punctuated by three special days and nights whose names I knew: Saturday, Sunday, Monday" (Zobel 1950, 47), this is largely because he is expressing something of any child's typical relationship to time, which is perhaps universal and not specific to Martinique.

23. Significantly, too, only when Jojo arrives with his 100 cent note is José finally able to ride the carousel and to experience the "liberating intoxication from his childhood repression" (Zobel 1950, 153). Access to money and higher social status are tacitly confirmed as the most likely and enduring means of liberation.

24. As André says, the conclusion is also a kind of preface, "the hero promising himself to tell a story, the one that we have just read" (1981, 55).

25. Ralph Ludwig asserts that today's French Caribbean author "no longer presents the reality of his archipelago as a tropical encyclopedia would" but now brings the reader into contact with the "circular rhythm of narration" that comes from oral culture (1994, 19).

26. Glissant's extensive writings on history are directed and informed by the need he feels for a "creative approach" to retelling the past, removed from and distinct to the classical European approach, which can be a "paralyzing handicap" when it is applied to the Caribbean. If these methodologies are "passively assimilated," he says, "far from reinforcing a global consciousness or permitting the historical process to be established beyond the ruptures experienced, [they] will simply contribute to worsening the problem" (1989, 61). See also Glissant (1989, 61–96).

27. Both Mathieu Béluse and Papa Longoué had already featured in Glissant's first novel, *La Lézarde* (1958), and, like other characters, were to reappear in Glissant's subsequent fictional works.

28. Chris Bongie argues that Glissant's novel is "as much about the dialogic process through which . . . Mathieu and Papa Longoué vertiginously narrate their respective pasts and affirm their places of origin as they are about that which is being sought after through these acts of narration" (1998, 190).

29. As Colette Maximin says, the act of "diving into the past is a prodigious falling into an abyss" (1996, 158).

30. Gallagher argues that, though Glissant often values discontinuity positively, he also "writes primarily out of the desire to reconnect with lived time," a desire embodied in Mathieu's "analgesic" search for history (2002, 56).

31. Britton reads this nondescription of the slave revolts as a sign of their unrepresentable nature: "Insurrection, in other words, which is the only form of political action open to the slaves, cannot be made intelligible within the boundaries of conventional realist fictional discourse, and this 'silence' is another indication of the irretrievability of subaltern consciousness" (1999, 64).

32. This representation of the drum prefigures Glissant's later writing on the differences between Caribbean and African drumming. In Africa, Glissant says, drumming is often a communal, orchestral affair, whereas in the Caribbean the drummer usually plays alone, with a more limited range of rhythms. Glissant does not think Caribbean rhythms are inferior but does suggest that the drum been "defunctionalized" and that it "does not correspond any more to moments of collective existence" (1997, 386–87).

33. As Bongie says, in Le Quatrième siècle, "a veil is cast over Africa. . . . [T]he continent functions as an absent origin to which the reader is given no access" (1998, 147).

34. On the relationship between individual and collective narrative voice in Le Quatrième siècle, see Bongie (1998, 174) and Corzani (1978, 5: 236).

35. Carminella Biondi and Elena Pessini describe Glissant's storyteller figure as "the key character, the story's beacon [who] masters narrative, guiding its rhythms" (2004, 53).

36. Glissant's reworking of the historical novel owes a lot to the influence of William Faulkner, who has been a constant point of reference in Glissant's fictional and theoretical works. See Dash (1995, 74–79).

37. Glissant takes up similar issues in L'Intention poétique and argues that "the meticulous reporting of dates and facts masks from us the continuous movement . . . of our past" (1969, 187).

38. J. Michael Dash argues that the image of the wind suggests "the elusive, inscrutable and overpowering nature of the past and memory" (1995, 82). See also what Theodor Adorno says more generally about the wind: "We can tell whether we are happy by the sound of the wind. It warns the unhappy man of the fragility of his house, hounding him from shallow sleep and violent dreams. To the happy man it is the song of his protectedness: its furious howling concedes that it has power over him no longer" (1974, 49).

39. An exception to this rule occurs when Papa Longoué narrates the moment of the abolition of slavery and the text is characterized by repetitions and disordered syntax, apparently in an attempt to communicate some of the excitement and confusion of the moment (Glissant 1964, 169–71).

40. Bongie argues that Mycéa is "primarily concerned with issues of praxis" and "acknowledges the importance of digging into the past, but also knows that the memorial concerns of Mathieu and Papa Longoué will be fruitless if not oriented toward the future and made in the name of that acte which motivated the revolutionary group in La Lézarde" (1998, 148).

41. As Dash says, at the end of the novel Mathieu "represents the bridge to future

action" and adopts a role that inversely reflects that played by the original Longoué, in that Longoué's escape was aided by Louise, a slave woman, whereas Mathieu's future development will be in collaboration with Mycéa, who originated in the hills (1995, 85).

42. As Bongie states, Maximin's second novel, *Soufrières* (1987), rewrites *L'Isolé soleil* in ways that echo Glissant's own fiction and that read as "a belated and parodic homage to the self-referential world of Glissant's novels, with their cast of recurring characters and episodes" (1998, 357).

43. Glissant's evolution as a novelist and theorist has been characterized by an increasing interest in cultural relation and the broader effects of cultural and economic globalization. Yet he has retained a primary interest in the specific situation of Martinique.

44. Glissant's pessimistic critique of the state of Martinican popular music is implicitly contested in the work of ethnomusicologists such as Jocelyne Guilbault and Brenda F. Berrian. See, e.g., the former's contention that zouk from Martinique is "a major contemporary force in the popular music field" that is "helping shape economic, political, and social change" (Guilbault et al. 1993, xv).

45. To a certain extent, Maximin's novel is a Francophone version of what Kamau Brathwaite calls the "West Indian jazz novel." Brathwaite anticipates the coming of a future West Indian novel that will deal with a "specific, clearly-defined, folk-type community" and that "will try to express the essence of the community through its form." This novel will, moreover, "absorb its rhythms from the people of this community, and its concern will be with the community as a whole, its characters taking their place in that community, of which they are felt and seen to be an integral part" (1993, 107). See also Brathwaite's idea that the West Indian writer should enter "his own cultural New Orleans" where he expresses in words "that joy, that protest, that paradox of community and aloneness, that controlled mixture of chaos and order, hope and disillusionment, based in his New World experience, which is the heart of jazz" (1993, 63).

46. As Adlai Murdoch points out, Georges and Jonathan are doubled with "California's Soledad Brothers, George and Jonathan Jackson," and "these temporal intersections of resistance and revolt continue to widen and redefine the context of regional identity through its pan-American points of reference and recall the narrator's concept of Caribbean identity as the product of an ongoing cultural interaction between the transplanted blacks of the Americas" (2001, 129).

47. Of Maximin's French Caribbean predecessors, Ménil has shown an enduring interest in and engagement with jazz. See, e.g., Ménil (1944).

48. Adrien's prophecy has been largely and spectacularly confirmed in the subsequent history of black music in England and France. See, e.g., Gilroy (1993, 16).

49. Later, too, when the character Antoine plans to stage a production of Césaire's *Et les chiens se taisaient,* he wants to give a "big role" to music, but the rest of his dramatic group sees music's sole function as "illustration" (Maximin 1981, 266).

50. For an excellent critique of the "rhythmic mulatta" figure in Cuban culture, see Aparicio (2000).

51. Nesbitt, drawing on Mireille Rosello, argues rightly that Maximin "undertakes a critique of the death-based sacrificial logic of texts such as Césaire's *Et les chiens se taisaient* and the various examples of phallocentric hero-worship that have marked the

growing historical attention paid to Louis Delgrès since 1946" (2003, 154). See also Rosello (1992, 41–70).

52. Nesbitt sees further affinities between Maximin and Hawkins in the former's extensive use of the anagram and the latter's penchant for the arpeggio: "More than mere aesthetic indulgence, both the anagram and its musical corollary the arpeggio rework the antinomies of black Atlantic historical experience" (2003, 161).

53. This salutary effect of jazz and of the jazzman's performance would seem to negate, to some extent, Nesbitt's argument that "the novel's explicit thematization of jazz artists focuses on the libidinal investments of its fictional listener at the expense of an appreciation of that artist's practice," and that jazz to Siméa functions much like it did for Parisian intellectuals of the 1920s—that is, as "a vehicle for the liberation of repressed sensuality and desires" (2003, 150). Nesbitt does seem to retreat somewhat from this critique in his subsequent analysis of the novel (2003, 150–63).

54. As John Erickson points out, "Marie Gabriel's/Maximin's rewriting of history involves not only a break from colonial history . . . but from patriarchal history and the dominant male narrative as well" (1992, 127).

55. On the history and evolution of the *gros-ka* drum in the French Caribbean, see Berrian (2000, 206–31).

4. JAMES BROWN, RHYTHM, AND BLACK POWER

1. LeRoi Jones (Amiri Baraka) argues that the most apparent African survivals in North American music are its rhythms: "not only the seeming emphasis in African music on rhythmic, rather than melodic or harmonic, qualities, but also the use of polyphonic, or contrapuntal, rhythmic effects" (1963a, 25).

2. Harry Weinger and Alan Leeds say that, with "Out of Sight," James Brown "wrapped a bass line around a street phrase and stepped into a whole new realm" (2008, 36).

3. Louis Jordan and Roy Brown were primary influences on James Brown. As Cynthia Rose says, they "personified innovation: what a person might *do* with dance music, with the vocabulary of the church-house, with his wardrobe and his emotional history" (1990, 77). In terms of rhythm, too, Jordan's Tympany Five was an important precursor to James Brown. By standardizing the size of the postwar dance band to seven members, Jordan created a band with fewer horns, which "made the rhythm more pronounced" and helped emphasize his "lean, emphatic beat in 2/4 time that he dubbed the 'shuffle boogie'" (George 1988, 19). Later, Chuck Berry would adapt Jordan's rhythm and humor and bring it to "teenland" (George 1988, 93).

4. For a contemporary description of James Brown's live performances, see Arbus (1966).

5. As a child, Brown often attended the church services of a traveling Baptist minister, Bishop "Daddy" Grace, who would talk and sing his sermons, sometimes to the accompaniment of drums. The first time Brown heard these drums, they "grabbed him by the ears and yanked him up straight" (Eliot 2005, 14).

6. On the influence of gospel music and the church on Brown's performances, see Rose (1990, 117–28).

7. As Douglas Wolk says, "The rhythmic explosion wouldn't take place for another few years, but something was happening, and everybody could feel it" (2004, 105).

8. For more on "Out of Sight," see G. Brown (2008, 86–87).

9. On Brown's screams in "Super Bad" (1975), see Brackett (1995, chap. 3).

10. Nelson George similarly states that, when listening to Brown's work from the late 1960s, "it is hard at times to distinguish the guitars from the congas because the band is so focused on rhythmic interplay" (1988, 101). In Craig Werner's words, Brown "pretty much abandoned melody and harmony. Everything moved to the demands of the rhythmic pulse" (2006, 138).

11. David Brackett questions (1995, 145) whether tracks like "Out of Sight" and "Papa's Got a Brand New Bag" are actually so free of melodic elements, and he identifies in these works classic blues progressions.

12. Later, to be "on the One," came to mean more generally to be in rhythmic harmony. As Rickey Vincent says, "When George Clinton is heard chanting onstage 'On the one, everybody on the one,' he isn't trying to get his band on the beat (they are already there), he is savoring the rhythmic lock that has brought the entire house together, as one" (1996, 37).

13. Werner similarly argues that "'Papa's Got a Brand New Bag' unleashed a polyrhythmic ferocity that eventually reconfigured every corner of the American soundscape" (2006, 138).

14. According to Jerry Wexler, then producer of Aretha Franklin and other major soul stars at Atlantic Records, "Cold Sweat" had a profound effect on contemporary musicians: "It just freaked them out. For a time, no one could get a handle on what to do next" (quoted in White and Weinger 1991, 31).

15. As George puts it, Brown's rhythms became the "motherlode" and his staccato lyrics the starting point for early hip-hop artists (1991, 5). In the late 1960s, the second period of what Guthrie Ramsey calls "Afro-modernism," characterized by the ongoing urbanization of African American communities, their sociopolitical advances, and their encounter with the mass media, Brown came to epitomize the moment. "James Brown ruled the private and public spaces of black Chicago," Ramsey writes. "You heard him constantly on the radio, at the block party, in roller rinks, homes, clubs, and stores. Everywhere" (2003, 149).

16. See also Olly Wilson's interpretation of James Brown's "Super Bad" as a work figured around African cross-rhythms (1974, 12–13).

17. See also the contemporary judgment of the journalist Mel Ziegler that Brown's movements were "sometimes brutal, always with a suggestion of the primitive" (1968, 46).

18. Wolk says that when Brown pronounced in 1968 that he was "more than an artist," that he was "a black man, a soul brother," it was "as if he *had* to say it" (2004, 114).

19. Henry Louis Gates, Jr. writes of how the Black Aesthetic movement during this period tended to accentuate the political potential of black literature, as opposed to its stylistic qualities. "How useful was our literature to be in this centuries-old political struggle," he writes, "and exactly how was our literature to be useful?" (1987, xxv–xxvi).

20. As White and Weinger put it, "James Brown was born to lose. He refused to accept that fate" (1991, 15).

21. See Gates (1988, 123).

22. On Brown's jazz (and other New Orleans) influences, see Stewart (2000).

23. Brown's first influence was gospel, but jazz was, he says, his "second influence." "I have pretty big jazz feelin's," he says,"I been right through the book" (Rose 1990, 46). Brown himself said in 1986 that he had never been an R&B act. "My music," he said, "always came from gospel and jazz, which is called funk and soul. You see funk and soul is really jazz" (quoted in Vincent 1996, 73).

24. Vincent also sees similarities between the "hard-hitting stomp" of Brown's rhythms and the French Quarter marching bands of New Orleans (1996, 61).

25. As Anne Danielsen says of Brown's vocal in "Sex Machine," "He never lets the sound loose but instead improvises in a style of focused restraint" (2006, 84).

26. This period of renewed creativity with the new band further advanced and diversified the rhythm revolution that had started with "Out of Sight." In 1970–71, the James Brown catalog was bolstered by classic works such as "Sex Machine," "Super Bad," "Give It Up Or Turnit A Loose," "Talkin' Loud & Saying Nothing," "Get Up, Get Into It And Get Involved," and "Soul Power." As White and Weinger say, it was a "staggering" period that "did no less than define a new order" (1991, 38).

27. It is important, however, not to overemphasize the spontaneous, improvisational quality of Brown's music. Although seminal works such as "Papa's Got a Brand New Bag" and "The Payback" were recorded quickly, the final products were only released after being remixed and improved technically. Brian Ward critiques the "crude reification of black spontaneity," which he says is "linked to the enduring belief that all real black music must be visceral rather than cerebral in character, springing from the instinctual needs of the body, rather than the intellectual or meditative workings of the mind" (1998, 265).

28. Danielsen says that Brown was an "icon" for Baraka (2006, 15).

29. Baraka's enthusiasm for Brown was echoed by Stokely Carmichael, who declared in 1966 that African Americans were not culturally deprived, that they were in fact "the only people who have a culture in America," and that "we don't have to be ashamed of James Brown" (quoted in Ward 1998, 211).

30. In his autobiography, Brown speaks of how his taste for repetition came partly from his gospel upbringing and partly from the music he had heard as a child, such as Louis Jordan and the Tympany Five (2005, 101). He also recounts his first visit to Africa in 1968 and how he felt as if he were "returning somewhere rather than stepping onto the soil of a land I'd never been to before" (145). Although there are apparently no records of his attributing his rhythms to African sources in the 1960s, in this autobiography he does say that he combined the "drums of Africa and the drums of the American Indian," from both of whom he claimed heritage (216). Therefore, the African element was always fused with American influences.

31. In 1982, Brown said to the journalist Christina Patoski that he was "never into black power." As he explained, "I was black pride. It's different, power and pride. That's why I always pushed the word pride. What influence I had over people is not power. Power's what ruins people. *God* has power; human bein' has influence" (quoted in Rose 1990, 55).

32. Ronald Radano similarly critiques the racial essentialisms that characterized the

Black Aesthetic movement, arguing that they "constrained the comprehension of black music's more fundamental insurgencies, particularly with reference to the undermining of racial categories" (2003, 53).

33. See also Stewart (2000) for an excellent analysis of rhythmic developments in the R&B and funk periods.

34. Marc Eliot also links Brown's new rhythms to the increased confidence of African Americans: "Gone along with the excess was the timidity, the apologetic head-down shuffle of Black musical passivity. James Brown's 'One' represented pride and authority, a sound that stepped up to the mike with strength and conviction" (2005, 31).

35. Baraka suggests a similar close relationship between musical and social change: "At each juncture, twist, and turn, as Black people were transformed, so was their characteristic music. It became emphatically clear to me that by analyzing the music, you could see with some accuracy what and why that change had been" (1963a, x).

36. As Ward says, although during the decade after Montgomery relatively few soul singers openly embraced the struggle, audiences sometimes bestowed political meanings onto ostensibly apolitical songs in acts of "creative consumption" (1998, 203).

37. It is also possible to interpret seemingly apolitical aspects of the music—the emphasis on love, romance, work, the everyday, the dance crazes—as implicitly political gestures. As Ward says, "The very act of claiming, naming and evaluating distinctive elements of a shared black world according to black standards in a uniquely black musical and lyrical form was enormously empowering for the black community in a psychological sense" (1998, 211). He also argues that, by the late 1960s, it became commercially advisable for soul artists to pronounce on social and racial issues (1998, 361).

38. Danielsen similarly argues that "contrary to what was often the case in the 'older school' of cultural studies and subculture theory, where music was assumed to mirror underlying social structures and relations, the formative role of music in *shaping* such cultural and social matters must be taken into account" (2006, 33).

39. This is, of course, only one side of the story. The early 1970s also saw the increasing ghettoization of many black neighborhoods: as prosperous blacks left the inner cities for the suburbs, poverty became more concentrated in the cities. On the problems this created, see Wilson (1987).

40. On this period, see George (1988).

41. As George notes of the mid- to late 1970s, "Millie Jackson and Cameo: too black. The phrase echoed with the sound of self-hatred: too black. A retreat from the beauty of blackness. Too black. The sound of the death of R&B" (1988, 160).

42. The late 1960s and early 1970s were marked by experimentation in black music, from the "psychedelic soul" of the Temptations to the expansive ballads of Isaac Hayes's *Hot Buttered Soul* and the richly orchestrated yet sparse sound of Marvin Gaye's *What's Going On*. Rhythm continued to play an important part in these new forms, as George says: "Latin percussion, in the form of cow bells, congas, and bongos, suddenly became rhythmic requirements, adding a new layer of polyrhythmic fire to the grooves" (1988, 124).

43. As Werner says, the African enthusiasm for soul and funk risked limiting the African artists' creativity and "enforcing a particular conception of what a black sound was" (2006, 139).

44. Brown's own reflections on visiting Africa further suggest that he did not see his work as an echo of African music. "I went over there and I heard their thing, and I felt their thing," he says, "but I honestly hadn't heard their thing in mine" (1991, 126).

45. Ward similarly argues that, though Vincent "rides his African-retentions hobby-horse too hard and too far," he recognizes that "it was what happened to those African practices and sensibilities during the course of several centuries in America which generated a distinctively African-American culture and the mighty funk he celebrates" (Ward 1998, 351).

CONCLUSION

1. See, e.g., Synnott (1991, esp. 68–70).

2. See M. Smith (2003b), McLuhan (1962),and Ong (1988). On the *Annales* school, see Febvre (1982, 423–42) and Mandrou (1976).

3. See also Leigh Eric Schmidt's argument that "almost all of history is eerily silent and so, to evoke those stilled and faded voices, the historian must act as a kind of necromancer" (2003, 41).

4. For an argument against the idea that Renaissance print culture rendered modernity entirely visual, see Woolf (2004).

5. On the bell as a "lieu de mémoire," see Corbin (1998).

6. Fred Moten, drawing on Cecil Taylor, similarly proposes that "anything is music as long as you apply certain principles of organization to it" (2003, 25). For a counter argument, see Cutler (1988).

7. Nathaniel Mackey hears echoes of the old gospel moan in the falsetto of Al Green, which, he says, functions like the moan or the shout and "explores a redemptive, unworded realm—a meta-word if you will—where the implied critique of the momentary eclipse of the word curiously rescues, restores and renews it: new word, new world" (1986, 52).

8. For more on slaves' strategic use of silence, see M. Smith (2003a, 145–49).

9. See, e.g., John Shepherd's work on the importance of sounds in oral cultures and his argument that "pre-literate people seem to sense themselves as being at the centre of a sound universe, which is dynamic and bounding with energy" (1991, 20–21).

10. Amiri Baraka writes of a similar process in North America, arguing that it was the "foreignness" and visual difference of the African that set him apart from the rest of society "blatantly and permanently" (1963a, 4).

11. As Michael Bull and Les Back say, "It would be impossible to think about the history of racism without its scopic component" (2003, 14).

12. The idea, suggested in Schafer (2004)and emphatically promoted in Attali (2004), that sound—and music in particular—are prophetic and herald times to come is also applicable to the Caribbean. Innovations in music seem to precede changes in society. Although Caribbean music is often rooted in the past (in terms of rhythm and style), it is almost always present- or future-oriented in the way it often projects forward in time, foreseeing and foreshadowing changes in society and thereby empowering music makers in ways denied to them by political and social elites.

13. Gérard Barthélemy agrees that "there is nothing in rhythm that is due to a par-

ticular morphology, and even less to race; genetics clearly have nothing to do with it. Everything is on the contrary the result of automatisms, themselves due to a long apprenticeship in the course of growing up" (2000, 173).

14. Henri Lefebvre writes of how modern (Western) music has been shaped by a "massive irruption of exotic rhythms" (1992, 58).

15. See also Paul Gilroy's argument that purpose-built reggae sound systems in English inner cities "disperse and suspend the temporal order of the dominant culture." As the sound-system wires "are strung up and the lights go down," Gilroy says, "dancers could be transported anywhere in the diaspora without altering the quality of their pleasures" (2002, 284). See also Bull and Back (2003, 13) and Hesmondhalgh and Negus (2002, 8).

16. Craig Werner argues that, when disc jockeys and dancers came together in the Chicago house scene, the dance floor "signified much the same thing as the 'threshing floors' of the sanctified churches" and that "when the spirit moved through the house clubs, it was almost as if disco had returned to its roots in gospel and soul and then followed those roots back to their West African sources" (2006, 283).

17. See the diverse essays in the excellent volume edited by Graham St. John (2003).

18. See, e.g., the argument that the rhythms of rave and techno music have led to the questioning of "assumed difference" among young people in the north of Ireland and have helped bridge the cultural divide between them (Moore 2003, 271–72).

19. On the spiritual dimensions of funk, see Danielsen (2006, 107–8, 204–18).

REFERENCES

Adams, Jessica, Michael P. Bibler, and Cécile Accilien, eds. 2007. *Just Below South: Intercultural Performance in the Caribbean and the U.S. South.* Charlottesville: University of Virginia Press.

Adorno, Theodor. 1974. *Minima Moralia: Reflections on a Damaged Life.* London: New Left Books.

Alexis, Jacques-Stephen. 1956. "Du réalisme merveilleux des Haïtiens." *Présence africaine* 8–10: 245–71.

Alonso, A. M. 1990. "Men in 'Rags' and the Devil on the Throne: A Study of Protest and Inversion in the Carnival of Post-Emancipation Trinidad." In *Carnival in Perspective,* 73–120. Ed. Thomas M. Fiehrer and Michael W. Lodwick. New York: Athens Printing.

André, Jacques. 1981. *Caraïbales: Études sur la littérature antillaise.* Paris: Éditions Caribéennes.

Aparicio, Frances R. 2000. "Ethnifying Rhythm, Feminizing Cultures." In *Music and the Racial Imagination,* 95–112. Ed. Ronald Radano and Philip V. Bohlman. Chicago: University of Chicago Press.

Arbus, Doon. 1966. "James Brown Is Out of Sight." *The New York Herald Tribune,* March 20. Reprinted in George and Leeds, eds., *The James Brown Reader,* 18–34.

Arnedo-Gomez, Miguel. 2006. *Writing Rumba: The Afrocubanista Movement in Poetry.* Charlottesville: University of Virginia Press.

Arnold, A. James. 2008. "Beyond Postcolonial Césaire: Reading *Cahier d'un retour au pays natal* historically." *Forum for Modern Language Studies* 44, no. 3: 258–75.

Arom, Simha. 1991. *African Polyphony and Polyrhythm: Musical Structure and Methodology.* Cambridge, Engl.: Cambridge University Press.

Arthur, Charles, and J. Michael Dash, eds. 1999. *Libète: A Haiti Anthology.* London: Latin America Bureau.

Asbury, Herbert. 1936. *The French Quarter: An Informal History of the New Orleans Underworld*. New York: Knopf.

Attali, Jacques. 2004. "Listening." In *Hearing History: A Reader*, 10–22. Ed. Mark M. Smith. Athens: University of Georgia Press.

Averill, Gage. 1997. *A Day for the Hunter, A Day for the Prey: Popular Music and Power in Haiti*. Chicago: University of Chicago Press.

Averill, Gage, and Yuen-Ming David Yih. 2000. "Militarism in Haitian Music." In *The African Diaspora: A Musical Perspective*, 267–93. Ed. Ingrid Monson. New York: Garland Publishing.

Bailey, Peter. 2004. "Breaking the Sound Barrier." In *Hearing History: A Reader*, 23–35. Ed. Mark M. Smith. Athens: University of Georgia Press.

Bakhtin, Mikhail. 1984. *Rabelais and His World*. Trans. Hélène Iswolsky. Bloomington: Indiana University Press.

Baraka, Amiri. 1963a. *Blues People*. New York: Harper Collins, 2002.

———. 1963b. "The Sullen Art: Le Roi Jones in Conversation with David Ossman." In *The Sullen Art: Interviews with Modern American Poets*, 77–81. Ed. David Ossman. New York: Corinth.

———. 1964. *The Dead Lecturer*. New York: Grove Press.

———. 1965. *Slave Ship: A Historical Pageant*. Newark, NJ: Jihad Productions.

———. 1966. *Home: Social Essays*. New York: William Morrow.

———. 1967. *Black Music*. Westport, CT: Greenwood Press, 1980.

———. 1971. *Raise Race Rays Raze: Essays Since 1965*. New York: Random House.

———. 1974. *The Autobiography of LeRoi Jones/Amiri Baraka*. New York: Freundlich Books.

———. 1979. *Selected Plays and Prose of Amiri Baraka/LeRoi Jones*. New York: William Morrow.

———. 1984. *Daggers and Javelins: Essays, 1974–1979*. New York: William Morrow.

Baraka, Amiri, and Larry Neal, eds. 1968. *Black Fire: An Anthology of Afro-American Writing*. New York: Morrow.

Barthélemy, Gérard. 2000. *Créoles-Bossales: Conflit en Haïti*. Petit-Bourg, Guadeloupe: Ibis Rouge.

Batson, Dawn K. 2004. "Voices of Steel: A Historical Perspective." In *Culture in Action—The Trinidad Experience*, 195–203. Ed. Milla Cozart Riggio. New York: Routledge.

Beauvoir-Dominique, Rachel. 1991. *L'Ancienne cathédrale de Port-au-Prince: Perspectives d'un vestige de Carrefours*. Port-au-Prince, Haiti: Éditions Henri Deschamps.

Bebey, Francis. 1975. *African Music: A People's Art*. London: Harrap.

Bechet, Sidney. 1960. *Treat It Gentle*. New York: Hill and Wang.

Bell, Beverly. 2001. *Walking on Fire: Haitian Women's Stories of Survival and Resistance*. Ithaca, NY: Cornell University Press.

Bell, Madison Smartt. 2007. *Toussaint Louverture: A Biography*. New York: Random House.

Bellour, Hélène, Kim Johnson, and Milla Riggio. 2002. *Renegades: The History of the Renegades Steel Orchestra of Trinidad and Tobago*. Oxford, Engl.: Macmillan.

Bellour, Hélène, and Samuel Kinser. 2004. "Amerindian Masking in Trinidad Carnival:

The House of Black Elk in San Fernando." In *Culture in Action—The Trinidad Experience*, 129–45. Ed. Milla Cozart Riggio. New York: Routledge.

Benítez-Rojo, Antonio. 1992. *The Repeating Island: The Caribbean and the Postmodern Perspective*. Trans. James E. Maraniss. Durham, NC: Duke University Press.

———. 1999. "The Role of Music in the Emergence of Afro-Cuban Culture." Trans. James E. Maraniss. In *The African Diaspora: African Origins and New World Identities*, 197–203. Ed. Isidore Okpewho, Carole Boyce Davies, and Ali A. Mazrui. Bloomington: Indiana University Press.

Benston, Kimberly W., ed. 1978a. *Imamu Amiri Baraka (LeRoi Jones): A Collection of Critical Essays*. Englewood Cliffs, NJ: Prentice-Hall.

———. 1978b. "Vision and Form in *Slave Ship*." In *Imamu Amiri Baraka (LeRoi Jones)*, 174–85. Ed. Kimberly W. Benston. Englewood Cliffs, NJ: Prentice-Hall.

Berrian, Brenda F. 2000. *Awakening Spaces: French Caribbean Popular Songs, Music, and Culture*. Chicago: University of Chicago Press.

Biondi, Carminella, and Elena Pessini. 2004. *Rêver le monde, Écrire le monde*. Bologna, Italy: CLUEB.

Blumin, Stuart M., ed. 1990. *New York by Gas-Light and Other Urban Sketches by George G. Foster*. Berkeley: University of California Press.

Bona, Dénètem Touam. 2004. "Negros cimarrones 2." *Africultures* (December 24). www .africultures.com/index.asp?menu= affiche_article&no = 3696.

Bongie, Chris. 1998. *Islands and Exiles: The Creole Identities of Post/Colonial Literature*. Stanford, CA: Stanford University Press.

Boomert, Arie. 2000. *Trinidad, Tobago and the Lower Orinoco Interaction Sphere*. Alkmaar, Netherlands: Cairi Publications.

Borde, Pierre Gustave Louis. 1982. *The History of the Island of Trinidad under the Spanish Government*. 2 vols. Port of Spain: Paria Publishing Company. (Orig. pub. 1876, 1882.)

Born, Georgina, and David Hesmondhalgh, eds. 2000. *Western Music and Its Others: Difference, Representation, and Appropriation in Music*. Berkeley: University of California Press.

Bracken, Harry M. 1978. "Philosophy and Racism." *Philosophia* 8, nos. 2–3 (November): 241–60.

Brackett, David. 1995. *Interpreting Popular Music*. Cambridge, Engl.: Cambridge University Press.

Branson, Susan, and Leslie Patrick. 2001. "Étrangers dans un Pays Étrange: Saint-Domingan Refugees of Color in Philadelphia." In *The Impact of the Haitian Revolution in the Atlantic World*, 193–208. Ed. David P. Geggus. Columbia: University of South Carolina Press.

Brathwaite, Kamau. 1993. "Jazz and the West Indian Novel." In Brathwaite, *Roots*, 55–110. Ann Arbor: University of Michigan Press.

Brereton, Bridget. 1979. *Race Relations in Colonial Trinidad 1870–1900*. Cambridge, Engl.: Cambridge University Press.

———. 1981. *A History of Modern Trinidad 1783–1962*. Kingston, Jamaica: Heinemann.

———. 2005. "History and Myth in Narratives of Trinidad and Tobago's Past." *UWI Today*, March 20. http://sta.uwi.edu/uwitoday/2005/march/histmyth.asp.

———. 2006. "'Hé St Domingo, songé St Domingo': Haiti and the Haitian Revolution in the Political Discourse of Nineteenth-Century Trinidad." In *Reinterpreting the Haitian Revolution and Its Cultural Aftershocks 1804–2004,* 123–49. Ed. Martin Munro and Elizabeth Walcott-Hackshaw. Kingston, Jamaica: University of the West Indies Press.

Britton, Celia. 1999. *Édouard Glissant and Postcolonial Theory: Strategies of Language and Resistance.* Charlottesville: University of Virginia Press.

———. 2002. *Race and the Unconscious: Freudianism in French Caribbean Thought.* Oxford, Engl.: Legenda.

Brown, Geoff. 2008. *The Life of James Brown.* London: Omnibus Press. (Orig. pub. 1996.)

Brown, James. 1991. "Introduction." Liner notes to *Star Time.* Polygram 849 108–2.

———. 2005. *I Feel Good: A Memoir of a Life of Soul.* New York: New American Library.

Brown, Karen McCarthy. 1995. "Serving the Spirits: The Ritual Economy of Haitian Vodou." In *Sacred Arts of Haitian Vodou,* 205–23. Ed. Donald Cosentino. Los Angeles: UCLA Fowler Museum of Cultural History.

Brown, Sarah, and John Morthland. 1994. "Now Free to Dance Themselves." Liner notes to *Roots of Funk* CD compilation, Rhino R271615.

Brunetière, Ferdinand. 1895. *L'Évolution de la poésie lyrique en France au 19e siècle.* Paris: Hachette.

Buck-Morss, Susan. 2000. "Hegel and Haiti." *Critical Inquiry* 26 (Summer): 821–65.

———. 2009. *Hegel, Haiti, and Universal History.* Pittsburgh, PA: University of Pittsburgh Press.

Bull, Michael, and Les Back. 2003. "Introduction." In *The Auditory Culture Reader,* 1–18. Ed. Michael Bull and Les Back. Oxford, Engl.: Berg.

Canez, Velério. 1942. "Notre folklore Musical." *Haïti Journal,.* November 26.

Carmichael, Gertrude. 1961. *The History of the West Indian Islands of Trinidad and Tobago 1498–1900.* London: Alvin Redman.

Carpentier, Alejo. 1961. *La Música en Cuba.* Havana: Luz-Hilo.

Carrington, Selwyn. 2000. "The State of the Debate on the Role of Capitalism in the Ending of the Slave System." In *Caribbean Slavery in the Atlantic World,* 1031–41. Ed. Verene Shepherd and Hilary McDonald Beckles. Kingston, Jamaica: Ian Randle Publishers.

Cartwright, Keith. 2006. "Re-creolizing Swing: Saint-Domingue Refugees in the *Govi* of New Orleans." In *Reinterpreting the Haitian Revolution and Its Cultural Aftershocks 1804–2004,* 102–22. Ed. Martin Munro and Elizabeth Walcott-Hackshaw. Kingston, Jamaica: University of the West Indies Press.

"Ce que nous voulons faire." 1931. *La Revue du monde noir* 1 (November): 3.

Césaire, Aimé. 1945. "Poésie et connaissance." *Tropiques* 12 (January): 157–70.

———. 1983. *Aimé Césaire, the Collected Poetry.* Trans. Clayton Eshleman and Annette Smith. Berkeley: University of California Press.

———. 2001. *Notebook of a Return to the Native Land.* Trans. and ed. Clayton Eshleman and Annette Smith. Middletown, CT: Wesleyan University Press. (Orig. pub. 1939.)

Chamoiseau, Patrick. 1993. *Antan d'enfance.* Paris: Gallimard. (Orig. pub. 1990.)

Chernoff, John Miller. 1979. *African Rhythm and African Sensibility.* Chicago: University of Chicago Press.

Cleaver, Eldridge. 1968. *Soul On Ice.* New York: Dell.

Clifford, James. 1989. "Negrophilia." In *A New History of French Literature*, 901–8. Ed. Denis Hollier. Cambridge, MA.: Harvard University Press.

Confiant, Raphaël. 1993. *Ravines du devant-jour: Récit.* Paris: Gallimard.

Connor, Steven. 2003. "The Help of Your Good Hands: Reports on Clapping." In *The Auditory Culture Reader*, 67–76. Ed. Michael Bull and Les Back. Oxford, Engl.: Berg.

———. 2004. "Sound and the Self." In *Hearing History: A Reader*, 54–66. Ed. Mark M. Smith. Athens: University of Georgia Press.

Corbin, Alain. 1998. *Village Bells: Sound and Meaning in the 19th-Century French Countryside.* Trans. Martin Thom. New York: Columbia University Press.

Corvington, Georges. 1987. *Port-au-Prince au cours des ans: La capitale d'Haïti sous l'occupation, 1922–1934.* Port-au-Prince, Haiti: Imprimerie Henri Deschamps.

Corzani, Jack. 1978. *La Littérature des Antilles-Guyane françaises.* 6 vols. Fort-de-France, Martinique: Désormeaux.

Cowley, John. 1992. "Music and Migration: Aspects of Black Music in the British Caribbean, the United States, and Britain, before the Independence of Jamaica and Trinidad and Tobago." Ph.D. diss., University of Warwick.

———. 1996. *Carnival, Canboulay, and Calypso: Traditions in the Making.* Cambridge, Engl.: Cambridge University Press.

Cozart Riggio, Milla, ed. 2004a. "Time Out or Time In? The Urban Dialectic of Carnival." In *Culture in Action—The Trinidad Experience*, 13–30. Ed. Milla Cozart Riggio. New York: Routledge.

———. 2004b. "We Jamming It." In *Culture in Action—The Trinidad Experience*, 183–86. Ed. Milla Cozart Riggio. New York: Routledge.

Craige, John Houston. 1933. *Black Bagdad.* New York: Minton, Balch.

Creecy, James R. 1860. *Scenes in the South, and Other Miscellaneous Pieces.* Philadelphia: J. B. Lippincott.

Crowley, Daniel J. 1956. "The Traditional Masques of Carnival." *Caribbean Quarterly* 4, nos. 2–3: 194–223.

Cutler, Chris. 1988. "Editorial Afterword." *ReRecords Quarterly Magazine* 2, no. 3: 46–47.

Damas, Léon-Gontran. 1956. *Black-Label.* Paris: Gallimard.

———. 1972. *Pigments/Névralgies.* Paris: Présence Africaine.

Daniels, Douglas Henry. 2003. "Vodun and Jazz: 'Jelly Roll' Morton and Lester 'Pres' Young—Substance and Shadow." *Journal of Haitian Studies* 9, no. 1 (Spring): 110–23.

Danielsen, Anne. 2006. *Presence and Pleasure: The Funk Grooves of James Brown and Parliament.* Middletown, CT: Wesleyan University Press.

Dash, J. Michael. 1981. *Literature and Ideology in Haiti, 1915–1961.* Totowa, NJ: Barnes and Noble.

———. 1995. *Édouard Glissant.* Cambridge, Engl.: Cambridge University Press.

———. 1998. *The Other America: Caribbean Literature in a New World Context.* Charlottesville: University Press of Virginia.

Dauphin, Claude. 1986. *Musique du Vodou.* Sherbrooke, Canada: Editions Namaan.

Davis, Thulani. 1980. "J-a-a-a-ames Brown!" *The Village Voice*, June 9. Reprinted in George and Leeds, *The James Brown Reader*, 148–51.

Day, Charles William. 1852. *Five Years' Residence in the West Indies*. 2 vols. London: Colburn.

Dayan, Joan. 1995. *Haiti, History, and the Gods*. Berkeley: University of California Press.

Depestre, René. 1998. *Ainsi parla le fleuve noir*. Grigny: Paroles d'aube.

Deren, Maya. 1953. *Divine Horsemen: The Living Gods of Haiti*. London: Thames and Hudson.

Derrida, Jacques. 1996. *Le Monolinguisme de l'autre*. Paris: Éditions Galilée.

Desmangles, Leslie G. 1992. *The Faces of the Gods: Vodou and Roman Catholicism in Haiti*. Chapel Hill: University of North Carolina Press.

Dessens, Nathalie. 2008. "Saint-Domingue Refugees in New Orleans: Identity and Cultural Influences." In *Echoes of the Haitian Revolution 1804–2004*, 28–40. Ed. Martin Munro and Elizabeth Walcott-Hackshaw. Kingston, Jamaica: University of the West Indies Press.

Dessons, Gérard, and Henri Meschonnic. 1998. *Traité du rythme: Des vers et des proses*. Paris: Dunod.

Determeyer, Eddy. 2006. *Rhythm Is Our Business: Jimmy Lunceford and the Harlem Express*. Ann Arbor: University of Michigan Press.

Drescher, Seymour. 2000. "The Antislavery Debate: Capitalism and Abolitionism as a Problem in Historical Interpretation." In *Caribbean Slavery in the Atlantic World*, 1042–54. Ed. Verene Shepherd and Hilary McDonald Beckles. Kingston, Jamaica: Ian Randle Publishers.

Dubois, Laurent. 2001. "The Promise of Revolution: Saint-Domingue and the Struggle for Autonomy in Guadeloupe, 1797–1802." In *The Impact of the Haitian Revolution in the Atlantic World*, 112–34. Ed. David P. Geggus. Columbia: University of South Carolina Press.

————. 2004. *Avengers of the New World: The Story of the Haitian Revolution*. Cambridge, MA: Harvard University Press.

Dubois, Laurent, and John D. Garrigus. 2006. *Slave Revolution in the Caribbean 1789–1804: A Brief History with Documents*. Boston, MA: Bedford/St. Martin's.

Dudley, Shannon. 1996. "Judging 'By the Beat': Calypso versus Soca." *Ethnomusicology* 40, no. 2 (Spring/Summer): 269–98.

Dumervé, Etienne Constantin Eugène Moïse. 1968. *Histoire de la musique haïtienne*. Port-au-Prince, Haiti: Imprimerie des Antilles.

Durand, Oswald. 1896. *Rires et pleurs*. Corbeil: Imprimerie E. Crété.

Du Tertre, Jean-Baptiste. 1973. *Histoire générale des Antilles habitées par les Français*. 3 vols. Fort-de-France, Martinique: Editions des Horizons Caraïbes. (Orig. pub. 1667–71.)

Edwards, Bryan. 1797. *An Historical Survey of the French Colony in the Island of St Domingo*. London: John Stockdale.

Elder, Jacob D. 1969. "From Congo Drum to Steelband: A Sociohistorical Account of the Emergence and Evolution of the Trinidad Steel Orchestra." Pamphlet. St. Augustine, Trinidad: University of the West Indies.

————. 2004. "Cannes Brûlées." In *Culture in Action—The Trinidad Experience*, 48–52. Ed. Milla Cozart Riggio. New York: Routledge.

Eldridge, Michael S. 2005. "Bop Girl Goes Calypso: Containing Race and Youth Culture in Cold War America." *Anthurium* 3, no.2 (Fall). http://scholar.library.miami.edu/anthurium/volume_3/issue_2/eldridge-bop.htm

Eliot, Marc. 2005. "Introduction." In *I Feel Good: A Memoir of a Life of Soul*, 1–37. By James Brown. New York: New American Library.

Ellison, Ralph. 1964. *Shadow and Act*. New York: Random House.

———. 1978. "Blues People" [1964]. In *Imamu Amiri Baraka (LeRoi Jones): A Collection of Critical Essays*, 55–63. Ed. Kimberly W. Benston. Englewood Cliffs, NJ: Prentice-Hall.

Erickson, John D. 1992. "Maximin's *L'Isolé soleil* and Caliban's Curse." *Callaloo* 15, no. 1 (Winter): 119–30.

Espinet, Charles S., and Harry Pitts. 1944. *Land of the Calypso: The Origin and Development of Trinidad's Folk Song*. Port of Spain: Guardian Commercial Printery.

Falassi, Allesandro. 1987. "Festival: Definition and Morphology." In *Time out of Time*, 1–7. Ed. Allesandro Falassi. Albuquerque: University of New Mexico Press.

Fanon, Frantz. 1952. *Peau noire, masques blancs*. Paris: Seuil.

Febvre, Lucien. 1982. *The Problem of Unbelief in the Sixteenth Century: The Religion of Rabelais*. Trans. Beatrice Gottlieb. Cambridge, MA: Harvard University Press.

Fick, Carolyn. 1990. *The Making of Haiti: The Saint-Domingue Revolution from Below*. Knoxville: University of Tennessee Press.

Filmer, Paul. 2003. "Songtime: Sound Culture, Rhythm and Sociality." In *The Auditory Culture Reader*, 91–111. Ed. Michael Bull and Les Back. Oxford, Engl.: Berg.

Firmin, Anténor. 2002. *The Equality of the Human Races*. Trans. Asselin Charles. Champaign: University of Illinois Press. (Orig. pub. 1885.)

Floyd, Samuel A., Jr. 1995. *The Power of Black Music: Interpreting Its History from Africa to the United States*. Oxford, Engl.: Oxford University Press.

Forbath, Peter. 1977. *The River Congo: Discovery, Exploration, and Exploitation of the World's Most Dramatic River*. Boston, MA: Houghton Mifflin.

Fouchard, Jean. 1955. *Le Théâtre à Saint-Domingue*. Port-au-Prince, Haiti: Imprimerie de l'Etat.

Franco, Pamela R. 2004. "The Martinican: Dress and Politics in Nineteenth-Century Trinidad Carnival." In *Culture in Action—The Trinidad Experience*, 64–75. Ed. Milla Cozart Riggio. New York: Routledge.

Fraser, Lionel Mordaunt. 1971. *History of Trinidad (First Period) from 1781 to 1803*. 2 vols. London: Frank Cass. (Orig. pub. 1891.)

Friedman, Robert Lawrence. 2000. *The Healing Power of the Drum*. Reno, NV: White Cliffs Media.

Frith, Simon. 1983. *Sound Effects: Youth, Leisure, and the Politics of Rock 'n' Roll*. London: Constable.

———. 1996. *Performing Rites: On the Value of Popular Music*. Oxford, Engl.: Oxford University Press.

Gallagher, Mary. 2002. *Soundings in French Caribbean Writing Since 1950: The Shock of Space and Time*. Oxford, Engl.: Oxford University Press.

———. 2004. "Contemporary French Caribbean Poetry: The Poetics of Reference." *Forum for Modern Language Studies* 40, no. 4 (October): 451–62.

Garraway, Doris L. 2005. *The Libertine Colony: Creolization in the Early French Caribbean*. Durham, NC: Duke University Press.

Garret, Naomi M. 1963. *The Renaissance of Haitian Poetry*. Paris: Présence Africaine.

Gates, Henry Louis, Jr. 1987. *Figures in Black: Words, Signs, and the "Racial" Self*. New York: Oxford University Press.

———. 1988. *The Signifying Monkey: A Theory of African-American Literary Criticism*. New York: Oxford University Press.

Gauthier, François. 2003. "Rapturous Ruptures: The 'Instituant' Religious Experience of Rave." In *Rave Culture and Religion*, 65–84. Ed. Graham St. John. London: Routledge.

Gayle, Addison, Jr., ed. 1972. *The Black Aesthetic*. New York: Anchor Books.

Geggus, David P. 2001a. "The Caradeux and Colonial Memory." In *The Impact of the Haitian Revolution in the Atlantic World*, 231–46. Ed. David P. Geggus. Columbia: University of South Carolina Press.

———. 2001b. "Preface." In *The Impact of the Haitian Revolution in the Atlantic World*, ix–xviii. Ed. David P. Geggus. Columbia: University of South Carolina Press.

———. 2002. *Haitian Revolutionary Studies*. Bloomington: Indiana University Press.

Genovese, Eugene D. 1979. *From Rebellion to Revolution: Afro-American Slave Revolts in the Making of the Modern World*. Baton Rouge: Louisiana State University Press.

George, Nelson. 1988. *The Death of Rhythm and Blues*. New York: Plume.

———. 1991. "'Right On!' to 'Word Up.'" Liner notes to *Star Time*. Polygram 849 108–2.

George, Nelson, and Alan Leeds, eds. 2008. *The James Brown Reader: 50 Years of Writing About the Godfather of Soul*. London: Penguin.

Gibbons, Rawle. 2007. "Trinidad Sailor Mas." In *Just Below South: Intercultural Performance in the Caribbean and the U.S. South*, 146–66. Ed. Jessica Adams, Michael P. Bibler, and Cécile Accilien. Charlottesville: University of Virginia Press.

Gilroy, Paul. 1993. *The Black Atlantic: Modernity and Double Consciousness*. London: Verso.

———. 2001. *Between Camps: Nations, Cultures and the Allure of Race*. London: Penguin.

———. 2002. *There Ain't No Black in the Union Jack: The Cultural Politics of Race and Nation*. London: Routledge. (Orig. pub. 1987.)

Gisler, Antoine. 1965. *L'Esclavage aux Antilles françaises (XVIIe–XIXe siècles)*. Fribourg: Éditions Universitaires Fribourg Suisse.

Gitelman, Lisa. 2004. "Recording Sound, Race, and Property." In *Hearing History: A Reader*, 279–94. Ed. Mark M. Smith. Athens: University of Georgia Press.

Glissant, Édouard. 1958. *La Lézarde*. Paris: Seuil.

———. 1964. *Le Quatrième siècle*. Paris: Gallimard.

———. 1965. *Les Indes*. Paris: Seuil.

———. 1969. *L'Intention poétique*. Paris: Seuil.

———. 1981. *Le Discours antillais*. Paris: Seuil.

———. 1989. *Caribbean Discourse: Selected Essays*. Trans. J. Michael Dash. Charlottesville: University Press of Virginia.

———. 1997. *Poetics of Relation*. Trans. Betsy Wing. Ann Arbor: University of Michigan Press.

———. 2000. *Faulkner, Mississippi*. Trans. Barbara B. Lewis and Thomas C. Spear. Chicago: University of Chicago Press, 2000.

Glissant, Édouard, and Patrick Chamoiseau. 2007. *Quand les murs tombent: L'identité nationale hors-la-loi?* Paris: Galaade.

Gobineau, Artur de. 1983. *Œuvres*. Ed. Jean Gaulmier. Paris: Gallimard.

Goldberg, David Theo. 1993. *Racist Culture: Philosophy and the Politics of Meaning.* Oxford, Engl.: Blackwell.

Gonzáles-Wippler, Migene. 1985. *Tales of the Orishas.* New York: Original Publications.

Guilbault, Jocelyne. 2007. *Governing Sound: The Cultural Politics of Trinidad's Carnival Musics.* Chicago: University of Chicago Press.

Guilbault, Jocelyne, with Gage Averill, Edouard Benoit, and Gregory Rabess. 1993. *Zouk: World Music in the West Indies.* Chicago: University of Chicago Press.

Guralnick, Peter. 2002. *Sweet Soul Music: Rhythm and Blues and the Southern Dream of Freedom.* Edinburgh: Mojo Books. (Orig. pub. 1986.)

Handelman, Don, and David Shulman. 1991. *Myths of Caribbean Identity.* Coventry: University of Warwick, Centre for Caribbean Studies.

Handy, W. C. 1991. *Father of the Blues: An Autobiography by W.C. Handy.* Ed. Arna Bontemps. New York: Da Capo. (Orig. pub. 1941.)

Hardwick, Louise. 2008. "Dancing the Unspeakable: Rhythms of Communication in 'Laghia de la mort' by Joseph Zobel." In *Rhythms: Essays in French Literature, Thought and Culture*, 119–31. Ed. Elizabeth Lindley and Laura McMahon. Bern, Switzerland: Peter Lang.

Harris, William J. 1985. *The Poetry and Poetics of Amiri Baraka: The Jazz Aesthetic.* Columbia: University of Missouri Press.

Hegel, Georg Wilhelm Friedrich. 1956. *The Philosophy of History.* Trans J. Sibree. New York: Dover Publications. (Orig. pub. 1837.)

———. 1977. *Phenomenology of Spirit.* Trans A. V. Miller. Oxford: Clarendon Press. (Orig. pub. 1807.)

Herbeck, Jason. 2005. "'Jusqu'aux limites de l'improvisation': Caribbean Identity and Jazz in Daniel Maximin's *L'Isolé soleil.*" *Dalhousie French Studies* 71 (Summer): 161–75.

Hérisson, Lélia J. 1955. *Manuel de littérature haïtienne.* Port-au-Prince, Haiti: Département de l'Éducation Nationale.

Herskovits, Melville J., and Frances S. Herskovits. 1976. *Trinidad Village.* New York: Octagon. (Orig. pub. 1947.)

Hesmondhalgh, David, and Keith Negus. 2002. *Popular Music Studies.* London: Edward Arnold.

Highfield, Arnold R. 1997. "Some Observations on the Taino Language." In *The Indigenous People of the Caribbean*, 154–68. Ed. Samuel M. Wilson. Gainesville: University Press of Florida.

Hill, Donald R. 1993. *Calypso Calaloo: Early Carnival Music in Trinidad.* Gainesville: University Press of Florida.

Hill, Errol. 1972. *The Trinidad Carnival: Mandate for a National Theatre.* Austin: University of Texas Press.

Hoffmann, Léon-François. 1993. "Un Mythe national: La cérémonie du Bois-Caïman." In *La République haïtienne: Etat des lieux et perspectives*, 434–48. Ed. Gérard Barthélemy and Christian Girault. Paris: Karthala.

———. 2003. "Introduction du Coordinateur." In Jacques Roumain. *Œuvres complètes*, xxxi–li. Ed. Léon-François Hoffmann. Madrid, Spain: ALLCA XX, Collection Archivos.

Holmes, Anne. 2008. "'De Nouveaux Rythmes': The Free Verse of Laforgue's 'Solo de Lune.'" *French Studies* 62, no. 2 (April): 162–72.

Hughes, Langston. 1956. *I Wonder as I Wander: An Autobiographical Journey*. New York: Hill and Wang.

Hunt, Alfred. 1988. *Haiti's Influence on Antebellum America: Slumbering Volcano in the Caribbean*. Baton Rouge: Louisiana State University Press.

Huntington, Julie Ann. 2005. "Transcultural Rhythms: An Exploration of Rhythm, Music and the Drum in a Selection of Francophone Novels from West Africa and the Caribbean." PhD diss., Vanderbilt University.

Innis, Lewis Osborn. 1910. *Trinidad and Trinidadians*. Port of Spain: Mirror Printing Works.

James, C. L. R. 1932. *Life of Captain A. A. Cipriani*. Nelson, Lancashire, Engl.: Coulton.

Jay, Martin. 1993. *Downcast Eyes: The Denigration of Vision in Twentieth-Century French Thought*. Berkeley: University of California Press.

Johnson, Barbara. 1989. "The Liberation of Verse." In *A New History of French Literature*, 798–801. Ed. Denis Hollier. Cambridge, MA: Harvard University Press.

Johnson, James H. 2004. "Listening and Silence in Eighteenth- and Nineteenth-Century France." In *Hearing History: A Reader*, 169–83. Ed. Mark M. Smith. Athens: University of Georgia Press.

Johnson, James Weldon. 1929. *God's Trombones: Some Negro Sermons in Verse*. London: George Allen and Unwin.

Johnson, Kim. 2004. "Notes on Pan." In *Culture in Action—The Trinidad Experience*, 204–12. Ed. Milla Cozart Riggio. New York: Routledge.

Johnson, Sara E. 2005. "Cinquillo Consciousness: The Formation of a Pan-Caribbean Aesthetic." In *Music, Writing, and Cultural Unity in the Caribbean*, 35–58. Ed. Timothy J. Reiss. Trenton NJ: Africa World Press.

Joseph, Edward Lanzer. 1970. *History of Trinidad*. London: Frank Cass. (Orig. pub. 1838.)

Jost, Ekkehard. 1981. *Free Jazz*. New York: Da Capo Press. (Orig. pub. 1974.)

Kebede, Ashenafi. 1982. *Roots of Black Music*. Englewood Cliffs, NJ: Prentice Hall.

Kingsley, Charles. 1889. *At Last: A Christmas in the West Indies*. London: MacMillan.

Klingfors, Gunno. 1991. *Bach går igen—Källkritiska studier i J S Bachs uppförandepraxis*. Gothenburg: Skrifter från Musikvetenskapliga Institutionen.

Kodat, Catherine Gunter. 2003. "Conversing with Ourselves: Canon, Freedom, Jazz." *American Quarterly* 55, no. 1: 1–28.

Labat, Jean-Baptiste. 1722. *Nouveau voyage aux isles de l'Amérique*. 8 vols. Paris: Cavelier.

Lachance, Paul. 2001. "Repercussions of the Haitian Revolution in Louisiana." In *The Impact of the Haitian Revolution in the Atlantic World*, 209–30. Ed. David P. Geggus. Columbia: University of South Carolina Press.

Laguerre, Michel S. 1993. *The Military and Society in Haiti*. Basingstoke, Engl.: MacMillan.

Lahens, Yanick. 1998. "Afterword." In *Caribbean Creolization: Reflections on the Cultural Dynamics of Language, Literature, and Identity*, 155–64. Ed. Kathleen M. Balutansky and Marie-Agnès Sourieau. Gainesville: University Press of Florida.

———. 2000. *Dans la maison du père*. Paris: Le Serpent à Plumes.

Largey, Michael. 2006. *Vodou Nation: Haitian Art Music and Cultural Nationalism*. Chicago: University of Chicago Press.

Leeds, Alan. 1991. "From the Inside." Liner notes to *Star Time*. Polygram 849 108–2.

Lefebvre, Henri. 1992. *Eléments de Rythmanalyse*. Paris: Editions Syllepse.

Leon, Rafael de. 1988. *Calypso, from France to Trinidad: 800 Years of History*. San Juan, Trinidad: General Printers of San Juan.

Levitin, Daniel J. 2007. *This Is Your Brain on Music: The Science of a Human Obsession*. New York: Plume.

Leyburn, James G. 1972. *The Haitian People*. New Haven, CT: Yale University Press.

Linton, Ralph. 1943. "Nativistic Movements." *American Anthropologist* 45: 230–40.

Lomax, Alan. 1975. "Africanisms in New World Music." In *The Haitian Potential: Research and Resources of Haiti*, 38–53. Ed. Vera Rubin and Richard P. Schaedel. New York: Teachers College Press.

Lovelace, Earl. 2004. "The Emancipation Jouvay Tradition." In *Culture in Action—The Trinidad Experience*, 187–94. Ed. Milla Cozart Riggio. New York: Routledge.

Lubin, Maurice A. 1965. *L'Afrique dans la poésie haïtienne*. Port-au-Prince, Haiti: Editions Panorama.

Ludwig, Ralph, ed. 1994. *Écrire la parole de nuit: La nouvelle littérature antillaise*. Paris: Gallimard.

Macey, David. 2000. *Frantz Fanon: A Life*. London: Granta.

Mackey, Nathaniel. 1986. *Bedouin Hornbook*. Lexington: University of Kentucky Press.

Madiou, Thomas. 1989. *Histoire d'Haïti*. 8 vols. Port-au-Prince, Haiti: Henri Deschamps. (Orig. pub. 1847–48.)

Malik, Kenan. 1996. *The Meaning of Race: Race, History and Culture in Western Society*. Basingstoke, Engl.: MacMillan.

Mallarmé, Stéphane. 1976. *Igitur, Divagations, Un coup de dès*. Paris: Gallimard.

Mandrou, Robert. 1976. *Introduction to Modern France, 1500–1640: An Essay in Historical Psychology*. Trans. R. E. Hallmark. New York: Holmes and Meier.

Manuel, Peter, Kenneth Bilby, and Michael Largey. 1995. *Caribbean Currents: Caribbean Music from Rumba to Reggae*. Philadelphia: Temple University Press.

Marsh, Dave. 1989. *The Heart of Rock and Soul: The 1001 Greatest Singles Ever Made*. London: Penguin.

Martins, Bayo. 1983. *The Message of African Drumming*. Brazzaville, Republic of the Congo: P. Kinouvou.

Maximilien, Louis. 1952. "Considérations sur le folklore: A propos de la musique de Werner Jaegerhuber." *Le National*, April 25: 3; April 27: 6; April 28: 3; April 29: 3; April 30: 5; and May 1: 3.

Maximin, Colette. 1996. *Littératures caribéennes comparées*. Paris: Jasor et Karthala.

Maximin, Daniel. 1981. *L'Isolé soleil*. Paris: Seuil.

———. 1986. "Entretien." *Les Nouvelles du sud* 3: 35–50.

Mayfield, Julian. 1972. "You Touch My Black Aesthetic and I'll Touch Yours." In *The Black Aesthetic*, 23–30. Ed. A. J. Gayle. New York: Anchor Books.

McCallum, Pierre F. 1805. *Travels in Trinidad During the Months of February, March and April 1803*. Liverpool, Engl.: W. Jones.

McClary, Susan. 2000. *Conventional Wisdom: The Content of Musical Form*. Berkeley: University of California Press.

McLellan, James E., II. 1992. *Colonialism and Science: Saint Domingue in the Old Regime*. Baltimore, MD: Johns Hopkins University Press.

McLuhan, Marshall. 1962. *The Gutenberg Galaxy: The Making of Typographic Man*. Toronto: University of Toronto Press.

McNeill, William Hardy. 1995. *Keeping Together in Time: Dance and Drill in Human History*. Cambridge, MA: Harvard University Press.

Ménil, René. 1943. "Notes sur Mallarmé." *Tropiques* 6–7 (February): 49–52.

———. 1944. "Situation de la poésie aux Antilles." *Tropiques* 11 (May): 127–33.

———. 1981. *Tracées: Identité, Négritude, esthétique aux Antilles*. Paris: Robert Laffont.

Meschonnic, Henri. 1982. *Critique du rythme, anthropologie historique du langage*. Lagrasse, France: Verdier.

Métraux, Alfred. 1958. *Le Vaudou haïtien*. Paris: Gallimard.

———. 1960. *Haiti: Black Peasants and Their Religion*. Trans. Peter Leyngel. London: Harrap.

Meyer, Leonard B. 1989. *Style and Music: Theory, History, and Ideology*. Chicago: University of Chicago Press.

———. 1994. *Music, the Arts, and Ideas: Patterns and Predictions in Twentieth-Century Culture*. Chicago: University of Chicago Press. (Orig. pub. 1967.)

Miller, Christopher L. 2008. *The French Atlantic Triangle: Literature and Culture of the Slave Trade*. Durham, NC: Duke University Press.

Miller, Paul B. 2005. "Reading Caribbean Music: Reflections on the Music of Leo Brouwer." In *Music, Writing, and Cultural Unity in the Caribbean*, 59–74. Ed. Timothy J. Reiss. Trenton, NJ: Africa World Press.

Moore, Paul. 2003. "Sectarian Sound and Cultural Identity in Northern Ireland." In *The Auditory Culture Reader*, 265–79. Ed. Michael Bull and Les Back. Oxford, Engl.: Berg.

Moore, Robin D. 1997. *Nationalizing Blackness: Afrocubanismo and Artistic Revolution in Havana, 1920–1940*. Pittsburgh, PA: University of Pittsburgh Press.

Moreau de Saint-Méry, Médéric-Louis-Élie. 1958. *Description topographique, physique, civile, politique et historique de la partie française de l'isle de Saint-Domingue*. 3 vols. Paris: Société de l'histoire des colonies françaises et Librairie Larose. (Orig. pub. 1796.)

Mosse, George L. 1978. *Toward the Final Solution: A History of European Racism*. London: J. M. Dent and Sons.

Moten, Fred. 2003. *In the Break: The Aesthetics of the Black Radical Tradition*. Minneapolis: University of Minnesota Press.

Munro, Martin. 2000. *Shaping and Reshaping the Caribbean: The Work of Aimé Césaire and René Depestre*. Leeds, Engl.: Maney Publishing for the Modern Humanities Research Association.

Murdoch, H. Adlai. 2001. *Creole Identity in the French Caribbean Novel*. Gainesville: University Press of Florida.

Naipaul, V. S. 1982. *The Loss of El Dorado.* Harmondsworth, Engl.: Penguin. (Orig. pub. 1969.)

———. 1985. *Finding the Centre.* Harmondsworth, Engl.: Penguin.

Nardal, Paulette. 1932. "Éveil de la conscience de race." *La Revue du monde noir* 6 (April): 25–31.

Nau, Émile. 1894. *Histoire des caciques d'Haiti.* Paris: Gustave Guérin.

Neptune, Harvey R. 2007. *Caliban and the Yankees: Trinidad and the United States Occupation.* Chapel Hill: University of North Carolina Press.

Nesbitt, Nick. 2003. *Voicing Memory: History and Subjectivity in French Caribbean Literature.* Charlottesville: University of Virginia Press.

———. 2005. "The Idea of 1804." *Yale French Studies* 107 (Spring): 6–38.

Newson, Linda A. 1976. *Aboriginal and Spanish Colonial Trinidad: A Study in Culture Contact.* London: Academic Press.

Ngal, Georges. 1994. *Aimé Césaire: Un homme à la recherché d'une patrie.* 2nd ed. Paris: Présence Africaine.

Nicholls, David. 1979. *From Dessalines to Duvalier: Race, Colour, and National Independence in Haiti.* Cambridge, Engl.: Cambridge University Press.

———. 1985. *Haiti in Caribbean Context: Ethnicity, Economy and Revolt.* Basingstoke, Engl.: MacMillan.

Nketia, J. H. Kwabena. 1974. *The Music of Africa.* New York: Norton.

Ong, Walter J. 1967. *The Presence of the Word: Some Prolegomena for Cultural and Religious History.* New Haven, CT: Yale University Press.

———. 1988. *Orality and Literacy: The Technologizing of the Word.* New York: Routledge.

Palmer, Robert. 1992. "James Brown." In *The Rolling Stone Illustrated History of Rock & Roll,* 163–70. Ed. A. DeCurtis and J. Henke. New York: Random House.

Pearse, Andrew. 1956a. "Carnival in Nineteenth Century Trinidad." *Caribbean Quarterly* 4, nos. 2–3: 175–93.

———. 1956b. "Mitto Sampson on Calypso Legends of the Nineteenth Century." *Caribbean Quarterly* 4, nos. 2–3: 250–62.

Petit, Georges, and Jacques Roumain. 2003. "À la jeunesse" [1928]. In Jacques Roumain, *Œuvres complètes,* 463. Ed. Léon-François Hoffmann. Madrid, Spain: ALLCA XX, Collection Archivos.

Pettinger, Alasdair. 2004. "From Vaudoux to Voodoo." *Forum for Modern Language Studies* 40, no. 4 (October): 415–25.

Pluchon, Pierre. 1989. *Toussaint Louverture: Un révolutionnaire noir d'Ancien Régime.* Paris: Fayard.

Popkin, Jeremy D. 2007. *Facing Racial Revolution: Eyewitness Accounts of the Haitian Insurrection.* Chicago: University of Chicago Press.

Popkin, Richard H. 1973. "The Philosophical Basis of Modern Racism." *Studies in Eighteenth Century Culture* 3: 245–62.

Powrie, Barbara E. 1956. "The Changing Attitude of the Coloured Middle Class Towards Carnival." *Caribbean Quarterly* 4, nos. 2–3: 224–32.

Price-Mars, Jean. 1929. *Le Bilan des études ethnologiques en Haïti et le cycle du nègre.* Port-au-Prince, Haiti: Imprimerie de La Presse.

———. 1932. "A propos de 'La Renaissance Nègre aux États-Unis.'" *La Relève* 1, no. 3: 8–14.

———. 1959. *De Saint-Domingue à Haïti: Essai sur la culture, les arts et la littérature.* Paris: Présence Africaine.

———. 1973. *Ainsi parla l'oncle.* Ottawa: Éditions Leméac. (Orig. pub. 1928.)

Quevedo, Raymond. 1983. "Attila's Kaiso: A Short History of Trinidad Calypso." Pamphlet. St. Augustine, Trinidad and Tobago: University of the West Indies.

Raboteau, Albert J. 1978. *Slave Religion: The "Invisible Institution" in the Antebellum South.* New York: Oxford University Press.

Radano, Ronald. 2003. *Lying up a Nation: Race and Black Music.* Chicago: University of Chicago Press.

Rainsford, Marcus. 1805. *An Historical Account of the Black Empire of Hayti.* London: Albion Press.

Ramsey, Guthrie P., Jr. 2003. *Race Music: Black Cultures from Bebop to Hip-Hop.* Berkeley: University of California Press.

Rath, Richard Cullen. 2004. "Acoustics and Social Order in Early America." In *Hearing History: A Reader,* 207–20. Ed. Mark M. Smith. Athens: University of Georgia Press.

Raymond, M. 1978. Letter to the editor. *Trinidad Guardian,* January 18.

Reiss, Timothy J. 2005. "Introduction: Music, Writing, and Ocean Circuits." In *Music, Writing, and Cultural Unity in the Caribbean,* 1–34. Ed. Timothy J. Reiss. Trenton, NJ: Africa World Press.

Renda, Mary A. 2001. *Taking Haiti: Military Occupation and the Culture of U.S. Imperialism, 1915–1940.* Chapel Hill: University of North Carolina Press.

Reynolds, Simon. 1999. *Generation Ecstacy: Into the World of Techno and Rave Culture.* London: Routledge.

Rigaud, Milo. 1953. *La Tradition vaudoo et le vaudoo haïtien.* Paris: Niclaus.

Robinson, Ray, and Allen Winold. 1976. *The Choral Experience: Literature, Materials, and Methods.* New York: Harper & Row.

Rohlehr, Gordon. 1990. *Calypso and Society in Pre-Independence Trinidad.* Port of Spain: Gordon Rohlehr.

———. 2001. "The Calypsonian as Artist: Freedom and Responsibility." *Small Axe* 9, no. 1 (March): 1–26.

———. 2004. "Calypso Reinvents Itself." In *Culture in Action—The Trinidad Experience,* 213–27. Ed. Milla Cozart Riggio. New York: Routledge.

———. 2005. "Drum and Minuet: Music, Masquerade and the Mulatto of Style." In *Music, Writing, and Cultural Unity in the Caribbean,* 149–79. Ed. Timothy J. Reiss. Trenton, NJ: Africa World Press.

Rommen, Timothy. 2007. *"Mek Some Noise": Gospel Music and the Ethics of Style in Trinidad.* Berkeley: University of California Press.

Rose, Cynthia. 1990. *Living in America: The Soul Saga of James Brown.* London: Serpent's Tail.

Rosello, Mireille. 1992. *Littérature et identité aux Antilles.* Paris: Karthala.

Rosemain, Jacqueline. 1986. *La Musique dans la société antillaise.* Paris: L'Harmattan.

———. 1990. *La Danse aux Antilles, des rythmes sacrés au zouk.* Paris: L'Harmattan.

Roumain, Jacques. 1944. *Gouverneurs de la rosée*. Paris: Éditeurs Français Réunis.

———. 2003a. "A propos de la campagne anti-superstitieuse: Las supersticiones" [1944]. In *Œuvres complètes*, 745–59.

———. 2003b. "Défense de Paul Morand" [1928]. In *Œuvres complètes*, 469–71.

———. 2003c. "Entre nous: Jacques Roumain" [1927]. In *Œuvres complètes*, 435–41.

———. 2003d. "L'Afrique" [1929]. In *Œuvres complètes*, 558.

———. 2003e. *La Proie et l'ombre* [1930]. In *Œuvres complètes*, 105–34.

———. 2003f. "*La Trouée*" [1927]. In *Œuvres complètes*, 433–34.

———. 2003g. "Le Sacrifice du tambour assôtô(r)" [1943]. In *Œuvres complètes*, 1071–1144.

———. 2003h. *Les Fantoches* [1931]. In *Œuvres complètes*, 135–91.

———. 2003i. "Présentation de Langston Hughes" [1931]. In *Œuvres complètes*, 635–36.

Russell, Peter Edward Lionel. 1973. "Towards an Interpretation of Rodrigo de Reinosa's 'poesía negra.'" In *Studies in Spanish Literature of the Golden Age Presented to Edward M. Wilson*, 225–45. Ed. R. O. Jones. London: Tamesis.

Saba Saakana, Amon. 2005. "Africanity and Continuum in Sacred and Popular Trinidadian Musical Forms." In *Music, Writing, and Cultural Unity in the Caribbean*, 75–89. Ed. Timothy J. Reiss. Trenton, NJ: Africa World Press.

Sachs, Curt. 1965. *The Wellsprings of Music*. Ed. Jaap Kunst. New York: McGraw Hill.

Sala-Moulins, Louis. 1987. *Le Code Noir, ou le calvaire de Canaan*. Paris: Presses Universitaires de France.

Sankeralli, Burton. 2004. "Indian Presence in Carnival." In *Culture in Action—The Trinidad Experience*, 76–84. Ed. Milla Cozart Riggio. New York: Routledge.

Sartre, Jean-Paul. 1948. "Orphée Noir." In *Situations, III*, 227–86. Paris: Gallimard.

Savary, Jacques. 1675. *Le Parfait négociant, ou instruction générale pour ce qui regarde le commerce*. Paris: Chez Jean Guignard Fils.

Schafer, R. Murray. 1980. *The Tuning of the World: Toward a Theory of Soundscape Design*. Philadelphia: University of Pennsylvania Press.

———. 2003. "Open Ears." In *The Auditory Culture Reader*, 25–39. Ed. Michael Bull and Les Back. Oxford, Engl.: Berg.

———. 2004. "Soundscapes and Earwitnesses." In *Hearing History: A Reader*, 3–9. Ed. Mark M. Smith. Athens: University of Georgia Press.

Schechner, Richard. 2004. "Carnival (Theory) After Bakhtin." In *Culture in Action—The Trinidad Experience*, 3–11. Ed. Milla Cozart Riggio. New York: Routledge.

Schmidt, Hans. 1971. *The United States Occupation of Haiti, 1915–1934*. New Brunswick, NJ: Rutgers University Press.

Schmidt, Leigh Eric. 2003. "Hearing Loss." In *The Auditory Culture Reader*, 41–59. Ed. Michael Bull and Les Back. Oxford, Engl.: Berg.

———. 2004. "Sound Christians and Religious Hearing." In *Hearing History: A Reader*, 221–46. Ed. Mark M. Smith. Athens: University of Georgia Press.

Senghor, Léopold Sédar. 1990. *Œuvre poétique*. Paris: Éditions du Seuil.

Shepherd, John. 1991. *Music as Social Text*. Cambridge, Engl.: Polity Press.

Sieger, Jacqueline. 1961. "Entretien avec Aimé Césaire." *Afrique* 5 (October): 64–67.

Singh, Kelvin. 1988. *Bloodstained Tombs: The Muharram Massacre 1884*. Basingstoke, Engl.: MacMillan.

Small, Christopher. 1987. *Music of the Common Tongue: Survival and Celebration in Afro-American Music*. London: Calder/Riverrun Press.

Smith, Bruce R. 2003. "Tuning into London c. 1600." In *The Auditory Culture Reader*, 127–35. Ed. Michael Bull and Les Back. Oxford, Engl.: Berg.

———. 2004. "How Sound Is Sound History?" In *Hearing History: A Reader*, 389–94. Ed. Mark M. Smith. Athens: University of Georgia Press.

Smith, Mark M. 1996. "Time, Slavery, and Plantation Capitalism in the Ante-Bellum American South." *Past and Present* 150 (February): 142–68.

———. 1997. *Mastered by the Clock: Time, Slavery, and Freedom in the American South*. Chapel Hill: University of North Carolina Press.

———. 2003a. "Listening to the Heard Worlds of Antebellum America." In *The Auditory Culture Reader*, 137–63. Ed. Michael Bull and Les Back. Oxford, Engl.: Berg.

———. 2003b. "Making Sense of Social History." *Journal of Social History* 37 (September): 165–86.

———. 2004a. "Introduction. Onward to Audible Pasts." In *Hearing History: A Reader*, ix–xxii. Ed. Mark M. Smith. Athens: University of Georgia Press.

———. 2004b. "Listening to the Heard Worlds of Antebellum America." In *Hearing History: A Reader*, 365–84. Ed. Mark M. Smith. Athens: University of Georgia Press.

Snead, James A. 1984. "Repetition as a Figure of Black Culture." In *Black Literature and Literary Theory*, 59–79. Ed. Henry Louis Gates, Jr. London: Metheun.

Stein, Robert Louis. 1979. *The French Slave Trade in the Eighteenth Century: An Old Regime Business*. Madison: University of Wisconsin Press.

Stewart, Alexander. 2000. "'Funky Drummer': New Orleans, James Brown and the Rhythmic Transformation of American Popular Music." *Popular Music* 19, no. 3: 293–318.

St. John, Graham, ed. 2003. *Rave Culture and Religion*. London: Routledge.

St. John, Spencer. 1884. *Hayti, or the Black Republic*. London: Smith Elder.

St.-Louis, Carlos, and Maurice A. Lubin. 1950. *Panorama de la poésie haïtienne*. Port-au-Prince, Haiti: Éditions Henri Deschamps.

Stuempfle, Stephen. 1995. *The Steelband Movement: The Forging of a National Art in Trinidad and Tobago*. Philadelphia: University of Pennsylvania Press.

Sublette, Ned. 2007. *Cuba and Its Music: From the First Drums to the Mambo*. Chicago: Chicago Review Press.

———. 2008. *The World That Made New Orleans: From Spanish Silver to Congo Square*. Chicago: Chicago Review Press.

Sylvain, Normil. 1927. "La Jeune littérature haïtienne." *La Revue Indigène* 2 (August): 42–53.

Synnott, Anthony. 1991. "Puzzling Over the Senses: From Plato to Marx." In *The Varieties of Sensory Experience: A Sourcebook in the Anthropology of the Senses*, 61–76. Ed. David Howes. Toronto: University of Toronto Press.

Tallant, Robert. 1965. *Voodoo in New Orleans*. New York: Collier Books. (Orig. pub. 1946.)

Taylor, Daphne Pawan. 1977. *Parang of Trinidad*. Port of Spain: National Cultural Council of Trinidad and Tobago.

Thaut, Michael. 2005. *Rhythm, Music, and the Brain: Scientific Foundations and Clinical Applications*. London: Routledge.

Tomich, Dale. 2000. "Slavery in Martinique in the French Caribbean." In *Caribbean Slavery in the Atlantic World*, 413–36. Ed. Verene Shepherd and Hilary McDonald Beckles. Kingston, Jamaica: Ian Randle Publishers.

Torres-Saillant, Silvio. 2006. *An Intellectual History of the Caribbean*. New York: Palgrave.

Trouillot, Lyonel. 2010. "To the Text." In *A Reader's Guide to Edwidge Danticat*. Ed. Martin Munro. Charlottesville: University of Virginia Press.

Turner, Richard Brent. 2003. "Mardi Gras Indians and Second Lines/Sequin Artists and Rara Bands: Street Festivals and Performances in New Orleans and Haiti." *Journal of Haitian Studies* 9, no. 1 (Spring): 124–56.

van Koningsbruggen, Peter. 1997. *Trinidad Carnival: A Quest for National Identity*. London : MacMillan.

Vaval, Duraciné. 1971. *Histoire de la littérature haïtienne ou l'âme noire*. Nendeln, Liechtenstein: Kraus Reprint. (Orig. pub. 1933.)

Ventura, Michael. 1985. *Shadow Dancing in the U.S.A.* New York: St. Martin's Press.

Verschueren, J. 1948. *La République d'Haïti: Le culte Vaudou*. Paris: Lethielleux.

Verteuil, Anthony de. 1973. *Sir Louis de Verteuil, His Life and Times, Trinidad 1800–1900*. Port of Spain: Columbus Publishers.

———. 1975. *The Years Before*. Port of Spain: Imprint Caribbean Ltd.

———. 1978. *Trinidad's French Verse 1850–1900*. Port of Spain: Instant Print.

Vincent, Rickey. 1996. *Funk: The Music, the People, and the Rhythm of the One*. New York: St. Martin's Griffin.

Voltaire, François Marie Arouet de. 1876–83. *Œuvres complètes*. 52 vols. Paris: Garnier.

Walsh, Martin W. 2004. "The Blue Devils of Paramin: Tradition and Improvisation in a Village Carnival Band." In *Culture in Action—The Trinidad Experience*, 146–56. Ed. Milla Cozart Riggio. New York: Routledge.

Ward, Brian. 1998. *Just My Soul Responding: Rhythm and Blues, Black Consciousness, and Race Relations*. Berkeley: University of California Press.

Warner-Lewis, Maureen. 1995. *Yoruba Songs of Trinidad*. London: Karnak House.

Weinger, Harry, and Alan Leeds. 2008. Liner notes to *Foundations of Funk*. Polygram/Universal PLG53116e. (Orig. pub. 1996.) Reprinted in George and Leeds, *The James Brown Reader*, 36–38.

Werner, Craig. 2006. *A Change Is Gonna Come: Music, Race, and the Soul of America*. Revised and updated. Ann Arbor: University of Michigan Press. (Orig. pub. 1998.)

West, Cornel. 1994. *Race Matters*. New York: Vintage.

Whisnant, David. 1983. *All That Is Native and Fine: The Politics of Culture in an American Region*. Chapel Hill: University of North Carolina Press.

White, Cliff, and Harry Weinger. 1991. "Are You Ready for Star Time?" Liner notes to *Star Time*. Polygram 849 108-2.

White, Shane, and Graham White. 2004. "Listening to Southern Slavery." In *Hearing History: A Reader*, 247–66. Ed. Mark M. Smith. Athens: University of Georgia Press.

———. 2005. *The Sounds of Slavery: Discovering African American History Through Songs, Sermons, and Speech*. Boston, MA: Beacon Press.

Wilder, Gary. 2005. *The French Imperial Nation-State: Negritude and Colonial Humanism between the Two World Wars*. Chicago: University of Chicago Press.

Williams, Eric. 1962. *History of the People of Trinidad and Tobago*. Port of Spain: PNM Publishing.

Wilson, Olly. 1974. "The Significance of the Relationship Between Afro-American Music and West African Music." *The Black Perspective in Music* 2, no. 1: 3–22.

———. 1992. "The Heterogeneous Sound Ideal in African-American Music." In *New Perspectives on Music: Essays in Honor of Eileen Southern*, 326–37. Ed. Josephine Wright, with Samuel A. Floyd, Jr. Warren, MI: Harmonie Park Press.

Wilson, William Julius. 1987. *The Truly Disadvantaged: The Inner City, the Underclass, and Public Policy*. Chicago: University of Chicago Press.

Wolk, Douglas. 2004. *Live at the Apollo*. New York: Continuum.

Wood, Donald. 1968. *Trinidad in Transition: The Years After Slavery*. Oxford, Engl.: Oxford University Press.

Woolf, D. R. 2004. "Hearing Renaissance England." In *Hearing History: A Reader*, 112–35. Ed. Mark M. Smith. Athens: University of Georgia Press.

Yarrow, Richard. 1923. "Jazz Ruining Girls, Declares Reformer." Illinois Vigilance Association Report, January 21. http://saintvitus.com/Jazz.html.

Ziegler, Mel. 1968. "James Brown Sells His Soul." *The Miami Herald*, August 18. Reprinted in George and Leeds, *The James Brown Reader*, 44–51.

Zimra, Clarisse, trans. 1989. "Introduction to *Lone Sun*." In Daniel Maximin. *Lone Sun*, xii–lix. Charlottesville: University Press of Virginia.

Zobel, Joseph. 1950. *La Rue Cases-Nègres*. Paris: Présence Africaine.

———. 1978. *Laghia de la mort*. Paris: Présence Africaine. (Orig. pub. 1946.)

INDEX

adjountò drum, 35
Adorno, Theodor, 242n38
African Americans, 45, 74, 137, 182–213, 225, 228n8, 236n47; Black Aesthetic of, 195–98, 203, 245n19, 247n32; Black Power movement of, 3, 168, 173, 182–84, 195, 204, 223; in civil rights era, 3, 209–11; religious practice of, 218–19; roots of music of, 169, 184–88
Africanism, 62, 139, 144, 145, 184–90
Africanity, 74–75, 134, 139, 142, 144
Afro-Creoles, 9, 43, 44
Afrocubanista, 126, 237n61
aguinaldos (seasonal Christian songs), 82
Akan people, 13
Alexis, Jacques-Stephen, 54–55
Algeria, 182, 183
Alonso, A. M., 233n14
Amerindians, 44, 75, 80–82, 166, 232n4, 233n6
André, Jacques, 241n22, n24
Anglican church, 218
Annales school, 215
Antillean writers, 132–34, 156, 166, 176. *See also names of specific authors*
Arawaks, 80
Arcade, Eugene, 42
Ardouin, Coriolan, 54
Argos (newspaper), 118–19, 237n51
arietos (Amerindian dances), 80–81
Arima (Trinidad), 80

Armstrong, Louis, 136; *Hot Five,* 188
Arnold, A. James, 240n9
Arom, Simha, 13
Artillery Company, 113
art nègre, 133
assoto drum, 36–37
Assyria, 11
Atlantic Records, 191, 245n14
Attali, Jacques, 210
Attila the Hun, 122; "The Horrors of War," 124
Audain, Léon, 64
Austin, Leon, 197
Austro-Hungarian empire, 217

Back, Les, 248n11
Bailey, Peter, 216
Bailly, Pierre, 41
Baker, Arthur Wybrow, 101, 109
Bakhtin, Michael, 95, 234n21
balanse (swinging), 42
Ballard, Hank, 194
bamboo bands, 119, 120. *See also* tamboo-bamboo bands
bamboula drum and dance, 31, 43, 88, 238n65
banza (musical instrument), 31
Baptists, 93, 196, 244n5
Baraka, Amiri, 22, 195–98, 200–208, 225, 244n1, 246n28, 247n35, 248n10; *Black Music,* 200–202; *Blues People,* 203; *Daggers and Javelins,*

Baraka, Amiri (*continued*)
201; *The Dead Lecturer*, 197; "New Black
Music," 200, 202; "A Poem for Willie Best,"
197; *Slave Ship*, 202
Barbados, 39, 100; migrants in Trinidad from,
92, 102, 112, 117
Barthélemy, Gérard, 20, 248n13
Basie, Count, 169
bat tenèb (beating back darkness), 77
Baudelaire, Charles, 60
bay manger tambour (Vodou ceremony), 36
Beats, the, 196
Beauvoir, Simone de, *Le Deuxième sexe*,
240n12
Bebey, Francis, 13, 14
Bechet, Sidney, 43–44
Beginner, 237n57
Belafonte, Harry, 210
belair dance, 12, 88, 94, 106, 234n20, 238n65
Bell, Beverly, 76–77
Bellegarde, Dantès, 57
Benítez-Rojo, Antonio, 10, 229n26
Benveniste, Émile, 52
Berrian, Brenda F., 243n44
Berrio, Antonio de, 81
Berry, Chuck, 244n3
Best, Willie, 197
Biassou, 46
Biondi, Carminella, 242n35
Black Aesthetic movement, 196–98, 203; 245n19,
247n32
Black Arts movement, 196
Black Atlantic, 227n1
black nationalism, 203, 225
Black Panther party, 194, 195, 197, 204
Black Power movement, 3, 168, 173, 182–84, 195,
204, 223
Blaikie, Lord, "Steelband Clash," 129
blues, 169, 175, 176, 184, 187, 188, 191, 197, 203,
245n11; origins of, 185; poetry and, 137, 143,
197, 198, 202
Boer War, 113
Bois-Caïman ceremony, 28, 66
Bois d'Inde, 100
Bonaparte, Napoleon, 21, 40, 168
Bongie, Chris, 241n28, 242n33, n40, 243n42
Bonnet, General Guy-Joseph, 72
boogie-woogie, 121, 187, 225
Borde, P. G. L., 234n23
Born, Georgia, 206
Borno, Louis, 74

Boston, 185
Boukman, Dutty, 28–29
boula drum, 35
Boyer, Jean-Pierre, 48, 50
Boys Town, 129
Brackett, David, 229n18, 245n11
Brathwaite, Kamau, 243n45
Brazil, 38, 133, 139, 183, 215, 221, 238n69
Brereton, Bridget, 86, 93, 233n17, 236n43
Breton, André, 201; *Union libre*, 176
Brigade Union, 113
Briggs, E., 119
Britain, 49, 126, 217, 220; colonies of, 21, 30, 38,
184. *See also* Trinidad; popular music in, 119;
raves in, 225, 226; in War of 1812, 40, 93; in
World War II, 123, 124
Britton, Celia, 240n10, 242n31
Brouard, Carl, 75
Brown, Elaine, *Seize the Time*, 197
Brown, James, 2, 22, 184, 188–95, 197–205, 207–
213, 219, 225, 228n8, 244n3, n5, 245n10, n15,
n17, n18, n20, 246nn23–31, 247n34, 248n44;
"Ain't That a Groove," 192; "America Is
My Home," 204; "Bring It Up," 192; "Cold
Sweat," 192, 193, 208, 213, 225, 245n14;
"Don't Be a Dropout," 204; "Get on the
Good Foot," 212; "Get Up, Get Into It
And Get Involved," 246n26; "Get Up Offa
That Thing," 199; "Give It Up Or Turnit
A Loose," 246n26; "How You Gonna Get
Respect (When You Haven't Cut Your
Process Yet)," 195; "I Don't Care," 188; *I Feel
Good*, 188, 246n27; "I Found You," 188; "I
Got You (I Feel Good)," 192; "Let Yourself
Go," 192; *Live at the Apollo*, 189; "Lost Some-
one," 184, 189; "Maybe the Last Time," 184;
"Money Won't Change You," 192; "Oh Baby
Don't You Weep," 184; "One," 247n34; "Out
of Sight," 184, 188–90, 209, 244n2, 245n11,
n13, 246n26; "Papa's Got a Brand New Bag,"
190–93, 209, 245n11, 246n27; "The Payback,"
225; "Please, Please, Please," 188, 199; "Say
It Loud (I'm Black and Proud)," 2, 195,
204, 209; "Sex Machine," 199, 246n25, n26;
"Soul Power," 246n26; "Super Bad," 245n16,
246n26; "Talkin' Loud & Sayin' Nothing,"
246n26
Brown, Roy, 244n3
Brown, Sarah, 194
Brunetière, Ferdinand, 57
Buck-Morss, Susan, 228n12

Bull, Michael, 248n11
Bullet, Jeannot, 29, 30
Burke, Solomon, 189
Burr-Reynaud, Frédéric, 64; "Trahison," 64–65
Byrd, Bobby, 199

cacos (peasant guerillas), 61
calenda dance, 6, 27, 30–32, 43, 44, 72, 88
caliso songs, 112
call-and-response, 13, 16, 93, 115, 160, 162, 166, 179, 188, 200, 218
calypso, 104, 107, 119, 121–27, 168, 173–75, 229n15, 233n4, 235n29, n34, n37, 237n52, n54, n57, n59, 238n65; dances to, 2–3; early, 112–14; precursors to, 81, 83, 92, 95, 100, 233n15; recordings of, 117, 121, 233n7, 236n49; steelbands and, 129–30
Canboulay, 88, 101–2, 104, 107–9, 233n8, n9, n12, 235n32, 237n54
Canez, Velério, 74
Carenage (Trinidad), 85
Caresser, Lord, 229n15
Caribs, 80
Carib Tokyo, 129
carieto songs, 81
cariso songs, 112
Carmichael, Gertrude, 234n22
Carmichael, Stokely, 173, 182, 246n29
Carnival, 79, 84, 88–105, 107, 109, 118–21, 230n34, n35, 233n6, 235n28, 238n67, n73; attempts at suppression of, 21–22, 74, 94–96, 101–2, 118, 224; calypso and, 113–14, 237n52; Canboulay and, 88, 101, 102, 107, 109, 233n9, n12; European visitors' perceptions of, 91–92; jamette, 98–101, 108, 110–12, 114–16, 233n12, n12, 234n24; post-Emancipation, 88–91, 93–94; recordings of songs of, 117; sailor dances in, 2, 237n60; Saint-Dominguan refugees and, 40; tamboo-bamboo music in, 127–28; during World War II, 124, 130
Carpentier, Alejo, 237n61
Carriacou, 233n8
Casséus, Maurice, "Le Tambour Racial," 66
Catholicism, 9, 62, 133, 223, 231n18, 234n27. See also Carnival; anti-superstition campaign and, 36, 75, 231n12; creolization of Amerindian beliefs and, 44; parodies of, 38, 87; in Saint-Domingue, 18, 27–28, 46–50; of Toussaint Louverture, 25, 77; in Trinidad, 82, 84, 91, 92; in United States, 39–40
Cedulas, 82–84, 96, 131

Cervantes, Miguel de, 6
Césaire, Aimé, 3, 132–48, 152, 154–55, 177, 181, 201–2, 205, 207, 239n3, n6, 240n8, n10; Les Armes miraculeuses, 134, 139; "Batouque," 139–42, 162; Cahier d'un retour au pays natal, 67, 134, 139, 142, 144, 175, 176, 201, 240n9; Corps perdu, 134; Et les chiens se taisaient, 136, 243n49, n51; Ferrements, 134; Moi, Laminaire, 134; Soleil cou coupé, 134; in Tropiques group, 134, 143, 167, 168, 170
Chamoiseau, Patrick, 148, 207–8, 240n16
chantwelles (folk artists and singers), 100, 111, 115, 121, 160
Charles X, King of France, 54
Charles, Ray, 184
Charleston (South Carolina), 39
Chen, Sylvia, 126
Chernoff, John Miller, 13, 14
chica dance, 6, 20, 32, 232n2
Chicago, 169, 184, 186, 245n15; house scene, 225, 249n16
Chinese immigrants, 78, 80, 129
Christianity, 9, 10, 12, 82, 87, 140. See also Catholicism; Afro-, 93; baptismal sacrament in, 36; calendar of, 18; poetry and, 53–54, 60; saints' identities in, 28, 49–50; Toussaint Louverture's promotion of family values of, 25
Christophe, Henri, 45–48, 50, 61
Cipriani, Captain A. A., 122
civil rights movement, 3, 209, 210
Cleaver, Eldridge, 182, 187
Clifford, James, 239n2
Clinton, George, 208, 211, 245n12
Cock of the North Highlanders, 113
Code Noir (1685), 27–29
Coicou, Massillon, 57
Collins, Phelps "Catfish," 208, 211
Collins, William "Bootsy," 208, 211
Coltrane, John, 198–200
Columbia Gramophone Company, 117
Columbia Phonograph Company, 116
Columbus, Christopher, 79
Confiant, Raphaël, 148, 240n16
Congo orchestra, 35
Congos, 37, 92
Connor, Steven, 220, 229n20
convois (dancing societies), 85, 99
Cooke, Sam, 210; "A Change Is Gonna Come," 209
"coon songs," 121

Corde-à-violon, "Sur le projet de loi contre la musique, le soir," 103
Coro rebellion (Venezuela, 1795), 39
corvée system, 61
coujaille dance, 43
Council of Racial Equality (CORE), 194
Courlander, Harold, 37
Cowley, John, 114, 119, 233n8
Creoles, 6, 36, 177, 221, 222; in Charleston, 39; in Guadeloupe, 170–72, 180; in Louisiana, 42, 236n47; in Martinique, 149, 151, 154, 156, 161, 169; in Saint-Domingue, 28, 31, 32, 231n9; in Trinidad, 21, 82–84, 88, 92, 93, 95–98, 100–109, 111, 112, 114, 116, 117, 126, 224, 238n73
Créolité writers, 173
Criminal Justice and Public Order Act (Britain, 1994), 226
Crowley, Daniel, 236n42, n45, 237n60
Cuba, 44, 57, 74, 75, 97, 170, 177, 229n25, 231n17, 238n69; Afrocubanista in, 126; Baraka in, 201; Saint-Dominguan migrants in, 40, 41
Cullen, Countee, 73–74, 137
Curaçao, 39

Dahomey, 35, 37, 234n27
Damas, Léon-Gontran, 132, 134–38, 143, 148; Black-Label, 138; Pigments, 136; "Trêve," 137
Damiens (Haiti), School of Agrigulture at, 61
Danielsen, Anne, 199, 228n10, 246n25, n28, 247n38
Danticat, Edwidge, 232n30
Dario, Rubén, 57
Dash, J. Michael, 53, 54, 231n23, 242n38, n41
Davis, Angela, 182
Davis, Thulani, 193, 195
Day, Charles William, 91–92, 94
Debergue, Constant, 42
De Boissiere, Jean, 126
Decca Records, 233n7
Dédé, Edmond, 42
Dédé, Sanité, 44
Delafosse, Maurice, 63, 145
Delgrès, Louis, 167, 172, 244n51
Denis, Lorimer, 74
Depestre, René, 64, 136
Deren, Maya, 21
Derrida, Jacques, 12, 205
Descartes, René, 216
Descourtilz, Michel Étienne, 29
Desdunes, Rodolphe, 42
Desmangles, Leslie G., 231n18

Dessalines, Jean-Jacques, 27, 45–48, 50, 51, 61, 78
Dessons, Gérard, 231n22
Destination Tokyo (film), 129
Detroit, 196, 208
Devenish, Sylvester, "La Canne à sucre—Chant du planteur trinidadicn," 96–97
devil mas, 127–28
Devot, Justin, 53
Dibango, Manu, 212; "Soul Makossa," 212
djouba drum and dance, 35
Dominican order, 105
Dorsainvil, J. C., 64
Douglas, Emory, 204
Dubois, Laurent, 19, 26, 33, 229n30
Dupré, Antoine, "Hymne à la liberté," 53–54
Durand, Oswald, 55, 231n23; "Choucoune," 55; "Le Vaudoux," 55–58, 231n24
Durkheim, Émile, 62
Du Tertre, Jean-Baptiste, 19, 228n9
Duval, Amilcar, 57
Duvalier, François, 49, 63, 75

Earth, Wind and Fire, 212
East Indian immigrants, 78, 80, 108–9, 233n12
École Nationale de Musique (Haiti), 72
Edward, Bryan, 85
Egypt, ancient, 11
Elder, Jacob, 81, 83, 233n9, 238n71
Eldridge, Michael, 237n54
Elie, Justin, 75
Eliot, Marc, 247n34
Ellington, Duke, 198
Ellis, Alfred "Pee Wee," 198
Ellison, Ralph, 180, 203–4
English immigrants, 80
Enlightenment, 10, 216
Erickson, John, 244n54
Ertegun, Ahmet, 191
Espinet, Charles, 233n7, 238n62
Essor, L' (newspaper), 74
Étudiant martiniquais, L' (journal), 134
Étudiant noir, L' (journal), 134
evangelical movement, 218

Fair Play (newspaper), 104, 105, 111
Falassi, Allesandro, 230n36
Fame recording studio, 208
Famous Flames, 184, 188
Fancy Bands, 113, 115, 117
"Fancy Sailor" bands, 2
Fanon, Frantz, 3–4, 22, 132, 144–48, 182, 224,

240n10; *Les Damnés de la terre,* 240n13; *Peau noire, masques blancs,* 3, 144, 145, 155
Faubert, Pierre, 54
Faulkner, William, 168, 242n36
festive laughter, 95, 234n21
Fireman dance, 2
Firmin, Anténor, 51, 57, 64
Fisk Jubilee Singers, 236n40
Fleury-Battier, Alcibiade, "Le Bamboula," 231n24
Floyd, Samuel A., 196
Forbes Commission, 61
Fort-de-France, 151, 239n3; Lycée Schœlcher, 136, 149, 155
Fort Matouba (Guadeloupe), 168
Foster, George, 185
France, 56, 135, 138, 151–52, 216; Ancien Régime, 84; balloon flight in, 19; Caribbean colonies of, 7, 9, 10, 18, 21–22, 82, 126, 136 (*See also* Guadeloupe; Martinique; Saint-Domingue); jazz in, 73; National Convention, 27, 40; poetry in, 51–53, 55; recognition of Haitian independence by, 54; Republican, 26; in World War II, 168–70
Franco, Pamela, 234n20
Francophilia, 21, 64, 71
Franklin, Aretha, 189, 245n14
Fraser, L. M., 86–87
Freeling, Sanford, 102, 103
Freemasonry, 41
French Revolution, 25, 82, 183
Freud, Sigmund, 134, 240n10
Frith, Simon, 187
Frobenius, Leo, 63, 134, 144, 145, 148, 239n2
funk, 187, 191, 199, 208, 211–13, 228n8, 246n23, 247n43, 248n45

Gallagher, Mary, 149, 240n18, 242n30
Gallifet plantation (Saint-Domingue), 19, 28
Garraway, Doris, 231n9
Garret, Naomi, 58
Garvey, Marcus, 183
Gates, Henry Louis, Jr., 245n19
Gaye, Marvin, *What's Going On,* 247n42
gayap songs, 92–93
Gayle, Addison, Jr., 196
Geffrard, Fabre Nicolas, 49, 51
Genovese, Eugene, 45
George, Nelson, 187, 191–93, 245n10, n15, 247n41
Germany, 123, 124
ghouba dance, 88
Gibbons, Rawle, 235n32, 237n60

Gilroy, Paul, 172–73, 177, 227n1, 230n33, 236n40, 249n15
Glissant, Édouard, 22, 51, 132, 146–48, 157, 171, 173, 181, 183, 207–8, 221, 224–25, 240n16, 241n26, 242n32, n36, 243nn42–44; *Caribbean Discourse,* 146, 168–69; *Les Indes,* 148; *L'Intention poétique,* 242n37; *La Lézarde,* 241n27; *Le Quatrième siècle,* 157–68, 241n28, 242n30, n33, n35, nn39–41
Gobineau, Artur de, 11–12, 63, 64, 222, 232n27
Gomes, Albert, 126, 127
Gordon, Arthur, 92
Gorki, Maxim, 229
gospel music, 169, 184, 188, 189, 219, 246n23, n30, 248n7, 249n16
Gouly, Marie-Benoît-Louis, 27
Grace, Bishop "Daddy," 244n5
Greece, 91; ancient, 9, 62
Green, Al, 248n7
Greene, Burton, 205
Grenada, 82
Griot movement, 74–75
gros-ka drum, 169–71, 173, 179–80
Growler, 124, 237n57
Growling Tiger, 123
Guadeloupe, 22, 39, 133, 166–183, 224, 233n8
Guilbault, Jocelyne, 243n44
Guillén, Nicolás, 201; *Motivos de Son,* 201
Guinean rhythm, 29, 66, 90
guineo dance, 6
Guitar Slim, "The Things That I Used to Do," 184
Guralnick, Peter, 193, 195
Guyana, 80

Haiti, 3, 21, 24–25, 27, 30, 45–79, 127, 170, 172, 205, 230n5, 231n20, 236n48, 238n69. *See also* Saint-Domingue; anti-superstition campaign in, 36, 75, 231n12; indigenism in, 3, 11, 21, 62, 66–69, 71–76, 126, 132, 195, 201, 202, 223; National Bank of, 60; poetry in, 50–60, 64–68, 136; postrevolution rhythms in, 45–50, 93; revolution in. *See* Haitian Revolution; U.S. occupation of, 60–72, 125, 232n25; Vodou in, 21, 25, 34–38, 42, 45–50, 199, 230n37
haïtianisme (Haitianity), 62
Haitian Revolution, 3, 21, 24–31, 45, 53, 78, 182, 183; dissemination of idea of, 38–41, 85–86; refugees from, 38–45
Handelman, Don, 235n30
Handy, W. C., 185

Harlem, 183, 195; Black Arts Repertory School, 196
Harlem Renaissance, 73, 133, 239n2
Harris, William, 200
Hawkins, Coleman, 244n52; *Body and Soul*, 177, 178
Hayes, Isaac, *Hot Buttered Soul*, 247n42
Hegel, Georg Wilhelm Friedrich, 11, 12, 145, 222, 228n10
Heidegger, Martin, 205, 207, 220
Heilbut, Anthony, 219
Hell, Henri, 136, 239n4
Hell Yard, 128
Herskovits, Frances S., 234n19
Herskovits, Melville J., 37, 234n19
Hesmondhalgh, David, 206
Highfield, Arnold, 81
Hill, Donald, 236n49, 238n72
Hill, Errol, 128
Hippolyte, Dominique, 64
Hislop, Thomas, 86
Hispaniola, 85
Hosein, 108–9, 235n38, n39
Houma Indians, 43
houmfo (Vodou temple), 37
houngan (Vodou priest), 35, 46
hounsi (Vodou initiates), 37
hountò drum, 35
Hughes, Langston, 73–74, 133, 137
Hugo, Victor, 55

Ibos, 30, 37, 92
Ignace, Joseph, 172
Ile-de-France, 27
Illinois Vigilance Association, 186
indigenism (in Haiti), 3, 21, 62, 133, 180–81, 195, 196, 201, 202, 223; literature inspired by, 65–71, 232n30; music and, 72–77, 126, 132
Innis, L. O., 111
Innocent, Antoine, 64
Invader, Lord, 125, 237n57; "A Bachelor Life," 125; "Rum and Coca Cola," 125; "Yankee Dollar," 126
Irish immigrants, 80
Italy, Carnival in, 81

Jackson, George, 243n46
Jackson, Jonathan, 243n46
Jackson, Millie, 247n41
Jaegerhuber, Werner Anton, 75
Jagger, Mick, 212

Jamaica, 38, 110, 169, 236n49, 238n69; Peace concert in, 214; Saint-Dominguans in, 39, 41
Jahn, Janheinz, 239n6
James, C. L. R., 236n43
jamettes (urban slum dwellers), 97–101, 103, 118–20, 235n29, 237n51; in Carnival, 97–98, 100–101, 108, 110–12, 114–16, 119, 233n12, n14, 234n24
Janvier, Louis-Joseph, 51
Japan, 129
Jay, Martin, 215
jazz, 168–70, 172–73, 177–80, 183, 186–87, 206, 237n60, 243n45, n47, 254n53; calypso and, 121, 127, 238n65; in Haiti, 73–75; in James Brown's music and, 193, 197, 199–200, 256n23; in Paris, 133, 239n2; poetry and, 132, 137, 143, 207, 208; R&B and, 209; roots of, 42; surrealism and, 202
Jazz des Jeunes, 75
Jean-Louis, Henri, 133
Jeanty, Occide, "1804," 69
Jersey City (New Jersey), 196
Jews, Nazirite, 62–63
John-John band, 128
Johnson, James Weldon, 218–19
Johnson, Kim, 239n73
Johnson, Sara E., 229n25
Jones, LeRoi. *See* Baraka, Amiri
Jones, Nat, 189
Jones, Patrick, 121; "Class Legislation," 121
Jones, Quincy, 187
Jordan, Louis, 188, 244n3, 246n30; "Caldonia," 184
Joseph, Edward Lanzer, 85
Jost, Ekkehard, *Free Jazz*, 206
Jules, Neville, 128
Julian, Henry, 117; "Iron Duke in the Land," 117
Jungian psychology, 205

kalinda songs, 100, 117, 160, 239
Karenga, Ron, 196
Keate, Robert William, 95–97
King, Martin Luther, Jr., 2
King Records, 184, 190
King Sailor dance, 2
Kingsley, Charles, 92
Kingston (Jamaica), 38, 110
Kitchener, Lord, 124, 237n57; "The Beat of the Steelband," 130; "My Wife Went Away with a Yankee," 125
konesans (knowledge), 43

Koningsbruggen, Peter van, 235n29, 238n73
Kool & the Gang, 212
Kuti, Fela, 212

Labat, Jean-Baptiste, 18, 49
Ladies' Home Journal, 42
Laforest, Edmond, 57
laghia dance, 149
Lamentin revolt (Guadeloupe, 1797), 39
Lamothe, Ludovic, 75
Lancaster, Burt, 1
Lanusse, Armand, 42
Last Poets, The, 204, 208; *Niggers Are Scared of Revolution,* 195
Laveaux, Étienne, 26, 46
Lebanese immigrants, 78, 80
Le Blanc, Norman, "Governor Jerningham," 113
Le Bon, Gustave, 232n26
Le Cap (Saint-Domingue), 19, 28, 33, 41
Lee, Don L., 196
Leeds, Alan, 191, 244n2
Lefebvre, Henri, 37, 227n4, 229n27, 240n19, 249n14
Légitime Défense (journal), 134
Lenoir, Jacques, "Maintenant 'Nous Nègres,'" 67–68
Leon, Rafael de, 235n34
Lescot, Émile, 75
Lévy-Bruhl, Lucien, 63, 239n2
Ligue de la Jeunesse Haïtienne, La, 61
Lion, 237n57
Locke, Alain, 133
London, 170, 173
Louisiana, 40–45, 183, 184, 238n69; dissemination of idea of Haitian revolution to, 38, 40–41; Saint-Dominguans in, 41–44
Lovelace, Earl, 238n66
Lovey's Band, 116, 117
Lowe, Sammy, 198
Lubin, Maurice A., 66
Ludlow, Henry, 103–5
Ludwig, Ralph, 241n25
lwas (deities), 35–37, 48, 50, 67

Macaya, 46
Mackey, Nathaniel, 248n7
Madhubuti, Haki R., 196
Madiou, Thomas, 48, 50
Malcolm X, 195, 196
Mallarmé, Stéphane, 51, 240n8
mambo (Vodou priest), 35

Mandingos, 92
Manley, Michael, 214
manman drum, 35, 37
Mannette, Ellie, 128, 129
maraca (Amerindian sacred rattle), 80, 81
Maria Theresa, Empress, 217
Maribones, 102, 105
Marie-Galante, 39
Marine Corps, U.S., 61, 73
Marley, Bob, 214
Marrico, 2
Marsh, Dave, 191
Martí, José, 57
Martinique, 3, 132–66, 182, 183, 205, 207, 229n25, 233n8, 241n22, 243n43, n44; Creole culture in, 149, 151, 154, 156, 161, 169; Negritude movement in, 22, 132–43, 224; post-Negritude period in, 143–49; St. Pierre volcano in, 169
Martinique drums, 35
Marxism, 68, 74, 168
Masakela, Hugh, 212
masquerades, 2–3, 89, 95, 98, 102–3, 118, 230n35, 233n6, 238n69; *jamette,* 100–101; upper-class, 91
Maximin, Colette, 241n21, 242n29
Maximin, Daniel, 22, 132, 148, 167, 168, 225, 240n14, 243n47, n51, 244n52, n54; *L'île et une nuit,* 167; *L'Isolé soleil,* 167–83, 243n42, n45; *Soufrières,* 167, 243n42
Mayfield, Curtis, 204
Mayfield, Julian, 196
McCallum, Pierre, 85
McClary, Susan, 8, 228n8
McKay, Claude, 133, 183
McLuhan, Marshall, 215
Memphis, 208
Men of Boys Town (film), 129
Mendes, Alfred, 126
Ménil, René, 22, 224, 240n8, 243n47; *Tracées,* 3, 143
Mentor, Ralph, 126
Mercury Records, 184
mereng dance, 73
Merleau-Ponty, Maurice, 145, 240n13
Merrick, Walter, 119
Meschonnic, Henri, 6, 52, 231n22
Meters, The, 208
Métraux, Alfred, 34–37, 43
Mexico, 44, 231n17
Meyers, Leonard B., 7–8; *Style and Music,* 7
Middle Passage, 20, 140, 166, 207, 212

Mighty Sparrow, "Jean and Dinah," 125, 126, 237n57
Miller, Christopher L., 229n16
Miller, Paul, 239n1
Millinder, Lucky, 188
Mingus, Charles, 198
Mirror (newspaper), 115, 116
Mississippi, 183, 185
Moravia, Charles, 57
Moreau de Saint-Méry, Médéric-Louis-Élie, 31–34, 37, 44, 62, 94, 231n9, 232n2
Mortland, John, 194
Moten, Fred, 22, 203–8, 212–13, 248n6
Motown, 210
Mozart, Wolfgang Amadeus, 217, 228n7
mulâtresse style, 88
Murdoch, H. Adlai, 243n45
Muscle Shoals (Alabama), 208
Musical Ordinance (Trinidad, 1882, 1883), 103, 105
music therapy, 227n2
Muslims, 108–9

Naipaul, V. S., 81
Nardal, Jane, 133
Nardal, Paulette, 133; "Éveil de la conscience de race," 133
National Broadcasting Company (NBC), 122
Native Americans, 43
Nau, Émile, 50; *Histoires des caciques d'Haïti*, 232n31
Nau, Ignace, 54
Nazirite Jews, 62–63
Neal, Larry, 196, 197, 200
nègres jardins (field slaves), 88, 101, 115
Negritude, 3, 22, 126, 132–34, 146, 207, 240n10; disalienation through evocation of past in, 152, 162, 180–81; Frobenius's influence on, 134, 144, 148; rhythm and, 134–43, 201, 223, 224
Neptune, Harvey, 237n58, n60
Nesbitt, Nick, 172, 231n20, 240n9, 243n51, 244n52, n53
Netherlands, colonies of, 38, 97
Newgates, 105
New Orleans, 121, 169, 186, 208, 212, 231n17, 236n47, 246n24; Congo Square, 43–45, 73; Saint-Dominguans in, 41–44, 73, 183
New York, 169, 170, 185; Apollo Theater, 193; CORE in, 194
New York Times, 128–29, 200

Ngal, Georges, 143–44
Nketia, J. H. Kwabena, 13
noiriste ideology, 75
Nolen, Jimmy, 211
North Carolina, 184

ochan drumming, 20–31
Odeluc, 19
okès bastreng (string orchestras), 72
Ong, Walter, 215
Oreste, Michel, 230n5
ouanga (fetishes), 29
Oval Boys, 128

Pacesetters, The, 208
Palmer, Robert, 190
pan-Africanism, 133
parang (Trinidadian musical form), 82–83
Pareles, Jon, 200
Paris, 134, 170, 173–76, 239n1; Antillean writers in, 133, 136, 139, 232n26; Conservatoire Impérial de Musique, 72
Parker, Maceo, 189
Parker, Melvin, 189, 193
Parliament, 211
Parnassians, 132
Patois songs, 117
Patoski, Christina, 246n31
Patrie, La (newspaper), 61
Peace Preservation Ordinance (Trinidad, 1884), 107
Pearse, Andrew, 81, 233n12, 234n26, n27
Peau de Canelle, 100
Péguy, Charles, 240n9
Péralte, Charlemagne, 61
Perez, Ralph, 233n7
Perse, Saint-John, *Éloges*, 240n16
Pessini, Elena, 242n35
Pétion, Alexandre, 27, 47, 61, 71
Petit, Georges J., 61
Petro rituals, 21, 35, 230n37
Pettinger, Alasdair, 49
Philadelphia, 185, 196; Saint-Dominguans in, 39–40
Pickett, Wilson, 189
pile chactas dance, 43
Pitts, Harry, 233n7, 238n62
plantations, 6, 8–9, 15, 39, 215, 221, 222, 229n29, 230n33, n36; in American South, 168–69, 193, 219, 221; fictional depictions of, 69–71,

149–53, 155–58, 160–62, 166, 171, 241n22; in post-revolutionary Haiti, 25–27, 47; in Saint-Domingue, 16–20, 28, 30, 34, 38, 229n30; in Trinidad, 40, 81–82, 84–85, 87, 88, 94, 97, 109, 123

Plato, 4

Pointe-à-Pitre (Guadeloupe), 172, 178

Police Rulings (Saint-Domingue, 1758, 1777), 27

Port-au-Prince, 30, 49, 61, 72; Lycée Pétion, 57; Notre-Dame cathedral, 48

Port of Spain, 79, 85, 100, 106, 109, 110, 119–20, 128–30; Borough Council, 113; Carnival Improvement Committee, 127

Port of Spain Gazette, 88–91, 93, 99, 107, 110–15, 118, 120

Portugal, 6; immigrants from, 78, 80

Powrie, Barbara, 236n32, 239n73

Pradel, Seymour, 57

Presbyterians, 218

Presley, Elvis, 212

Price, Hannibal, 64

Price-Mars, Jean, 53, 54, 58, 61, 66, 68, 76, 133, 205, 232n26; Ainsi parla l'oncle, 62–64, 73

Prospect, Andrew, 238n70

Protestantism, 40, 60, 90–92, 233n12

Puerto Rico, 97, 229n25

Quakers, 217

Quevedo, Francisco, 6

quimboiseur (storyteller), 158, 159, 162–66

Radano, Ronald, 186–88, 246n32

Rada rituals, 35, 230n37

Radas, 32, 92

Ramsey, Guthrie, 245n15

Ransford, Marcus, 85

Redding, Otis, 209

Redmond, Layne, 227n3

regiments (dancing societies), 85, 90, 94, 99, 111

Renaissance, 216, 220, 235n35, 248n4

Revue indigène, La, 68, 74

Revue du monde noir, La, 133

rhythm and blues (R&B), 183, 184, 187, 189–90, 195, 197–98, 204, 209–10, 246n23

Rigaud, André, 39

Rigaud, Milo, 36

Riggio, Milla Cozart, 230n34

Rodó, José Enrique, 57

Rohlehr, Gordon, 83, 121, 230n36, 233n7, n16, 234n24, 236n44, 237n55, n57, n59, 238n65

Roman Catholic Church. See Catholicism

Romanticism, 51, 53–55, 57, 132

Rome, ancient, 62

Ronde, La (literary review), 57, 58, 60, 65

Rose, Cynthia, 188–89, 194, 244n3

Rose, Julian White, 236n45

Rosello, Mireille, 243n51

Roumain, Jacques, 36, 37, 65, 68–71, 73–74, 76, 133, 136, 170, 183; Les Fantoches, 69–70; Gouverneurs de la rosée, 68, 70–71, 232n30; La Proie et l'ombre, 69

sailor mas, 12

Saint-Domingue, 16–21, 24–31, 37, 86–88, 212, 229n30, 231n10, 232n27. See also Haiti; Catholicism in, 18, 25, 27, 28, 46; European musical performances in, 72; migrants from, 38–45, 73, 85, 183, 199; music, dance, and ritual in, 31–34, 94

St. John, Spencer, 49

St. Joseph (Trinidad), 81

St. Lucia, 233n8

Sajous, Léo, 133

s'Amandes, 100

Sampson, Mitto, 81, 232n4

San Fernando (Trinidad), 109

San José de Oruña (Trinidad), 81

Sankeralli, Burton, 235n38

Santamaria, Mongo, 212

Santarém (Portugal), 6

Sartre, Jean-Paul; Critique de la raison dialectique, 240n13; "Orphée noir," 145; Réflexions sur la question juive, 240n12

Savannah Grande (Trinidad), 80, 93

Schafer, R. Murray, 210, 216, 217, 248n12

Schechner, Richard, 235n28

Schmidt, Hans, 232n25

Schmidt, Leigh Eric, 248n3

Schœlcher, Victor, 145

Scott, Robert W., "L'Africain," 65–66

Scott-Heron, Gil, 204

Scottish immigrants, 80

Seaga, Edward, 214

ségond drum, 35

Séjour, Louis Victor, 42

Séligny, Michel, 42

Senegambian slaves, 44

Senghor, Léopold Sédar, 134–38, 143, 144, 148, 201, 239n5; "C'est le temps de partir," 134; Chants d'ombre, 134; "Comme les lamantins

Senghor, Léopold Sédar *(continued)*
vont boire à la source," 138; "Congo," 134–35;
Éthiopiques, 134, 135; "Lettre à trois poètes
de l'Hexagone," 135; "Vacances," 134
serviteur (one who serves the gods), 35, 42–44
Shakers, 93
Shand Estate Revolt (Trinidad, 1805), 39, 85–87
Shango, 229n15, 235n36, 238n70
Shapiro, Brad, 192
Shepherd, John, 248n9
Shouters, 93, 234n19
Shrovetide, 84, 101, 107, 113
Shulman, David, 235n30
Sieger, Jacqueline, 138–39
Simon, Winston "Spree," 128
Singh, Kelvin, 235n39
slavery, institution of, 4, 15, 16, 26, 38, 78, 79,
150, 184, 215, 228n9; abolition of, 39, 40, 149,
242n39; Hegel on, 11, 12, 228n12; legacies of,
94, 97, 108, 111, 147, 151, 235n35; memory of,
21, 66, 224; "natural" hierarchies of, 219;
untenable practices of, 17; Voltaire on, 10
slaves, 3, 6, 9–12, 17–21, 54, 83, 99, 108, 111, 185,
219–21, 229n16, 230n33, 231n10, 234n22, n23,
236n44; Canboulay celebrations of, 88, 101,
233n9; Carnival parodies of, 90, 91; dances
of, 6, 12, 16, 20–21, 31–34, 37–38, 85, 87, 94,
209, 215, 222, 230n36; emancipation of, 89;
insurgencies of, 12, 19–20, 24, 37–41, 84–87,
159, 184, 215, 242n31. *See also* Haitian Revolution; literary evocations of, 65, 69, 71, 150,
157, 159, 161–65, 167, 168, 171, 173, 181, 201,
241n22, 242n39, 243n41; religious rituals
of, 27, 32–33, 218, 225, 230n37, 231n9; Saint-
Dominguan migrants, 38, 39, 41–44, 183, 199;
songs of, 16, 232n4; on sugar plantations, 17–
20, 96, 97, 229n30; transported to New World,
15–17
Smash record label, 184
Smith, Mark, 215–16, 219, 222
Snaër, Samuel, 42
Social Unions, 111, 113
Société d'Histoire et de Géographie d'Haïti, La,
61
Soledad Brothers, 243n46
Soul magazine, 194
soul music, 183, 184, 189, 194, 197, 198, 205, 209,
212, 245n14, 246n23, 247n36, n37, n42, n43,
249n16
Soulouque, Faustin, 48–50

South Carolina, 184; Saint-Dominguans in, 39
Spain, 6; colonies of, 9, 30, 38, 40, 80–84, 97
Spanish Inquisition, 6
Spiritual Baptists, 93
Spoiler, 125
steelbands, 127–31, 173, 174, 190, 235n29, 238n68,
239n73
stick-fighting, 98, 100–103, 105, 107–9, 111, 115,
127, 235n39
Stone, Sly, 204
Stono slave rebellion (South Carolina, 1739), 184
Strauss, Johann, II, 217
Stubblefield, Clyde, 193
Student Non-violent Coordinating Committee
(SNCC), 194
Stuempfle, Stephen, 233n10, 235n36, 236n48,
238n68
sugar production, 16–20, 40, 61, 84, 96–97,
229–30
Summary Offences Ordinance (Trinidad, 1945),
130
"Surisma the Carib," 81
surrealism, 134, 136, 139–41, 145, 148, 168, 176,
201–2, 240n8, n10
Swimmer, The (film), 1–3, 22
Sylvain, Georges, 57, 61
Sylvain, Normil, 74
Syrian immigrants, 78, 80

tamboo-bamboo bands, 100, 114–15, 120, 127–28,
238n70
Tam-tam (journal), 144
Taylor, Cecil, 200, 248n6
Taylor, Daphne, 83
tchatcha (musical instrument), 35
Temptations, The, 204, 247n42

Tennessee Jubilee Singers, 110, 111
Theatre and Dance Halls Ordinance (Trinidad,
1934), 122–23
Thierry, Camille, 42
Thomas, Fred, 211
Tobago, 85, 234n22
Toco (Trinidad), 80
Tolstoy, Leo, 229n24
Torch Ordinance (Trinidad, 1884), 107
Torres-Saillant, Silvio, 214–215
Toussaint Louverture, François Dominique,
25–27, 32–34, 38, 45–47, 77
Trinidad, 78–131, 160, 173, 184, 202, 223–24,

232n4, 233n16, 234n22, 236n44, 238n66;
American jubilee and minstrel music in,
109–11; British rule of, 82–84, 86–88, 95–99,
101–7, 109, 113, 121, 122, 125, 131, 224; calypso
in, 81, 83, 92, 95, 100, 104, 107, 112–14, 117,
119, 121–30, 229n15, 347n57; Canboulay in,
88, 101–9, 237n54; Carnival in, 2–3, 21–22,
40, 79, 84, 88–105, 107, 109–16, 118–21, 124,
127, 130, 224, 237n60, 238n67; dissemination of idea of Haitian revolution to, 38, 39;
Emancipation in, 89–90, 93, 94; French Creoles in, 82–84, 88, 92, 95–98, 100–105, 107–9,
112, 114, 117, 224; Hosein massacre in, 108–9;
poetry in, 96–97; recordings in, 116–18,
233n7; revolts in, 84–87; Saint-Dominguan
refugees in, 40; Spanish colonization of, 80–
84; steelbands in, 127–32, 174, 190; during
World War II, 123–26, 129
Trinidad Chronicle, 98, 102, 107
Trinidad Gazette, 87
Trinidadian Guardian, 118–20, 131
Trinidad Review, 107
Trinidad Sentinel, 95, 98
Trinidad Spectator, 91
Trinidad and Tobago Steel Band Association, 130
Tropiques (journal), 134, 143, 167, 168, 170, 178
Trouillot, Lyonel, 232n30
Tutwiler (Mississipppi), 185
twoubadou music, 74
Tympany Five, 244n3, 246n30
Tzara, Tristan, 201

U.S. Baptist Mission, 93
Union Patriotique, 61
United States, 22, 50, 119, 133, 216, 220, 237n54.
    See also African Americans; Caribbean
    influence of, 58; civil rights movement in, 3,
    209, 210; jubilee and minstrel music from,
    109–11; occupation of Haiti by, 60–72, 125,
    232n25; plantations in, 168–69, 193, 219,
    221; recorded music in, 116, 118; religion
    in, 217–19; Saint-Dominguans in, 39–44,
    73, 183; sounds of progress versus sounds
    of frontier in, 216; Vodou worship in, 44;
    during World War II, 123–26
Université d'Haïti, 61
Urich, Frederick, 89

Valéry, Paul, 52
vaudoux dance, 32–34

Vega, Lope de, 6
Venezuela, 39, 80, 82, 236n48
Ventura, Michael, 43
Verteuil, Anthony de, 234n23
Vesey, Denmark, 39
Vichy France, 168–70, 231n12
Victoria, Queen of England, 113
Victorianism, 84, 94, 98, 111, 115, 216
Victor Talking Machine Company, 116, 117
Vietnam War, 204
Vieux, Damoclès, 57
Vilaire, Etzer, 57; "Les Martyrs," 58–60
Village Voice, 193
Vincent, Rickey, 188, 192, 208, 210, 212, 245n12,
    246n24
Virginia, 38, 39, 215, 221
Vodou, 28, 30, 62, 71, 72, 136, 199, 223, 230n37;
    anti-superstition campaign against, 75; in
    Louisiana, 42–44; poetry and, 51, 54–60,
    67–68; and post-independence Haitian
    state, 27, 47–50; rhythms of, 31, 34–38;
    slaves and, 19, 21; Toussaint Louverture's
    antagonism toward, 25–27, 45–47
Vodou Jazz, 75
Voltaire, 10

Walker, Junior, and the Allstars, 209
War of 1812, 40, 93
Ward, Brian, 194, 209, 210, 246n27, 247n36, n37,
    248n45
Warner-Lewis, Maureen, 233n15
Washington, D.C., 196
Water Riot, 114
Weinger, Harry, 193, 244n2, 245n20,
    246n26
Werleigh, Christian, 64
Werner, Craig, 245n10, n13, 247n43, 249n16
Wesley, Fred, 208, 211, 212
West, Cornel, 211
Westermann, Diedrich Hermann, 145
Wexler, Jerry, 245n14
White, Cliff, 193, 245n20, 246n26
White, Graham, 218, 219, 228n10
White, Shane, 218, 219, 228n10
White Rose Fancy Band, 117
White Rose Special Union, 113
Wilder, Gary, 239n5
Williams, Eric, 82
Wilson, Olly, 14, 187, 188, 245n16
Wolk, Douglas, 245n7, n18

Wonder, Stevie, 209
Wood, Donald, 235n35, n39
Woodford, Ralph, 87, 95
Wordsworth, William, 55
World War I, 118, 123
World War II, 2, 123–24, 129, 168–70
Wright, Richard, 137
Wulfe, Beau, 104

Yarrow, Richard, 186
Yorubas, 92, 234n27
Young, Hubert, 124

Ziegler, Mel, 245n17
Zobel, Joseph, 22, 132, 173, 181, 224; *Lughia de la mort,* 149; *La Rue Cases-Nègres,* 149–57, 159, 162, 241n22, n23

TEXT
10/12.5 Minion Pro

DISPLAY
Minion Pro

COMPOSITOR
Bookmatters, Berkeley

INDEXER
Ruth Elwell

PRINTER AND BINDER
Maple-Vail Book Manufacturing Group